QoS for IP/MPLS Networks

Santiago Alvarez

Cisco Press

800 East 96th Street
Indianapolis, IN 46240 USA

QoS for IP/MPLS Networks

Santiago Alvarez

Copyright© 2006 Cisco Systems, Inc.

Published by:
Cisco Press
800 East 96th Street
Indianapolis, IN 46240 USA

Printed in the United States of America 1 2 3 4 5 6 7 8 9 0

First Printing   June 2006

Library of Congress Cataloging-in-Publication Number: 2004117089

ISBN: 1-58705-233-4

Trademark Acknowledgments

Warning and Disclaimer

This book is designed to provide information about quality of service in IP/MPLS networks using Cisco IOS and Cisco IOS XR. Every effort has been made to make this book as complete and as accurate as possible, but no warranty or fitness is implied.

The information is provided on an "as is" basis. The authors, Cisco Press, and Cisco Systems, Inc. shall have neither liability nor responsibility to any person or entity with respect to any loss or damages arising from the information contained in this book or from the use of the discs or programs that may accompany it.

The opinions expressed in this book belong to the author and are not necessarily those of Cisco Systems, Inc.

Corporate and Government Sales

Cisco Press offers excellent discounts on this book when ordered in quantity for bulk purchases or special sales.

For more information please contact: **U.S. Corporate and Government Sales**   1-800-382-3419
corpsales@pearsontechgroup.com

For sales outside the U.S. please contact: **International Sales**   international@pearsoned.com

Feedback Information

At Cisco Press, our goal is to create in-depth technical books of the highest quality and value. Each book is crafted with care and precision, undergoing rigorous development that involves the unique expertise of members from the professional technical community.

Readers' feedback is a natural continuation of this process. If you have any comments regarding how we could improve the quality of this book, or otherwise alter it to better suit your needs, you can contact us through e-mail at feedback@ciscopress.com. Please make sure to include the book title and ISBN in your message.

We greatly appreciate your assistance.

Publisher	Paul Boger
Cisco Representative	Anthony Wolfenden
Cisco Press Program Manager	Jeff Brady
Production Manager	Patrick Kanouse
Development Editor	Jill Batistick
Senior Project Editor	San Dee Phillips
Copy Editor	Keith Cline
Technical Editors	Mark Gallo, Raymond Zhang
Book and Cover Designer	Louisa Adair
Composition	Mark Shirar
Indexer	Keith Cline

CISCO SYSTEMS

Corporate Headquarters
Cisco Systems, Inc.
170 West Tasman Drive
San Jose, CA 95134-1706
USA
www.cisco.com
Tel: 408 526-4000
   800 553-NETS (6387)
Fax: 408 526-4100

European Headquarters
Cisco Systems International BV
Haarlerbergpark
Haarlerbergweg 13-19
1101 CH Amsterdam
The Netherlands
www-europe.cisco.com
Tel: 31 0 20 357 1000
Fax: 31 0 20 357 1100

Americas Headquarters
Cisco Systems, Inc.
170 West Tasman Drive
San Jose, CA 95134-1706
USA
www.cisco.com
Tel: 408 526-7660
Fax: 408 527-0883

Asia Pacific Headquarters
Cisco Systems, Inc.
Capital Tower
168 Robinson Road
#22-01 to #29-01
Singapore 068912
www.cisco.com
Tel: +65 6317 7777
Fax: +65 6317 7799

Cisco Systems has more than 200 offices in the following countries and regions. Addresses, phone numbers, and fax numbers are listed on the **Cisco.com Web site at www.cisco.com/go/offices.**

Argentina • Australia • Austria • Belgium • Brazil • Bulgaria • Canada • Chile • China PRC • Colombia • Costa Rica • Croatia • Czech Republic Denmark • Dubai, UAE • Finland • France • Germany • Greece • Hong Kong SAR • Hungary • India • Indonesia • Ireland • Israel • Italy Japan • Korea • Luxembourg • Malaysia • Mexico • The Netherlands • New Zealand • Norway • Peru • Philippines • Poland • Portugal Puerto Rico • Romania • Russia • Saudi Arabia • Scotland • Singapore • Slovakia • Slovenia • South Africa • Spain • Sweden Switzerland • Taiwan • Thailand • Turkey • Ukraine • United Kingdom • United States • Venezuela • Vietnam • Zimbabwe

About the Author

Santiago Alvarez, CCIE No. 3621, is a technical marketing engineering for Cisco Systems working on MPLS and QoS since 2000. He joined Cisco in the blazing days of 1997. Prior to Cisco, Santiago worked in software development for Lucent Technologies. He has been involved with computer networking since 1991. Santiago is a frequent speaker at Cisco Networkers and a periodic contributor to *Cisco Packet* Magazine. He holds a bachelor of science degree in computer science from EAFIT University, a master of Science degree in computer science from Colorado State University, and a master of science in telecommunications from the University of Colorado at Boulder. Outside work, he enjoys the outdoors, fine food, and exploring the world as an independent traveler. He can be reached at saalvare@cisco.com.

About the Technical Reviewers

Mark Gallo is a systems engineering manager at Cisco Systems within the channels organization. He has led several engineering groups responsible for positioning and delivering Cisco end-to-end systems, as well as designing and implementing enterprise LANs and international IP networks. He has a B.S. degree in electrical engineering from the University of Pittsburgh and holds Cisco CCNP and CCDP certifications. Mark resides in northern Virginia with his wife, Betsy, and son, Paul.

Raymond Zhang is a senior network architect for BT Infonet in the areas of Global IP backbone infrastructure, routing architecture design, planning, and its evolutions. Currently, his main areas of interest include large-scale backbone routing, traffic engineering, performance and traffic statistical analysis, and MPLS-related technologies (including interdomain traffic engineering, GMPLS, metro Ethernet, Diffserve, IPv6, and Multicast). Raymond participates in several IETF drafts relating to MPLS, BGP-based MPLS VPN, Inter-AS TE, and, more recently, PCE-based work.

Dedications

Thanks for withstanding long, long working hours.

Acknowledgments

I would like to give special thanks to Bob Olsen and Sandeep Bajaj for sharing their technical expertise through so many years. They have patiently tolerated my constant interruptions and have provided useful insight on different topics included in the book.

Special thanks to the reviewers, Mark Gallo and Raymond Zhang. I appreciate your detailed comments. I am to blame for any remaining inaccuracies or omissions.

Big thanks to Bruce Davie, whose responsiveness at key points encouraged me to persist in my goal. I highly regard his unusual ability to abstract complexity and clearly illustrate the essence of intricate technology concepts. Much of his work has directly and indirectly influenced the content of this book. Similarly, I extend my gratitude to François Le Faucheur and Jean Philippe Vasseur. They have had the patience to discuss with me many aspects of these technologies in numerous occasions. *Merci!*

Thanks to Ramesh Uppili for contributing to the presentation of key topics in multiple ways.

I also want to thank Rakesh Gandi, Prashanth Yelandur, Ashish Savla, Bobby Kaligotla, Lawrence Wobker, Ashok Ganesan, Jay Thontakudi, and Scott Yow for facilitating the discussion of Cisco IOS XR in this book.

Special thanks to the Cisco Press team: John Kane, Chris Cleveland, Jill Batistick, San Dee Phillips, and Elizabeth Peterson. I really appreciate your attention to detail and extraordinary patience with me. I wish John the best in his new endeavors.

Finally, if you have read this far in search of your name, this paragraph is for you. I have to acknowledge that numerous individuals contributed through insightful discussions. They unhappily or maybe happily remain anonymous. Thanks!

This Book Is Safari Enabled

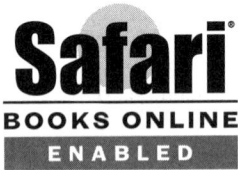

The Safari® Enabled icon on the cover of your favorite technology book means the book is available through Safari Bookshelf. When you buy this book, you get free access to the online edition for 45 days.

Safari Bookshelf is an electronic reference library that lets you easily search thousands of technical books, find code samples, download chapters, and access technical information whenever and wherever you need it.

To gain 45-day Safari Enabled access to this book:

- Go to http://www.ciscopress.com/safarienabled
- Complete the brief registration form
- Enter the coupon code 2ML4-YT1N-YR8J-D5NQ-DAH4

If you have difficulty registering on Safari Bookshelf or accessing the online edition, please e-mail customer-service@safaribooksonline.com.

Contents at a Glance

Contents

Icons Used in This Book

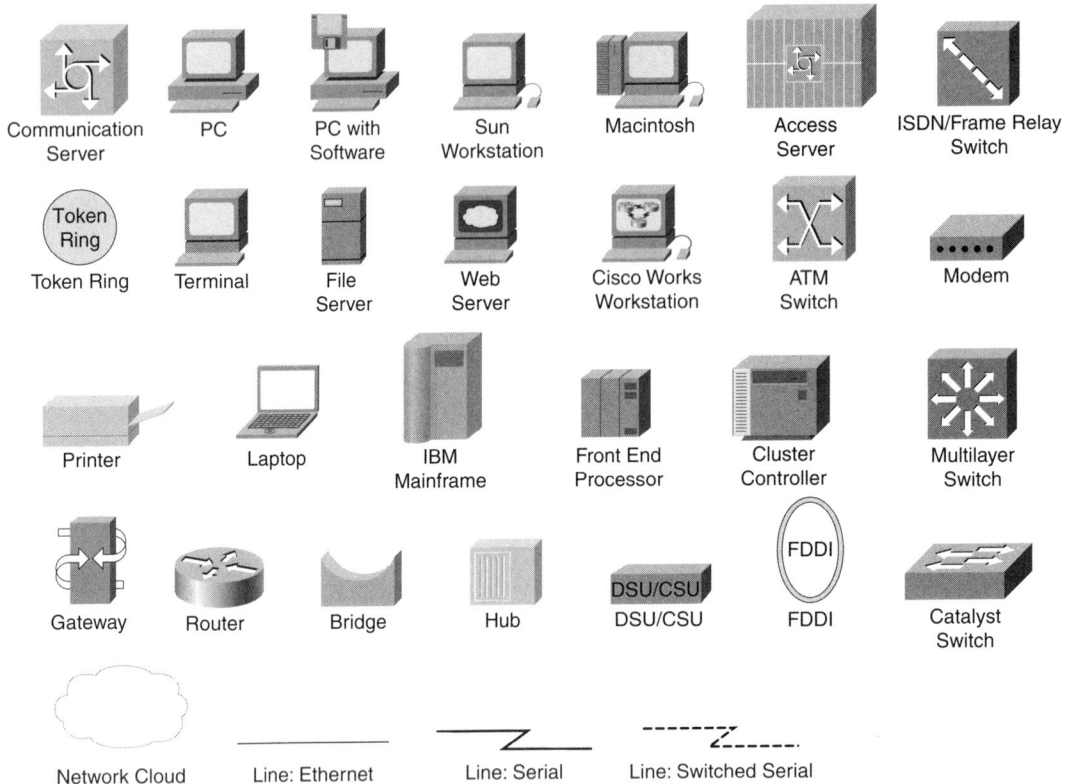

Communication Server

PC

PC with Software

Sun Workstation

Macintosh

Access Server

ISDN/Frame Relay Switch

Token Ring

Terminal

File Server

Web Server

Cisco Works Workstation

ATM Switch

Modem

Printer

Laptop

IBM Mainframe

Front End Processor

Cluster Controller

Multilayer Switch

Gateway

Router

Bridge

Hub

DSU/CSU

FDDI

Catalyst Switch

Network Cloud

Line: Ethernet

Line: Serial

Line: Switched Serial

Command Syntax Conventions

The conventions used to present command syntax in this book are the same conventions used in the IOS Command Reference. The Command Reference describes these conventions as follows:

- **Boldface** indicates commands and keywords that are entered literally as shown. In actual configuration examples and output (not general command syntax), boldface indicates commands that are manually input by the user (such as a **show** command).

- *Italics* indicate arguments for which you supply actual values.

- Vertical bars (|) separate alternative, mutually exclusive elements. Note, however, that the vertical bar (pipe operand) is also used to filter command-line interface command output; in that scenario, the operand (|) precedes the **begin**, **exclude**, or **include** keywords, which are then followed by a regular expression.

- Square brackets [ ] indicate optional elements.

- Braces { } indicate a required choice.

- Braces within brackets [{ }] indicate a required choice within an optional element.

Foreword

The phrase "IP QoS" was for many years considered an oxymoron. Indeed, much of the success of the IP architecture could be traced to its adoption of a "best effort" service model, enabling IP to run over just about any underlying network technology. Best effort service, however, is defined by a lack of assurance that packets will be delivered in a timely manner, or even delivered at all. Such a service model limits the potential of IP networks to support applications that demand timely packet delivery, such as interactive telephony and multimedia applications.

As far back as 1979, there were proposals to extend the IP service model to support applications with stronger QoS requirements. However, this remained a research topic until the early 1990s. By that point, the idea of convergence—carrying many applications with diverse QoS needs on a single network—was gaining currency, although the word "convergence" would not become a buzzword for several years. ATM was widely expected to be the packet switching technology that would enable this convergence, but a concerted effort to add QoS to IP was also getting underway. The seminal 1992 paper by Clark, Shenker, and Zhang on support of real-time applications in the Internet put a serious stake in the ground for IP QoS, and work at the IETF to standardize a set of IP QoS mechanisms began shortly thereafter. The Integrated Services architecture and Resource Reservation Protocol resulted, and the Differentiated Services architecture followed.

Another technical development with big implications for IP QoS was Multiprotocol Label Switching, which grew out of work on Tag Switching at Cisco begun in 1996. There was considerable confusion about exactly what impact MPLS would have on IP QoS, in part because of the resemblances between MPLS and ATM, which had its own QoS model. In reality, the biggest single effect MPLS had on QoS was to add another tool to the QoS toolbox, in the form of traffic engineering with constraint-based routing. It is for this reason more than any other that MPLS and QoS deserve to be covered in a single book.

Which brings us to the current volume. IP QoS can now be considered a mature technology, not just something for the bleeding edge. It is also notoriously complex to understand and to configure correctly. Some of this complexity is intrinsic; some is an accident of history. On the intrinsic side, understanding QoS is hard because it requires the ability to operate at many different levels of abstraction. One needs to understand the high level QoS architectures, to have a behavioral model of QoS features inside a router, to know how those features map onto a particular piece of hardware, and to understand the CLI that is used to control those features. This is where this book sets itself apart from the pack of QoS books. Some cover QoS architecture and IETF standards. Some provide information on CLI commands. But this is the only book I've found that walks the reader through the levels of abstraction from high level architecture to low level CLI, with a clear explanation of the abstract QoS behavior model that all routers support providing the bridge between the levels. By reading this book, you will understand both the big picture of QoS and the details necessary to deploy it in a real network.

Another factor that made QoS difficult to manage in the past was a somewhat ad hoc approach to its implementation. Combinations of features were sometimes implemented in a monolithic way, and inconsistency across platforms was the norm. This situation has improved massively in recent years, notably with the adoption of the Modular QoS CLI across most of the Cisco product line. Thus, QoS deployment is much more straightfoward than it once was, and this book's timely coverage of the MQC and its underlying behavioral model will make it even easier.

Many readers may be tempted to jump straight to the last chapter's guidance on how to design and deploy a QoS strategy in a backbone network. Santiago's extensive real-world deployment experience certainly makes this chapter especially valuable. However, the preceding four chapters are the ones that will provide you with a fundamental understanding of QoS. Thus, rather than blindly following a QoS "recipe," you'll be able to make the right design decisions to meet the needs of your own applications and customers. If you really want to understand QoS fully, this is the book to read, from start to finish.

Bruce Davie
Cisco Fellow

Introduction

The motivation behind this book is the continued interest in the implementation of *quality of service* (QoS) in IP/MPLS networks. QoS arises as a key requirement for these networks, which have become the preferred technology platform for building converged networks that support multiple services. The topic can be one of the most complex aspects of the network design, implementation, and operation. Despite the importance of and interest in this topic, no other Cisco Press title provides a detailed discussion of this subject. A significant amount of the content of this book also applies to pure IP networks that do not have immediate plans to migrate to a full IP/MPLS network.

This material covers both QoS and *Multiprotocol Label Switching Traffic Engineering* (MPLS TE). In particular, it covers MPLS TE as a technology that complements traditional QoS technologies. MPLS TE can be an instrumental tool to improve the QoS guarantees that an IP/MPLS network offers. As such, it can contribute to improving both network performance and availability. However, this book provides a concise discussion of MPLS TE. Those readers interested in further information should consult the Cisco Press title *Traffic Engineering with MPLS*.

The book takes the point of view of those individuals responsible for the IP/MPLS network. Other Cisco Press titles describe the details of the QoS implementation for those devices receiving the services that the network offers.

You should have a basic understanding of both IP and MPLS to obtain the most benefit from this book. That understanding should include basic IP addressing and routing, along with the basics of MPLS forwarding. However, the book provides a technology overview of QoS and MPLS TE to help those with less exposure to these technologies or to serve as a review/reference to those more familiar with those topics.

This book touches a broad topic and does not pretend to address all QoS aspects of interest. You can expect future Cisco Press books to cover important areas, including the following:

- Implementation of QoS for specific services (for instance, IP, Ethernet, ATM)

- QoS management (including monitoring and provisioning)

- Interprovider QoS

Visit this book's website, http://www.ciscopress.com/title/1587052334, for further information.

Who Should Read This Book?

This book's primary audience is the technical staff of those organizations building IP/MPLS networks as an infrastructure to provide multiple services. The material includes technology, configuration, and operational details to help in the design, implementation, and operation of QoS in IP/MPLS networks. Service providers are a prime example of the organizations that this book targets. However, government agencies, educational institutions, and large enterprises pursuing IP/MPLS will find the material equally useful.

A secondary audience for this book is those individuals in charge of service definition or those individuals subscribing to network services. Both types can benefit from a better understanding of the differentiation capabilities that IP/MPLS networks can offer.

How This Book Is Organized

Although this book could be read cover to cover, it is designed to be flexible and allow you to easily move between chapters and sections of chapters to cover just the material that you need more work with. The content is roughly divided into three parts:

- Chapters 1 and 2 provide a technology overview.

- Chapters 3 and 4 discuss Cisco implemenation.

- Chapter 5 covers different backbone design options.

Here is a brief synopsis of each chapter:

Chapter 1, "QoS Technology Overview"—This chapter provides a review of QoS technology for IP and IP/MPLS networks. The chapter initially discusses the IP QoS architectures and how they apply to MPLS. Multiple sections elaborate on MPLS support for *Differentiated Services* (DiffServ), including a detailed discussion on *EXP-inferred-class link switched path* (E-LSP), *Label-inferred-class LSP* (L-LSP), and DiffServ tunneling models (pipe, short pipe, and uniform). This dicussion leads into a summary of traffic-management mechanisms with a detailed look at traffic policing, traffic shaping, traffic scheduling, active queue manangemt, and so on. The chapter also discusses QoS signaling with a focus on the *Resource Reservation Protocol* (RSVP).

Chapter 2, "MPLS TE Technology Overview"—This chapter reviews the basic operation of this technology with its DiffServ extensions and applicability as a traffic-protection alternative. This review elaborates on the concepts of contraint-based routing, *DiffServ-aware Traffic Engineering* (DS-TE) and *fast reroute* (FRR) (including link, shared-risk link group, and node protection).

Chapter 3, "Cisco QoS"—This chapter covers the Cisco QoS behavioral model and the *modular QoS command-line interface* (MCQ). The chapter abstracts the platform specifics to facilitate the understanding of Cisco QoS and provides a complete reference of the configuration commands. In addition, the chapter includes numerous examples to illustrate the configuration and verification of different traffic-management mechanisms in Cisco IOS and Cisco IOS XR. This material is equally relevant to IP and IP/MPLS networks.

Chapter 4, "Cisco MPLS Traffic Engineering"—This chapter presents Cisco implementation of MPLS Traffic Engineering in both Cisco IOS and Cisco IOS XR. It includes multiple configuration and verification examples illustrating the implementation of basic MPLS TE, DS-TE, and FRR.

Chapter 5, "Backbone Infrastructure"—This chapter discusses the backbone performance requirements and the different design options. The chapter reviews different designs, ranging from a best-effort backbone to the most elaborate scenarios combining DiffServ, DS-TE, and FRR. Numerous configuration examples illustrate their implementation using Cisco IOS and Cisco IOS XR.

CHAPTER 1

QoS Technology Overview

In this chapter, you review the following topics:

- IP QoS Architectures
- MPLS Support for IntServ
- MPLS Support for DiffServ
- Traffic-Management Mechanisms
- QoS Signaling

This chapter provides a review of the key technology components of *quality of service* (QoS) in IP/MPLS networks. This review discusses the IntServ and DiffServ architectures including their relationship with MPLS. The chapter covers the traffic management mechanisms that enable QoS implementation and reviews different QoS signaling alternatives in IP/MPLS with a special focus on RSVP protocol.

This book assumes that you are already familiar with the basic concepts behind these topics. You should also be familiar with the basics of *Multiprotocol Label Switching* (MPLS) in general. This chapter and Chapter 2, "MPLS TE Technology Overview," serve as a technology review and quick reference for later content. Chapter 3, "Cisco QoS," covers the specifics on Cisco implementation of QoS technology. The "References" section at the end of this chapter lists sources of additional information on the topics that this chapter covers.

IP QoS Architectures

Originally, IP was specified a best-effort protocol. One of the implications of this service definition was that the network would attempt to deliver the traffic to its destination in the shortest time possible. However, the network would provide no guarantee of achieving it.

This service definition proved successful during the early Internet years, when data applications constituted the bulk of Internet traffic. Generally, these applications used TCP and therefore adapted gracefully to variations in bandwidth, latency, jitter, and loss. The amount of interactive traffic was minimal, and other applications requiring stricter guarantees were at an experimental stage.

However, a new generation of applications with new service requirements emerged as the Internet grew in success. The increasing reach and capacity of the Internet made it an attractive infrastructure to support an increasing number of applications. In addition, corporations, governments, and educational institutions, among others, found the IP protocol an appealing option to build their private data networks. Many of the new IP applications (for example, voice and video) had a real-time nature and limited tolerance to variations in bandwidth, latency, jitter, and loss. The service expectations of network users and their application requirements made the best-effort service definition insufficient.

The definition of a QoS architecture started in the middle of the 1990s. Since then, the *Internet Engineering Task Force* (IETF) has defined two QoS architectures for IP: *Integrated Services* (IntServ) and *Differentiated Services* (DiffServ). The IntServ architecture was the initial proposed solution. Subsequently, the DiffServ architecture came to life. MPLS later incorporated support for the DiffServ architecture, which the IETF had defined exclusively for IP.

These two architectures use different assumptions and take different approaches to bringing QoS to IP. Although sometimes considered opposite and competing architectures, they tend to complement each other. Moreover, the QoS mechanisms used ultimately to manipulate traffic are essentially the same in both architectures.

Integrated Services

The IntServ working group was responsible for developing the specifications of this architecture at the IETF. The group met for the first time during the twenty-ninth IETF in 1994. The architecture specifications have a close relationship with the work of the *IntServ over Specific Link Layers* (ISSLL) and the *Resource Reservation Protocol* (RSVP) working groups. The ISSLL working group defined the implementation of IntServ over different link-layer protocols (for example, Ethernet and ATM). The RSVP working group defined the RSVP protocol that the IntServ group selected as the signaling protocol. The three working groups collectively produced 32 RFCs, of which 24 are in the IETF standards track. The working groups eventually closed between the years 2000 and 2002.

The IETF decided to modify the original Internet architecture to support real-time applications. The IETF considered simpler alternatives, but they offered less-complete solutions. For instance

- Fair-queuing algorithms solved the unfairness between data and real-time applications, but they could not guarantee the delay and jitter.
- The use of separate networks for separate services was less efficient due to the lower levels of statistical multiplexing.
- Bandwidth overprovisioning was not a realistic solution when bandwidth was offered as a service.

- A simple priority mechanism could not prevent a growing number of real-time flows from causing degradation of all flows.

- The rate and delay adaptation of real-time applications had limits, especially when no admission control was used.

IntServ Terminology

This section lists several important terms that IntServ introduces. The next two sections provide more detail about these abstractions:

- **Flow**—An identifiable stream of packets that a network node associates with the same request for QoS. A flow may span a single or multiple application sessions.

- **Traffic specification (TSpec)**—Characterization of the traffic pattern of a flow over time.

- **Service request specification (RSpec)**—Characterization of the QoS a flow desires.

- **Flow specification (flowspec)**—Combination of a TSpec and an RSpec. Network nodes use the flowspec as input for admission-control decisions.

Architecture Principles

A crucial principle of the IntServ architecture is the requirement for resource reservation. This requirement implies admission control to manage finite resources. IntServ nodes need to avoid accepting unauthorized requests or requests that can affect existing reservations with service commitments. Different types of users are expected to have different rights to reserve network resources. In addition, the network load has to be controlled to meet the quantitative specification of the service-quality commitments of existing flows. IntServ leaves the selection of the QoS to the application rather than the network.

The architecture defines a flow as the basic service unit. This abstraction represents a distinguishable stream of packets that requires the same QoS. Flows are unidirectional. They have a single source and one or many destinations. IntServ requires the use of per-flow state in network nodes. This requirement results from the flow granularity and the use of resource reservation with admission control. Having network nodes maintaining per-flow state represents a significant change to the original IP architecture that left per-flow state to end systems. The architecture recommends the use of a signaling protocol to set up and refresh the state to preserve the robustness of the IP protocol. RFC 1633 introduces the architecture. Figure 1-1 shows a simple example of an IntServ network.

Figure 1-1   *Overview of a Network Implementing IntServ*

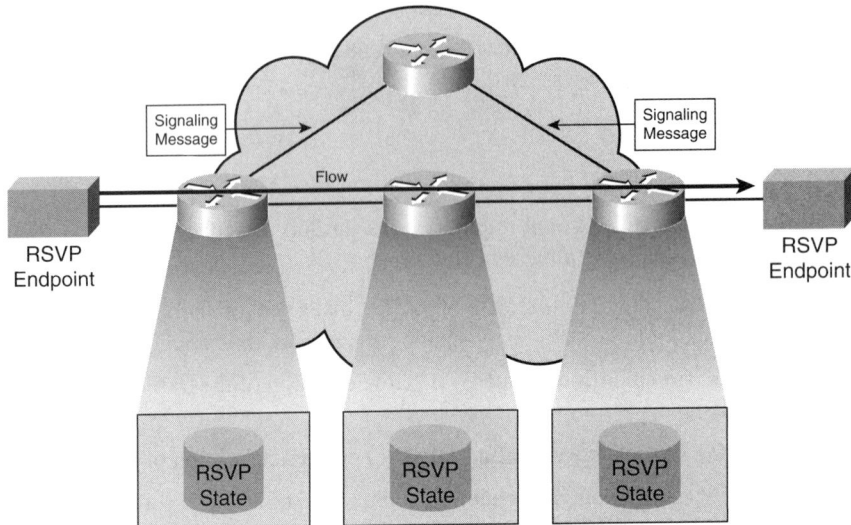

Service Model

The IntServ architecture defines an extensible service model with a common framework. An important component of the definition of a service is the information that the receiver, which requests the service, must specify to the network. A service request includes a TSpec and, possibly, an RSpec. When a service request is accepted, the network nodes must guarantee the service as long as the TSpec continues to describe the flow. The combination of a TSpec and an RSpec receives the name of flowspec.

The architecture service model uses a common TSpec definition. Four parameters characterize the traffic:

- **A token bucket (r, b)**—The token bucket includes a token rate (r) and a token bucket size (b).

- **A peak rate (p)**—Flow traffic may not arrive at a rate higher than the peak rate.

- **A minimum policed unit (m)**—Network nodes treat packets of a size smaller than the minimum policed unit as packets of size m. This term facilitates the estimation of the actual bandwidth that a flow requires (including the Layer 2 header overhead).

- **A maximum packet size (M)**—A node considers packets with a size larger than M as packets that do not conform to the traffic specification. Those nonconforming packets might not receive the same service as conforming packets.

Table 1-1 summarizes the TSpec parameters.

Table 1-1   *TSpec Parameters*

Parameter	Description
r	Token rate
b	Token bucket size
p	Peak rate
m	Minimum policed unit
M	Maximum packet size

NOTE   The token bucket is an important concept in traffic management. The sections "Traffic Policing" and "Traffic Shaping" describe it in more detail later in this chapter.

The architecture defined two services: *Guaranteed Service* (GS) and *Controlled Load Service* (CLS). They complement the best-effort service that is part of the definition of the IP protocol. IntServ does not introduce any changes to the operation of the best-effort service. In addition, the IntServ service model does not mandate a particular implementation for the traffic-management mechanisms that implement a service. The next two sections explain the GS and CLS services, focusing on their end-to-end behavior and their flow specifications.

NOTE   RFC 2997 later defined a Null Service type. Applications can use this service to let the network determine the appropriate service parameters for the flow. This service type has special applicability for the integration of IntServ and DiffServ architectures.

Guaranteed Service

GS provides flows with a delay and bandwidth guarantee. GS ensures a firm bound on the maximum end-to-end queuing delay for packets that conform to the flowspec. Furthermore, a properly policed flow should not experience queuing drops in the absence of network failures or routing changes. The service does not consider fixed-delay components that are a property of the flow path (for example, propagation delay or serialization delay). A flow receives guaranteed service if all nodes along the path support the service. GS does not guarantee an average or minimum delay, just a maximum bound. Therefore, this service does not provide any jitter guarantees. RFC 2212 defines GS.

A receiver provides a TSpec and an RSpec when requesting GS. The RSpec contains a *service rate* (R) and a *time slack* (S). Network nodes must approximate the service that a dedicated line at that rate would provide to the flow. Nodes make available the margin of error of their approximation. Applications can use this information to compute the maximum end-to-end delay that the flow will experience. The slack term in the RSpec specifies the incremental end-to-end delay that the sender can tolerate if a node modifies the flow resource allocation. Applications can adjust the flowspec if the delay bound is not acceptable. Table 1-2 summarizes the RSpec parameters.

Table 1-2   *RSpec Parameters*

Parameter	Description
R	Service rate
S	Time slack

Control Load Service

CLS approximates the behavior of best-effort service during unloaded conditions. Network nodes satisfy this behavior even in the presence of congestion. Applications can assume that the network will deliver a high percentage of all packets to their final destination. In addition, applications can assume that a high percentage of the delivered packets will experience a delay that will not greatly exceed the minimum delay of any packet. Applications do not receive any target values for packet delay or loss. This service supports those applications that operate satisfactorily with a best-effort service but are highly sensitive to congestion conditions. Applications do not require an RSpec to request CLS, only the flow TSpec. RFC 2211 introduces CLS.

Use of RSVP in IntServ

IntServ can use RSVP as the reservation setup protocol. One of the principles of this architecture is that applications communicate QoS requirements for individual flows to the network. These requirements are used for resource reservation and admission control. RSVP can perform this function. However, RSVP is frequently but inaccurately equated to IntServ. RSVP and IntServ share a common history, but they are ultimately independent. Two separate working groups at the IETF developed their specifications. RSVP has applicability as a signaling protocol outside IntServ. Similarly, IntServ could use other signaling mechanisms. The section "Resource Reservation Protocol" explains the protocol details later in this chapter. RFC 2210 describes how IntServ uses RSVP and defines the RSVP objects to implement the IntServ service model.

Differentiated Services

The DiffServ working group was responsible for the definition of this architecture at the IETF. The group met for the first time during the forty-first IETF in 1998. The working group was created with a charter to produce an architecture with a simple and coarse QoS approach that applied to both IPv4 and IPv6. The charter explicitly excluded microflow identification and signaling mechanisms (marking an explicit departure from the approach taken by IntServ). The working group produced 12 RFCs, with five of them being in the standards track and the rest being informational. The group eventually closed after its last meeting in 2001.

NOTE   An IP traffic stream with a unique combination of source address, destination address, protocol, source port, and destination port defines a microflow.

DiffServ Terminology

The DiffServ architecture introduces many new terms. This section presents a simplified definition of a selected few of them. The upcoming sections explain the terms in more detail. RFC 2475 and 3260 introduce the complete list of terms:

- **Domain**—A network with a common DiffServ implementation (usually under the same administrative control).
- **Region**—A group of contiguous DiffServ domains.
- **Egress node**—Last node traversed by a packet before leaving a DiffServ domain.
- **Ingress node**—First node traversed by a packet when entering a DiffServ domain.
- **Interior node**—Node in a DiffServ domain that is not an egress or ingress node.
- **DiffServ field**—Header field where packets carry their DiffServ marking. This field corresponds to the six most significant bits of the second byte in the IP header (formerly, IPv4 TOS [*Type-of-Service*] octet and IPv6 Traffic Class octet).
- **Differentiated Services Code Point (DSCP)**—A specific value assigned to the DiffServ field.
- **Behavior aggregate (BA)**—Collection of packets traversing a DiffServ node with the same DSCP.
- **Ordered aggregate (OA)**—A set of BAs for which a DiffServ node must guarantee not to reorder packets.
- **BA classifier**—Classifier that selects packets based on DSCP.
- **Multifield (MF) classifier**—Classifier that selects a packet based on multiple fields in the packet header (for example, source address, destination address, protocol, and protocol port).

- **Per-hop behavior (PHB)**—Forwarding behavior or service that a BA receives at a node.

- **Per-hop behavior group**—One or more PHBs that are implemented simultaneously and define a set of related forwarding behaviors.

- **PHB scheduling class (PSC)**—A set of PHBs for which a DiffServ node must guarantee not to reorder packets.

- **Traffic profile**—Description of a traffic pattern over time. Generally, in terms of a token bucket (rate and burst).

- **Marking**—Setting the DSCP in a packet.

- **Metering**—Measuring of a traffic profile over time.

- **Policing**—Discarding of packet to enforce conformance to a traffic profile.

- **Shaping**—Buffering of packets to enforce conformance to a traffic profile.

- **Service level agreement (SLA)**—Parameters that describe a service contract between a DiffServ domain and a domain customer.

- **Traffic-conditioning specification**—Parameters that implement a service level specification.

- **Traffic conditioning**—The process of enforcing a traffic conditioning specification through control functions such as marking, metering, policing, and shaping.

NOTE   This DiffServ section is consistent with the original architecture terms. Note, however, that Cisco documentation considers metering an implicit component of traffic shaping and policing. Furthermore, it regards dropping as just one of three possible actions (transmit, drop, mark) of a policer. The remainder of the book follows the policing and shaping definitions used in Cisco documentation.

Architecture Principles

The DiffServ architecture relies on the definition of classes of traffic with different service requirements. A marking in the packet header captures the traffic classification. Further network nodes inspect this marking to identify the packet class and allocate network resources according to locally defined service policies. The service characteristics are unidirectional with a qualitative description in terms of latency, jitter, and loss. DiffServ nodes are stateless from a QoS point of view and have no knowledge of individual flows. Relatively few packet markings are possible with respect to the number of microflows that a node may be switching at a given point in time. However, the concept of grouping or aggregating traffic into a small number of classes is inherent to DiffServ. The architecture intentionally makes a tradeoff between granularity and scalability. RFC 2475 introduces the architecture.

Providing different levels of service using aggregate classification and marking is not a novel concept. As an analogy, consider a transoceanic commercial flight with multiple classes of service. During the check-in process, the passenger needs to provide some identification information (classification criteria). Based on this information, the agent identifies the passenger class (for instance, first, business, or tourist) and provides a boarding pass that reflects the assigned class (marking). The customer class influences the service the passenger receives during the duration of the flight (including access to airline lounge, boarding priority, in-flight service, and deboarding priority). The reduced number of classes allows the airline to provide some differentiation to customers without having to provide a totally individualized service to each passenger. As you can probably recognize, this is not the only instance of aggregate classification and marking used in real life.

Differentiated Services Code Point

Previous specifications of the IP protocol had already reserved header bits for QoS purposes. The IP version 4 specifications in RFC 791 defined the second header octet as the TOS octet. Also, the IP version 6 specifications in RFC 2460 defined the second header octet as the Traffic Class octet but with an undefined structure. In the original TOS octet in IP version 4, the three most significant bits specified the packet precedence (an indication of the relative importance or priority). The next 3 bits in the TOS octet indicated the delay, throughput, and reliability requirements. The final two (least significant) bits were undefined and set to zero. RFC 1349 introduced a small change in the TOS octet by defining a field that included a cost bit plus the existing delay, throughput, and reliability bits. Similarly, the IP version 6 specifications in RFC 2460 define the second header octet as the Traffic Class octet but with an undefined structure. Figure 1-2 illustrates these now-obsolete definitions.

The DiffServ architecture redefines the IPv4 TOS octet and the IPv6 Traffic Class octet. RFC 2474 and RFC 3260 name the DiffServ field as the six most significant bits in the previous IPv4 TOS and IPv6 Traffic Class octets. A particular value of the DiffServ field represents a DSCP. A DiffServ node services packets according to this code point. A group of packets sharing the same DSCP and traversing a link in a specific direction constitutes a BA. A class of traffic may include one or more BAs.

The architecture defines three code point pools for the DiffServ field. Two pools, representing 32 out of the 64 possible values, are reserved for experimental or local use. The existing DiffServ specifications provide recommendations for 21 out of the 32 code points available in the third pool.

The section "Per-Hop Behaviors" in this chapter introduces these values and their service definitions. Eight (class selector) code points provide backward compatibility with the previous Precedence field in the TOS octet. The DiffServ field does not provide any backward compatibility with the TOS field (delay, throughput, and reliability bits) previously defined in the TOS octet. Figure 1-3 shows the structure of the new DiffServ field, the code point pools, and the class selector code points.

Figure 1-2 *Previous Definitions of the TOS Octet for IPv4 and IPv6 That DiffServ Makes Obsolete*

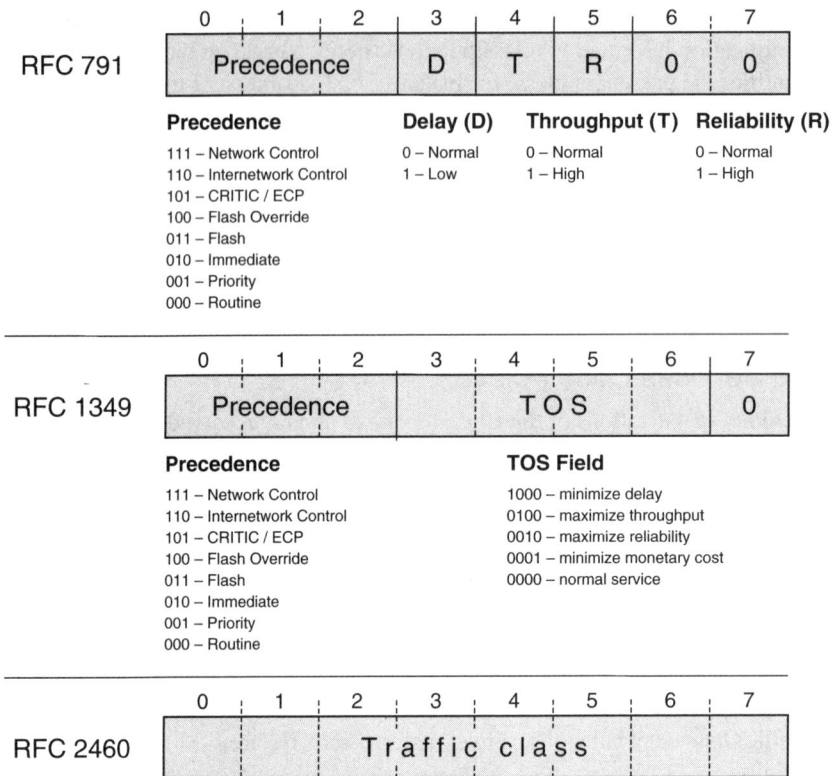

	0	1	2	3	4	5	6	7
RFC 791	\multicolumn{3}{Precedence}	D	T	R	0	0

Precedence

111 – Network Control
110 – Internetwork Control
101 – CRITIC / ECP
100 – Flash Override
011 – Flash
010 – Immediate
001 – Priority
000 – Routine

Delay (D)

0 – Normal
1 – Low

Throughput (T)

0 – Normal
1 – High

Reliability (R)

0 – Normal
1 – High

	0	1	2	3	4	5	6	7
RFC 1349	Precedence			T O S				0

Precedence

111 – Network Control
110 – Internetwork Control
101 – CRITIC / ECP
100 – Flash Override
011 – Flash
010 – Immediate
001 – Priority
000 – Routine

TOS Field

1000 – minimize delay
0100 – maximize throughput
0010 – maximize reliability
0001 – minimize monetary cost
0000 – normal service

	0	1	2	3	4	5	6	7
RFC 2460	Traffic class							

Figure 1-3 *DiffServ Field, Code Point Pools, and Class Selector Code Points*

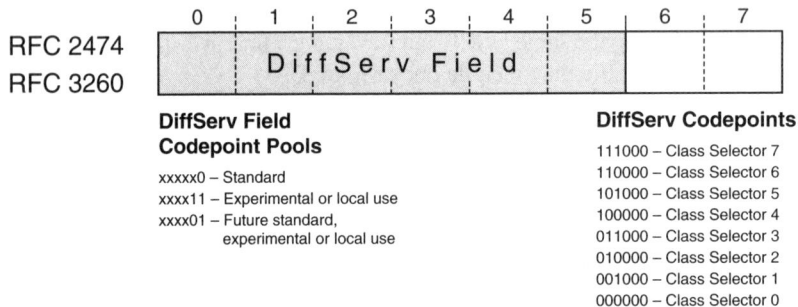

	0	1	2	3	4	5	6	7
RFC 2474 / RFC 3260	DiffServ Field							

DiffServ Field
Codepoint Pools

xxxxx0 – Standard
xxxx11 – Experimental or local use
xxxx01 – Future standard,
       experimental or local use

DiffServ Codepoints

111000 – Class Selector 7
110000 – Class Selector 6
101000 – Class Selector 5
100000 – Class Selector 4
011000 – Class Selector 3
010000 – Class Selector 2
001000 – Class Selector 1
000000 – Class Selector 0

Nodes, Domains, and Regions

The DiffServ architecture defines a hierarchy that goes from a single device, to a network, to a group of networks. A set of nodes with a common DiffServ implementation forms a domain. The nodes inside a domain perform similar service definitions and policies. A domain is typically under a single administrative control. A set of contiguous domains defines a DiffServ region. The domains within the region must be able to provide DiffServ to traffic traversing the different domains in the region. Individual domains may use different service definitions, policies, and packet markings. In those cases, the domains must have peering agreements that specify how traffic is handled when crossing domains.

Boundary nodes and interior nodes constitute the two main types of nodes that reside in a DiffServ domain. Boundary nodes interface with the outside of the domain and ensure that any traffic is properly classified, marked, and within the agreed amounts. DiffServ defines these operations as traffic classification and conditioning. Boundary and interior nodes implement local service policies according to the packet marking. These local policies provide different levels of service to each BA that DiffServ calls PHBs. The section "Per-Hop Behaviors" discusses this concept in detail. A domain may have some nodes that do not support DiffServ. The service impact of these nodes depends on their number and their location within a domain. Figure 1-4 illustrates a DiffServ region with two domains.

Traffic enters a domain at an ingress boundary node and leaves the domain at an egress boundary node. The ingress boundary node typically performs the traffic-classification and conditioning function according to a specification or contract. Boundary nodes generally act as both ingress and egress nodes because traffic differentiation is desirable for the traffic that flows in both directions.

Traffic Classification and Conditioning

Traffic classification and conditioning identifies the traffic that will receive a differentiated service and ensures that it conforms to a service contract. Outside nodes connecting to the DiffServ domain have agreed to some service terms that the architecture defines as an SLA. The boundary node enforces this SLA, or contract, using traffic classification and conditioning. This enforcement uses a combination of packet classification, marking, metering, shaping, and policing to ensure that the traffic conforms to the contract terms.

Figure 1-4 *Functional View of Nodes and Domains in a DiffServ Region*

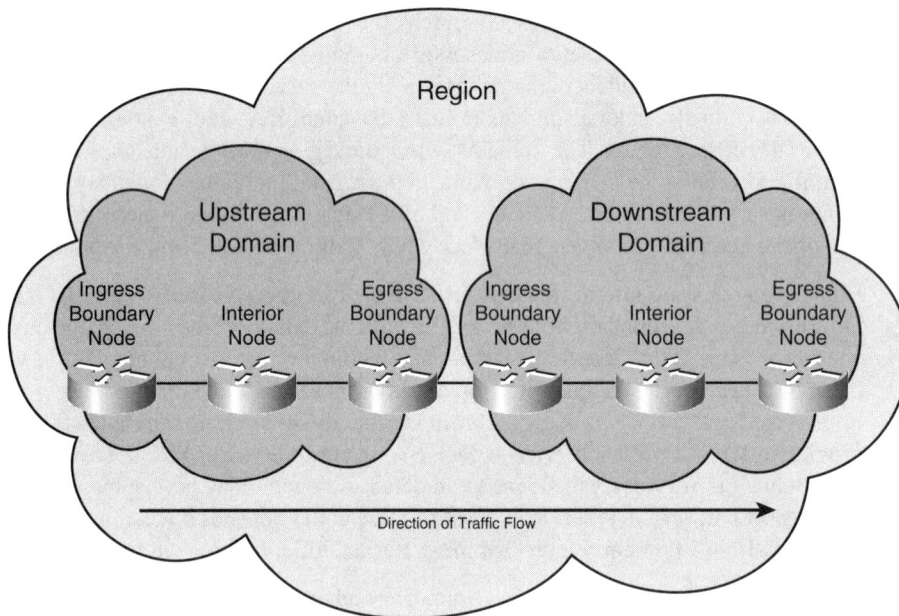

NOTE   RFC 3260 refined the initial DiffServ definition of SLA and introduced a new term, *service level specification* (SLS). Even though the term clarification is useful, this book uses the term SLA (which is more commonly used).

Traffic classification is the first action that a boundary node performs on traffic entering the domain. The boundary node examines the packet and, according to the SLA terms, implements an appropriate action (for example, marking, metering, policing). The architecture describes two types of classifiers: BA classifier and MF classifier. The BA classifier classifies packets using the DSCP in the packet. The MF classifier classifies packets using one or more fields of the packet header (for example, source IP address, destination IP address, protocol, source port, destination port) and other packet information (for example, input interface). The final result of packet classification is the local association of each packet with a class.

NOTE   The DiffServ architecture did not consider packet payload as input for packet classification. Actual implementations support packet classification using payload inspection and other classification criteria. You can consider those classifiers as an extension of the MF classifiers.

The boundary node conditions packets according to the SLA after classification. Traffic conditioning involves a combination of one or more of the following mechanisms: metering, marking, policing, or shaping. This conditioning process uses the result of the packet classification as input. Conditioning may vary from class to class. SLAs typically define a limit on the amount of traffic that the boundary node will take for each class. In those cases, the boundary node measures the traffic and makes a marking, dropping, or buffering decision on the packet. Conditioning must set the DSCP of each packet to an appropriate value. Downstream nodes typically rely on this DSCP for fast packet classification. The sections "Traffic Policing" and "Traffic Shaping" provide more details on conditioning mechanisms.

Traffic classification and conditioning may happen at different points of a packet path. In general, boundary nodes perform these tasks. However, the architecture does not preclude interior nodes from doing complex classification and conditioning if needed (for example, on international links). Figure 1-5 shows an example in which the ingress boundary node of the upstream domain uses MF classifiers and conditions separately the traffic that A and B generate. Marking packets close to the source facilitates application differentiation and simplifies classification on downstream nodes. In this example, the ingress boundary node of the downstream domain conditions the aggregate traffic that it receives. The ingress node relies on the classification and marking that the upstream domain performed. The egress boundary nodes may also perform traffic conditioning.

Figure 1-5   *Illustration of SLA Enforcement Across Two DiffServ Domains*

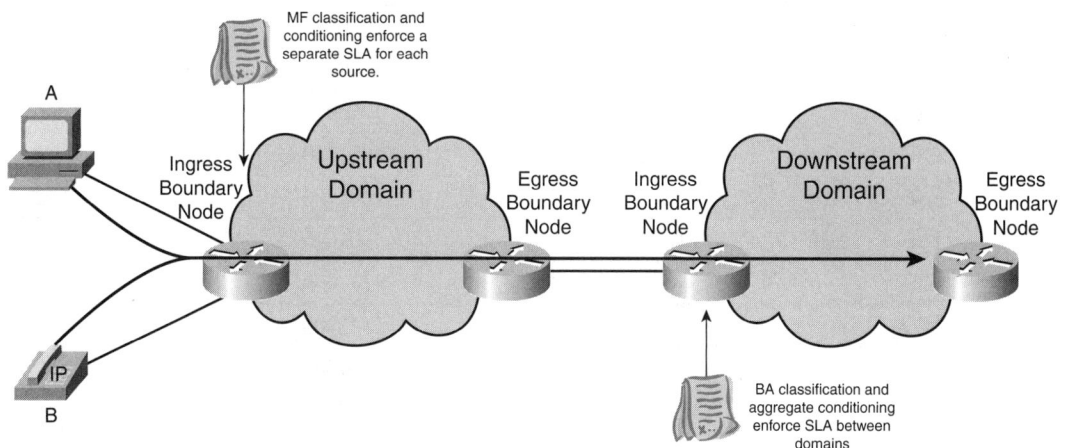

Per-Hop Behaviors

The DiffServ architecture defines a PHB as the forwarding behavior that a node applies to a BA. It represents a qualitative description of the latency, jitter, or loss characteristics that a BA will experience while traversing a DiffServ node. The PHB definition does not quantify these characteristics. A PHB group contains one or more related PHBs that are implemented simultaneously.

DiffServ nodes map packets to PHBs according to their DSCP. Table 1-3 shows the mappings that the architecture specifications recommend. DiffServ does not mandate these DSCP-to-PHB mappings. It provides the flexibility to confiugure arbitrary mappings if desired. Class selectors are the only exception, because the architecture defines them for backward compatibility with the use of the Precedence field in the IPv4 TOS octet. DiffServ domains not using the recommended mappings are more likely to have to re-mark traffic when interfacing with other DiffServ domains and experience greater operational complexity.

Table 1-3   *IETF-Recommended Mapping Between PHBs and DSCPs*

PHB	DSCP (Decimal)	DSCP (Binary)
EF	46	101110
AF43	38	100110
AF42	36	100100
AF41	34	100010
AF33	30	011110
AF32	28	011100
AF31	26	011010
AF23	22	010110
AF22	20	010100
AF21	18	010010
AF13	14	001110
AF12	12	001100
AF11	10	001010
CS7	56	111000
CS6	48	110000
CS5	40	101000
CS4	32	100000
CS3	24	011000
CS2	16	010000
CS1	8	001000
Default	0	000000

A number of PHB or PHB groups are part of the current DiffServ specifications: *Expedited Forwarding* (EF), *Assured Forwarding* (AF1, AF2, AF3, and AF4), *Class Selector* (CS), and Default. A node may support multiple PHB groups simultaneously. Nodes implement these PHBs using packet-buffering and scheduling mechanisms that the section "Traffic-Management Mechanisms" discusses.

Expedited Forwarding

The EF PHB defines a low-latency, low-jitter, and low-loss behavior that a DiffServ node may implement. This PHB acts as a building block for the transport of real-time traffic over a DiffServ domain. To support this behavior, a DiffServ node must serve EF traffic at a rate that is higher than its arrival rate, independently of the amount of non-EF traffic. This difference between the EF arrival and service rate helps ensure that EF traffic encounters empty or near-empty queues, which minimizes the queuing latency. This type of latency is generally the main contributor to packet latency and jitter during normal node operation. Minimization of queuing latency results in not only low latency and low jitter but also in low loss, because it prevents exhaustion of packet buffers. A DiffServ node should not cause any packet reordering within EF microflows. RFC 3246 and RFC 3247 define and discuss this PHB in detail.

Assured Forwarding

The AF family of PHB groups defines four different levels of forwarding guarantee that a DiffServ node may support. In simpler terms, these groups define how a DiffServ node may support different packet-loss guarantees. The AF PHB groups receive the names: AF1, AF2, AF3, and AF4. Each of these groups supports three drop-precedence levels. The higher the drop precedence, the more likely a DiffServ node will drop the packet if the group exhausts its allocated resources (bandwidth and buffers).

A total of 12 PHBs are associated with AF. Table 1-4 lists these PHBs with their respective drop precedence. RFC 2597 provides the detailed specifications for this set of PHB groups.

Table 1-4   *AF PHBs and Their Respective Drop Precedence*

Drop Precedence	AF1	AF2	AF3	AF4
Low	AF11	AF21	AF31	AF41
Medium	AF12	AF22	AF32	AF42
High	AF13	AF23	AF33	AF43

The AF PHB groups operate independently of each other. No implied ordering of forwarding guarantee exists between them. Furthermore, AF groups do not have an implicit latency or jitter characterization. The actual guarantees provided by each group depend on the forwarding resources that the node allocated, the amount of traffic of that group arriving at the node, and the relative drop precedence of the packet. The resources the node allocates are bandwidth and buffering space. The specifications mandate that nodes forward with higher probability those packets within an AF group that have lower drop precedence. A DiffServ node must not reorder packets of the same microflow within an AF group.

Class Selectors

DiffServ defines CS PHBs to offer backward compatibility with the use of IP precedence in the IPv4 TOS octet. Class selectors maintain the same relative ordering of IP precedence (a higher value implies a higher relative order). A node should provide a higher probability of forwarding to higher CSs. There is no latency, jitter, or loss characterization. Table 1-5 shows the mapping between CSs and IP precedence.

Table 1-5 *Relationship Between IP Precedence Values and DiffServ CSs*

PHB	DSCP (Decimal)	DSCP (Binary)	Precedence Name	Precedence (Binary)	Precedence (Decimal)
CS7	56	111000	Network Control	111	7
CS6	48	110000	Internetwork Control	110	6
CS5	40	101000	Critic/ECP	101	5
CS4	32	100000	Flash Override	100	4
CS3	24	011000	Flash	011	3
CS2	16	010000	Immediate	010	2
CS1	8	001000	Priority	001	1
CS0	0	000000	Routine	000	0

Default PHB

A DiffServ domain must provide a Default PHB that offers best-effort service. More precisely, the architecture defines the Default PHB as the existing best-effort service that RFC 1812 specifies. That is, the DiffServ domain will forward as many packets as possible, as soon as possible. There is no latency, jitter, and loss characterization. The implementation of other PHBs should preclude the operation of applications that rely on best-effort service.

MPLS Support for IntServ

MPLS support for IntServ remains undefined. The fact that RSVP can perform MPLS label distribution does not imply support for IntServ. As mentioned previously, the IntServ architecture makes use of RSVP, but the protocol signaling capabilities go beyond the IntServ requirements. However, you can find current efforts at the IETF to specify the interaction of aggregate IntServ reservations with MPLS networks. This proposal allows aggregate reservations to take advantage of the capabilities of MPLS networks without forcing those networks to provide full IntServ support. The "References" section at the end of this chapter lists reading material on the subject that currently constitutes work in progress.

MPLS Support for DiffServ

MPLS supports DiffServ with minimal adjustments to the MPLS and DiffServ architectures. MPLS does not introduce any modifications to the traffic-conditioning and PHB concepts defined in DiffServ. A *label switching router* (LSR) uses the same traffic-management mechanisms (metering, marking, shaping, policing, queuing, and so on) to condition and implement the different PHBs for MPLS traffic. An MPLS network may use traffic engineering to complement its DiffServ implementation. RFC 3270 defines MPLS support for the DiffServ architecture.

An MPLS network may implement DiffServ to support a diverse range of QoS requirements and services in a scalable manner. MPLS DiffServ is not specific to the transport of IP traffic over an MPLS network. An MPLS network may be carrying other types of traffic for which DiffServ does not apply (for example, ATM or Frame Relay). An MPLS DiffServ implementation is concerned only with supporting the PHBs that can satisfy the QoS requirements of all the types of traffic it carries. In addition, an MPLS network can grow without having to introduce major changes to its DiffServ design as the number of *label switched paths* (LSPs) in the network increases. These characteristics play an important role in the implementation of large MPLS networks that can transport a wide spectrum of traffic.

MPLS support for DiffServ introduces two types of LSPs with different service characteristics and operation. The first type, *EXP-inferred-class LSP* (E-LSP), can transport simultaneously multiple classes of traffic. The second type, *Label-inferred-class LSP* (L-LSP), transports a single class. They rely on different mechanisms to encode the DiffServ marking of the packet. In general, MPLS uses a label stack encoding based on shim headers that RFC 3032 defines. Figure 1-6 illustrates the fields contained in the shim header. The specifications for MPLS DiffServ define two encodings for the DiffServ code point. In addition, these LSP types impose different LSP signaling requirements. The changes in the encoding of DiffServ marking and the use of signaling are the two important areas where MPLS DiffServ differs from the original specification.

NOTE   RFC 3270 formally defines E-LSPs as EXP-inferred-PSC LSPs and L-LSP as Label-only-inferred-PSC LSPs. The section "DiffServ Terminology" provided a formal definition of a PSC earlier in this chapter. You can simply equate the term to a class of traffic.

Figure 1-6 *MPLS Shim Header*

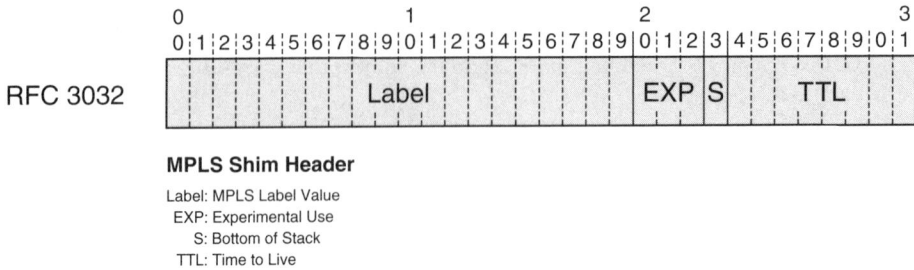

MPLS Shim Header
Label: MPLS Label Value
EXP: Experimental Use
S: Bottom of Stack
TTL: Time to Live

NOTE   ATM LSRs, Frame Relay LSRs, and LSRs with *label switching controlled ATM* (LC-ATM) interfaces use a native encoding for the top label rather than the shim header. This has important implications for the implementation of DiffServ on those devices. Given their decreasing use, this book does not focus on their details.

E-LSP

MPLS support for DiffServ defines E-LSP as a type of LSP that can carry simultaneously multiple classes of traffic. LSRs use the EXP field in the shim header to infer the PHB that a packet requires. As Figure 1-6 shows, the EXP contains three bits that can take eight possible values. The size of this field implies that an E-LSP can transport up to eight classes of service. An E-LSP carries fewer classes if some of those classes consume multiple markings (for example, AF1 which may use two or three markings). The specifications do not define recommended EXP values for the existing DiffServ PHBs (EF, AFn, CSn, Default). Furthermore, they do not define any structure on the three-bit field. LSRs may set up E-LSPs with bandwidth reservation (generally for the purpose of admission control).

Figure 1-7 illustrates a network using E-LSPs. In this case, there are two E-LSPs between node A and D. The network supports three classes: EF, AF1, and AF2. From top to bottom, the first E-LSP carries EF traffic; the second LSP multiplexes traffic of the three classes. Even though E-LSPs may carry multiple classes, the first E-LSP transports only EF traffic in this scenario. According to the E-LSP rules, all nodes perform PHB determination based on the EXP value of the packet. Notice that some EF traffic follows one E-LSP, whereas the rest follows the other E-LSP. Node A can split EF traffic if the node does not split EF microflows. Node C serves EF traffic without consideration of what LSP carries the EF traffic.

Figure 1-7   *MPLS Network Using an E-LSP*

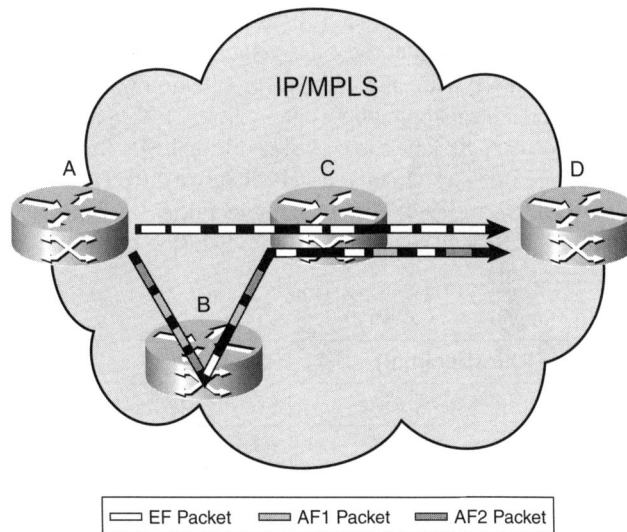

MPLS support for DiffServ defines mechanisms for E-LSPs to signal mappings between EXP values and PHBs. An LSR associates EXP-to-PHB mappings for input labels and PHB-to-EXP mappings for output labels. Signaling is optional and takes place during LSP setup. RFC 3270 defines extensions to LDP (DiffServ TLV [*Type, Length, Value*] for Label Request, Label Mapping, Label Release, and Notification messages) and RSVP (DiffServ object for Path messages) and their appropriate processing. The signaling identifies the LSP as an E-LSP and specifies the mappings between EXP values and PHBs that it will use. LSRs can use static but configurable mappings to avoid these signaling extensions for E-LSPs. An LSR should map all EXP values to the Default PHB if the LSP signaling did not specify a mapping and no preconfigured mapping exists.

NOTE   ATM LSRs, Frame Relay LSRs, and LSRs with LC-ATM interfaces do not forward packets using an MPLS shim header encapsulation. The absence of a shim header implies the absence of the EXP field. Therefore, those devices cannot support E-LSPs. This restriction also applies to nonpacket networks that use *generalized MPLS* (GMPLS).

L-LSP

MPLS support for DiffServ defines L-LSP as a type of LSP that can only transport of a single class of traffic. LSRs infer the class associated with the a packet from the label and determine the exact PHB using the label in combination with the EXP field. Table 1-6 illustrates the mandatory mapping between <classes, EXP> and PHBs. LSRs learn the association between L-LSP labels and classes during LSP setup. L-LSPs require the use of DiffServ signaling extensions. In this case, LSRs use a different format of the LDP DiffServ TLV and RSVP DiffServ object. The signaling identifies the LSP as an L-LSP and specifies the class that the L-LSP will transport. As with E-LSPs, LSRs may set up L-LSPs with bandwidth reservation.

Table 1-6 *Mandatory PHB Mappings for L-LSPs*

Class	EXP (Decimal)	EXP (Binary)	PHB
EF	0	000	EF
AF4	3	011	AF43
AF4	2	010	AF42
AF4	1	001	AF41
AF3	3	011	AF33
AF3	1	010	AF32
AF3	3	001	AF31
AF2	2	011	AF23
AF2	1	010	AF22
AF2	3	001	AF21
AF1	2	011	AF13
AF1	1	010	AF12
AF1	1	001	AF11
CS7	0	000	CS7
CS6	0	000	CS6
CS5	0	000	CS5
CS4	0	000	CS4

Table 1-6   *Mandatory PHB Mappings for L-LSPs (Continued)*

Class	EXP (Decimal)	EXP	PHB
CS3	0	000	CS3
CS2	0	000	CS2
CS1	0	000	CS1
Default	0	000	Default

Figure 1-8 illustrates an MPLS network using L-LSPs. In this case, there are four L-LSPs between node A and D. The network supports three classes: EF, AF1, and AF2. From top to bottom, the first L-LSP carries AF2, the second and third ones carry EF, and the fourth and last L-LSP carries AF1 traffic. Notice that node A splits EF traffic over two L-LSPs. Node A can divide EF traffic if the node does not split EF microflows. Even though Node C identifies EF traffic using the labels, that node serves EF traffic without consideration of what L-LSP is carrying the traffic (that is, the node does not provide a PHB per L-LSP, but per class).

Figure 1-8   *MPLS Network Using L-LSPs*

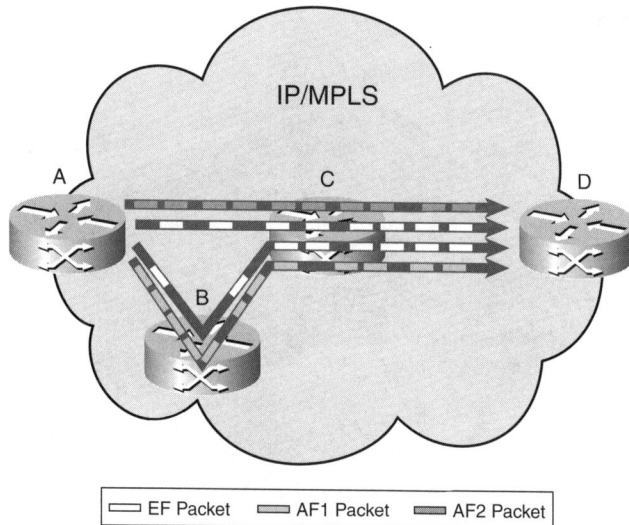

The use of E-LSPs and L-LSPs on an MPLS network is not mutually exclusive. LSRs maintain a DiffServ label context. This context indicates the LSP type (E-LSP or L-LSP), the PHBs that the LSP supports, and a mapping between the packet encapsulation and a PHB. For input labels, that mapping defines how the LSR can infer the PHB from the packet encapsulation. For output labels, that mapping defines how the LSR encodes the PHB. This context is populated with preconfigured mappings or through DiffServ information learned during LSP setup. Table 1-7 compares E-LSPs and L-LSPs.

Table 1-7 *Comparing E-LSPs and L-LSPs*

E-LSP	L-LSP
One or more classes per LSP	One class per LSP
PHB inferred from EXP field	PHB inferred from Label and EXP field
Signaling optional	Signaling required

Figure 1-9 shows an MPLS network using L-LSPs and E-LSPs simultaneously. In this example, there are two E-LSPs between node E and node D and two L-LSPs between node A and D. The network supports three classes: EF, AF1, and AF2. In this example, node C transports both E-LSPs and L-LSPs. This node uses the DiffServ label context to determine the LSP type and the exact mapping that it should use to infer the PHB from the packet encapsulation. LSRs serve the packets according to their PHB regardless of the LSP and its type. The LSP details influence the PHB determination, but the PHB ultimately determines the packet treatment. In this example, nodes A and E use one type of LSPs exclusively. However, each of them could alternatively use a combination of E-LSPs and L-LSPs to reach node D.

Figure 1-9 *MPLS Network Combining L-LSPs and E-LSPs*

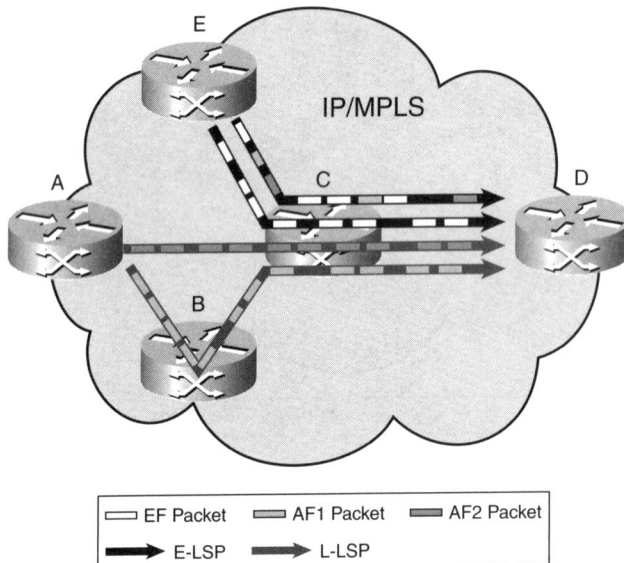

NOTE   ATM LSRs, Frame Relays LSRs, and LSRs with LC-ATM interfaces do not forward packets using an MPLS shim header encapsulation. The absence of a shim header implies the absence of the EXP field. However, those devices can still support DiffServ using their native encapsulation to implement L-LSPs. ATM LSRs and LSRs with LC-ATM interfaces use the native label encoding and the ATM CLP (*Cell Loss Priority*) bit for PHB determination. Frame Relay LSRs use their native label encoding and the Frame Relay DE bit for PHB determination. RFC 3270 describes in detail the procedures that apply in those cases.

DiffServ Tunneling Models over MPLS

MPLS LSPs support for DiffServ defines three models of interaction between DiffServ markings in different layers of encapsulation. A simple example is an IP packet that has received the MPLS encapsulation. There is one PHB marking in the MPLS encapsulation and a PHB marking in the DiffServ field of the IP packet. There are three models to handle the interaction between multiple markings: the pipe, short-pipe, and uniform models. The models define the procedures that an LSR can apply when a packet (either IP or MPLS) with an existing PHB marking enters and exits an LSP. The three models do not introduce any changes to the normal label swapping behavior of an LSR or any signaling requirements. These models apply equally to E-LSPs and L-LSPs.

NOTE   The MPLS DiffServ tunneling models extend the concepts introduced in RFC 2983. That RFC defines the operation of DiffServ over IP tunnels. In many aspects, LSPs resemble IP tunnels.

NOTE   RFC 3270 defines the MPLS DiffServ tunneling models for the transport of IP and MPLS traffic. However, the underlying concepts can apply to the transport of other types of traffic (for example, Ethernet) over an MPLS network.

Pipe Model

The pipe model conceals the tunneled PHB marking between the LSP ingress and egress nodes. This model guarantees that there are no changes to the tunneled PHB marking through the LSP; even if an LSR along the path performs traffic conditioning and re-marks the traffic. All LSRs that the LSP traverses use the LSP PHB marking and ignore the tunneled PHB marking. This model proves useful when an MPLS network connects other DiffServ domains. The MPLS network can implement DiffServ and still be transparent for the connected domains. RFC 3270 defines this model as mandatory for MPLS networks supporting DiffServ.

Figure 1-10 illustrates the operation of the pipe model. The LSP ingress determines the LSP PHB marking it will encode in the pushed encapsulation. It may consider the existing PHB marking of the packet for this purpose. It preserves the tunneled PHB marking when pushing the new label encapsulation. Be aware that the packet entering the LSP may be an IP or an MPLS packet. The LSP egress serves the packet according to the LSP PHB marking. This action implies that this node infers the packet PHB before the pop operation. Moreover, the LSP egress does not modify the tunneled PHB marking that the pop operation exposes. An LSP using the pipe model cannot use *penultimate hop popping* (PHP) because the LSP egress will not have access to the LSP PHB marking.

Figure 1-10 *Pipe Tunneling Model*

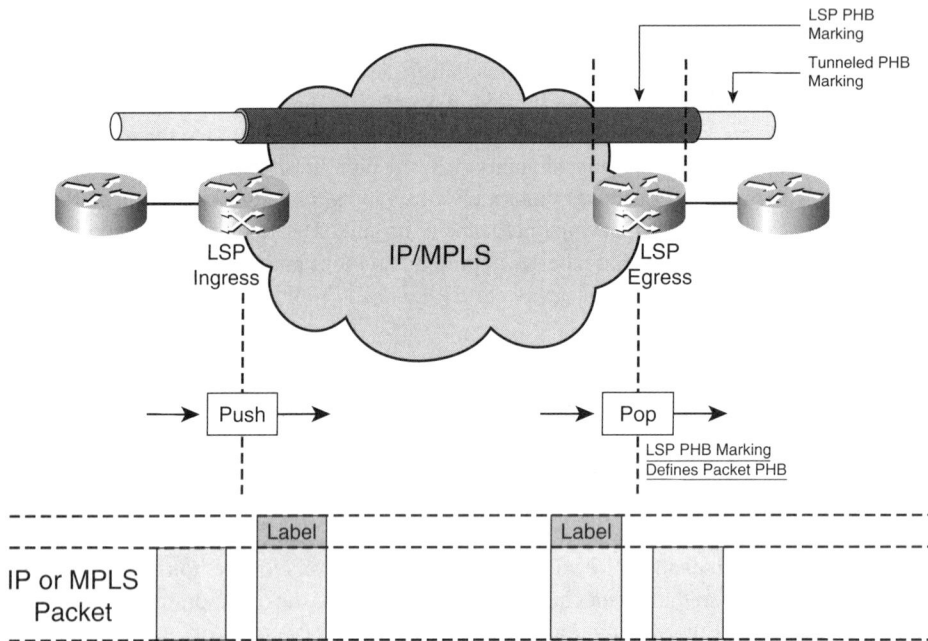

Short-Pipe Model

The short-pipe model represents a small variation of the pipe model. It also guarantees that there are no changes to the tunneled PHB marking, even if an LSR re-marks the LSP PHB marking. The short-pipe model shares the same ability of the pipe model to allow an MPLS network to be transparent from the DiffServ point of view. The short-pipe model differs, however, on how the LSP egress infers the packet PHB. The LSP egress uses the tunneled PHB marking to infer the packet PHB and serve the packet consequently. Given this difference with the pipe model, an MPLS network may implement LSPs using the short-pipe model regardless of whether LSRs perform PHP.

Figure 1-11 demonstrates the details of the operation of the short-pipe model with PHP. The LSP ingress must determine the LSP PHB marking it will encode in the pushed encapsulation. It may consider the existing PHB marking of the packet. The LSP ingress also preserves tunneled PHB marking when pushing the new label encapsulation. The short-pipe and pipe models share the same procedure for the LSP ingress. It infers the packet PHB from the LSP PHB marking before performing the pop operation. The penultimate hop does not modify the tunneled PHB marking that the pop operation exposes. The LSP egress infers the packet PHB from the tunneled PHB marking in the header used for packet forwarding.

Figure 1-11 *Short-Pipe Tunneling Model with PHP*

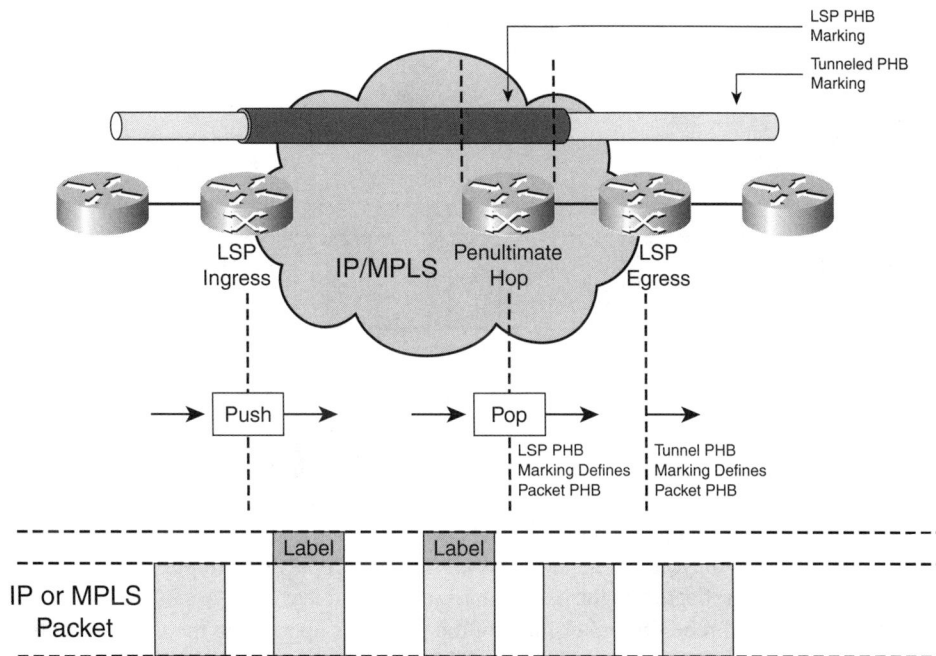

Figure 1-12 shows the details of the short-pipe model for LSPs that do not experience PHP. The operation of the LSP ingress remains the same as before. The penultimate hop performs the label swapping operation and serves the packet according to the corresponding E-LSP or L-LSP procedures. The LSP egress infers the packet PHB from the tunneled PHB marking in the header used for packet forwarding. This action implies that the LSP egress infers the packet PHB after the label pop. As with all previous models, this node forwards the tunneled PHB marking unmodified. The short-pipe model offers the external behavior regardless of whether PHP happens.

Figure 1-12 *Short-Pipe Tunneling Model Without PHB*

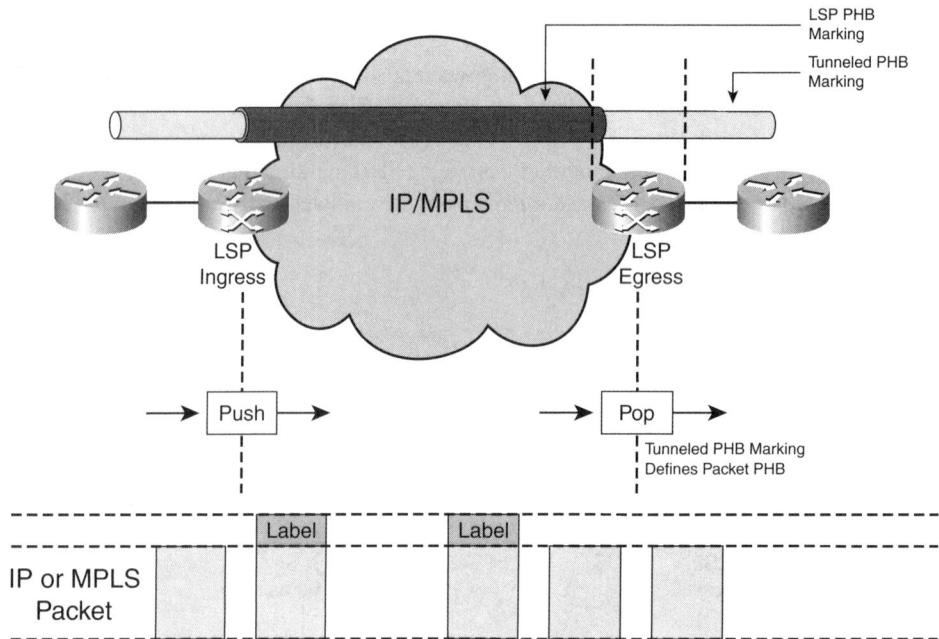

Uniform Model

The uniform model makes the LSP an extension of the DiffServ domain of the encapsulated packet. In this model, a packet only has a single meaningful PHB marking (which resides in the most recent encapsulation). LSRs propagate the packet PHB to the exposed encapsulation when they perform a pop operation. This propagation implies that any packet re-marking is reflected on the packet marking when it leaves the LSP. The LSP becomes an integral part of the DiffServ domain of the packet as opposed to the transparent transport that the pipe and short-pipe models provided. This model proves useful when an MPLS network connects other DiffServ domain and all networks (including the MPLS network) need to behave as a single DiffServ domain.

Figure 1-13 illustrates the operation of the uniform model with PHP. The LSP ingress encodes the existing packet PHB marking in the pushed encapsulation. When the packet receives the new encapsulation, the encapsulated PHB marking becomes irrelevant. The penultimate hop infers the packet PHB before the pop operation and encodes it in the exposed encapsulation.

Figure 1-13 *Uniform Tunneling Model with PHP*

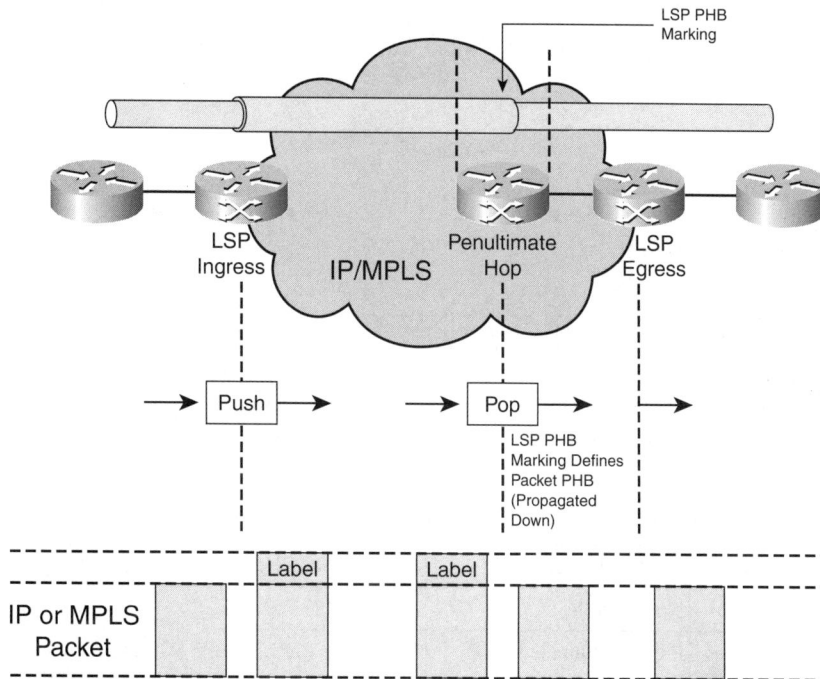

Figure 1-14 shows the details of the uniform model for LSPs without PHP. The operation of the LSP ingress remains the same. The penultimate hop performs a regular label swapping operation. The LSP egress always infers the PHB before the pop operation and propagates the PHB marking to the exposed encapsulation. The uniform model offers the same external behavior regardless of whether the LSP uses PHP. Tables 1-8 and 1-9 summarize the operation of the three tunneling modes with PHP and without PHP, respectively.

Figure 1-14 *Uniform Tunneling Model Without PHP*

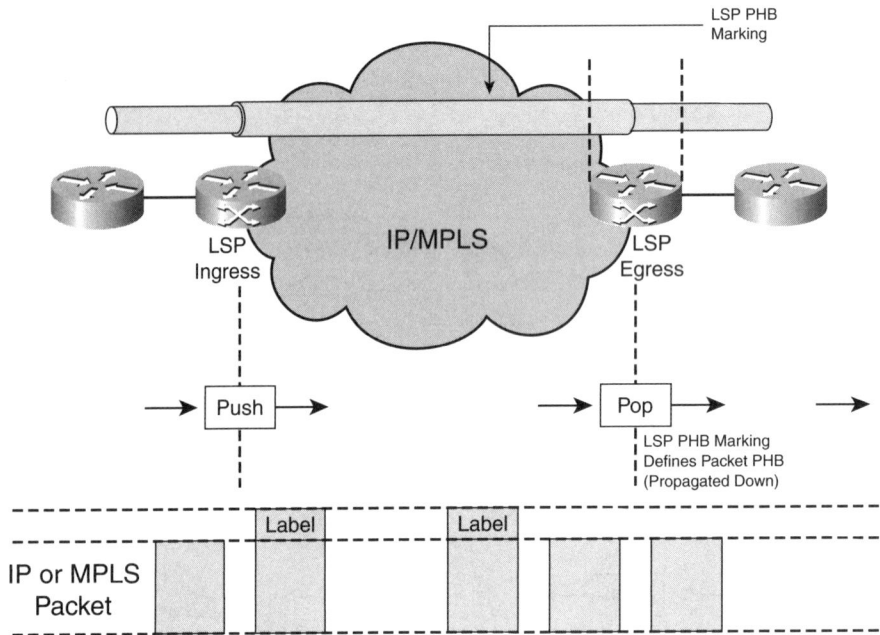

Table 1-8 *DiffServ Tunneling Models over MPLS with PHP*

Model	LSP Ingress	Penultimate Hop	LSP Egress
Pipe	Not possible.	Not possible.	Not possible.
Short-pipe	Preserve tunneled PHB and set PHB in pushed encapsulation.	Determine PHB before pop.	Determine PHB using forwarding header.
Uniform	Copy existing packet PHB to pushed encapsulation.	Determine PHB before pop and propagate it down.	Determine PHB using received header.

Table 1-9 *Tunneling Models over MPLS Without PHP*

Model	LSP Ingress	LSP Egress
Pipe	Preserve tunneled PHB and set PHB in pushed encapsulation.	Determine PHB before pop operations.
Short-pipe	Preserve tunneled PHB and set PHB in pushed encapsulation.	Determine PHB after pop using forwarding header.
Uniform	Copy existing packet PHB to pushed encapsulation.	Determine PHB before pop and propagate it down.

Traffic-Management Mechanisms

The implementation of QoS ultimately relies on a collection of traffic-management mechanisms. The evolution of packet switched networks introduced the need for the development of suitable traffic-management mechanisms. These mechanisms help network nodes avoid and manage congestion. Frame Relay and, especially, ATM networks make use of some of these or similar techniques. This section summarizes the key concepts behind traffic management within the context of IP and MPLS networks. These mechanisms represent the building blocks that network nodes use to implement QoS using both the DiffServ and IntServ architectures.

Traffic Classification

Network nodes generally perform traffic classification before applying traffic-management mechanisms. The aggregate traffic that traverses a node typically combines traffic with different QoS requirements. In those cases, network nodes need to classify the traffic to provide the expected level of differentiation.

Traffic classification can be in the form of an MF or BA classifier in the context of DiffServ. Classification can also be in the form of filter specification in IntServ. Traffic classification typically involves stateless inspection of packet headers. In some cases, nodes perform packet payload inspection or even stateful inspection of packets. However, the complexity and processing impact of those two types of classification limits its applicability to particular devices in the network.

Traffic Marking

Packet marking involves assigning a new value to a QoS-related field in the header of a packet. This marking typically associates the packet with a class or a drop precedence. As discussed earlier, the DiffServ architecture relies on packet marking to indicate the PHB for each packet. Several Layer 2 technologies also make use of packet marking for QoS purposes, as follows:

- Ethernet uses a 3-bit priority field in the VLAN header.
- ATM uses a 1-bit field to indicate the drop precedence of a cell (cell loss priority or CLP).
- Frame Relay uses an equivalent 1-bit field to capture the drop precedence of a frame (*Discard Eligible* or DE).

Table 1-10 summarizes the most common fields used for packet marking.

Table 1-10   *Examples of Header Fields Used for Packet Marking for QoS Purposes*

Header Field	Field Size (Bits)	Field Function
IP DiffServ Code Point (DSCP)	6	PHB
MPLS Experimental Bits (EXP)	3	PHB or drop precedence
Ethernet VLAN User Priority	3	Queue selection
ATM Cell Loss Priority (CLP)	1	Drop precedence
Frame Relay Discard Eligible (DE)	1	Drop precedence

NOTE   The term *drop precedence* is synonymous with *drop priority*.

Traffic Policing

Traffic policing is a commonly used scheme for rate control. In different situations, a network node might need to control the amount of a particular traffic stream. A policer measures the traffic and compares the measurement with a predefined traffic profile. The comparison result determines the action the policer takes on the packet. The three main actions are transmitting, marking, or dropping the packet. The marking action indicates implicitly that the node will transmit the packet after marking it.

Policing is essential to the traffic-conditioning function in DiffServ. It is not exclusive to this architecture. Many technologies make use of traffic policing (for example, ATM and Frame Relay). In general, traffic policing is a popular mechanism at boundaries between administrative domains.

Policers generally use a token bucket as the traffic profile description. A token bucket has two parameters: token rate and bucket size. The token rate specifies the rate at which new tokens arrive. The bucket size defines the highest number of tokens that the bucket can accumulate. The algorithm is simple: The policer constantly adds tokens to the bucket at the token rate. The policer checks whether the bucket holds B tokens when a packet of size B arrives. A positive or negative result triggers two different actions. If the result is positive (the bucket holds B tokens or more), the policer removes B tokens and executes a predetermined action. Otherwise, the policer executes an alternative action. Figure 1-15 shows three different traffic streams with the same average rate (10 Mbps) but with different token bucket definitions.

Figure 1-15 *Three Traffic Streams with the Same Average Rate but Different Token Bucket Descriptions*

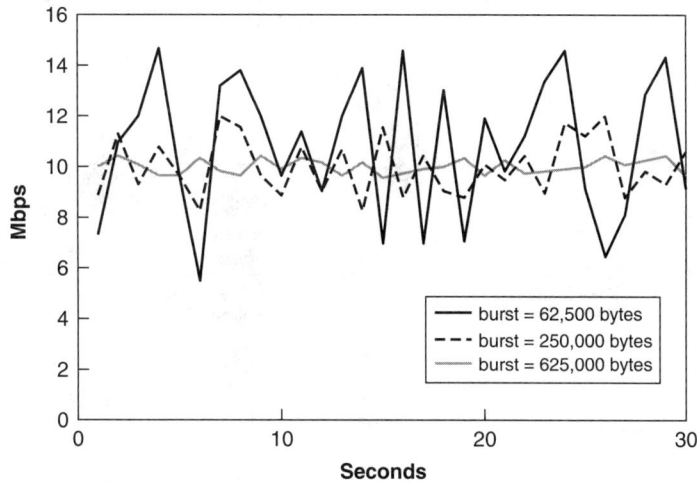

RFC 2697 defines a single-rate policer for DiffServ. This policer uses two token buckets, C and E. Tokens arrive at bucket C at a *committed information rate* (CIR). Tokens overflow into bucket E when bucket C is full. The policer can operate in two modes: color blind and color aware. In color-blind mode, the policer does not consider the current packet marking. In color-aware mode, the existing packet marking influences the operation of the policer. The policer configuration identifies the traffic colors (that is, markings) as conform or exceed.

Figure 1-16 shows the token buckets and the two modes of operation. This policer can trigger three different actions: conform, exceed, and violate. Each of those actions can be transmitting, marking, or dropping the packet.

Figure 1-16 *Single-Rate Policer Defined in RFC 2697*

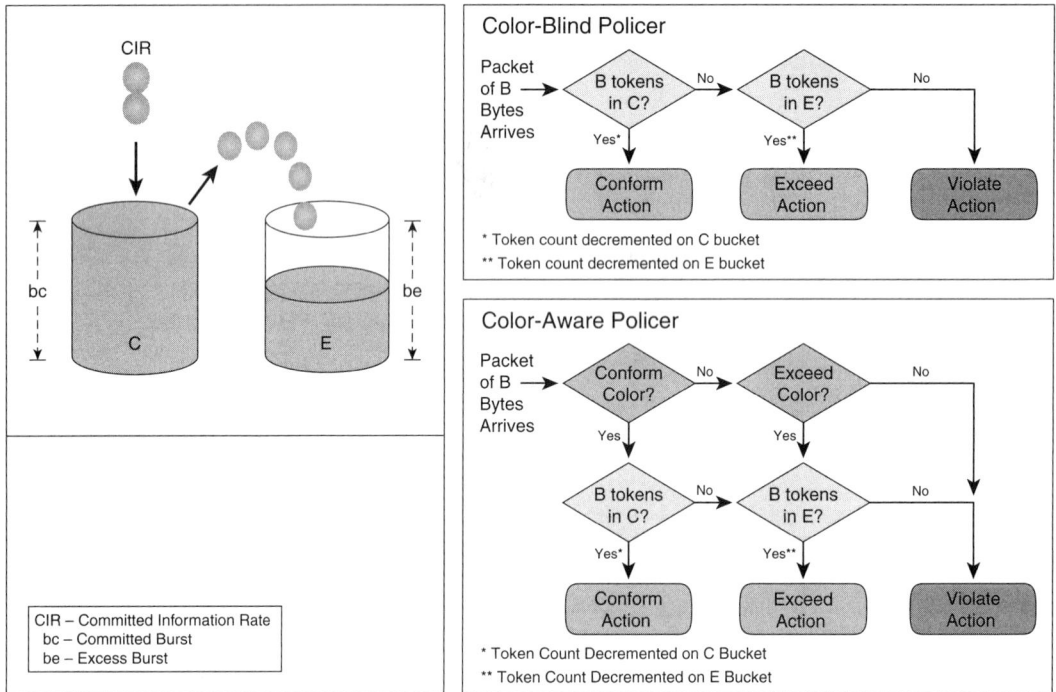

RFC 2698 proposes a similar dual-rate policer for DiffServ. This policer also uses two token buckets, C and P. Tokens arrive at bucket P at a *peak information rate* (PIR). Similarly, tokens arrive at bucket C at a CIR. Tokens do not overflow between buckets in this case. The policer can also operate in a color-blind or color-aware mode. These two modes have the same characteristics described earlier.

Figure 1-17 illustrates the token bucket structure and the policer operation in its two modes. Similar to the single-rate policer described earlier, this policer can trigger three actions: conform, exceed, and violate. Again, each of those actions can be transmitting, marking, or dropping the packet.

Figure 1-17 *Dual-Rate Policer Defined in RFC 2698*

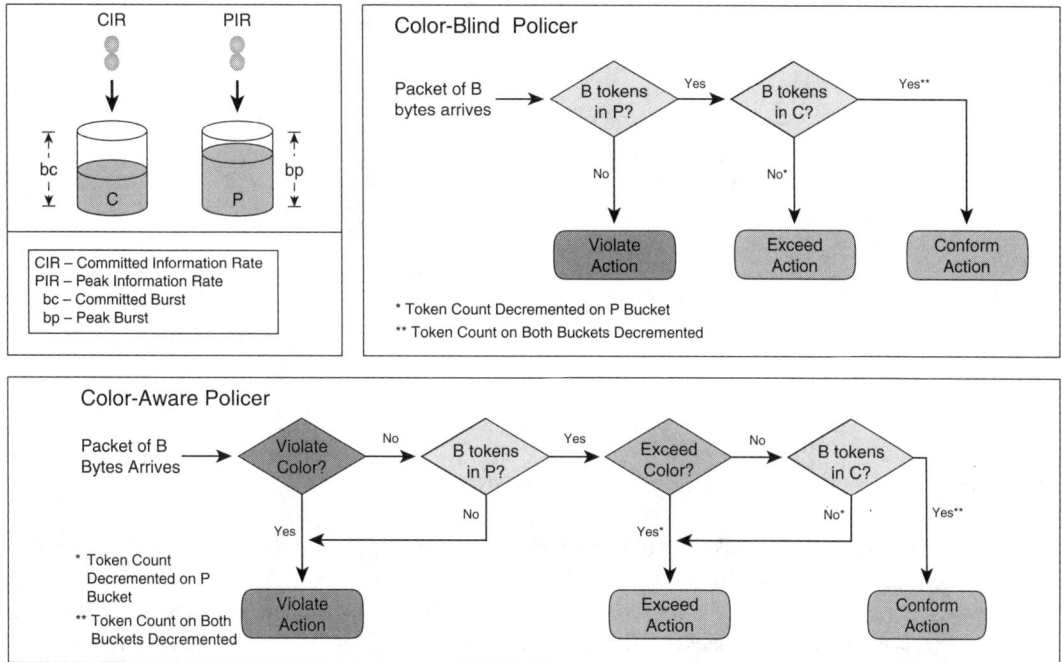

NOTE   The description of these policers uses Cisco terminology that differs somewhat from the
            terms in the original specifications. However, the policer operation is the same.

Traffic Shaping

Shaping is another commonly used mechanism for rate control. Similar to a policer, a
shaper measures traffic and compares the measurement with a profile. In this case, the
comparison result determines whether the shaper should delay the packet or permit further
processing. Therefore, shaping requires the buffering or queuing of packets that exceed the
profile. Shaping allows a node to absorb bursts in a traffic stream and smooth these bursts
by serving the stream according to the profile. Shaping might result in packet loss if the
traffic stream drastically exceeds the profile or might not smooth the traffic if the stream
never exceeds the profile. Shaping is also essential to traffic-conditioning in DiffServ.
Figure 1-18 shows the smoothing effect of a (10-Mbps) shaper on a sample traffic stream.

Figure 1-18 *Effect of Shaping on a Sample Traffic Stream*

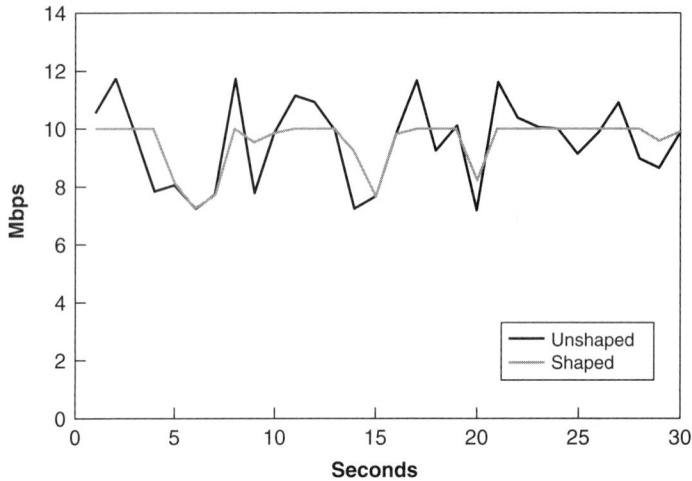

Shaping can also make use of a token bucket as a traffic profile. The token bucket algorithm remains the same: Tokens go into the bucket at the token rate. The bucket size defines the maximum number of tokens that the bucket can hold. The shaper checks whether B tokens are available in the bucket when a packet of size B arrives. If the current token count is greater than or equal to B tokens, the shaper serves the packet and removes B tokens from the bucket. If less than B tokens are in the bucket, the shaper queues the packet. If the packet encounters a queue when arriving at the shaper, it waits its turn at the end of the queue. The smaller the bucket size, the smoother the shaper output is. Figure 1-19 shows a packet shaper using a token bucket.

Figure 1-19 *Example of a Packet Shaper Using a Token Bucket*

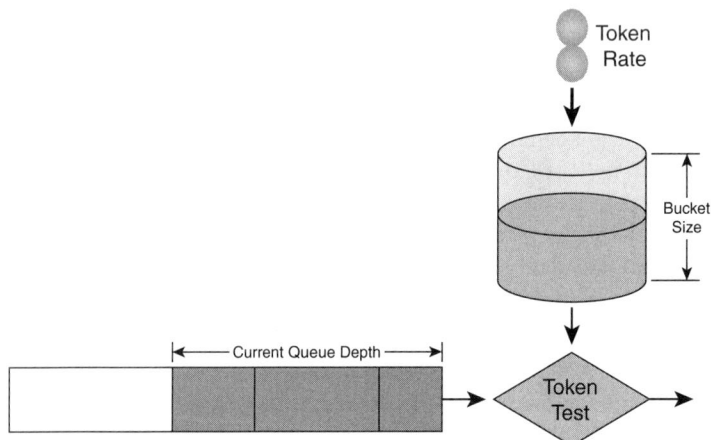

Congestion Management

Buffer allocation and traffic scheduling are two popular mechanisms for congestion management. Suppose, for instance, that a node switches traffic to an interface at a rate that exceeds the capacity of that interface at that specific time. When congestion occurs, the interface manages the excess traffic by buffering or queuing the traffic. A scheduler decides how to serve the queue (that is, it decides which packet to transmit next). A node may create multiple queues at a given congestion point. Each queue can receive a different allocation of buffers and bandwidth. This resource allocation, along with the scheduling discipline between queues, provides different latency, jitter, and loss characteristics for the traffic in the different queues.

Congestion may happen at different points within a network node. Each congestion point represents a potential source of delay, jitter, and loss for traffic streams. The most common points subject to congestion are output interfaces. However, nodes do experience congestion at other points. For example, nodes with a distributed architecture might face congestion at the interface between a line card and the switch fabric. Other service modules (for example, encryptors and compressors) can also experience congestion. The exact list of points subject to a relevant level of congestion depends on the device architecture and the traffic patterns across the device.

A simple approach to congestion management uses a single queue with a *first-in, first-out* (FIFO) scheduler. With a FIFO queue, an interface transmits packets in the order they arrive. New packets are appended to the end of the queue. The queue grows as long as packets arrive faster than the interface can send them. At some point, the queue might exceed the maximum buffering capacity (in which case, the interface needs to discard a packet). A common policy is to drop the arriving new packets in favor of those packets already waiting in the queue. This dropping policy receives the name of tail drop. In this case, the maximum queue size limits the maximum queuing delay that a packet will experience on this interface. Tail drop is one of several mechanisms that could be used. The next section discusses other methods of managing queue size.

Weighted fair queuing (WFQ) is a popular scheduler for fair bandwidth sharing. A simple scheduler that served nonempty queues in a round-robin order can provide bandwidth sharing. However, bandwidth distribution would not be fair because those queues with larger packets would eventually get a larger share. A bit-by-bit round-robin scheduler would be fair to packets of all sizes, but nodes transmit entire packets at a time and not individual bits. WFQ approximates the ideal behavior by computing the departure time of the packet as if a bit-by-bit round-robin scheduler were in use. The scheduler selects packets for transmission in the order of their departure times. A weight associated with queues can scale the departure time and ultimately scales the bandwidth share for the queue.

Figure 1-20 illustrates the operation of WFQ with three sample queues. The packet number identifies the order in which each packet arrived. The scheduler orders packets by their departure time and serves them in that order. In this case, the first queue has a weight two times the weight of the other two queues. The weight has the effect of reducing the departure time in half for packets in that queue. This weight provides that queue a guarantee of half the bandwidth in the worst case. The scheduler still guarantees a quarter of the bandwidth to each of the other two queues. Queues may get more than their fair share of the bandwidth if other queues are empty. The bottom part of the figure shows the transmission order that WFQ creates in comparison with a FIFO scheduler.

Figure 1-20 *WFQ Scheduler with Three Sample Queues*

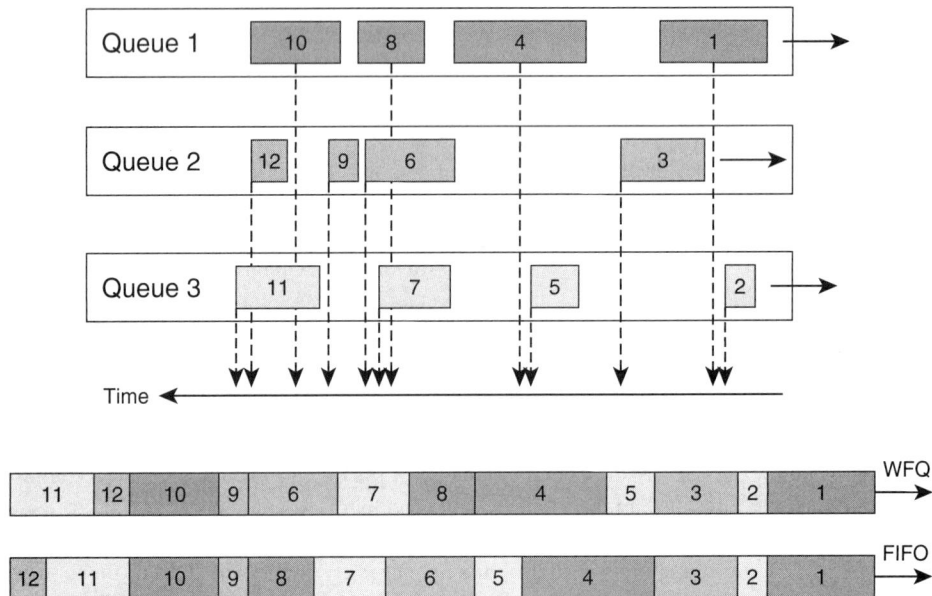

Deficit round robin (DRR) is an alternative scheduler that can provide bandwidth sharing. Similarly to WFQ, DRR provides fair bandwidth sharing for variable-length packets and a weighting mechanism to influence bandwidth distribution. However, this scheduler results in a simpler hardware implementation that facilitates its use at higher speeds. The scheduler maintains a deficit (byte) counter for all nonempty queues. During each round, the scheduler selects the next nonempty queue, adds a quantum (byte) value to the queue deficit counter, and serves as many packets as the result permits. The deficit counter receives any remainder after serving the queue. The scheduler can scale the bandwidth share of a queue by scaling the quantum value for that queue.

Figure 1-21 shows the operation of DRR with three sample queues. As in the previous figure, the packet number identifies the order in which each packet arrived. The first queue uses a quantum of 600, which is two times the quantum of 300 used for the other two queues. That configuration guarantees that the first queue gets half of the bandwidth in the worst case. Each of the other two queues gets a quarter of the bandwidth in the worst case. As with WFQ, queues may get more than their fair share of the bandwidth if other queues are empty. The scheduler uses the packet size and the deficit counter to determine the next packet to transmit in each round. The bottom part of the figure shows the transmission order that DRR generates in comparison with a FIFO scheduler.

Figure 1-21 *DRR Scheduler with Three Sample Queues*

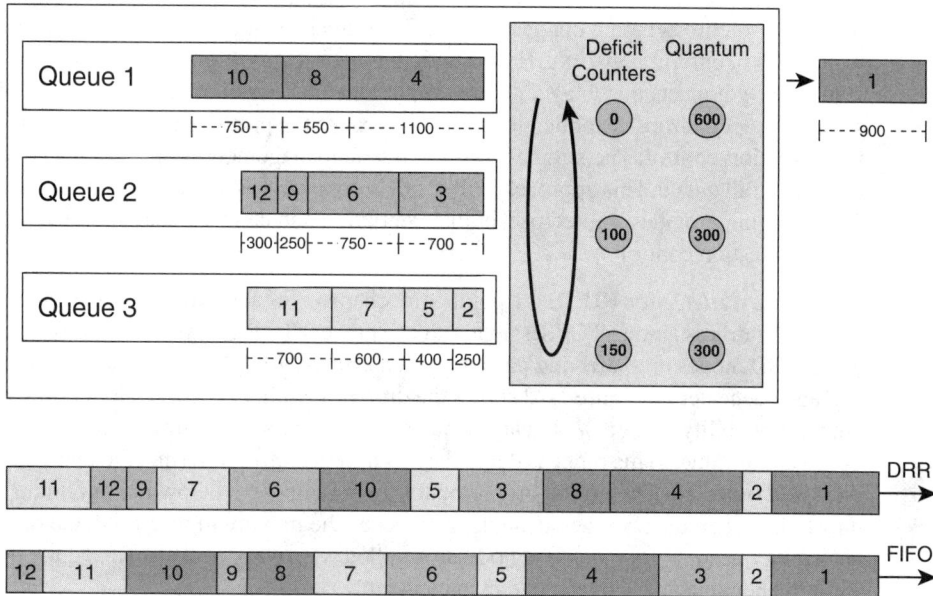

Schedulers operate independently from the classification process that selects a queue for arriving packets. The granularity of that classification process and its corresponding number of queues can vary greatly. Classifying and queuing microflows separately provides a high level of isolation; as the number of microflows increases, however, the processing complexity of the scheduler increases. A microflow hashing function with a fixed number of buckets reduces this complexity with a lower level of isolation between individual microflows. A scheme based on DiffServ BAs reduces the processing complexity even further while providing coarse traffic isolation.

Actual scheduler implementations regularly include the ability to serve some traffic with strict priority. Schedulers such as WFQ or DRR can provide bandwidth guarantees and latency bounds for each queue. However, they cannot guarantee low latency in general terms. A hybrid scheduler can compensate for this limitation with the addition of at least one priority queue. The scheduler serves this queue with strict priority until the queue becomes empty. Only at that point does the scheduler serve other queues. The priority queue does not preempt the transmission of a nonpriority packet, but the presence of a single packet in the priority queue forces the scheduler to serve that queue next.

Active Queue Management

Network nodes need to manage queues to control their length. Active queue management consists in dropping or marking packets before a queue becomes full and is independent of the type of scheduler serving the queue. Dropping and in some cases marking play an important role in signaling congestion to TCP sources, which consume most of the bandwidth in current networks. How a node indicates congestion to traffic sources significantly impacts the delay and throughput that TCP sessions experience. How UDP sessions react to drops is application specific because the protocol does not provide a built-in congestion-control. The simplest form of queue management drops new packets that arrive to a full queue. This approach, called tail dropping, uses a fixed maximum queue size. Tail dropping provides limited packet differentiation and can have suboptimal effects on TCP congestion control.

Random early detection (RED) is a popular mechanism for active queue management. RED improves fairness among TCP sessions and can prevent TCP global synchronization. When using RED, nodes drop arriving packets with a *probability* (p) that is a function of the average queue depth. Figure 1-22 shows the drop probability function. Nodes drop packets with a probability that grows linearly from zero to a maximum within a range of average queue depth values. This range is defined by a *minimum threshold* (minTh) and a *maximum threshold* (maxTh). The packet drop probability remains zero below the minimum threshold. When the average queue depth exceeds the maximum threshold, the drop probability becomes one, and the node drops all new arriving packets. RFC 2309 contains recommendations for active queue management.

Figure 1-22 *Drop Probability Function for RED*

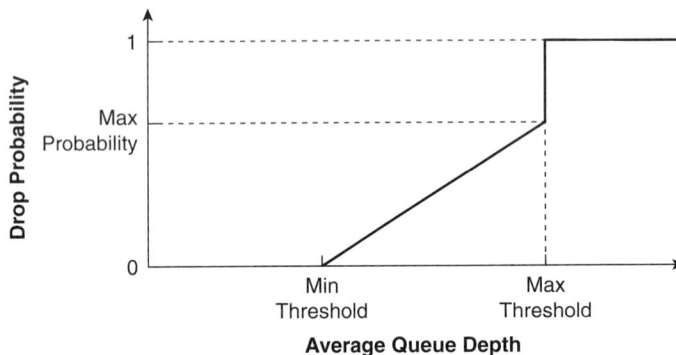

RED relies on the computation of the average queue depth. The use of the average depth rather than the instantaneous depth allows the node to accommodate traffic bursts but react to persistent congestion. RED uses a moving average as a simple approximation of the actual average depth. This moving average is computed with the following equation:

$$a_i = (1 - w)\, a_{i-1} - w q_i$$

where

- a_i = Average queue depth for the i-th packet
- w = Averaging weight, ranging between zero and one
- q_i = Instantaneous queue depth for the i-th packet

Figure 1-23 illustrates the impact that different averaging weights depth have on the average queue depth estimation. The average is smoother with lower weight values. The higher the weight, the closer the average queue depth tracks the instantaneous size. A weight value of one produces an estimated average queue depth that equals the instantaneous queue.

Figure 1-23 *RED Average Queue Depth Estimation with Different Weights*

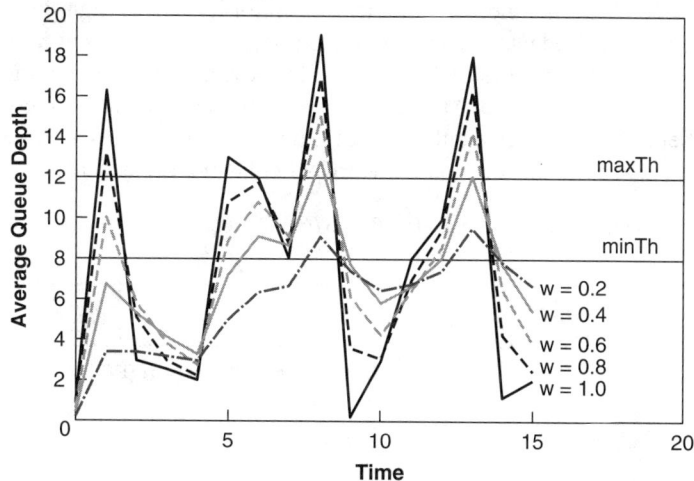

A network node can use multiple RED profiles to perform active queue management using different probability functions. This particular use of RED receives the name of *weighted RED* (WRED). The word *weight* refers to the drop profile selection mechanism. The network node uses a packet marking (for example, IP DSCP or MPLS EXP) for the drop profile selection. WRED can use that drop precedence of a packet to apply different WRED profiles. This drop precedence can be the result of traffic policing marking some packets differently based on whether they exceeded a traffic profile. Figures 1-24 shows three sample drop profiles that a node could use for queue management. The definition of each WRED profile is independent from the others. For example, they may overlap or have different slopes. However, network nodes should use a more aggressive profile for packets with a higher drop precedence.

NOTE   The weight (or marking) that WRED uses to select a drop profile is different from the averaging weight it uses to compute the average queue depth.

Figure 1-24 *Sample WRED Design with Three Drop Profiles*

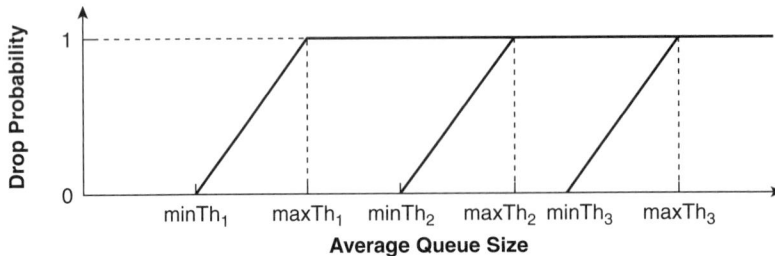

Active queue management can use packet marking as an alternative to packet dropping. A node can use packet marking for congestion notification. Although packet dropping is an acceptable congestion-notification mechanism for long-lived high-throughput TCP sessions, short-lived interactive TCP sessions react better to *explicit congestion notification* (ECN). RFC 3168 defines ECN for IP. MPLS has no standard congestion-notification specification. Definition of MPLS ECN would probably require using a bit in the MPLS EXP field. This approach would reduce the number of PHBs that an E-LSP could transport. Figure 1-25 shows the location of the ECN field in the IP header.

Figure 1-25 *ECN Field in IP Header as Defined in RFC 3168*

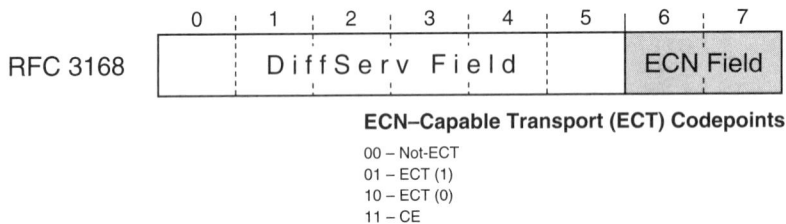

Link Fragmentation and Interleaving

A network node may require performing *link fragmentation and interleaving* (LFI) to reduce latency for priority traffic. Schedulers that use a priority queue do not preempt the current transmission of nonpriority packets. A priority packet may arrive right after the transmission of a nonpriority packet starts. In that case the priority packet must wait for the complete transmission of the nonpriority packet before the scheduler serves the priority packet. Depending on packet sizes and transmission rates, priority packets might experience an unacceptable amount of latency. Fragmentation of large nonpriority packets and interleaving of fragments with priority packets bounds the latency for priority traffic. Table 1-11 shows the latency that different packet sizes create at various rates.

Table 1-11   *Transmission Latency in Milliseconds for Different Packet Sizes at Multiple Rates*

	256 kbps	512 kbps	768 kbps	1024 kbps	1280 kbps	1536 kbps
64 bytes	2.0	1.0	0.7	0.5	0.4	0.3
128 bytes	4.0	2.0	1.3	1.0	0.8	0.7
256 bytes	8.0	4.0	2.7	2.0	1.6	1.3
384 bytes	12.0	6.0	4.0	3.0	2.4	2.0
512 bytes	16.0	8.0	5.3	4.0	3.2	2.7
640 bytes	20.0	10.0	6.7	5.0	4.0	3.3
768 bytes	24.0	12.0	8.0	6.0	4.8	4.0
896 bytes	28.0	14.0	9.3	7.0	5.6	4.7
1024 bytes	32.0	16.0	10.7	8.0	6.4	5.3
1152 bytes	36.0	18.0	12.0	9.0	7.2	6.0
1280 bytes	40.0	20.0	13.3	10.0	8.0	6.7
1408 bytes	44.0	22.0	14.7	11.0	8.8	7.3
1500 bytes	46.9	23.4	15.6	11.7	9.4	7.8
4096 bytes	128.0	64.0	42.7	32.0	25.6	21.3

LFI uses Layer 2 fragmentation mechanisms that the network node applies to influence packet scheduling. Layer 2 fragmentation is a more generic and efficient approach than other alternatives (for example, IP fragmentation). The most common fragmentation mechanism is *Multilink PPP* (MLP). It can be used on PPP, Frame Relay, and ATM links. Frame Relay links can also use native fragmentation mechanisms (FRF.11 and FRF.12).

Figure 1-26 demonstrates how link fragmentation integrates with the packet scheduler managing congestion. Notice that the scheduler continues to serve individual packets and fragmentation and interleaving happens after the scheduling of nonpriority packets. This approach prevents interleaving of nonpriority traffic and simplifies the reassembly of packets at the receiving side of the link.

Figure 1-26 *Congestion Management with LFI*

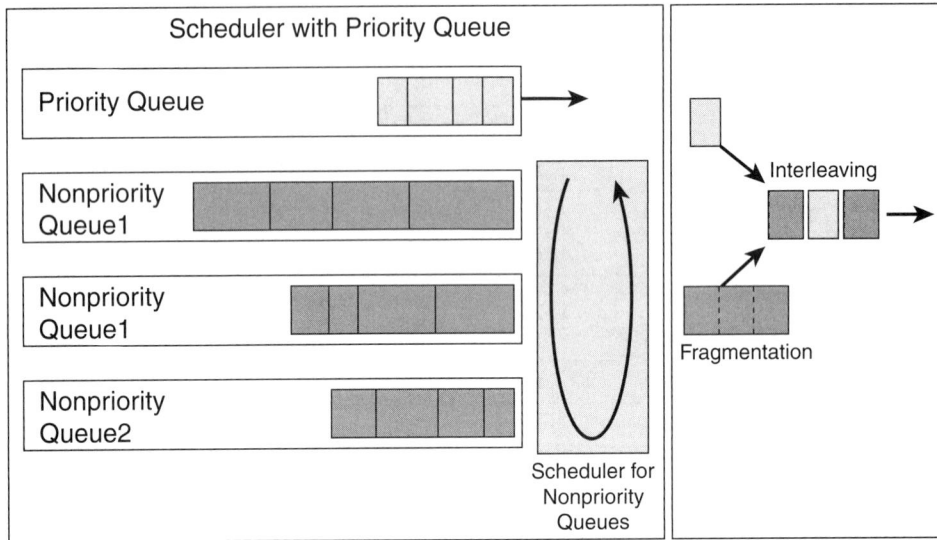

Header Compression

Header compression provides higher bandwidth efficiency and reduces transmission latency. Real-time traffic generally relies on the *Real-Time Transport Protocol* (RTP). These traffic streams also receive an UDP and IP encapsulation. Depending on the type of real-time traffic, header information can be larger than the actual real-time payload. To reduce the overhead, a node can use *RTP header compression* (cRTP) to compact IP, UDP, and RTP headers. The remote end of the link reconstructs the headers before continuing packet forwarding. The reduction in packet size saves link bandwidth and reduces the transmission latency due to the node having to transmit fewer bits to forward the RTP packet. RFC 2508 defines cRTP. The IETF is working in the definition of cRTP operation over MPLS.

Figure 1-27 illustrates the effect of cRTP on a sample RTP packet. In this case, the original RTP packet consists of 40 bytes of header information and 20 bits of RTP payload. The packet overhead accounts for two thirds of the total packet size. For this packet, cRTP converts the header information into 3 bytes. After compression, the packet overhead accounts for slightly higher than one third of the packet. The smaller packet size can also save a few milliseconds of transmission latency in low-speed links. The size of the compressed headers can actually range between 2 and 4 bytes depending on the contents of the original headers.

Figure 1-27 *Example of the Effect of RTP Header Compression on the Overall Packet Size*

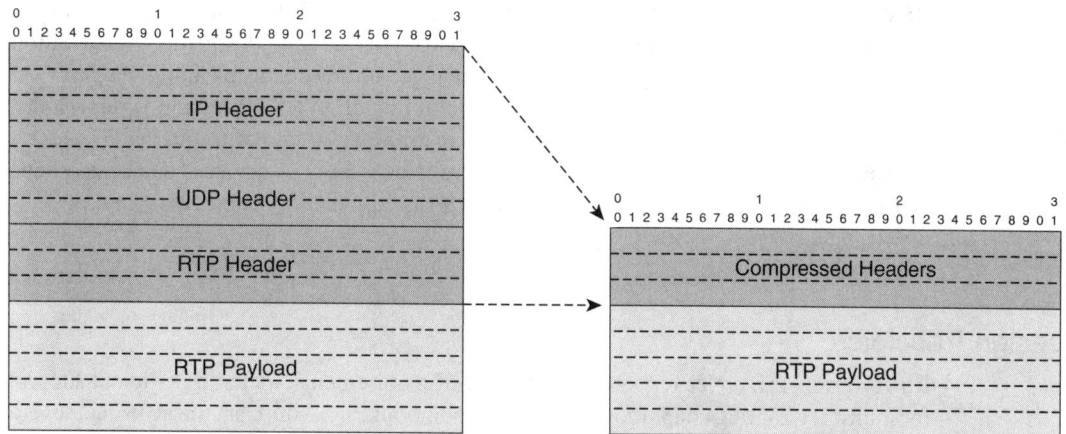

QoS Signaling

IP/MPLS networks perform QoS signaling using RSVP and extensions to other IP protocols. Signaling brings dynamic behavior to the QoS behavior in the network. Although QoS signaling proves useful in some scenarios, it is not a requirement for QoS deployment. The definition of the IntServ architecture resulted in the development of RSVP for the purpose of resource reservation. RSVP is the protocol of choice for QoS signaling in IP networks, but it is also applicable outside the context of QoS as a signaling protocol for traffic-engineering LSPs. In addition to the RSVP capabilities, there are proposed extensions to other IP protocols (for instance, *Open Shortest Path First* [OSFP], *Border Gateway Protocol* [BGP], *Label Distribution Protocol* [LDP]) that bring some QoS or QoS-related signaling capabilities to those protocols. This section provides an overview of RSVP and briefly mentions extensions in other protocols.

Resource Reservation Protocol

RSVP is an IP protocol for setting up resource reservations. The definition of the IntServ architecture prompted the creation of the protocol. However, the modularity of RSVP makes the protocol independent from the architecture and enables its use for other signaling applications. Today, networks can use RSVP to signal LSPs or IntServ reservations. RSVP supports resource reservation for both unicast and multicast applications. A network node processing a reservation request may apply admission control and policy control. Admission control determines whether the node has enough resources available to support the reservations. Policy control determines whether the user has administrative permission to make the reservation. RFC 2205 defines RSVP.

RSVP uses the concept of a session that includes a number of senders and receivers. An RSVP session is a data flow with a particular destination and transport layer protocol. A session may contain multiple reservations in the case of multicast destination. Reservations are unidirectional. They may trigger traffic-management mechanisms along the path depending on the signaling application. The definition of an RSVP session varies when RSVP signals LSPs. In that case, a session is an arbitrary stream of traffic that a sender transmits to one or more receivers. In general, a wide variety of devices can act as senders and receivers (for example, routers, switches, hosts, application gateways, signaling proxies).

Design Principles

RSVP design principles respond to a number of requirements, including efficient support for multicast, routing adaptability, and protocol modularity. Multicast traffic brings several challenges, such as heterogeneous receivers, changes in group membership, reservation sharing, and selection among multiple sources. In addition, RSVP has the requirement of adapting gracefully to IP routing changes and being modular and extensive enough to serve as a general soft-state signaling protocol. As a consequence of these requirements, RVSP relies on the following design principles:

- **Receiver-initiated reservation**—Receivers choose the level of resources that network nodes should reserve for the flow. Similarly, they are responsible for initiating and maintaining active the reservation as long as they want to receive data. The motivation for this approach is that the receiver knows locally its capacity limitations and is the only one who experiences it. Thus, the receiver is directly concerned with the QoS of incoming packets.

- **Reservation and packet filter separation**—A reservation does not determine which packets can use the resources that the receiver reserved (for example, buffers and bandwidth). A separate packet filtering function selects the packets that can use those resources. This filtering function is dynamic, allowing the receiver to adjust it during the course of the reservation.

- **Different reservation styles**—Service requests of multicast applications dictate how the reservation request from individual receivers should be aggregated inside the network. To satisfy this requirement, RSVP provides different reservations styles that control reservation sharing and sender selection.

- **Soft state**—Network nodes maintain RSVP state information that the sender and receiver must refresh. This soft state expires in the absence or periodic refreshing. The choice of soft rather than hard state contributes to the robustness of the network by preventing orphaned reservations and helping reservations adapt to routing changes.

- **Control of protocol overhead**—Network nodes can merge protocol messages as they traverse the network. The initial intent was to control the number of messages sent for multicast sessions. More recent changes to the protocol have optimized, in general, the processing and the amount of information in messages without affecting the responsiveness of the protocol.

- **Modularity**—RSVP does not make any assumptions about flowspecs it carries. Protocol messages carry flowspecs as uninterpreted information between senders, receivers, and admission-control modules in network nodes. These modules return an admit or reject signal after examining the flowspec that the RSVP message carries. This characteristic gives RSVP flexibility and extensibility.

Protocol Messages

RSVP messages consist of a message header and a number of objects. RSVP messages and objects are of variable length. A message type identifies each RSVP message, and a class number identifies each object. A particular object may have different classes. A class type identifies the object class. Ultimately, the combination of a class number and a class type uniquely defines all objects. Some objects contain subobjects. A subobject type identifies each subobject.

Figure 1-28 illustrates the high-level view of a sample RSVP message containing three objects. In this example, the second object carries a list of three subobjects. Table 1-12 lists the most commonly used RSVP messages and their function. The next section discusses them in more detail in the context of the protocol operation.

NOTE   Multiple RFCs define the complete list of current RSVP messages with their respective objects. The "References" section at the end of this chapter lists the main RFCs that define the most commonly used RSVP messages and their structure. Several groups in the IETF continue to extend RSVP.

Figure 1-28 *High-Level View of a Sample RSVP Message*

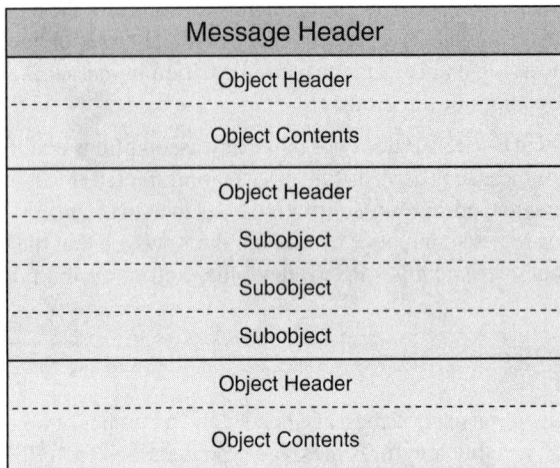

| Message Header |
| Object Header |
| Object Contents |
| Object Header |
| Subobject |
| Subobject |
| Subobject |
| Object Header |
| Object Contents |

Table 1-12 *Most Commonly Used RSVP Messages*

RSVP Message	Message Function
Path	Initiates session signaling. Generates Path state along the data path from sender to receiver.
Resv	Signals actual reservation. Generates Resv state along the data path from receiver to sender.
ResvConf	Confirms a successful reservation.
PathTear	Tears down Path state.
ResvTear	Tears down Resv state.
PathErr	Reports error conditions upstream.
ResvErr	Reports error conditions downstream.
Integrity Challenge	Starts a handshake to initialize sequence numbers for message authentication.
Integrity Response	Responds to an Integrity Challenge message.
Bundle	Aggregates a number of standard RSVP messages.
Ack	Explicitly acknowledges the reception of a message when piggybacking the acknowledgment would delay the response.
Srefresh	Performs a summary refresh of a list of Path and Resv state entries using Message-Id objects.
Hello	Provides rapid detection of neighbor failures when signaling LSPs.

Protocol Operation

Reservation setup and teardown represent the most important part of the protocol operation. In some cases, the processing aspects of the protocol may seem complex because of its support for multicast. The following sections discuss the basic protocol operation and its protocol messages to provide an overall understanding of the protocol capabilities and operation.

This book does not cover all aspects of the RSVP protocol, particularly aggregation and operation over DiffServ networks. Note, however, that these topics still have limited implementation and deployment. RFC 2209 discusses how a network node processes RSVP messages and maintains RSVP soft state.

Reservation Setup

RSVP operation primarily consists of periodic transmission and processing of Path and *Reservation* (Resv) messages to establish and maintain a reservation. Senders generate Path messages destined to receivers. Path messages signal the sender flowspec. Receivers transmit Resv messages back to senders. The Resv messages travel back performing resource reservation. Network nodes forward Resv messages hop by hop using the reversed path. A ResvConf message provides a receiver with a confirmation of a success reservation when it requests such confirmation. Nodes store and maintain Path and Resv state based on the Path and Resv messages they receive. Figure 1-29 shows the flow of Path and Resv messages in an RSVP session with two senders (A and B) and two receivers (E and F).

Figure 1-29 *Flow of Path and Resv Messages in an RSVP Session*

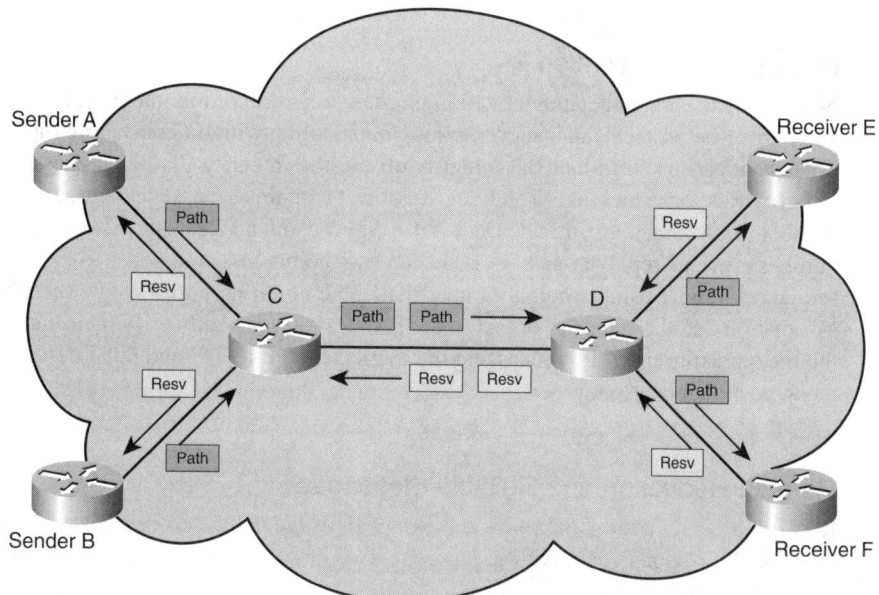

Reservation Teardown

RSVP provides a mechanism for explicitly tearing down soft state. This mechanism improves the protocol responsiveness when compared with the alternative of allowing the soft state to time out. RSVP uses the PathTear and ResvTear messages to tear down soft state. A PathTear travels toward all receivers from its creation point and it deletes all Path and associated Resv states. ResvTear messages travel toward all senders from its initiation point. Both senders and receivers can tear down a reservation. Network nodes can also initiate a teardown (for example, as a result of a timeout in Path or Resv state).

NOTE	Cisco uses a ResvTearConf message to provide confirmation of a successful reservation teardown. This message uses contents and procedures similar to the ResvConf message.

Error Signaling

RSVP defines the ResvErr and PathErr messages for error notification. Nodes send PathErr messages toward the sender that created the error. These messages may remove Path state along the path depending on the RSVP application. A network node sends ResvErr messages downstream toward all receivers. A node generates PathErr and ResvErr messages when it finds an error while processing a message (for example, detection of a mandatory but unknown object). In addition, nodes generate ResvErr messages when preempting an existing reservation or when admission control fails. RFC 3473 introduces new enhancements to RSVP error signaling.

Message Authentication

Nodes may use message authentication to guarantee reservation integrity. Message authentication protects against corruption and spoofing without encrypting the message. The specifications introduce the Integrity object, the Integrity Challenge message and the Integrity Response message. The Integrity object contains a message digest and a sequence number. A hashing algorithm computes the digest using a secret shared key. The sequence number prevents replay attacks. A node can use the Integrity messages to initialize the sequence number using a neighbor handshake. Neighboring nodes with a security association add the Integrity object to the RSVP messages and verify their integrity using the message digest before processing the message. RFCs 2747 and 3097 describe RSVP message authentication.

Refresh Reduction and Reliable Messages

RSVP refresh reduction and reliable message delivery reduce processing overhead and increase the responsiveness of the protocol. Two new messages, *Bundle* and *Summary refresh* (Srefresh), reduce the amount of information that RSVP neighbors exchange to refresh the soft state. The Bundle message aggregates multiple standard RSVP messages in a single message. Alternatively, two neighboring nodes can use a Srefresh message to refresh Path and Resv state and avoid the transmission of additional Path and Resv messages. Neighbors identify the state using a *message identification* (Message-Id) object they learned when the state was initially installed. The summary refresh reduces the amount of information that neighbors have to exchange and reduces message processing.

RVSP also provides extensions for reliable message delivery. In general, RSVP messages are encapsulated in a raw IP packet with the respective RSVP protocol ID. The protocol operation is tolerant to message loss, but those losses reduce the responsiveness of the protocol. RSVP can use message acknowledgment to enhance message delivery. A network node can request a neighbor to acknowledge a specific message. The node includes a Message-Id object and sets a flag requesting an acknowledgment. The neighbor can piggyback the acknowledgment in an RSVP message using a *Message-Identification-Acknowledgment* object (Message-Id-Ack). Alternatively, the node can reduce the response delay using an *acknowledgment* (Ack) message. RFC 2961 defines RSVP refresh reduction and reliable messages.

NOTE   Reliable message delivery obviates the need for the ResvTearConf message.

Detection of Neighbor Failures

RSVP uses a Hello message for rapid detection of neighbor failures. The definition of this extension is exclusive to the use of RSVP as an LSP signaling protocol. The Hello message provides rapid neighbor failure detection for two purposes: protection and graceful restart. A network node can provide fast traffic restoration in the event of a failure. RSVP provides the LSP signaling capabilities and supports faster failure detections to trigger the restoration. This *fast reroute* (FRR) functionally is described in Chapter 2. Nodes also use the Hello message to allow a neighbor to gracefully recover from a failure. The use of Hello messages is optional. RFC 3209 introduced the Hello message. RFC 3473 modifies the Hello message to support RSVP graceful restart.

Other QoS Signaling Mechanisms

QoS signaling for IP/MPLS is more prevalent as extensions to existing protocols than as separate signaling protocols. You will find LDP and RSVP extensions to signal L-LSPs in the context of MPLS support for DiffServ. In addition, other IETF working groups are proposing routing extensions to existing protocols to support multiple topologies within a routing domain. These extensions do not signal QoS information explicitly, but they allow a network to compute different paths for different classes of service. You will also find additional proposals for QoS extensions to LDP in the *Pseudo Wire Emulation Edge to Edge* (PWE3) working group at the IETF. In addition to these extensions, network nodes can use existing protocols (such as BGP) to trigger local QoS policies.

A new IETF working group is also discussing additional QoS signaling mechanisms. The group is called the *Next Steps in Signaling* (NSIS) working group and targets IP signaling in general with the initial goal of producing new proposals for QoS signaling. It is not clear that the developments in this working group will be more suitable to satisfy QoS signaling requirements than what RSVP can offer today. Therefore, it is still uncertain the acceptance that these new proposals will have and whether they will eventually experience significant implementation and deployment.

Summary

Two QoS architectures have been defined for IP: IntServ and DiffServ. IntServ provides granular QoS guarantees with explicit resource reservation. IntServ uses RSVP as signaling protocol. DiffServ provides a coarse QoS approach based on aggregates (classes) of traffic. MPLS does not define new QoS architectures. Currently, MPLS provides support for DiffServ. MPLS DiffServ introduces the concepts of E-LSP and L-LSP, along with the concept of tunnel modes (pipe, short-pipe, and uniform). Both architectures use a collection of traffic-control mechanisms that include classification, marking, policing, shaping, congestion management, active queue management, fragmentation/interleaving, and header compression.

This chapter provided a technology overview that serves as a reference for later chapters. The following "References" section includes a detailed list of documents that provide further details on particular subjects. All discussions in this chapter focused on technology aspects without making any reference to what components are available in Cisco products and how they implement those components. Chapter 2 provides a technology overview of MPLS traffic engineering. This technology can be an important tool to build MPLS networks that can provide more elaborate SLAs. Chapter 3 covers the details of the Cisco implementation of QoS technology. The remainder of the book favors the technology terminology in Cisco implementation uses. This chapter favored the terminology used in the technology specifications to maintain technical accuracy and to facilitate the reading of the original specifications.

References

IP

RFC 791, *Internet Protocol*

RFC 1349, *Type of Service in the Internet Protocol Suite*

RFC 1812, *Requirements for IP Version 4 Routers*

RFC 2460, *Internet Protocol, Version 6 (IPv6) Specification*

IntServ

RFC 1633, *Integrated Service in the Internet Architecture: an Overview*

RFC 2210, *The Use of RSVP with IETF Integrated Services*

RFC 2211, *Specification of the Controlled-Load Network Element Service*

RFC 2212, *Specification of Guaranteed Quality of Service*

RFC 2215, *General Characterization Parameters for Integrated Service Network Elements*

RFC 2216, *Network Element Service Specification Template*

DiffServ

RFC 2474, *Definition of the Differentiated Services Field (DS Field) in the IPv4 and IPv6 Headers*

RFC 2475, *An Architecture for Differentiated Services*

RFC 2597, *Assured Forwarding PHB Group*

RFC 2697, *A Single Rate Three Color Marker.txt*

RFC 2698, *A Two Rate Three Color Marker*

RFC 2983, *Differentiated Services and Tunnels*

RFC 3246, *An Expedited Forwarding PHB (Per-Hop Behavior)*

RFC 3247, *Supplemental Information for the New Definition of the EF PHB (Expedited Forwarding Per-Hop Behavior)*

RFC 3260, *New Terminology and Clarifications for DiffServ*

RFC 3270, *Multi-Protocol Label Switching (MPLS) Support of Differentiated Services*

Traffic Management

RFC 2309, *Recommendations on Queue Management and Congestion Avoidance in the Internet*

RFC 3168, *The Addition of Explicit Congestion Notification (ECN) to IP*

Shreedhar, M. and Varghese, G., "Efficient Fair Queuing Using Deficit Round-Robin," IEEE/ACM Transactions on Networking, Vol. 4, No. 3, 1996

MPLS

RFC 3032, *MPLS Label Stack Encoding*

RSVP

draft-ietf-tsvwg-rsvp-dste-01 - RSVP Aggregation over MPLS TE tunnels (work in progress)

draft-ietf-avt-hc-over-mpls-protocol-04 – Protocol Extensions for Header Compression over MPLS (work in progress)

RFC 2209, *Resource ReSerVation Protocol (RSVP) -- Version 1 Message Processing Rules*

RFC 2747, *RSVP Cryptographic Authentication*

RFC 2961, *RSVP Refresh Overhead Reduction Extensions*

RFC 2996, *Format of the RSVP DCLASS Object*

RFC 3097, *RSVP Cryptographic Authentication -- Updated Message Type Value*

RFC 3175, *Aggregation of RSVP for IPv4 and IPv6 Reservations*

Zhang, L., Deering, S., Estrin, D., Shenker, S., and D. Zappala, D "RSVP: A New Resource ReSerVation Protocol," IEEE Network, September 1993. RFC 2205, *Resource ReSerVation Protocol (RSVP) -- Version 1 Functional Specification*

CHAPTER 2

MPLS TE Technology Overview

In this chapter, you review the following topics:

- MPLS TE Introduction
- Basic Operation of MPLS TE
- DiffServ-Aware Traffic Engineering
- Fast Reroute

This chapter presents a review of *Multiprotocol Label Switching Traffic Engineering* (MPLS TE) technology. MPLS TE can play an important role in the implementation of network services with *quality of service* (QoS) guarantees. The initial sections describe the basic operation of the technology. This description includes the details of TE information distribution, path computation, and the signaling of TE LSPs. The subsequent sections present how *Differentiated Services (DiffServ)-Aware traffic engineering* (DS-TE) helps integrate the implementation of DiffServ and MPLS TE. This chapter closes with a review of the *fast reroute* (FRR) capabilities in MPLS TE. Chapter 4, "Cisco MPLS Traffic Engineering," covers in depth the Cisco implementation of MPLS TE in Cisco IOS and Cisco IOS XR. In addition, Chapter 5, "Backbone Infrastructure," discusses the different network designs that can combine QoS with MPLS TE.

MPLS TE Introduction

MPLS networks can use native TE mechanisms to minimize network congestion and improve network performance. TE modifies routing patterns to provide efficient mapping of traffic streams to network resources. This efficient mapping can reduce the occurrence of congestion and improves service quality in terms of the latency, jitter, and loss that packets experience. Historically, IP networks relied on the optimization of underlying network infrastructure or *Interior Gateway Protocol* (IGP) tuning for TE. Instead, MPLS extends existing IP protocols and makes use of MPLS forwarding capabilities to provide native TE. In addition, MPLS TE can reduce the impact of network failures and increase service availability. RFC 2702 discusses the requirements for TE in MPLS networks.

MPLS TE brings explicit routing capabilities to MPLS networks. An originating *label switching route* (LSR) (or headend) can set up a TE *label switched path* (LSP) to a terminating LSR (or tail end) through an explicitly defined path containing a list of intermediate LSRs (or midpoints). IP uses destination-based routing and does not provide a general and scalable method for explicitly routing traffic. In contrast, MPLS networks can support destination-based and explicit routing simultaneously. MPLS TE uses extensions to RSVP and the MPLS forwarding paradigm to provide explicit routing. These enhancements provide a level of routing control that makes MPLS suitable for TE.

Figure 2-1 shows a sample MPLS network using TE. This network has multiple paths from nodes A and E toward nodes D and H. In this figure, traffic from A and E toward D follows explicitly routed LSPs through nodes B and C. Traffic from A and E toward H follows explicitly routed LSPs through nodes F and G. Without TE, the IGP would compute the shortest path using only a single metric or cost. You could tune that metric, but that would provide you limited capabilities to allocate network resources when compared with MPLS TE (specially, when you consider larger more complex network topologies). This chapter describes those routing and signaling enhancements that make MPLS TE possible.

Figure 2-1 *Sample MPLS Network Using TE*

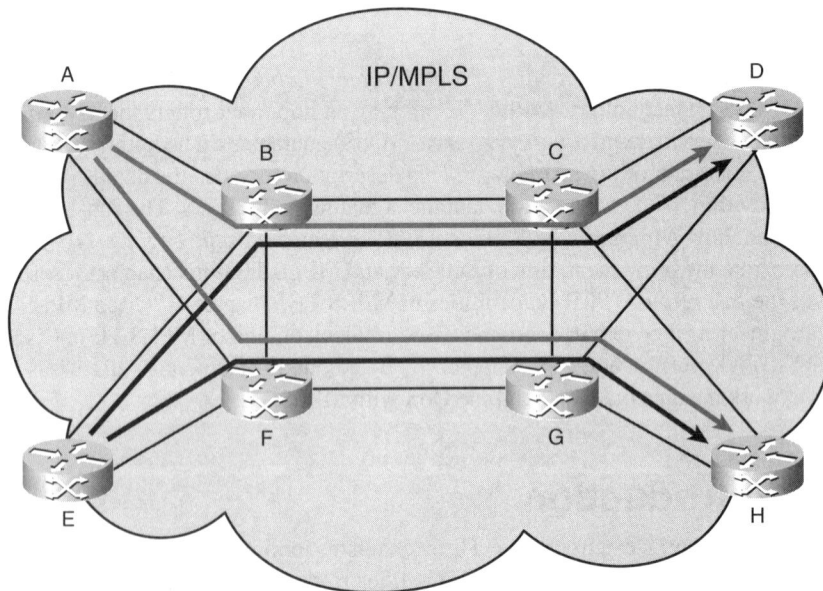

MPLS TE also extends the MPLS routing capabilities with support for constraint-based routing. As mentioned earlier, IGPs typically compute routing information using a single metric. Instead of that simple approach, constraint-based routing can take into account more detailed information about network constraints, and policy resources. MPLS TE extends current link-state protocols (IS-IS and OSPF) to distribute such information.

Constraint-based routing and explicit routing allow an originating LSR to compute a path that meets some requirements (constraints) to a terminating LSR and then set up a TE LSP through that path. Constraint-based routing is optional within MPLS TE. An offline tool can perform path computation and leave TE LSP signaling to the LSRs.

MPLS TE supports preemption between TE LSPs of different priorities. Each TE LSP has a setup and a holding priority, which can range from zero (best priority) through seven (worst priority). When a node signals a new TE LSP, other nodes throughout the path compare the setup priority of the new TE LSPs with the holding priority of existing TE LSPs to make a preemption decision. A better setup priority can preempt worse-holding priorities a TE LSP can use hard or soft preemption. A node implementing hard preemption tears down the existing TE LSP to accommodate the new TE LSP. In contrast, a node implementing soft preemption signals back the pending preemption to the headend of the existing TE LSP. The headend can then reroute the TE LSP without impacting the traffic flow. RFC 3209 and draft-ietf-mpls-soft-preemption-07. define TE LSP preemption.

Basic Operation of MPLS TE

The operation of MPLS TE involves link information distribution, path computation, LSP signaling, and traffic selection. This section explains the most important concepts behind each of these four steps. LSRs implement the first two steps, link information distribution and path computation, when they need perform constraint-based routing. MPLS networks that do not use constraint-based routing (or use an offline tool for that purpose) perform only LSP signaling and traffic selection. MPLS TE does not define any new protocols even though it represents a significant change in how MPLS networks can route traffic. Instead, it uses extensions to existing IP protocols.

Link Information Distribution

MPLS TE uses extensions to existing IP link-state routing protocols to distribute topology information. An LSR requires detailed network information to perform constraint-based routing. It needs to know the current state of an extended list of link attributes to take a set of constraints into consideration during path computation for a TE LSP. Link-state protocols (IS-IS and OSPF) provide the flooding capabilities that are required to distribute these attributes. LSRs use this information to build a TE topology database. This database is separate from the regular topology database that LSRs build for hop-by-hop destination-based routing.

MPLS TE introduces available bandwidth, an administrative group (flags), and a TE metric as new link attributes. Each link has eight amounts of available bandwidth corresponding to the eight priority levels that TE LSPs can have. The administrative group (flags) acts as a classification mechanism to define link inclusion and exclusion rules. The TE metric is a second link metric for path optimization (similar to the IGP link metric). In addition, LSRs distribute a TE ID that has a similar function to a router ID. The OSPF and IS-IS extensions mirror each other and have the same semantics. Table 2-1 shows the complete list of link attributes. RFC 3784 and RFC 3630 define the IS-IS and OSPF extensions for TE respectively.

Table 2-1   *Extended Link Attributes Distributed for TE*

Link Attribute	Description
Interface address	IP address of the interface corresponding to the link
Neighbor address	IP address of the neighbor's interface corresponding to the link
Maximum link bandwidth	True link capacity (in the neighbor direction)
Reservable link bandwidth	Maximum bandwidth that can be reserved (in the neighbor direction)
Unreserved bandwidth	Available bandwidth at each of the (eight) preemption priority levels (in the neighbor direction)
TE metric	Link metric for TE (may differ from the IGP metric)
Administrative group	Administratively value (flags) associated with the link for inclusion/ exclusion policies

NOTE   In addition to the attributes listed in Table 2-1, OSPF advertises the link type (point-to-point or multi-access) and a link ID. OSPF uses type 10 opaque (area-local scope) *link-state advertisements* (LSA) to distribute this information.

MPLS TE can still perform constraint-based routing in the presence of multiple IGP areas or multiple autonomous systems. OSPF and IS-IS use the concept of areas or levels to limit the scope of information flooding. An LSR in a network with multiple areas only builds a partial topology database. The existence of these partial databases has some implications for path computation, as the next section describes. LSRs in an inter-autonomous system TE environment also need to deal with partial network topologies. Fortunately, inter-area TE and inter-autonomous system TE use similar approaches for constraint-based routing in the presence of partial topology information.

Path Computation

LSRs can perform path computation for a TE LSP using the TE topology database. A common approach for performing constraint-based routing on the LSRs is to use an extension of the *shortest path first* (SPF) algorithm. This extension to the original algorithm generally receives the name of *constraint-based, shortest path first* (CSPF). The modified algorithm executes the SPF algorithm on the topology that results from the removal of the links that do not meet the TE LSP constraints. The algorithm may use the IGP link metric or the link TE metric to determine the shortest path. CSPF does not guarantee a completely optimal mapping of traffic streams to network resources, but it is considered an adequate approximation. MPLS TE specifications do not require that LSRs perform path computation or attempt to standardize a path computation algorithm.

Figure 2-2 illustrates a simplified version of CSPF on a sample network. In this case, node E wants to compute the shortest path to node H with the following constraints: only links with at least 50 bandwidth units available and an administrative group value of 0xFF. Node E examines the TE topology database and disregards links with insufficient bandwidth or administrative group values other than 0xFF. The dotted lines in the topology represent links that CSPF disregards. Subsequently, node E executes the shortest path algorithm on the reduced topology using the link metric values. In this case, the shortest path is {E, F, B, C, H}. Using this result, node E can initiate the TE LSP signaling.

Figure 2-2   *Path Computation Using the CSPF Algorithm*

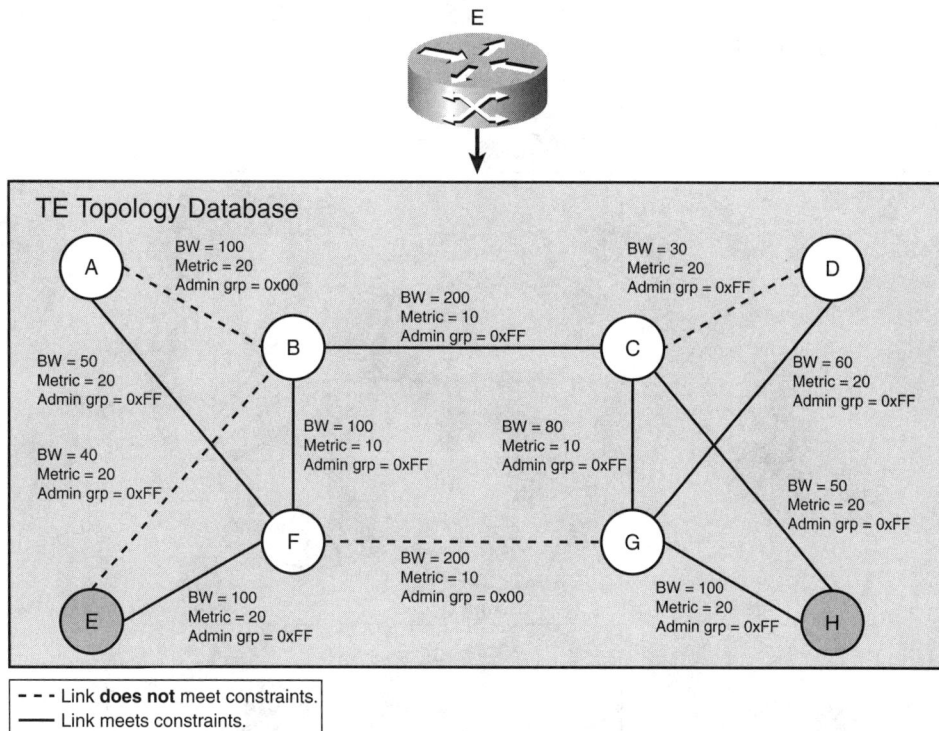

Path computation in multi-area or inter-autonomous system environments may involve several partial computations along the TE LSP. When the headend does not have a complete view of the network topology, it can specify the path as a list of predefined boundary LSR (*Area Border Router* [ABR] in the case of inter-area and *Autonomous System Boundary Router* [ASBR] in the case of inter-autonomous system). The headend can compute a path to the first boundary LSR (which must be in its topology database and initiate the signalling of the TE LSP signaling can be initiated). When the signaling reaches the boundary LSR, that LSR performs the path computation to the final destination if it is in its topology. If the destination is not in the topology, the signaling should indicate the next exit boundary LSR, and the path computation will take place to that boundary LSR. The process continues until the signaling reaches the destination. This process of completing path computation during TE LSP signaling is called loose routing.

Figure 2-3 shows path computation in a sample network with multiple IGP areas. All LSRs have a partial network topology. The network computes a path between nodes E and H crossing the three IGP areas in the network. Node E selected nodes F and G, which have as the boundary LSRs that the TE LSP will traverse. Node E computes the path to node F and initiates the TE LSP signaling. When node F receives the signaling message, it computes the next segment of the path toward node G. When the signaling arrives at node G, it completes the path computation toward node H in area 2. The next section explains how LSRs signal TE LSPs.

Figure 2-3 *Multi-Area Path Computation*

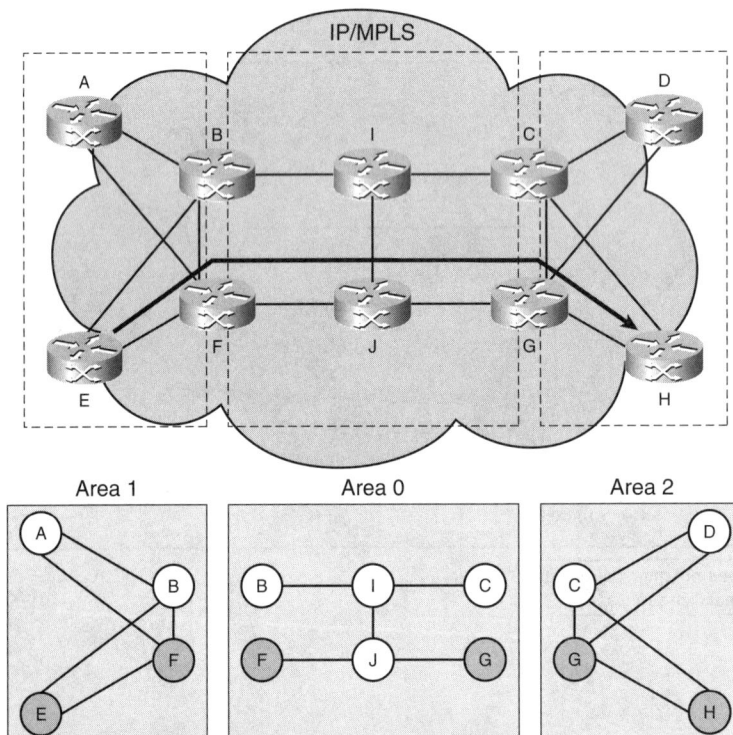

Signaling of TE LSPs

MPLS TE introduces extensions to RSVP to signal up LSPs. RSVP uses five new objects: LABEL_REQUEST, LABEL, EXPLICIT_ROUTE, RECORD_ROUTE, and SESSION_ATTRIBUTE. RSVP Path messages use a LABEL_REQUEST object to request a label binding at each hop. Resv messages use a LABEL object to perform label distribution. Network nodes perform downstream-on-demand label distribution using these two objects. The EXPLICIT_ROUTE object contains a hop list that defines the explicit routed path that the signaling will follow. The RECORD_ROUTE object collects hop and label information along the signaling path. The SESSION_ATTRIBUTE object lists the attribute requirements of the LSP (priority, protection, and so forth).

RFC 3209 defines these RSVP TE extensions. Table 2-2 summarizes the new RSVP objects and their function.

NOTE   The *Internet Engineering Task Force* (IETF) considered extensions to the *Label Distribution Protocol* (LDP) as a signaling protocol for TE LSPs in the early stages of MPLS TE. These protocol extensions were called *Constraint-based routed LDP* (CR-LDP). For some time, CR-LDP and RSVP TE specifications advanced simultaneously. In 2002, the MPLS working group at the IETF decided not to pursue new developments for CR-LDP and focused instead on RSVP TE as the prime protocol for MPLS TE.

Table 2-2   *New RSVP Objects to Support MPLS TE*

RSVP Object	RSVP Message	Description
LABEL_REQUEST	Path	Label request to downstream neighbor
LABEL	Resv	MPLS label allocated by downstream neighbor
EXPLICIT_ROUTE	Path	Hop list defining the course of the TE LSP
RECORD_ROUTE	Path, Resv	Hop/label list recorded during TE LSP setup
SESSION_ATTRIBUTE	Path	Requested LSP attributes (priority, protection, affinities)

Figure 2-4 illustrates the setup of a TE LSP using RSVP. In this scenario, node E signals a TE LSP toward node H. RSVP Path messages flow downstream with a collection of objects, four of which are related to MPLS TE (EXPLICIT_ROUTE, LABEL_REQUEST, SESSION_ATTRIBUTE, and RECORD_ROUTE). Resv messages flow upstream and include two objects related to MPLS TE (LABEL and RECORD_ROUTE). Each node performs admission control and builds the *LSP forwarding information base* (LFIB) when processing the Resv messages. The structure of the LFIB and the MPLS forwarding algorithm remain the same regardless of the protocols that populated the information (for example, RSVP in the case of MPLS TE).

Figure 2-4   *TE LSP Setup Using RSVP*

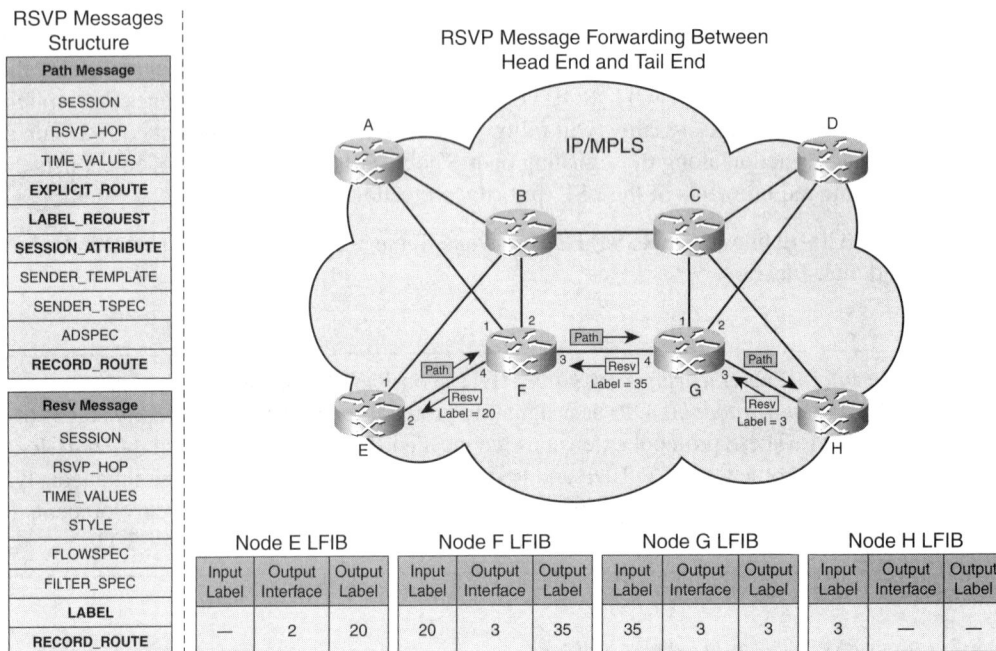

Traffic Selection

MPLS TE separates TE LSP creation from the process of selecting the traffic that will use the TE LSP. A headend can signal a TE LSP, but traffic will start flowing through the LSP after the LSR implements a traffic-selection mechanism. Traffic can enter the TE LSP only at the headend. Therefore, the selection of the traffic is a local head-end decision that can use different approaches without the need for standardization. The selection criteria can be static or dynamic. It can also depend on the packet type (for instance, IP or Ethernet) or packet contents (for example, class of service). An MPLS network can make use of several traffic-selection mechanisms depending on the services it offers.

DiffServ-Aware Traffic Engineering

MPLS DS-TE enables per-class TE across an MPLS network. DS-TE provides more granular control to minimize network congestion and improve network performance. DS-TE retains the same overall operation framework of MPLS TE (link information distribution, path computation, signaling, and traffic selection). However, it introduces extensions to support the concept of multiple classes and to make per-class constraint-based routing possible. These routing enhancements help control the proportion of traffic of different classes on network links. RFC 4124 introduces DS-TE protocol extensions.

Both DS-TE and DiffServ control the per-class bandwidth allocation on network links. DS-TE acts as a control-plane mechanism, while DiffServ acts in the forwarding plane. In general, the configuration in both planes will have a close relationship. However, they do not have to be identical. They can use a different number of classes and different relative bandwidth allocations to satisfy the requirements of particular network designs. Figure 2-5 shows an example of bandwidth allocation in DiffServ and DS-TE for a particular link. In this case, the link rate equals the maximum reservable bandwidth for TE. Each class receives a fraction of the total bandwidth amount in the control and forwarding planes. However, the bandwidth proportions between classes differ slightly in this case.

DS-TE does not imply the use of *Label-inferred-class LSP* (L-LSPs). An MPLS node may signal a DS-TE LSP as an *EXP-inferred-class LSP* (E-LSP) or L-LSP. Furthermore, a DS-TE LSP may not signal any DiffServ information or not even count on the deployment of DiffServ on the network. You need to keep in mind that an instance of a class within DS-TE does not need to maintain a one-to-one relationship with a DiffServ class. Chapter 5 explains different models of interaction between TE and DiffServ.

Figure 2-5   *Bandwidth Allocation in DiffServ and DS-TE*

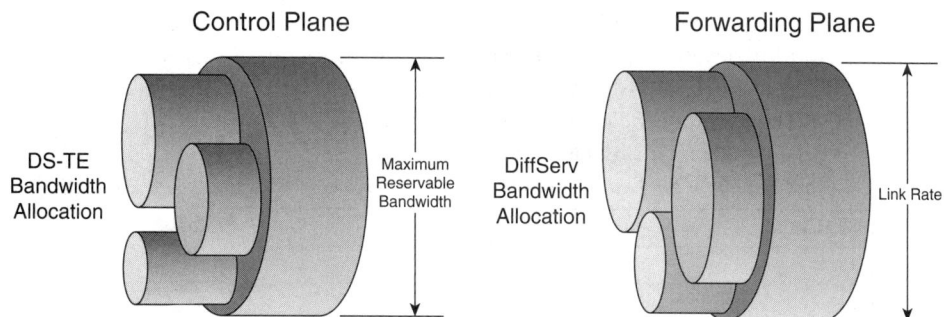

| Control Plane | Forwarding Plane |

DS-TE Bandwidth Allocation — Maximum Reservable Bandwidth — DiffServ Bandwidth Allocation — Link Rate

---

NOTE   This section uses the term *aggregate MPLS TE* to refer to MPLS TE without the DS-TE extensions. Even though that name might not be completely accurate in some MPLS TE designs, it differentiates TE with a single bandwidth constraint from the approach that DS-TE uses.

Class-Types and TE-Classes

DS-TE uses the concept of *Class-Type* (CT) for the purposes of link bandwidth allocation, constraint-based routing, and admission control. A network can use up to eight CTs (CT0 through CT7). DS-TE retains support for TE LSP preemption, which can operate within a CT or across CTs. TE LSPs can have different preemption priorities regardless of their CT. CTs represent the concept of a class for DS-TE in a similar way that *per-hop behavior* (PHB) *scheduling class* (PSC) represents it for DiffServ. Note that flexible mappings between CTs and PSCs are possible. You can define a one-to-one mapping between CTs and PSCs. Alternatively, a CT can map to several PSCs, or several CTs can map to one PSC.

DS-TE provides flexible definition of preemption priorities while retaining the same mechanism for distribution of unreserved bandwidth on network links. DS-TE redefines the meaning of the unreserved bandwidth attribute discussed in the section "Link Information Distribution" without modifying its format. When DS-TE is in use, this attribute represents the unreserved bandwidth for eight TE classes. A TE-Class defines a combination of a CT and a corresponding preemption priority value. A network can use any 8 (TE-Class) combinations to use out of 64 possible combinations (8 CTs times 8 priorities). No relative ordering exists between the TE-Classes, and a network can use a subset of the 8 possible values. However, the TE-Class definitions must be consistent across the DS-TE network.

Tables 2-3, 2-4, and 2-5 include examples of three different TE-Class definitions:

- Table 2-3 illustrates a TE-Class definition that is backward compatible with aggregate MPLS TE. In this example, all TE-Classes support only CT0, with 8 different preemption priorities ranging from 0 through 7.

- Table 2-4 presents a second example where the TE-Class definition uses 4 CTs (CT0, CT1, CT2, and CT3), with 8 preemption priority levels (0 and 7) for each CT. This definition makes preemption possible within CTs but not across CTs.

- Table 2-5 contains a TE-Class definition with 2 CTs (CT0 and CT1) and 2 preemption priority levels (0 and 7). 2 third example defines some TE-Classes as *unused*. In this case, preemption is possible within and across CTs. With this design, preemption is possible within and across CTs, but you can signal CT1 TE LSPs (using priority zero) that no other TE LSP can preempt.

Table 2-3   *TE-Class Definition Backward Compatible with Aggregate MPLS TE*

TE-Class	CT	Priority
0	0	0
1	0	1
2	0	2
3	0	3
4	0	4
5	0	5
6	0	6
7	0	7

Table 2-4   *TE-Class Definition with Four CTs and 8 Preemption Priorities*

TE Class	Class Type	Priority
0	0	7
1	0	6
2	1	5
3	1	4
4	2	3
5	2	2
6	3	1
7	3	0

Table 2-5   *TE-Class Definition with Two CTs and Two Preemption Priorities*

TE-Class	CT	Priority
0	0	7
1	1	7
2	Unused	Unused
3	Unused	Unused
4	0	0
5	1	0
6	Unused	Unused
7	Unused	Unused

Table 2-6   *TE-Class Definition with Two CTs and Eight Preemption Priorities*

TE-Class	CT	Priority
0	0	7
1	1	6
2	0	5
3	1	4
4	0	3
5	1	2
6	0	1
7	1	0

DS-TE introduces a new CLASSTYPE RSVP object. This object specifies the CT associated with the TE LSP and can take a value ranging form one to seven. DS-TE nodes must support this new object and include it in Path messages, with the exception of CT0 TE LSPs. The Path messages associated with those LSPs must not use the CLASSTYPE object to allow non-DS-TE nodes to interoperate with DS-TE nodes. Table 2-6 summarizes the CLASSTYPE object.

Table 2-7 *New RSVP Object for DS-TE*

RSVP Object	RSVP Message	FRR Function
CLASSTYPE	Path	CT associated with the TE LSP. Not used for CT0 for backward compatibility with non-DS-TE nodes.

Bandwidth Constraints

A set of *bandwidth constraints* (BC) defines the rules that a node uses to allocate bandwidth to different CTs. Each link in the DS-TE network has a set of BCs that applies to the CTs in use. This set may contain up to eight BCs. When a node using DS-TE admits a new TE LSP on a link, that node uses the BC rules to update the amount of unreserved bandwidth for each TE-Class. One or more BCs may apply to a CT depending on the model.

DS-TE can support different BC models. The IETF has primarily defined two BC models: *maximum allocation model* (MAM) and *Russian dolls model* (RDM). These are discussed in the following subsections of this chapter.

DS-TE also defines a BC extension for IGP link advertisements. This extension complements the link attributes that Table 2-1 already described and applies equally to OSPF and IS-IS. Network nodes do not need this BC information to perform path computation. They rely on the unreserved bandwidth information for that purpose. However, they can optionally use it to verify DS-TE configuration consistency throughout the network or as a path computation heuristic (for instance, as a tie breaker for CSPF). A DS-TE deployment could use different BC models throughout the network. However, the simultaneous use of different models increases operational complexity and can adversely impact bandwidth optimization. Table 2-8 summarizes the BC link attribute that DS-TE uses.

Table 2-8 *Optional BC Link Attribute Distributed for DS-TE*

Link Attribute	Description
BCs	BC model ID and BCs (BC0 through BCn) that the link uses for DS-TE

Maximum Allocation Model

The MAM defines a one-to-one relationship between BCs and Class-Types. BCn defines the maximum amount of reservable bandwidth for CTn, as Table 2-9 shows. The use of preemption does not affect the amount of bandwidth that a CT receives. MAM offers limited bandwidth sharing between CTs. A CT cannot make use of the bandwidth left unused by another CT. The packet schedulers managing congestion in the forwarding plane typically guarantee bandwidth sharing. To improve bandwidth sharing using MAM, you may make the sum of all BCs greater than the maximum reservable bandwidth. However, the total reserved bandwidth for all CTs cannot exceed the maximum reservable bandwidth at any time. RFC 4125 defines MAM.

Table 2-9   *MAM Bandwidth Constraints for Eight CTs*

Bandwidth Constraint	Maximum Bandwidth Allocation For
BC7	CT7
BC6	CT6
BC5	CT5
BC4	CT4
BC3	CT3
BC2	CT2
BC1	CT1
BC0	CT0

Figure 2-6 shows an example of a set of BCs using MAM. This DS-TE configuration uses three CTs with their corresponding BCs. In this case, BC0 limits CT0 bandwidth to 15 percent of the maximum reservable bandwidth. BC1 limits CT1 to 50 percent, and BC2 limits CT2 to 10 percent. The sum of BCs on this link is less than its maximum reservable bandwidth. Each CT will always receive its bandwidth share without the need for preemption. Preemption will not have an effect on the bandwidth that a CT can use. This predictability comes at the cost of no bandwidth sharing between CTs. The lack of bandwidth sharing can force some TE LSPs to follow longer paths than necessary.

Figure 2-6   *MAM Constraint Model Example*

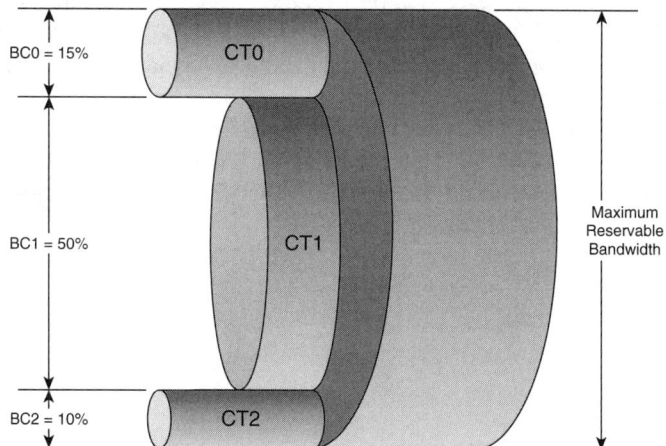

Russian Dolls Model

The RDM defines a cumulative set of constraints that group CTs. For an implementation with n CTs, BCn always defines the maximum bandwidth allocation for CTn. Subsequent lower BCs define the total bandwidth allocation for the CTs at equal or higher levels. BC0 always defines the maximum bandwidth allocation across all CTs and is equal to the maximum reservable bandwidth of the link.

Table 2-10 shows the RDM BCs for a DS-TE implementation with eight CTs. The recursive definition of BCs improves bandwidth sharing between CTs. A particular CT can benefit from bandwidth left unused by higher CTs. A DS-TE network using RDM can rely on TE LSP preemption to guarantee that each CT gets a fair share of the bandwidth. RFC 4127 defines RDM.

Table 2-10   *RDM Bandwidth Constrains for Eight CTs*

Bandwidth Constraint	Maximum Bandwidth Allocation For
BC7	CT7
BC6	CT7+CT6
BC5	CT7+CT6+CT5
BC4	CT7+CT6+CT5+CT4
BC3	CT7+CT6+CT5+CT4+CT3
BC2	CT7+CT6+CT5+CT4+CT3+CT2
BC1	CT7+CT6+CT5+CT4+CT3+CT2+CT1
BC0 = Maximum reservable bandwidth	CT7+CT6+CT5+CT4+CT3+CT2+CT1+CT0

Figure 2-7 shows an example of a set of BCs using RDM. This DS-TE implementation uses three CTs with their corresponding BCs. In this case, BC2 limits CT2 to 30 percent of the maximum reservable bandwidth. BC1 limits CT2+CT1 to 70 percent. BC0 limits CT2+CT1+CT0 to 100 percent of the maximum reservable bandwidth, as is always the case with RDM. CT0 can use up to 100 percent of the bandwidth in the absence of CT2 and CT1 TE LSPs. Similarly, CT1 can use up to 70 percent of the bandwidth in the absence of TE LSPs of the other two CTs. CT2 will always be limited to 30 percent when no CT0 or CT1 TE LSPs exist. The maximum bandwidth that a CT receives on a particular link depends on the previously signaled TE LSPs, their CTs, and the preemption priorities of all TE LSPs. Table 2-11 compares MAM and RDM.

Figure 2-7 *RDM Constraint Model Example*

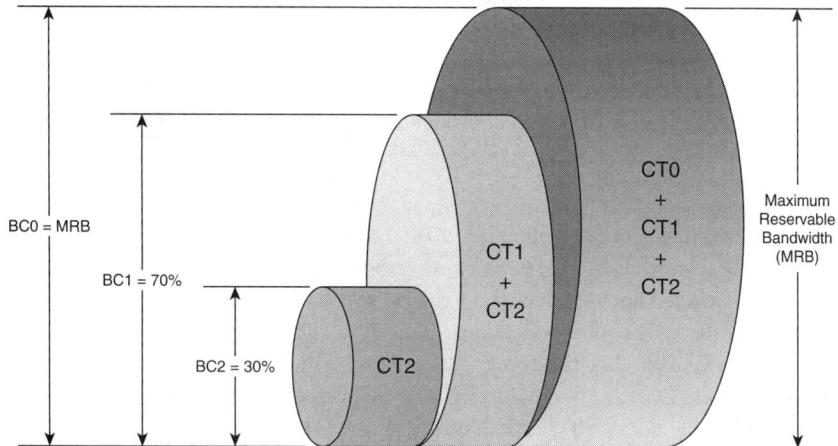

Table 2-11 *Comparing MAM and RDM BC Models*

MAM	RDM
1 BC per CT.	1 or more CTs per BC.
Sum of all BCs may exceed maximum reservable bandwidth.	BC0 always equals the maximum reservable bandwidth.
Preemption not required to provide bandwidth guarantees per CT.	Preemption required to provide bandwidth guarantees per CT.
Bandwidth efficiency and protection against QoS degradation are mutually exclusive.	Provides bandwidth efficiency and protection against QoS degradation simultaneously.

Fast Reroute

MPLS TE supports local repair of TE LSPs using FRR. Traffic protection in case of a network failure is critical for real-time traffic or any other traffic with strict packet-loss requirements. In particular, FRR uses a local protection approach that relies on a presignaled backup TE LSP to reroute traffic in case of a failure. The node immediately next to the failure is responsible for rerouting the traffic and is the headend of the backup TE LSP. Therefore, no delay occurs in the propagation of the failure condition, and no delay occurs in computing a path and signaling a new TE LSP to reroute the traffic. FRR can reroute traffic in tens of milliseconds. RFC 4090 describes the operation and the signaling extensions that MPLS TE FRR requires.

NOTE   MPLS TE FRR specifications offer two protection techniques: facility backup and one-to-
            one backup. Facility backup uses label stacking to reroute multiple protected TE LSPs
            using a single backup TE LSP. One-to-one backup does not use label stacking, and every
            protected TE LSP requires a dedicated backup TE LSP. The remainder of this section
            focuses on the facility backup approach because of its greater scalability and wider use.

Figure 2-8 shows an example of an MPLS network using FRR. In this case, node E signals
a TE LSP toward node H. The network protects this TE LSP against a failure of the link
between nodes F and G. Given the local protection nature of FRR, node F is responsible for
rerouting the traffic into the backup TE LSP in case the link between nodes F and G fails.
This role makes node F the *point of local repair* (PLR). It has presignaled a backup TE LSP
through node I toward node G to bypass the potential link failure. The PLR is always the
headend of the backup TE LSP. Node G receives the name of *merge point* (MP) and is the
node where the protected traffic will exit the backup TE LSP during the failure and retake
the original path of the protected TE LSP.

Figure 2-8   *MPLS Network Using FRR*

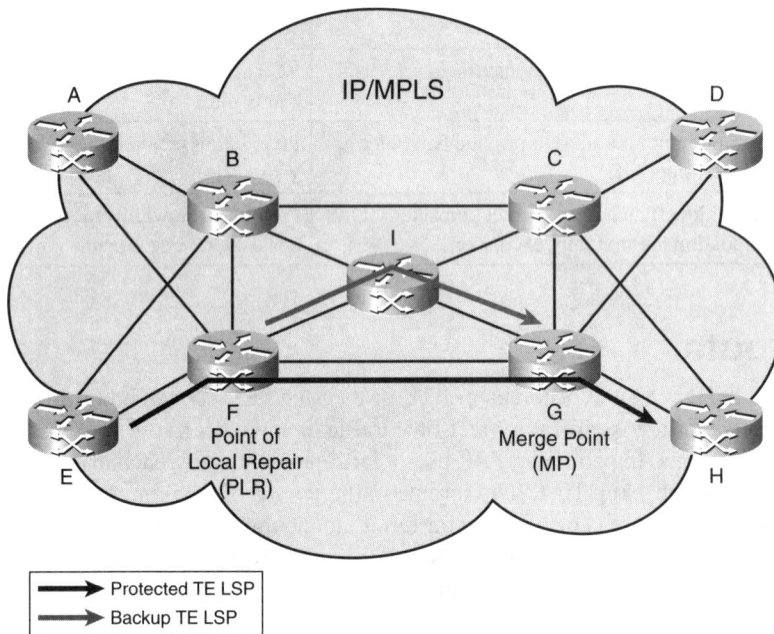

MPLS TE FRR introduces a few RSVP extensions for the signaling of the protected TE LSP, as follows:

- A new FAST_REROUTE object defines the characteristics for the backup TE LSP. These characteristics include priorities (setup and holding), hop limit, bandwidth, and attributes. The FAST_REROUTE object also specifies whether nodes should use facility backup or one-to-one backup to protect the TE LSP.

- The extended RECORD_ROUTE object indicates protection availability at each hop and its type (link, node, or bandwidth protection).

- The extended SESSION_ATTRIBUTE object signals whether the TE LSP desires protection and its type (link, node, or bandwidth protection).

Table 2-12 summarizes these extensions.

Table 2-12   *RSVP Objects Used for MPLS TE FRR*

RSVP Object	RSVP Message	FRR Function
FAST_REROUTE	Path	Specifies the desired FRR technique (facility backup or one-to-one backup) and the desired characteristics (priority, bandwidth, attributes, and so on) of the backup TE LSP
RECORD_ROUTE	Path, Resv	Records a list of hops/labels for the protected TE LSP, including protection status and type at each hop
SESSION_ATTRIBUTE	Path	Indicates whether the TE LSP requires protection and the type of protection

NOTE   The one-to-one backup technique uses an additional RSVP object (DETOUR).

MPLS TE FRR can use global or local restoration of the protected TE LSP as a result of a network failure. The global restoration approach relies on the headend rerouting the protected TE LSP. When the failure of a protected facility occurs, the PLR sends a PathErr message toward the headend of the protected TE LSP. In addition to the RSVP notification, the headend may also learn about the failure condition from IGP updates if the failure happens in the same IGP area. When the headend receives the failure notification, it can reroute the protected TE LSP permanently around the failure. When a PLR uses local restoration instead, it reroutes the protected TE LSPs through the backup while the failure persists. When the facility is back in service, the PLR resignals the protected TE LSP through its original path. Global restoration is more desirable as it relies on the headend to re-optimize the protected TE LSP. That node typically has a more complete view of the network resources and TE LSP constraints.

Link Protection

Link protection uses a backup TE LSP destined to the PLR *next hop* (NHOP). When a node signals a TE LSP with link protection desired, nodes along the path attempt to associate the TE LSP with a backup TE LSP to the NHOP downstream. The backup TE LSP could exist already, or the node may attempt to compute a suitable path and signal it. Any node that finds a TE backup LSP becomes a potential PLR and signals back to the protected TE LSP headend the protection availability at that location using the RECORD_ROUTE object. When a link fails, the PLR reroutes all the identified TE LSPs using the backup TE LSP. The rerouting process involves pushing the protected TE LSP label (as done before the failure) and then stacking the backup TE LSP label on top.

Figure 2-9 illustrates the operation of link protection. Node E signals a TE LSP toward node H, indicating in the SESSION_ATTRIBUTE that the TE LSP desires protection for link failures. When node F processes the object, it finds a suitable backup to the NHOP (node G) through node I. When the link between nodes F and G fails, node F detects the failure locally and modifies the output encapsulation of the protected TE LSP. It continues to push label 35 as expected by the NHOP and, in addition, it pushes label 16 to reroute the traffic through the backup TE LSP. Node I switches the backup TE LSP packets without any knowledge of the protected TE LSP. In this case, node I performs a PHP operation and the packets finally arrive at the MP (node G) with label 35 to continue toward node H.

Link protection can also protect against the failure of *shared-risk link groups* (SLRG). In some cases, multiple links in a network have a high probability of failing at the same time. Generally, these SRLGs are the result of multiple links sharing the same underlying infrastructure (Layer 2, Layer 1, or actual physical facilities). The path computation for the backup TE LSP should take into account these SLRGs to avoid using links that could fail at the same time as the protected link. PLRs can learn about SRLGs dynamically from IGP extensions or through local configuration. SRLGs affect the path computation that the PLR may perform the backup TE LSP. However, they do not impact the operation of link protection.

Node Protection

Node protection uses a backup TE LSP destined to the PLR next-next hop (NNHOP). When a node signals a TE LSP with node protection desired, nodes along the path attempt to associate it with a backup TE LSP to the NNHOP downstream. The backup TE LSP could exist already, or the node may attempt to compute a suitable path and signal it. Nodes that find a TE backup LSP become a potential PLR and signal back to the protected TE LSP headend the protection availability at their location using the RECORD_ROUTE object. When the NHOP fails, the PLR reroutes all the identified TE LSPs using the backup TE LSP. The rerouting process involves pushing the protected TE LSP label expected by the NNHOP and then stacking the TE backup LSP label on top. The PLR learns the NNHOP label from the RECORD_ROUTE object in Resv messages. Node protection can also protect against SRLG failures. As described in the previous section, SRLGs affect backup path computation but have no impact on the operation FRR, and in this case, node protection.

Figure 2-9 *MPLS TE FRR Link Protection Operation*

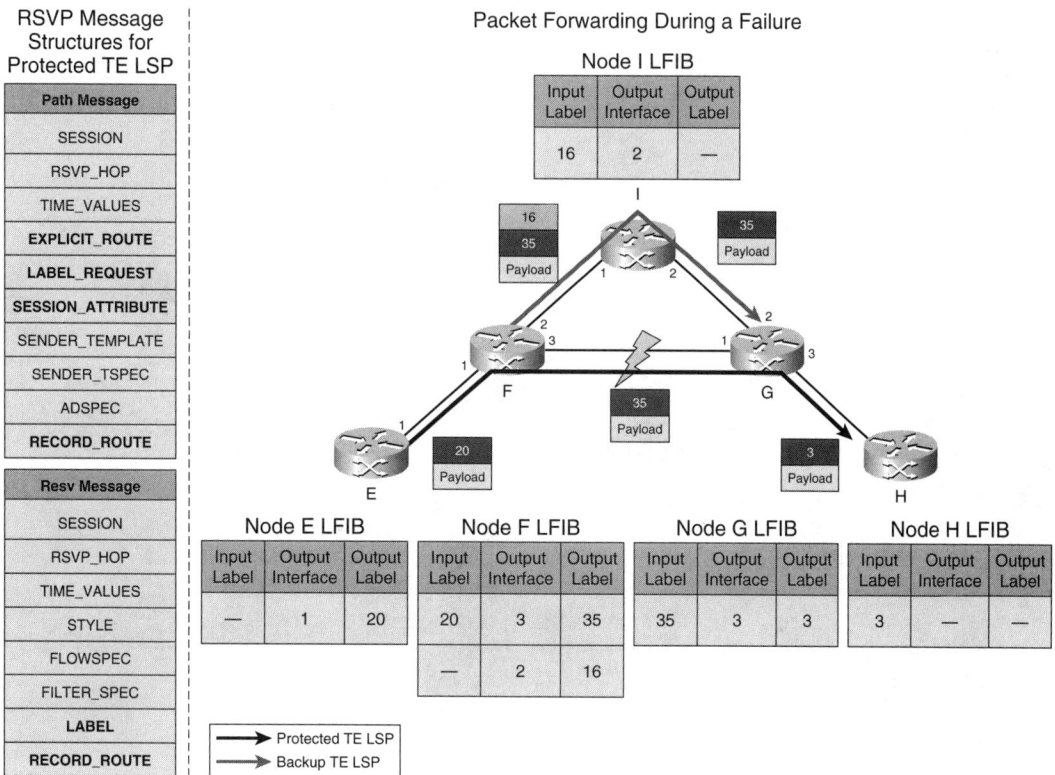

RSVP Message Structures for Protected TE LSP

Path Message
SESSION
RSVP_HOP
TIME_VALUES
EXPLICIT_ROUTE
LABEL_REQUEST
SESSION_ATTRIBUTE
SENDER_TEMPLATE
SENDER_TSPEC
ADSPEC
RECORD_ROUTE

Resv Message
SESSION
RSVP_HOP
TIME_VALUES
STYLE
FLOWSPEC
FILTER_SPEC
LABEL
RECORD_ROUTE

Packet Forwarding During a Failure

Node I LFIB

Input Label	Output Interface	Output Label
16	2	—

Node E LFIB

Input Label	Output Interface	Output Label
—	1	20

Node F LFIB

Input Label	Output Interface	Output Label
20	3	35
—	2	16

Node G LFIB

Input Label	Output Interface	Output Label
35	3	3

Node H LFIB

Input Label	Output Interface	Output Label
3	—	—

→ Protected TE LSP
→ Backup TE LSP

Figure 2-10 shows the operation of node protection. Node E signals a TE LSP toward node H, this time indicating in the SESSION_ATTRIBUTE that the TE LSP desires node protection. In this case, node E itself finds a suitable backup to the NNHOP (node G) through nodes B and I. When node F fails, node E detects the failure locally and modifies the output encapsulation of the protected TE LSP. Instead of pushing label 20 as performed before the failure, node E now pushes label 35 as expected by the node G and, in addition, it pushes label 16 to reroute the traffic through the backup TE LSP. Node B and I switch the backup TE LSP packets without any awareness of the protected TE LSP. Packets finally arrive at the MP (node G) with label 35 to continue toward node H.

Figure 2-10 *MPLS TE FRR Node Protection Operation*

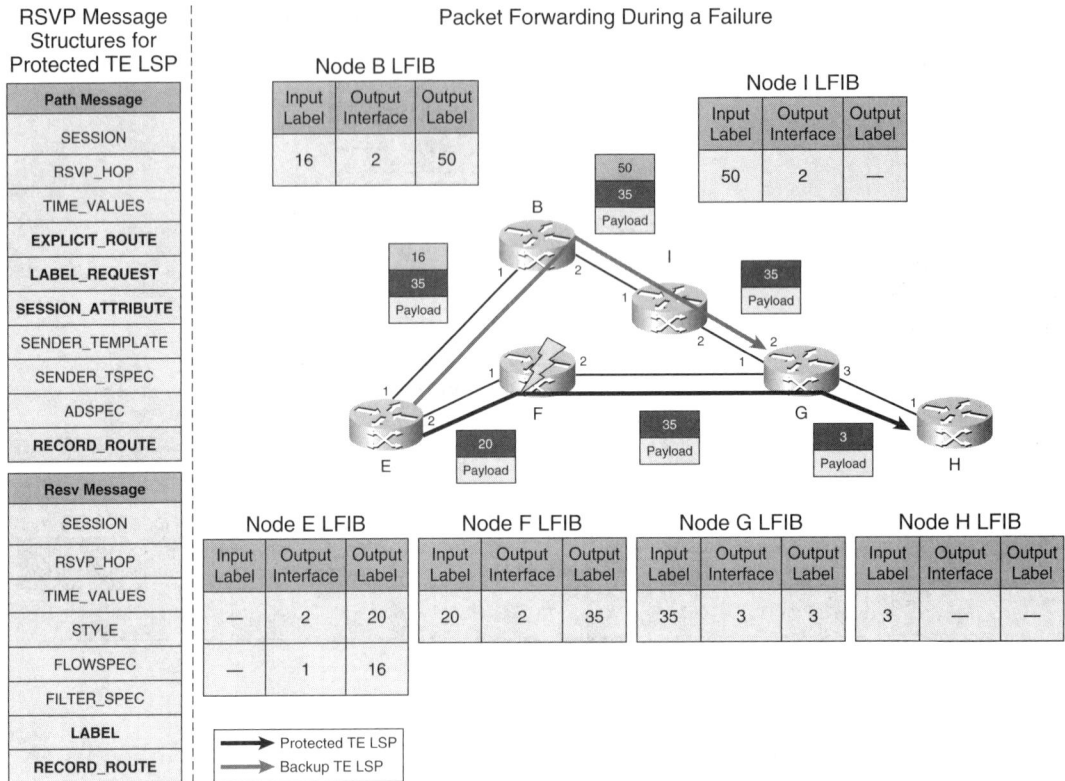

Summary

MPLS provides native TE capabilities that can improve network efficiency and service guarantees. These MPLS TE capabilities bring explicit routing, constraint-based routing, and bandwidth reservation to MPLS networks. MPLS TE relies on extensions to existing IP protocols (IS-IS, OSPF, and RSVP). MPLS TE also supports its routing and bandwidth-reservation capabilities per class through the DS-TE extensions. DS-TE retains the same overall operation characteristics of MPLS TE but introduces minor protocol extensions to accommodate multiple classes. DS-TE enforces BCs on network links that complement the bandwidth allocation that DiffServ can provide in the forwarding plane provides. DS-TE can use two different BC models (MAM and RDM). Last, MPLS TE provides a fast protection mechanism for link and node failures using FRR. This mechanism relies on presignaled backup TE LSPs to provide fast protection (in milliseconds) in a scalable manner to other TE LSPs.

References

MPLS TE

Draft-ietf-mpls-soft-preemption-03 – MPLS Traffic Engineering Soft Preemption

Osborne, E., and A. Simha. *Traffic Engineering with MPLS*. Cisco Press; 2003.

RFC 3209, *RSVP-TE: Extensions to RSVP for LSP Tunnels*

RFC4090, *Fast Reroute Extensions to RSVP-TE for LSP Tunnels*

RFC 3784, *IS-IS extensions for Traffic Engineering*

RFC 3630, *Traffic Engineering (TE) Extensions to OSPF Version 2*

RFC 4124, *Protocol extensions for support of Differentiated-services-aware MPLS Traffic Engineering*

RFC 4125, *Maximum Allocation bandwidth Constraints Model for Diffserv-aware MPLS Traffic Engineering*

RFC 4127, *Russian Dolls Bandwidth Constraints Model for Diffserv-aware MPLS Traffic Engineering*

RSVP

RFC 2205, *Resource Reservation Protocol (RSVP) -- Version 1 Functional Specification*

RFC 2209, *Resource Reservation Protocol (RSVP) -- Version 1 Message Processing Rules*

RFC 2747, *RSVP Cryptographic Authentication*

RFC 2961, *RSVP Refresh Overhead Reduction Extensions*

RFC 2996, *Format of the RSVP DCLASS Object*

RFC 3097, *RSVP Cryptographic Authentication—Updated Message Type Value*

RFC 3175, *Aggregation of RSVP for IPv4 and IPv6 Reservations*

RFC 3473, *Generalized Multi-Protocol Label Switching (GMPLS) Signaling Resource Reservation Protocol-Traffic Engineering (RSVP-TE) Extensions*

In this chapter, you learn the following topics:

- Cisco QoS Behavioral Model
- The Modular QoS Command-Line Interface

CHAPTER 3

Cisco QoS

This chapter provides an overview of the *quality of service* (QoS) implementation and configuration in Cisco products. This overview includes details about algorithms and configuration commands. The material includes simple examples to illustrate the use of the commands. Chapter 5, "Backbone Infrastrusture," provides more elaborate examples. You will find details about both Cisco IOS and Cisco IOS XR implementations. This chapter does not include platform or hardware details because of their constant evolution. The material assumes that you are already familiar with the technology aspects of QoS. Chapter 1, "QoS Technology Overview," includes a technology overview that you can use as a reference.

Cisco QoS Behavioral Model

Cisco uses an abstract QoS behavioral model that provides consistency across devices. Cisco platforms may ultimately use different internal QoS implementations. However, the Cisco QoS behavioral model provides a common abstraction that hides the implementation details and facilitates the implementation of QoS across different product families. The model is flexible enough to provide a wide range of possible QoS behaviors despite its simplicity. A good understanding of this model will help you comprehend QoS configuration on Cisco devices. Later sections in this chapter present an overview of QoS configuration commands and their relationship with this model.

The QoS behavioral model relies on the concept of a *traffic-management node* (TMN). This concept represents an abstraction of a collection of QoS actions that a device applies to traffic at a particular point during packet forwarding. The TMN identifies one or more traffic streams and defines the actions performed on each stream. The underlying implementation infers what structures and mechanisms (including possible queues) will provide the behavior that the TMN actions define.

The TMN has four components, in the following order: classification, pre-queuing, queuing, and post-queuing. All components are optional and user configurable. Figure 3-1 provides a functional view of a packet traversing a TMN. The next sections provide more details on these components.

Figure 3-1 *Components in a TMN*

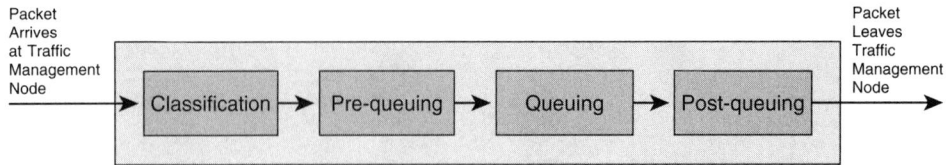

A packet might encounter zero or more TMNs while traversing a device. A TMN typically exists at points where congestion can happen. A device can have several congestion points in its forwarding path depending on its architecture. However, a TMN can also exist at other points where congestion does not occur. The input and output interfaces are the most common points where a packet might encounter a TMN. Some distributed platforms may support a TMN for traffic entering their switching fabric. A TMN can also exist at the interface to the route processor. This TMN manages the traffic that the route processor sends and receives. Figure 3-2 shows a packet passing through multiple TMNs.

Figure 3-2 *Packet Traversing Multiple TMNs*

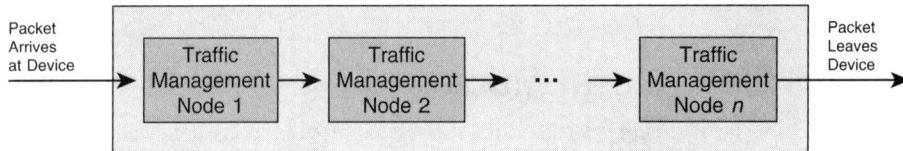

Classification Component

The classification component identifies traffic streams using packet contents or context information. The TMN associates each traffic stream with a class name. The TMN typically uses packet headers to classify traffic. These headers include Layer 2, Layer 3, and Layer 4 headers.

The classification component can also inspect (statefully or not) the packet payload or use packet context information such as input interface. All traffic that does not match any explicitly configured classification criteria becomes part of a default class that uses the **class-default** keyword. If the classification component does not exist, all traffic becomes part of this default class. In summary, the classification component receives a traffic aggregate and identifies one or more streams that it associates with class names.

Pre-Queuing Component

The pre-queuing component groups a set of QoS actions that must precede queuing in the TMN. This is the second entry in the list of TMN components. The pre-queuing component always follows the classification component. It includes actions such as policing, marking, dropping, and header compression. Despite its name, this component does not imply that a queuing component must exist in every TMN. However, the prequeuing component must precede a queuing component if one exists.

The pre-queuing component can affect the operation of subsequent components. For instance, a policing action may re-mark packets. The new packet marking would affect any active queue management in the queuing component. The pre-queuing component does not affect the result of the classification component. That is, the TMN does not reclassify packets.

Queuing Component

The queuing component provides bandwidth management during periods of congestion. Queuing is the third entry in the list of possible TMN components. It always precedes the post-queuing component and always follows the classification and pre-queuing components. The queuing component includes two subcomponents: enqueuing and dequeuing. These subcomponents use a set of parameters to control how traffic enters and leaves that queue. A TMN may process traffic at a point where congestion does not occur, and therefore, the queuing component will not exist. Figure 3-3 illustrates the structure of the queuing component.

Figure 3-3   *Queuing Component in the TMN*

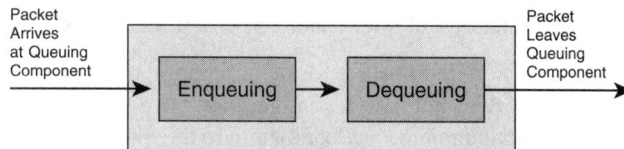

Enqueuing Subcomponent

Enqueuing controls the size of a queue by deciding which packets enter a queue. A maximum queue depth represents the simple form of control that implements a tail drop policy. That is, enqueuing of packets stops when the queue reaches the maximum queue size (that is, the tail of the queue).

Enqueuing can also use the queue management mechanism that section "Active Queue Management" in Chapter 1 described. In such a case, the enqueuing subcomponent is responsible for computing the packet-drop probability based on the average queue size and the minimum and maximum thresholds. It would make a dropping decision using the computed drop probability.

Dequeuing Subcomponent

The dequeuing subcomponent controls packet departure from queues. It represents an abstraction of the scheduling and shaping mechanisms that sections "Traffic Shaping" and "Congestion Management" presented in Chapter 1. Four attributes can influence traffic dequeuing:

- The minimum-bandwidth guarantee represents the worst-case bandwidth allocation that the queue will receive.

- The maximum bandwidth defines the best-case bandwidth allocation for the queue. In some cases, it corresponds to a shaper rate.

- The excess bandwidth defines the distribution of excess bandwidth beyond the minimum-bandwidth guarantee.

- The priority attribute defines whether the scheduler must service a queue ahead of all other queues of lower priority.

The configuration flexibility of the queue attributes defines two-parameter versus three-parameter schedulers. A TMN uses a two-parameter scheduler if the minimum and maximum bandwidth guarantees are independent, whereas the excess bandwidth depends on one of the other two guarantees (typically, the minimum guarantee). Therefore, the configuration of the minimum and excess bandwidths is mutually exclusive. One parameter implies the other. A TMN with a three-parameter scheduler supports the independent configuration of minimum, maximum, and excess bandwidth amounts for each queue. This configuration flexibility allows a TMN to offer more varied behaviors. In particular, a queue can provide better latency and jitter characteristics if it receives more excess bandwidth.

The TMN has implicit default values for the minimum, maximum, and excess-bandwidth attributes. If a queue does not have a configuration for a minimum-bandwidth guarantee, the scheduler will not guarantee any bandwidth to the queue. If the queue does not have a maximum bandwidth attribute, the queue can receive as much bandwidth as possible.

Two-parameter and three-parameter schedulers have a different default behavior for the excess-bandwidth attribute. Three-parameter schedulers share excess bandwidth equally among queues without an explicit excess-bandwidth configuration. Two-parameter schedulers share excess bandwidth proportionally to the minimum-bandwidth guarantee. If a minimum-bandwidth configuration does not exist, the scheduler shares the excess bandwidth equally.

Figure 3-4 shows a sample TMN with four queues. The first queue is a priority queue with a maximum-bandwidth guarantee. The second and third queues have explicit minimum- and maximum-bandwidth guarantees. The last queue has only a maximum-bandwidth guarantee. All nonpriority queues rely on the default excess-bandwidth configuration. The exact amount of bandwidth that each queue receives depends on the traffic patterns and the type of scheduler. Either a two-parameter or three-parameter scheduler could support this configuration given that none of the queues have an explicit minimum and excess-bandwidth configuration. Table 3-1 summarizes the four dequeuing attributes and their defaults.

Figure 3-4   *Sample Bandwidth Configuration for a TMN with Four Queues*

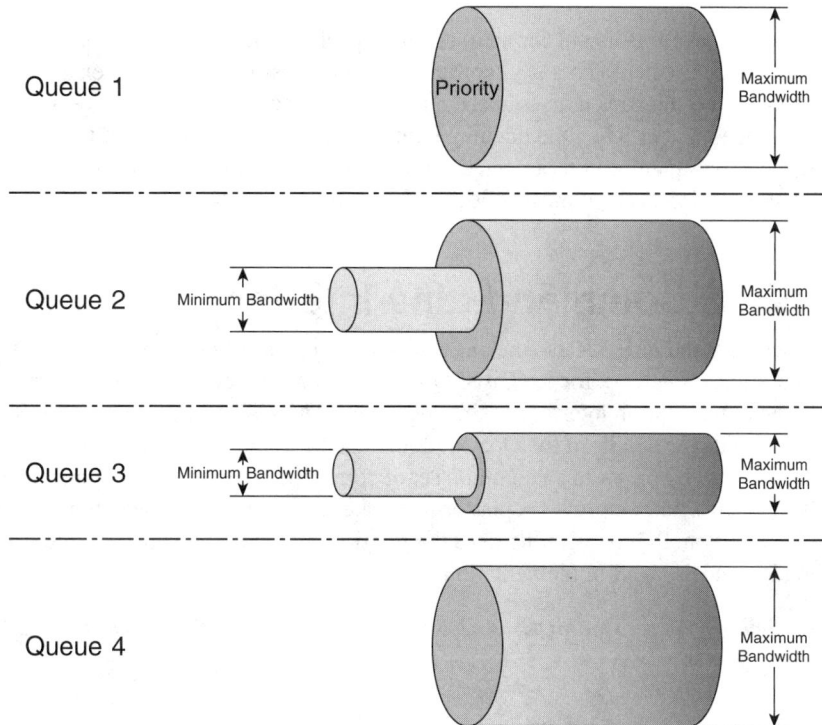

Table 3-1   *Dequeuing Attributes in the TMN*

Dequeuing Attribute	Description	Default
Minimum bandwidth	Worst-case bandwidth allocation.	No bandwidth is guaranteed.
Maximum bandwidth	Best-case bandwidth allocation.	As much bandwidth as possible is allocated.
Excess bandwidth	Distribution of excess bandwidth beyond the minimum-bandwidth guarantee.	Equal excess-bandwidth sharing for three-parameter schedulers. Proportional excess-bandwidth sharing for two-parameter schedulers.
Priority	Strict priority relative to other queues. Scheduler serves queues according to their priority.	No strict priority.

Post-Queuing Component

The post-queuing component defines the QoS actions that must follow queuing in the TMN. This is the fourth and last component of the TMN. It defines the last group of actions before the packet leaves the TMN.

This component is useful for actions where packet sequencing is important given that the queuing component generally reorders packets across queues. As an example, some compression mechanisms use sequence numbers and packets should receive their respective sequence number when the queuing component schedules the packet for transmission. As with the pre-queuing component, this component does not imply that a queuing component must exist. However, it must follow it if present.

Modular QoS Command-Line Interface

Cisco IOS and IOS XR use the *modular QoS command-line interface* (MQC) as the configuration framework for the Cisco QoS behavioral model. The MQC acts as a template-based configuration interface to the underlying TMN. The MQC and the QoS behavioral model hide the details of the QoS implementation from the user. The MQC facilitates QoS deployment by providing a common set of commands with the same syntax and semantics. At the same time, it provides platforms greater flexibility in the selection of their QoS implementation. Figure 3-5 illustrates the relationship between MQC, the QoS behavioral model, and the QoS implementation.

Figure 3-5 *Relationship Between the MQC, the QoS Behavioral Model, and the QoS Implementation*

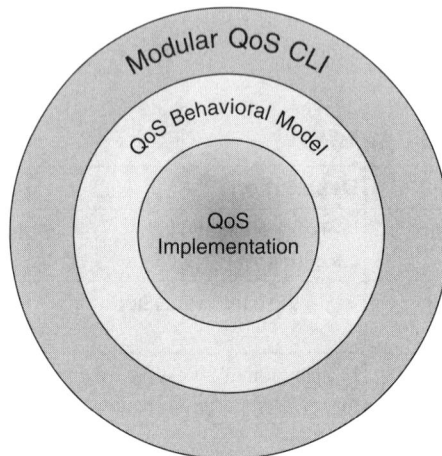

The MQC has three configuration components:

- **Class map**—Defines a class of traffic via matching rules. It corresponds to the classification component of the TMN.

- **Policy map**—Defines a policy that contains QoS actions to be applied to some classes of traffic. It typically references the classes that **class-map** commands defined. It provides the configuration for the pre-queuing, queuing, and post-queuing components of the TMN.

- **Service policy**—Associates a policy with a particular target and direction within a device. A **policy-map** command must have defined the policy previously. The separation of the policy definition from the policy invocation reduces the complexity of the QoS configuration.

NOTE   Class names and policy names are case-sensitive.

The configuration of the **service-policy** command determines both the direction and attachment point of the QoS policy. You can attach a policy to an interface (physical or logical), a *permanent virtual circuit* (PVC), or special points to control route processor traffic. Examples of logical interfaces include the following:

- **MFR** (*Multilink Frame Relay*)
- **Multilink** (*Multilink PPP*)
- **Port-channel** (Ethernet channel of interfaces)
- **POS-channel** (*Packet-over-SONET/SDH* channel of interfaces)
- **Virtual Template**

Two directions are possible for a policy: input and output. The policy direction is relative to the attachment point. The attachment point and direction influence the type of actions that a policy supports (for example, some interfaces may not support input queuing policies). This chapter and Chapter 5, "Backbone Infrastructure," provide numerous policy examples.

Example 3-1 shows an example of a QoS policy using the MQC. This example includes two explicit class definitions: CLASS1 and CLASS2. The policy with name POLICY1 references those two classes in addition to the default class (class-default). As mentioned previously, this class does not require configuration and represents all traffic that does not match the explicitly configured classes. The policy is attached to the interface GigabitEthernet3/0 in the input direction. Therefore, the policy will process packets entering the device through that interface. This particular example shows only placeholders for the **class-map** statements and the class actions in the policy map. The following section provides more details about the configuration syntax and options.

Example 3-1   *QoS Policy Configuration Using the MQC*

```
class-map match-all CLASS1
  match <statement-1>
class-map match-any CLASS2
  match <statement-2>
  match <statement-3>
  match <statement-4>
!
policy-map POLICY1
  class CLASS1
   police <action-1>
  class CLASS2
   <action-2>
   <action-3>
  class class-default
   <action-4>
!
interface GigabitEthernet3/0
 ip address 192.168.0.1 255.255.255.254
 service-policy input POLICY1
 !
```

The **show policy-map** command is the primary command for verifying the operation and configuration of a QoS policy. The output from this command displays the counters relative to all the actions configured on the policy. Those counters are a vital tool to troubleshoot QoS problems. The **clear counters** command resets all interface counters, including MQC counters, in Cisco IOS. The **clear qos counters** command clears the MQC counters in Cisco IOS XR. You will not find **debug** commands to monitor the operation of traffic-management mechanisms in the forwarding place because of the per-packet processing impact. Cisco IOS XR includes some debug options (using the debug qos command prefix), but those are useful to troubleshoot the internal details of the QoS implementation on a platform. They are not generally practical as an operational tool. In addition, the show qos interface command displays the hardware-programmed values for an interface with an attached policy, but does not display any counter information.

Table 3-2 summarizes the three most common forms of the **show policy-map** command. The following sections include specific examples of the output of this command. Formatting differences apply between Cisco IOS and Cisco IOS XR.

Table 3-2   *Policy Verification Using the **show policy-map** Command*

Syntax	Description
show policy-map *name*	Displays policy configuration
show policy-map interface [*name* [**dlci**|**vc**|**vp**]]|[{**input**|**output**} **class** *name*]	Displays counters for a policy attached to an interface, Frame Relay DLCI,[*] ATM PVC, or ATM PVP[*]

Table 3-2   *Policy Verification Using the **show policy-map** Command (Continued)*

Syntax	Description
show policy-map control-plane [**all**|**slot** *value*][{**input**|**output**} **class** *name*]	Displays counters for a policy controlling control-plane traffic
show policy-map switch-fabric { **unicast**	**multicast**}	Displays counters for a policy controlling traffic sent to the switch fabric

* DLCI = data-link connection identifier
  PVC = permanent virtual path

NOTE   Platforms with a distributed architecture might exhibit a delay in updating counters when compared with platforms with a centralized architecture.

Hardware Support for the MQC

MQC support has wide support in all products running Cisco IOS and Cisco IOS XR. New software releases have constantly enhanced this framework since it was first introduced in 1999. Before that time, Cisco switches and routers already offered a good amount of QoS functionality. MQC has gradually incorporated more features and today offers greater functionality than earlier, sometimes platform-specific, features. In some cases, you might still have to rely on non-MQC features. However, those cases should be the exception and not the rule. You should expect that most, if not all, future QoS enhancements will involve MQC.

This book does not include a detailed description of QoS support on specific Cisco equipment. Different devices play different roles in a network, and those roles define the functionality, performance, and scale those devices should provide. You will find differences depending on the device series, software release, hardware modules, and, sometimes, configured services. You should rely on the software and hardware documentation to understand what commands are available on a particular device and any deviations from the Cisco behavioral model.

Traffic-Management Mechanisms

This section covers the details of the configuration options in the MQC. It presents the commands that enable you to configure the components of the TMN (classification, pre-queuing, queuing, and post-queuing). You will find an explanation of each function with a brief syntax overview, configuration examples, and sample outputs of the **show policy-map interface** command. The information focuses on the most commonly used commands and gives you a good understanding about how to use the command and verify its operation. Do *not* consider it a complete command reference guide. For a complete description of all command options and a complete syntax, consult the Cisco IOS and Cisco IOS XR documentation.

Traffic Classification

You configure packet classification using **class-map** commands. Class maps define the classification component of the TMN. They can include one or more **match** commands. These commands provide a wide range of criteria for packet classification. They vary from Layer 2 (for example, MAC address, ATM *Cell Loss Priority* [CLP]) to application level criteria (for example, an URL). Within a policy the classification process for a packet ends when the packet matches a class. Therefore, the classification can associate only each packet with a single class.

Packets that do not satisfy the matching criteria of any class map become part of the implicit default class that you reference with the **class-default** command keyword. Tables 3-3 through 3-7 provide a summary of most of the matching criteria that the MQC supports.

Table 3-3   *Matching Criteria Using IP and MPLS[*] Headers*

Syntax	Matching Criteria
match access-group {*value*|**name** *value*}	Numbered or named access list (Cisco IOS only)
match access-group [**ipv4**|**ipv6**] *value*	Access list (Cisco IOS XR only)
match precedence *list*	List of precedence values (IPv4 and IPv6)
match dscp *list*	List of DSCP[*] values (IPv4 and IPv6)
match mpls experimental topmost *list*	List of EXP[*] values for MPLS
match packet length {**min** *value*[**max** *value*]|[**min** *value*] **max** *value*}	IP packet size (including IP header)

[*] MPLS = Multiprotocol Label Switching

DSCP = Differentiated Services Code Point

EXP = Experimental bit

NOTE   Earlier implementations of the **match mpls experimental topmost** command did not use the **topmost** keyword.

NOTE   Earlier implementations of the **match precedence** command used the **match ip precedence** syntax. Similarly, earlier implementations of the **match dscp** command used the **match ip dscp** syntax.

Table 3-4   *Matching Criteria on External Packet Characteristics*

Syntax	Matching Criteria
match input-interface *value*	Interface packet arrived at
match qos-group *list*	List of internal packet class marking
match discard-class *list*	List of nternal packet marking identifying drop profile

Table 3-5   *Matching Criteria for Ethernet, ATM, and Frame Relay*

Syntax	Matching Criteria
match cos *list*	List of Ethernet 802.1Q user priority values
match cos inner *list*	List of inner Ethernet 802.1Q user priority values for packets with double VLAN encapsulation
match source-address mac *value*	Ethernet source MAC address
match destination-address mac *value*	Ethernet destination MAC address
match spantree bpdu	Ethernet spanning-tree BPDU[*]
match vlan *range*	Range of Ethernet VLAN IDs
match vlan inner *range*	Range of inner VLAN IDs for packets with double VLAN encapsulation
match atm ilmi	ATM ILMI[*] packets
match atm oam	ATM OAM[*] cells
match atm clp	ATM CLP bit
match frame-relay dlci *range*	Frame Relay DLCI
match frame-relay de	Frame Relay DE[*] bit
match frame-relay lmi	Frame Relay LMI[*] packets

* BPDU = bridge protocol data unit

ILMI = interim local management interface

OAM = operation, administration, and maintenance

DE = Discard Eligibility bit

LMI = local management interface

NOTE Earlier implementations of the **match frame-relay dlci**, **match frame-relay de**, and **match frame-relay lmi** commands used the **match fr-dlci** syntax, **match fr-de** syntax, and **match fr-lmi** syntax respectively.

Table 3-6 *Matching Criteria for Protocols and Packet Payload*

Syntax	Matching Criteria
match ip rtp *start offset*	RTP[*] packets with UDP ports between *start* and *start+offset*
match protocol arp	ARP[*] packets
match protocol cdp	CDP[*] packets
match protocol clns	ISO CLNS[*] packets
match protocol clns_es	ISO CLNS ES[*] packets
match protocol clns_is	ISO CLNS IS[*] packets
match protocol cmns	ISO CMNS[*] packets
match protocol compressedtcp	Compressed TCP
match protocol ip	IPv4 packets
match protocol ipv6	IPv6 packets

[*] RTP = Real-Time mTransport Protocol

ARP = Address Resolution Protocol

CDP = Cisco Discovery Protocol

CLNS = Connectionless Network Service

ES = End System

IS = Intermediate System

CMNS = Connection-Mode Network Service

NOTE Table 3-6 includes only a small fraction of the protocols that the **match protocol** command supports. Depending on the platform and software, this command can match more than 80 different protocols and applications. Some of them provide stateful inspection of the packet payload to identify traffic that is not easily classified (for example, peer-to-peer applications). See the Cisco *network-based application recognition* (NBAR) documentation for more details.

Table 3-7   *Matching Criteria for Hierarchical Class Definitions*

Syntax	Matching Criteria
match class-map *name*	Class map name

A class map supports logical operations of **match** commands. You can define a logical OR, a logical AND, or a negation of match commands. The **match-any** keyword defines a logical OR of all the **match** statements in a class map. Similarly, the **match-all** keyword defines a logical AND. In addition, the **match not** command negates individual matching criteria. More-complex operations combining these operations require hierarchical configurations that the section "Hierarchical Classification" covers. Some **match** commands (for example, **match dscp** and **match mpls experimental topmost**) accept list of values. In those cases, a packet satisfies the statement if it matches any of the values in the list.

Example 3-2 shows four different class configurations. The first class, CLASS1, includes packets that match access list 99 or have a DSCP value of EF. CLASS2 matches packets with a DSCP of AF11, AF12, or AF13. MPLS packets with EXP values of 3 or 4 will match CLASS3. Notice that the **match-all** keyword in CLASS2 and CLASS3 does not change the logical OR operation that the multiple values in the **match** statements imply. CLASS4 matches ATM OAM cells and CLASS5 matches IPv6 packets with a DSCP of default. Multiple policies could reference these classes.

Example 3-2   *Traffic-Classification Configuration*

```
class-map match-any CLASS1
  match access-group 99
  match  dscp ef
class-map match-all CLASS2
  match  dscp af11  af12  af13
class-map match-all CLASS3
  match mpls experimental topmost 3  4
class-map match-all CLASS4
  match atm oam
class-map match-all CLASS5
  match protocol ipv6
  match  dscp default
!
```

Example 3-3 and 3-4 highlight the classification counters that a policy maintains. Example 3-3 illustrates the **show policy-map** output in Cisco IOS for a policy that references the CLASS1 and CLASS2 definitions in Example 3-2. There are three main classification counters:

- Classified packets
- Classified bytes
- Offered (average) rate (5 minutes by default)

You can see that the policy has classified 28,000 packets as CLASS1. Those packets amount to 41,608,000 bytes. The average arrival rate was 188,000 bps for CLASS1 in the past 5 minutes. Similarly, the policy has classified 14,000 packets (or 20,804,000 bytes) as CLASS2, which has an average arrival rate of 95,000 bps. The default class (class-default) received 42,000 packets representing 62,412,000 bytes. The average rate of packets arriving at this class is 282,000 bps. In this example, the same set of counters is available per **match** statement for those class maps using the **match-any** keyword.

NOTE   A number of platforms do not support separate classification counters for each **match** statement. Consult the platform documentation for details.

TIP   You can control the averaging interval for an interface using the load-interval command. This command impacts the calculation of average rates for the policies you apply to the interface and other average rates associated with the interface counters.

Example 3-3   *Classification Counters in Cisco IOS*

```
Router#show policy-map interface pos0/0/0

 POS0/0/0

  Service-policy output: POLICY1

    Class-map: CLASS1 (match-any)
      28000 packets, 41608000 bytes
      5 minute offered rate 188000 bps, drop rate 0 bps
      Match: access-group 99
        0 packets, 0 bytes
        5 minute rate 0 bps
      Match: dscp ef (46)
        28000 packets, 41608000 bytes
        5 minute rate 188000 bps
      QoS Set
        dscp cs5
          Packets marked 28000

    Class-map: CLASS2 (match-all)
      14000 packets, 20804000 bytes
      5 minute offered rate 95000 bps, drop rate 0 bps
      Match: dscp af11 (10) af12 (12) af13 (14)
      QoS Set
        dscp cs1
          Packets marked 14000
```

Example 3-3 *Classification Counters in Cisco IOS (Continued)*

```
      Class-map: class-default (match-any)
        42000 packets, 62412000 bytes
        5 minute offered rate 282000 bps, drop rate 0 bps
        Match: any
          42000 packets, 62412000 bytes
          5 minute rate 282000 bps
        QoS Set
          dscp default
            Packets marked 42000
Router#
```

Example 3-4 shows the **show policy-map** output for an equivalent policy using Cisco IOS XR. The same counters are present, but the output format differs. POLICY1 has classified 40,000 packets as CLASS1, 20,000 packets as CLASS2, and 60,000 packets in the default class (class-default). Those packets amount to 59,280,000, 29,640,000 and 88,920,000 bytes, respectively. The average arrival rates for these three classes are 758, 379, and 1136 kbps respectively.

Example 3-4 *Classification Counters in Cisco IOS XR*

```
RP/0/4/CPU0:Router#show policy-map interface pos0/3/0/3
POS0/3/0/3 input: POLICY1

Class CLASS1
  Classification statistics          (packets/bytes)     (rate - kbps)
    Matched                :             40000/59280000              758
    Transmitted            :             40000/59280000              758
    Total Dropped          :                        0/0                0
  Marking statistics (S/W only)      (packets/bytes)
    Marked                 :                        0/0
  Queueing statistics
    Vital            (packets)           : 0
    Queue ID                             : None (Bundle)
    Taildropped(packets/bytes)           : 0/0

Class CLASS2
  Classification statistics          (packets/bytes)     (rate - kbps)
    Matched                :             20000/29640000              379
    Transmitted            :             20000/29640000              379
    Total Dropped          :                        0/0                0
  Marking statistics (S/W only)      (packets/bytes)
    Marked                 :                        0/0
  Queueing statistics
    Vital            (packets)           : 0
    Queue ID                             : None (Bundle)
    Taildropped(packets/bytes)           : 0/0

Class class-default
  Classification statistics          (packets/bytes)     (rate - kbps)
    Matched                :             60000/88920000             1136
    Transmitted            :             60000/88920000             1136
    Total Dropped          :                        0/0                0
```

continues

Example 3-4 *Classification Counters in Cisco IOS XR (Continued)*

```
    Marking statistics (S/W only)      (packets/bytes)
      Marked              :                  0/0
    Queueing statistics
      Vital            (packets)        : 0
      Queue ID                          : None (Bundle)
      Taildropped(packets/bytes)        : 0/0
  RP/0/4/CPU0:Router#
```

Traffic Marking

Marking is one of the actions of the pre-queuing component in the TMN. The **set** command is the major method to mark a field associated with a packet. The **set** command supports a wide range of marking criteria, including Layer 2, Layer 3, and internal fields. A class can include multiple **set** commands for different fields (for example, one command marks Layer 3 header, and a second command marks Layer 2 header). In general, this command applies to both input and output policies.

Tables 3-8 through 3-12 provide a summary of the marking criteria that the MQC supports.

TIP   The **police** command can also mark packets. The next section describes that command in detail.

Table 3-8 *Marking Criteria for IP and MPLS Packets*

Syntax	Marking Criteria
set precedence *value*	IPv4 and IPv6 precedence
set precedence tunnel *value*	Precedence to be used by IP header
set dscp *value*	IPv4 and IPv6 DSCP
set dscp tunnel *value*	DSCP to be used by IP tunnel header
set mpls experimental imposition *value*	EXP bits to be used by push operation
set mpls experimental topmost *value*	EXP bits in MPLS header on top of the stack

NOTE   Earlier implementations of the **set mpls experimental imposition** command did not use the **imposition** keyword. If the device performs multiple simultaneous push operations, all headers receive the EXP value.

NOTE   Earlier implementations of the **set precedence** command used the **set ip precedence** syntax. Similarly, earlier implementations of the **set dscp** command used the **set ip dscp** syntax.

A node automatically marks MPLS and IP tunnel packets by default during some encapsulation operations. For MPLS, a node performing a label push operation will set the MPLS EXP in all imposed labels according to the marking in the encapsulated packet. That marking will correspond to the existing EXP for an MPLS packet, IP precedence for an IP packet and the 802.1Q user priority for an Ethernet frame. A label swap operation always preserves the existing MPLS EXP. A label pop operation does not have any effect on the marking of the exposed header. For IP tunnels, the DSCP in the tunnel header will reflect the encapsulated DSCP for IP over GRE or the encapsulated (topmost) EXP for MPLS over GRE. Those IP tunnels using L2TP will use a DSCP of default (zero) unless you configure reflection explicitly. The tunnel decapsulation will not modify the exposed header in any case. Note that the behavior described in this paragraph represents the default behavior when you do not configure marking explicitly. You can use the commands in Table 3-8 to override this behavior. Tables 3-38 and 3-39 summarize the default marking actions for MPLS and IP tunnels.

Table 3-9 *Default MPLS EXP Marking Actions*

MPLS Forwarding Operation	Default Marking Action
Push	Set MPLS EXP on all imposed labels using marking in encapsulated header (MPLS EXP, IP Precedence or Ethernet 802.1Q user priority).
Swap	Maintain MPLS EXP value.
Pop	Do not modify marking in exposed header.

NOTE   The set mpls experimental topmost command on an input policy always marks MPLS packets before the node performs all label forwarding operations (push, swap, or pop). When invoked in an output policy, the command marks MPLS packets after all label forwarding operations.

Table 3-10 *Default IP Tunnel Marking Actions*

IP Tunnel Operation	Default Marking Action
Tunnel Encapsulation	Set tunnel header DSCP using the encapsulated DSCP for IP over GRE or encapsulated EXP for MPLS over GRE. For L2TP, set DSCP to default (zero).
Tunnel Decapsulation	Do not modify DSCP in exposed header.

Table 3-11 *Criteria for Marking of Internal Device Fields*

Syntax	Marking Criteria
set qos-group *value*	Internal field for packet class
set discard-class *value*	Internal field for packet drop profile

Table 3-12 *Marking Criteria for Ethernet, ATM, and Frame Relay*

Syntax	Marking Criteria
set cos *value*	Ethernet 802.1Q user priority
set atm-clp	ATM CLP bit
set fr-de	Frame Relay DE bit

The MQC uses a QoS group ID and a discard class as internal fields that a device can associate with a packet. The QoS group ID field represents a class identifier. The discard class corresponds to a drop profile identifier on drop precedence. A device can set those fields without altering the packet contents. Both fields use integer numbers. The information is lost as soon as the device transmits the packet through the output interface. In most cases, the input policy sets the values and the output policy makes use of them. The section "Active Queue Management" in this chapter shows how to configure *weighted random early detection* (WRED) to select drop profiles using the value set in the discard class. Tables 3-4 and 3-11 showed how to use them to classify traffic and how to set these internal fields, respectively.

A policy can define the marking of a future packet header in advance. This is the case when you want to define the MPLS EXP bits in an input policy for a push operation in an input policy. The input policy indicates the upcoming MPLS EXP marking using the **set mpls experimental imposition** command. The marking does not take effect until the device performs the push operation and imposes a new MPLS header. A similar situation occurs when a packet is about to ingress an IP tunnel. In that case, you can use the **set dscp tunnel** and **set precedence tunnel** commands. The marking action does not affect the contents of the original packet. Figure 3-6 illustrates this beforehand marking for MPLS and IP tunnels.

Figure 3-6   *Marking During MPLS Push and IP Tunneling Operation*

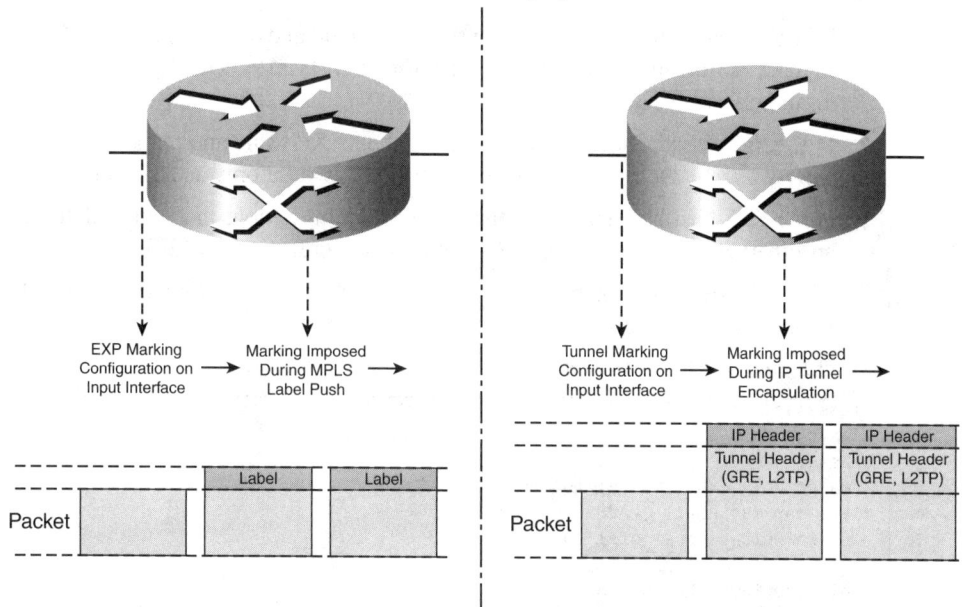

You can also use the **set** command to implement a mapping between two markings. You can define mappings between DSCP, IP precedence, MPLS EXP, internal markings, and 802.1Q user priority. By default, the command implements a one-to-one mapping. However, you can configure an arbitrary mapping using a *table map* that groups a series of **map** statements. Each statement specifies a map between two values. The **default** command defines a default mapping for values without and explicit map. Table 3-13 illustrates how to use the **set** command to map markings. In addition, Table 3-14 summarizes the **map** and **default** commands that are part of a table map.

Table 3-13   *Mapping Between Marking Criteria*

Syntax	Description
set to-field from-field [**table** *name*]	Mapping between two packet fields (for instance, DSCP, IP precedence, MPLS EXP, internal markings, 802.1Q user priority)

Table 3-14   *Mapping Statements in a Table Map*

Syntax	Description
map from *value* **to** *value*	Statement mapping two values
default {*value*|**copy**|**ignore**}	Default mapping action

Example 3-5 demonstrates where four different policies mark traffic:

- POLICY1 classifies IP traffic using the DSCP field and defines the MPLS EXP value to mark during an upcoming label push for each class. POLICY1 is valid only as an input policy.

- POLICY2 classifies MPLS packets using their EXP value and marks the packet locally using a QoS group ID value. POLICY2 is valid only as an input policy.

- POLICY3 illustrates a policy with multiple marking actions that marks all traffic with an Ethernet 802.1Q user priority value of 5 and an IP DSCP of EF.

- POLICY4 defines a mapping between MPLS EXP and QoS group ID using table map FROM-EXP-TO-QoS-GROUP.

Example 3-5 *Policies Performing Traffic Marking*

```
class-map match-all CLASS1
  match  dscp ef
class-map match-all CLASS2
  match mpls experimental topmost  5
class-map match-all CLASS3
  match mpls experimental topmost  3  4
!
table-map FROM-EXP-TO-QoS-GROUP
 map from 1 to 1
 map from 2 to 1
 map from 3 to 3
 map from 4 to 3
 map from 5 to 5
 default 0
!
policy-map POLICY1
  class CLASS1
   set mpls experimental imposition 5
  class class-default
   set mpls experimental imposition 0
!
policy-map POLICY2
  class CLASS2
   set qos-group 5
  class CLASS3
   set qos-group 3
  class class-default
   set qos-group 0
!
policy-map POLICY3
  class class-default
   set dscp ef
   set cos 5
!
policy-map POLICY4
 class class-default
   set qos-group mpls experimental topmost table FROM-EXP-TO-QoS-GROUP
 !
```

Examples 3-6 and 3-7 illustrate the accounting for packet marking in a policy. Some platforms provide marking counters that indicates the number of packets the policy has marked. Example 3-6 presents the output of the **show policy-map** command in Cisco IOS for the POLICY3 defined in Example 3-5. In this case you have explicit marking counters. The policy has received and successfully marked 104,993 packets. Some platforms may not display specific marking counters. In those cases, the classification counters serve as an indication of the number of packets the policy marked.

Example 3-6   *Marking Counters in Cisco IOS*

```
Router#show policy-map interface fastEthernet1/1/1.1
 FastEthernet1/1/1.1

  Service-policy output: POLICY3

    Class-map: class-default (match-any)
       104993 packets, 157489500 bytes
       5 minute offered rate 3196000 bps, drop rate 0 bps
      Match: any
        104993 packets, 157489500 bytes
        5 minute rate 3196000 bps
      QoS Set
        dscp ef
          Packets marked 104993
        cos 5
          Packets marked 104993
Router#
```

Example 3-7 shows the output in Cisco IOS XR for the policy POLICY1 in Example 3-5. The counters that show the number of transmitted packets indicates implicitly the number of marked packets. In the case of CLASS1, the policy marked 70,000 packets corresponding to 103,740,000 bytes. Similarly, the policy marked 140,000 packets in the default class (class-default) that correspond to 207,480,000 bytes. A separate marking counter shows the number of software-switched packets that the policy marked. In this example, no packets have been switched in software.

Example 3-7   *Marking Counters in Cisco IOS XR*

```
RP/0/4/CPU0:Router#show policy-map interface pos0/3/0/3
POS0/3/0/3 input: POLICY1
Class CLASS1
  Classification statistics          (packets/bytes)      (rate - kbps)
    Matched                 :         70000/103740000          1325
    Transmitted             :         70000/103740000          1325
    Total Dropped           :              0/0                    0
  Marking statistics (S/W only)      (packets/bytes)
    Marked                  :              0/0
  Queueing statistics
    Vital           (packets)                :  0
    Queue ID                                 :  None (Bundle)
    Taildropped(packets/bytes)               :  0/0
```

continues

Example 3-7 *Marking Counters in Cisco IOS XR (Continued)*

```
Class class-default
  Classification statistics          (packets/bytes)       (rate - kbps)
    Matched                :         140000/207480000            2650
    Transmitted            :         140000/207480000            2650
    Total Dropped          :              0/0                       0
  Marking statistics (S/W only)      (packets/bytes)
    Marked                 :              0/0
  Queueing statistics
    Vital             (packets)            : 0
    Queue ID                              : None (Bundle)
    Taildropped(packets/bytes)           : 0/0
RP/0/4/CPU0:Router#
```

Traffic Policing

The **police** command configures traffic policing to meter a traffic stream against a profile and process packets based on comparison. Policing is another of the actions of the pre-queuing component in the TMN and, therefore, it does not cause packet queuing. In its simplest form, the **police** command defines a rate threshold for a class and drops the traffic if it exceeds the rate.

The **police** command has a great number of options and provides great flexibility. It always includes a traffic profile, in terms of one or two token buckets (rate and burst), and a group of actions (implicitly or explicitly specified). The command has a single-line format (see Example 3-8) or a multiple-line format (see Example 3-9).

Example 3-8 *Single-Line Format for the **police** Command*

```
policy-map POLICY1
 class class-default
  police <traffic profile> <conform-action> <exceed-action> <violate-action>
 !
```

Example 3-9 *Multiple-Line Format for the **police** Command*

```
policy-map POLICY1
 class class-default
  police <traffic profile>
    <color-definition>
    <conform-action>
    <exceed-action>
    <violate-action>
 !
```

Table 3-15 shows the traffic profile definitions for single-rate policers. The command can use a compact syntax to define the profile rate and bursts. Alternatively, the **cir** and **bc** keywords define the first token bucket. The **be** keyword and the overflow of the first bucket define the second token bucket. You can define a single-rate policer with a single token bucket if you do not define an excess burst value. The **police cir** and **police rate** syntax is equivalent. The **rate** keyword is more general and supports ATM policing. The **rate** and **burst** keywords are equivalent to **cir** and **bc**. All rates are in bits per second, and bursts are in bytes by default. The device computes default bursts if not entered explicitly.

Table 3-15 *Single-Rate Policer Traffic Profile*

Syntax	Profile Definition
police *rate-value* [*bc-value* [*be-value*]]	Absolute terms with compact syntax
police cir *value* [**bc** *value* [**be** *value*]]	Absolute terms with keywords
police rate *value* [**burst** *value* [**peak-burst** *value*]]	Absolute terms with keywords (alternative syntax)
police cir percent *value* [**bc** *value* **ms** [**be** *value* **ms**]]	Relative to underlying bandwidth
police rate percent *value* [**burst** *value* **ms** [**peak-burst** *value* **ms**]]	Relative to underlying bandwidth (alternative syntax)

Table 3-16 shows the traffic profile definitions for dual-rate policers. As with the single-rate policer, the **cir** and **bc** keywords define the first token bucket. However, the **pir** and **be** keywords define the second token bucket. The equivalence between the **police cir** and **police rate** syntax also applies to the dual-rate policer, too. However, the keywords **peak-rate** and **peak-burst** are equivalent to **pir** and **be**. As with all forms of the **police** command, rates are in bits per second and bursts are in bytes by default. The device computes default bursts if not entered explicitly.

Table 3-16 *Dual-Rate Policer Traffic Profile*

Syntax	Profile Definition
police cir *value* [**bc** *value*] **pir** *value* [**be** *value*]	Absolute terms
police rate *value* [**burst** *value*] **peak-rate** *value* [**peak-burst** *value*]	Absolute terms (alternative syntax)
police cir percent *value* [**bc** *value* **ms**] **pir percent** *value* [**be** *value* **ms**]	Relative to underlying bandwidth
police rate percent *value* [**burst** *value* **ms**] **peak-rate percent** *value* [**peak-burst** *value* **ms**]	Relative to underlying bandwidth (alternative syntax)

You can define the policer traffic profile in relative terms. In this case, you specify a rate as a percentage of the underlying bandwidth rate of the policy attachment point. Similarly, you can specify burst sizes in time units (milliseconds by default) relative to the policer rate. The device computes the effective rate and burst sizes in bits per second and bytes, respectively. The **percent** keyword enables the definition of relative traffic profiles. The section "Percentage-Based Rates" explains what constitutes the underlying bandwidth rate that nodes use to interpret relative profile definitions. In its simplest form, the underlying bandwidth rate for a policy that you attach to a physical interface corresponds to the interface bandwidth rate.

TIP

The **police percent** command helps reuse policies across interfaces of different speeds. The reuse of policies has significant operational benefits on devices with a large number of interfaces.

A policer executes different actions depending on the traffic patterns it receives. There are three actions types: conform, exceed, and violate. Table 3-17 summarizes the events that trigger these actions. The section "Traffic Policing" in Chapter 1 previously illustrated the flowchart that both the single-rate and the dual-rate policers follow.

Table 3-18 lists all the specific actions that a policer can invoke. When you use the multiple-line format, you can configure more than one conform, exceed, and violate action. This option proves useful when you want to apply simultaneously more than one marking to the same packet (for example, Ethernet 802.10 user priority and DSCP). The default conform action is to transmit the packet as normal. The default exceed action is to drop the packet. The default violate action is to track the exceed action.

Table 3-17 *Policer Action Types*

Syntax	Trigger for Single-Rate Policer	Trigger for Dual-Rate Policer
conform-*action*	Enough tokens in first bucket	Enough tokens in both buckets
exceed-*action*	Enough tokens in second bucket only	Enough tokens in second bucket only
violate-*action*	Not enough tokens in both buckets	Not enough tokens in both buckets

Table 3-18 *Policer Actions*

Syntax	Description
drop	Drops packet
transmit	Transmits packet without modifications
set-prec-transmit *value*	IPv4 and IPv6 precedence
set precedence *value*	IPv4 and IPv6 precedence (alternative syntax)
set-prec-tunnel-transmit *value*	Precedence to be used by IP tunneling operation
set precedence tunnel *value*	Precedence to be used by IP tunneling operation (alternative syntax)
set-dscp-transmit *value*	IPv4 and IPv6 DSCP
set dscp *value*	IPv4 and IPv6 DSCP (alternative syntax)

Table 3-18 *Policer Actions (Continued)*

Syntax	Description
set-dscp-tunnel-transmit *value*	DSCP to be used by IP tunneling operation
set dscp tunnel *value*	DSCP to be used by IP tunneling operation (alternative syntax)
set-mpls-exp-imposition-transmit *value*	EXP bits to be used by push operation
set mpls experimental imposition *value*	EXP bits to be used by push operation (alternative syntax)
set-mpls-exp-topmost-transmit *value*	EXP bits in MPLS header on top of the stack
set mpls experimental topmost *value*	EXP bits in MPLS header on top of the stack (alternative syntax)
set-qos-transmit *value*	Internal field for packet class
set qos-group *value*	Internal field for packet class (alternative syntax)
set-discard-class-transmit *value*	Internal field for packet drop profile
set discard-class *value*	Internal field for packet drop profile (alternative syntax)
set-cos-transmit *value*	Ethernet 802.1Q user priority
set cos *value*	Ethernet 802.1Q user priority (alternative syntax)
set-clp-transmit	ATM CLP bit
set atm-clp	ATM CLP bit (alternative syntax)
set-frde-transmit	Frame Relay DE bit
set fr-de	Frame Relay DE bit (alternative syntax)

The color-aware policers use the **conform-color** and **exceed-color** commands. You can use these commands in the multiple-line format of the **police** command. Those commands reference a class previously defined using a class map. For a single-rate policer with one token bucket, you define only the conforming color. The policer automatically associates all other traffic with the exceeding color. For a single-rate policer with two token buckets or a dual-rate policer, you define the conforming and exceeding color. The policer automatically associates all other traffic with the violating color. POLICY4 in Example 3-10 illustrates an example of a color-aware policer. Table 3-19 summarizes the commands that define the traffic colors for color-aware policers.

Table 3-19 *Color Definition for Color-Aware Policers*

Syntax	Description
conform-color *name*	Class associated with conforming color
exceed-color *name*	Class associated with exceeding color

You can also use the **police** command to configure traffic policing in compliance with the ATM Forum Traffic Management (TM) specification version 4.0. You can use this command to enforce the different ATM conformance definitions (for example, *Constant Bit Rate* 1 [CBR.1], *Variable Bit Rate* 1 [VBR.1], VBR.2). Some of those definitions require the configuration of color-aware policing. You can specify the profile as a dual-token bucket with rates in cells per second and bursts in number of cells. Alternatively, you can define the policing profile in ATM terms (sustained cell rate, maximum burst size, peak cell rate, cell delay variation tolerance). ATM policing can also make use of the **percent** keyword. Table 3-20 shows the configuration alternatives for ATM traffic profiles.

Table 3-20   *ATM Traffic Profiles*

Syntax	Profile Definition
police rate *value* **cps** [**burst** *value* **cells**] [**peak-rate** *value* **cps**] [**peak-burst** *value* **cells**]	Absolute cells per second and cell units
police rate *value* **cps atm-mbs** *value* [**peak-rate** *value* **cps**] [**delay-tolerance** *value*]	ATM TM 4.0 terms
police rate percent *value* [**burst** *value* **ms**] [**peak-rate percent** *value*] [**peak-burst** *value* **ms**]	Cells per second and cell units relative to underlying bandwidth
police rate percent *value* **atm-mbs** *value* **ms|us** [**peak-rate** *value* **cps**] [**delay-tolerance** *value* **ms|us**]	ATM TM 4.0 terms relative to underlying bandwidth

Example 3-10 illustrates four different policies performing different types of traffic policing:

- POLICY1 specifies a single-rate and a dual-rate policer. The single-rate policer in CLASS1 uses the default actions. The dual-rate policer in CLASS2 uses default burst sizes but explicit actions that drop violating traffic and transmits all other traffic.

- POLICY2 uses a dual-rate policer with a profile specified in relative terms and with multiple actions for conforming traffic.

- POLICY3 shows an example of a policer that uses an ATM traffic profile specified in cells per second and number of cells.

- POLICY4 includes a color-aware dual-rate policer for CLASS5 and a color-blind dual-rate policer for all other traffic.

Example 3-10   *Policies Performing Traffic Policing*

```
class-map match-all CLASS1
  match dscp ef
class-map match-all CLASS2
  match dscp af11  af12  af13
class-map match-all CLASS3
  match dscp af31
class-map match-all CLASS4
  match dscp af32
class-map match-all CLASS5
  match dscp af31  af32  af33
!
policy-map POLICY1
  class CLASS1
   police rate 1000000 burst 31250
  class CLASS2
   police rate 2000000 peak-rate 4000000
     conform-action transmit
     exceed-action transmit
!
policy-map POLICY2
  class class-default
   police rate percent 10 peak-rate percent 20
     conform-action set-mpls-exp-imposition-transmit 5
     conform-action set-qos-transmit 5
     exceed-action drop
!
policy-map POLICY3
  class class-default
   police rate 10000 cps atm-mbs 2500 peak-rate 20000 cps
     conform-action set-mpls-exp-imposition-transmit 1
     exceed-action set-mpls-exp-imposition-transmit 2
!
policy-map POLICY4
  class CLASS5
   police rate 100000 peak-rate 200000
     conform-color CLASS3 exceed-color CLASS4
     conform-action set-dscp-transmit af31
     exceed-action set-dscp-transmit af32
     violate-action set-dscp-transmit af33
  class class-default
   police rate percent 10 peak-rate percent 20
!
```

Example 3-11 illustrates the counters displayed for policers in Cisco IOS. The output corresponds to POLICY4 Example 3-10. A basic set of counters specify the number of packets (and related bytes) on which the policy executed the conform, exceed, and violate actions. In this example, the CLASS5 policer had 22,153 conforming, 22,617 exceeding, and 46,066 violating packets. In the case of the default class (class-default), the policer executed the conform action on 76,858 packets. There were no exceeding or violating packets. The conforming packets represented 3,381,752 bytes. In addition, policers display the current rate of conforming, exceeding, and violating packets. CLASS5 shows 32,000 bps of conforming, 32,000 bps of exceeding, and 59,000 bps of violating traffic. The policer in the default class is currently receiving 85,000 bps of conforming traffic.

Example 3-11 *Policer Counters in Cisco IOS*

```
Router#show policy-map interface pos0/0/0
 POS0/0/0

  Service-policy input: POLICY4

    Class-map: CLASS5 (match-all)
      90836 packets, 3996784 bytes
      5 minute offered rate 112000 bps, drop rate 0 bps
      Match:  dscp 26  28  30  (1281)
      police:
          rate 100000 bps, burst 3125 bytes
          peak-rate 200000 bps, peak-burst 6250 bytes
        conformed 22153 packets, 974732 bytes; action:
          set-dscp-transmit af31
        exceeded 22617 packets, 995148 bytes; action:
          set-dscp-transmit af32
        violated 46066 packets, 2026904 bytes; action:
          set-dscp-transmit af33
        conform color
          conform action 22153 packets, 974732 bytes
          exceed action 19705 packets, 867020 bytes
          violate action 36691 packets, 1614404 bytes
        exceed color
          exceed action 2912 packets, 128128 bytes
          violate action 6030 packets, 265320 bytes
        violate color
          violate action 3345 packets, 147180 bytes
        conformed 32000 bps, exceeded 32000 bps violated 59000 bps

    Class-map: class-default (match-any)
      76858 packets, 3381752 bytes
      5 minute offered rate 85000 bps, drop rate 0 bps
      Match: any  (1284)
        76858 packets, 3381752 bytes
        5 minute rate 85000 bps
      police:
          rate 10 %
            (15500000 bps, burst 484375 bytes)
          peak-rate 20 %
            (31000000 bps, peak-burst 968750 bytes)
        conformed 76858 packets, 3381752 bytes; action:
          transmit
        exceeded 0 packets, 0 bytes; action:
          drop
        violated 0 packets, 0 bytes; action:
```

Example 3-11 *Policer Counters in Cisco IOS (Continued)*

```
            drop
         conformed 85000 bps, exceeded 0 bps violated 0 bps
Router#
```

The color-aware policer includes an additional set of counters that capture the number of packets (and bytes) per type of action according to their initial color classification. Out of all the packets classified initially as of conforming color, the policer executed the conform action on 22,153, the exceed action on 19,705, and the violate action on 36,691. Similarly, the policer executed the exceed action on 2912 packets and the violate action on 6030 packets that arrived with the exceed color, respectively. Finally, the policer executed the violate action on 3345 packets that arrived with the violate color. Each packet counter has an associated byte counter.

NOTE   Remember that in color-aware mode, the policer will not execute the conform action on packets that arrive with the exceed or violate colors. Similarly, the policer will not execute the exceed action on packets that arrive with the violate color.

Example 3-12 illustrates the counters that the **show policy-map** command displays for policers in Cisco IOS XR. The sample output corresponds to POLICY1 in Example 3-10. Both policers maintain the same set of counters. That is, packet, byte, and rate counts for the conform, exceed, and violate actions. In this example, the CLASS1 policer has had 3123 conforming packets (4,628,286 bytes) with a current rate of 60 kbps. The policer has measured 66,877 packets exceeding the profile for a total of 99,111,714 bytes. The current rate of exceeding packets is 1266 kbps. The policer has not executed the violate action for any packet. The CLASS2 policer has found 6,196 conforming packets (9,182,472 bytes) and is currently receiving 118 kbps of those packets. It has also measured 28,804 exceeding packets (42,687,528 bytes) with a current rate of 546 kbps. There have not been violating packets.

Example 3-12 *Policer Counters in Cisco IOS XR*

```
RP/0/4/CPU0:Router#show policy-map interface pos0/3/0/3
POS0/3/0/3 input: POLICY1

Class CLASS1
  Classification statistics          (packets/bytes)     (rate - kbps)
    Matched                :         70000/103740000              1325
    Transmitted            :         70000/103740000                59
    Total Dropped          :             0/0                      1266
  Policing statistics                (packets/bytes)     (rate - kbps)
    Policed(conform)       :          3123/4628286                  60
    Policed(exceed)        :         66877/99111714               1266
    Policed(violate)       :             0/0                         0
```

Example 3-12 *Policer Counters in Cisco IOS XR (Continued)*

```
    Policed and dropped :         66877/99111714
  Queueing statistics
    Vital         (packets)       : 0
    Queue ID                      : None (Bundle)
    Taildropped(packets/bytes)    : 0/0

Class CLASS2
  Classification statistics     (packets/bytes)     (rate - kbps)
    Matched       :               35000/51870000             663
    Transmitted   :               35000/51870000             663
    Total Dropped :               0/0                           0
  Policing statistics           (packets/bytes)     (rate - kbps)
    Policed(conform)  :           6196/9182472               118
    Policed(exceed)   :           28804/42687528             546
    Policed(violate)  :           0/0                          0
    Policed and dropped :         0/0
  Queueing statistics
    Vital         (packets)       : 0
    Queue ID                      : None (Bundle)
    Taildropped(packets/bytes)    : 0/0

Class default
  Classification statistics     (packets/bytes)     (rate - kbps)
    Matched       :               105000/155610000          1987
    Transmitted   :               105000/155610000          1987
    Total Dropped :               0/0                          0
  Queueing statistics
    Vital         (packets)       : 0
    Queue ID                      : None (Bundle)
    High watermark  (bytes)       : 0
    Taildropped(packets/bytes)    : 0/0
RP/0/4/CPU0:Router#
```

Traffic Shaping

The **shape** command configures traffic shaping and defines a maximum bandwidth rate for a class. Shaping implements the maximum bandwidth attribute in the queuing component of the TMN. It causes packet queuing when the arriving traffic pattern exceeds a traffic profile. You define the profile using a rate and one or two bursts. The rate is in bits per second, and the bursts are in bits by default.

The shaper enforces the rate during a time interval. Within the interval, the traffic can exceed the shaper rate. The smaller the interval, the smoother the shaper output. This interval also defines how frequently the shaper replenishes tokens in the bucket. Some forms of the **shape** command allow you to control this interval. Table 3-21 summarizes the configuration options for the **shape** command.

Table 3-21   *Average and Peak Packet Shaping*

Syntax	Description
shape average *rate-value* [*burst*]	Average shaper with token bucket definition in absolute terms and fixed shaping interval
shape average *rate-value* [*bc-value* [*be-value*]]	Average shaper with token bucket definition in absolute terms and configurable shaping interval
shape peak *rate-value* [*bc-value* [*be-value*]]	Peak shaper with token bucket definition in absolute terms and configurable shaping interval
shape average percent *rate-value* [*burst*] **ms**	Average shaper with token bucket definition relative to underlying bandwidth and fixed shaping interval
shape average percent *rate-value* [*bc-value* **ms** [*be-value* **ms**]]	Average shaper with token bucket definitions relative to underlying bandwidth and configurable shaping interval
shape peak percent *rate-value* [*bc-value* **ms** [*be-value* **ms**]]	Peak shaper with token bucket definition in relative to underlying bandwidth and configurable shaping interval

You use the **shape average** command to enforce a maximum average rate. There is a two-parameter and three-parameter version of this command. In the two-parameter version, the **shape average** command uses a rate and a burst to define a token bucket. The underlying implementation selects the shaping interval automatically. In the three-parameter version, the command uses **rate** (**bc** and **be**) values. The **rate** and (**bc**+**be**) define a token bucket. In this case, the shaper implements an interval of **bc** divided by the **rate**. That is, every interval, the shaper replenishes **bc** tokens into a bucket of size **bc**+**be**. In both cases, the shaper serves packets if the bucket holds enough tokens; otherwise, the packet waits in a queue. The device computes default bursts if you do not configure them explicitly.

The **shape peak** command enforces a maximum peak rate. This command uses three parameters: **rate**, **bc**, and **be**. The device computes default **bc** and **bc** values if you do not configure them explicitly. This shaper implements an interval of **bc** divided by the **rate**, but effectively replenishes **bc**+**be** tokens at each interval. This implies that the shaper can offer a peak rate that exceeds the configured rate.

You control the peak rate with the value of **be**. This shaping behavior is useful for Frame Relay environments making use of a *committed information rate* (CIR), an *excess information rate* (EIR), and a *peak information rate* (PIR). In this case, the shape rate equals the CIR. If **tc** is the shaper interval, the following relationships hold:

tc = bc / CIR
PIR = (bc + be) / tc
PIR = CIR + CIR (be / bc)
PIR = CIR + EIR
EIR = CIR (be / bc)

You can also define the shaping parameters in relative terms. In this case, you specify the shaper rate as a percentage of the underlying bandwidth rate of the policy attachment point. Similarly, you specify the burst, **bc**, and **be** values in time units (milliseconds by default) relative to the shaper rate. The device computes the effective parameters in absolute values. The **percent** keyword enables the definition of relative traffic profiles. Both the **shape average** and **shape peak** commands support this keyword. The section "Percentage-Based Rates" explains what constitutes the underlying bandwidth rate that the device uses to interpret relative profile definitions.

Figure 3-7 shows the output of three sample shapers for a given packet-arrival pattern. Each black box represents a packet, and each gray box represents a token. A stream of packets arrives at an average rate of 200 *packets per second* (pps). In this example, all parameters are normalized in packets and packets have the same size. These assumptions will help you understand the operation of the shapers, which in reality operate in bits and bits per second. The first configuration (from top to bottom) uses a two-parameter average shaper. This particular shaper implementation uses a 5-ms shaping interval (one token every 5 ms). The second configuration uses a three-parameter average shaper. The last configuration uses peak shaping. Notice how the first shaper smoothes traffic the most, and the last one has the least smoothing effect. These are the sequence of events for the two-parameter average shaper:

- **Initial state**—Bucket holds two tokens.
- **(0 ms, 5 ms)**—Three packets arrive. Two tokens are consumed and one packet is queued. Bucket becomes empty.
- **(5 ms, 10 ms)**—One token accumulates and is used to serve the queued packet. No new packets arrive. Bucket becomes empty.
- **(10 ms, 15 ms)**—One token accumulates. No new packets arrive. Bucket holds one token.
- **(15 ms, 20 ms)**—One token accumulates. No new packets arrive. Bucket holds two tokens.

- **(20 ms, 25 ms)**—Additional token discarded because bucket is full. One packet arrives and consumes one token. Bucket holds one token.

- **(25 ms, 30 ms)**—One token accumulates. No new packet arrives. Bucket holds two tokens.

- **(30 ms, 35 ms)**—Additional token discarded because bucket is full. One packet arrives and consumes one token. Bucket holds one token.

- **(35 ms, 40 ms)**—One token accumulates. One packet arrives and consumes one token. Bucket holds one token.

- **(40 ms, 45 ms)**—One token accumulates. Four packets arrive and consume two tokens. Two packets are queued. Bucket becomes empty.

- **(45 ms, 50 ms)**—One token accumulates and is used to serve one queued packet. Four packets arrive. Five packets are queued. Bucket becomes empty.

- **(50 ms, 55 ms)**—One token accumulates and is used to serve one queued packet. No new packets arrive. Four packets are queued. Bucket becomes empty.

- **(55 ms, 60 ms)**—One token accumulates and is used to serve one queued packet. No new packets arrive. Three packets are queued. Bucket becomes empty.

- **(60 ms, 65 ms)**—One token accumulates and is used to serve one queued packet. No new packets arrive. Two packets are queued. Bucket becomes empty.

- **(65 ms, 70 ms)**—One token accumulates and is used to serve one queued packet. No new packets arrive. One packet is queued. Bucket becomes empty.

- **(70 ms, 75 ms)**—One token accumulates and is used to serve one queued packet. No new packets arrive. No packets are queued. Bucket becomes empty.

The **shape adaptive** command adjusts the shaper rate in response to congestion notification. This command defines a reduced shaping rate. Adaptive shaping is useful for a Frame Relay environment where a device learns about network congestion from frames that arrive with the *backward explicit congestion notification* (BECN) flag set. When a device receives a congestion notification, the shaper decreases the shaping rate until it reaches the configured reduced rate. When the arrival of congestion notifications ceases, the shaper increases the shaping rate back to the original maximum rate. You can configure adaptive shaping with either the average or the peak shaping discussed earlier. Table 3-22 summarizes the **shape adaptive** command.

Figure 3-7 *Comparison Between Average and Peak Shaping*

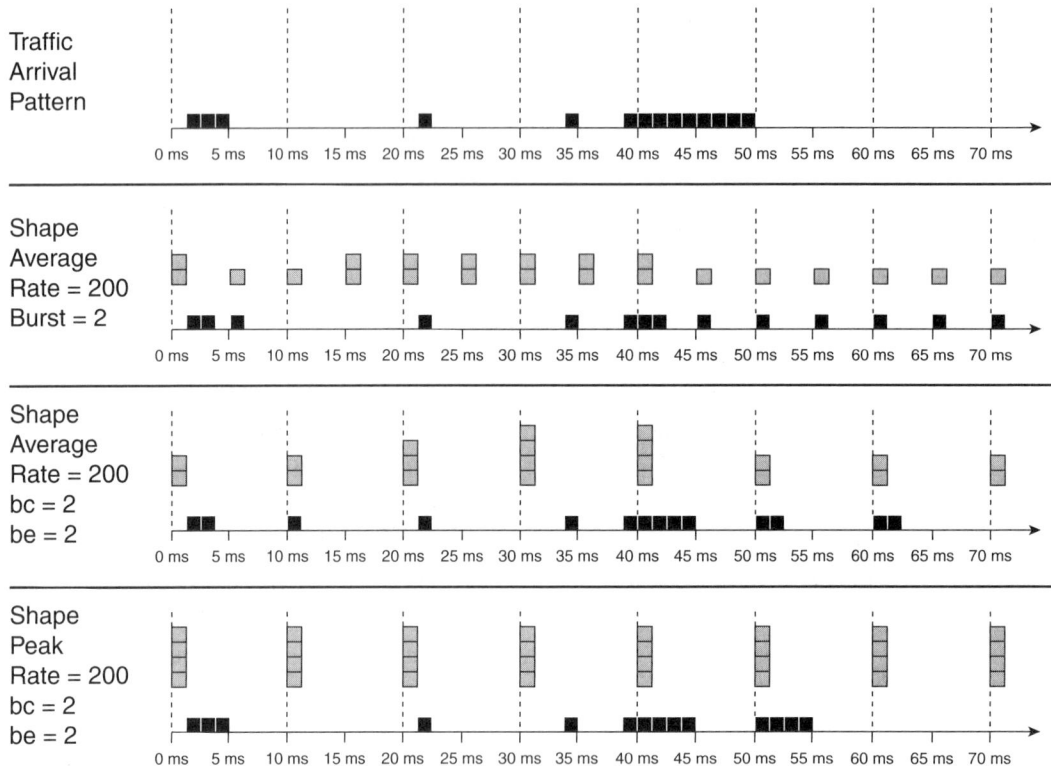

Table 3-22 *Adaptive Shaping for Frame Relay*

Syntax	Description
shape adaptive *value*	Reduce shaping rate upon arrival of congestion notifications
shape adaptive percent *value*	Reduce shaping rate (relative to underlying bandwidth) upon arrival of congestion notifications

Example 3-13 displays three different shaping policies:

• POLICY1 enforces an average rate of 1,000,000 bps on all traffic. That policy uses a two-parameter shaper with an implicit default burst size.

• POLICY2 describes an adaptive shaper with a peak rate for a Frame Relay circuit. The shaper uses a committed rate of 1,024,000 bps and a peak rate of 2,048,000 bps. When the Frame Relay network notifies of a congestion condition, the shaper adjusts the rate to 1,024,000 bps.

- POLICY3 uses average shaping for two classes. The policy classifies the traffic using the Ethernet 802.1Q user priority. Both classes use two-parameter average shapers that define the shaping rate in relative terms and rely on the default burst size.

Example 3-13 *Policies Performing Traffic Shaping*

```
class-map match-all CLASS1
  match cos  3  4
class-map match-all CLASS2
  match cos  1  2
!
policy-map POLICY1
  class class-default
    shape average 1000000
!
policy-map POLICY2
  class class-default
    shape peak 1024000 4096 4096
    shape adaptive 1024000
!
policy-map POLICY3
  class CLASS1
    shape average percent 5
  class CLASS2
    shape average percent 10
!
```

Example 3-14 illustrates the shaper counters available in Cisco IOS. The counters are not specific to shapers; they relate to the queue that the shaper enables. This example shows the output of **show policy-map** for POLICY2 in Example 3-13. A first set of counters provide information about the shaped queue. A second group of counters provides details about the number of transmitted packets and their respective byte count. For POLICY2, 235 packets are queued, and the shaper has dropped 54 packets because of the queue overflowing. (The maximum queue size is 256 packets.) There have not been packet drops due to buffer starvation. The second set of counters shows that the shaper has transmitted 56,493 packets or 83,947,146 bytes. The sum of transmitted and dropped packets matches the packet count for the policy (56,547 packets).

Example 3-14 *Shaper Counters in Cisco IOS*

```
Router#show policy-map interface pos0/0/0

 POS0/0/0

  Service-policy output: POLICY2

    Class-map: class-default (match-any)
      56547 packets, 84027390 bytes
      5 minute offered rate 882000 bps, drop rate 4000 bps
      Match: any
        56547 packets, 84027390 bytes
```

Example 3-14 *Shaper Counters in Cisco IOS (Continued)*

```
            5 minute rate 882000 bps
        Queueing
        queue limit 256 packets
        (queue depth/total drops/no-buffer drops) 235/54/0
        (pkts output/bytes output) 56493/83947146
        shape (peak) cir 1024000, bc 4096, be 4096
        target shape rate 2048000
          lower bound cir 1024000,  adapt to fecn 0
Router#
```

NOTE   Some platforms display a reduced number of counters that include the current, maximum, and average queue depths (that is, number of packets in the queue).

Example 3-15 shows the counters associated with traffic shaping in Cisco IOS XR. This example uses policy POLICY1 that Example 3-13 introduced. As in the preceding example, the counters most relevant to the shaper are associated with the shaping queue. The first queue counters shows a high watermark of 43,636 bytes. The next two counters show the instantaneous and average queue length (also called queue depth). For this policy, these two counters show 32 and 15 packets, respectively. The last counter shows the number of packets lost due to tail dropping. In this case, 340 packets found the queue full. The number of dropped plus transmitted packets equals the number of packets that the class matched.

Example 3-15 *Shaper Counters in Cisco IOS XR*

```
RP/0/4/CPU0:Router#show policy-map interface pos0/3/0/4
POS0/3/0/4 output: POLICY1

Class class-default
  Classification statistics          (packets/bytes)     (rate - kbps)
    Matched             :            42000/62244000           540
    Transmitted         :            41660/62244000           540
    Total Dropped       :              340/0                    0
  Queueing statistics
    Vital           (packets)         : 0
    Queue ID                          : 8
    High watermark  (bytes)           : 43636
    Inst-queue-len  (packets)         : 32
    Avg-queue-len   (packets)         : 15
    Taildropped(packets/bytes)        : 340/0
RP/0/4/CPU0:Router#
```

Congestion Management

The **bandwidth**, **bandwidth remaining percent**, and **priority** commands are the three main mechanisms that define a queuing policy in the MQC. These commands configure the minimum-bandwidth, excess-bandwidth, and priority attributes that the section "Dequeuing Subcomponent" described. The underlying implementation allocates the queues and configures the packet scheduling mechanisms to satisfy the bandwidth allocation and traffic prioritization that the policy defines. The **shape** command complements these commands by allowing you to define maximum bandwidth allocations.

The **bandwidth** command can define the minimum bandwidth that a queue receives. The simplest form of the **bandwidth** command specifies a minimum-bandwidth guarantee in absolute terms. The rates are in kilobits per second by default. You can also define the guarantee as a percentage of the underlying bandwidth rate using the **bandwidth percent** syntax. The **bandwidth remaining percent** command performs excess-bandwidth allocation. The excess bandwidth includes the bandwidth that is not part of minimum guarantees or bandwidth that other classes are not using within their minimum guarantees at a particular point in time. The explicit configuration of minimum- and excess-bandwidth allocations are mutually exclusive in platforms with two-parameter schedulers. See the section "Dequeuing Subcomponent" for a discussion of two-parameter and three-parameter schedulers. Table 3-23 summarizes the syntax of the **bandwidth** and **bandwidth remaining percent** command.

Table 3-23   *Bandwidth Allocation and Traffic Prioritization During Congestion*

Syntax	Description
bandwidth *value*	Minimum-bandwidth allocation
bandwidth percent *value*	Minimum-bandwidth allocation relative to the underlying bandwidth
bandwidth remaining percent *value*	Excess-bandwidth allocation
priority [**level** *value*][*rate-value* [*burst-value*]]	Low-latency prioritization with optional conditional policer
priority [**level** *value*] **percent** [*rate-value* [*burst-value*]]	Low-latency prioritization with optional conditional policer at a rate relative to the underlying bandwidth

The **priority** command indicates that a class requires low latency. The scheduler should serve the traffic with strict priority (that is, at the underlying full rate of the policy attachment point). The priority traffic is not part of the rate-allocation process that the scheduler performs for nonpriority classes. Therefore, the configuration of the **priority** and **bandwidth** commands is mutually exclusive within the same class. A policer can limit the amount of bandwidth that the priority traffic consumes. The policer acts as pre-queuing operation that does not affect the rate at which the scheduler serves the priority packets. The policer will limit the amount of packets that enter the priority queue. It does not reduce the service rate of the priority queue, which the scheduler will always serve at the full rate of the policy attachment point.

The configuration of a priority class influences the configuration of bandwidth to nonpriority classes. In its simplest form, the **priority** command does not use any parameters, and no upper bandwidth limit applies to the priority traffic. Therefore, you cannot allocate minimum-bandwidth guarantees to other classes in the same policy. However, you can allocate excess bandwidth using the **bandwidth remaining percent** command. Alternatively, you can configure an explicit policer to enforce a bandwidth limit on the priority traffic. In that case, other classes can receive minimum-bandwidth guarantees equal to the underlying bandwidth of the policy attachment point minus the sum of the policer rates of all priority classes.

The **priority** command may include an implicit conditional policer. You can define this command with an associated traffic profile in the form of a token bucket: rate and burst. These parameters can be in absolute terms (bits per second and bytes) or relative terms (rate percentage and milliseconds) with respect to the underlying bandwidth using the **priority percent** syntax. During periods of congestion, this conditional policer enforces the traffic profile. When congestion is not present, no limit applies to the amount of priority traffic. This behavior differs from the scenario that uses an explicitly configured policer. The explicit policer limits the priority traffic regardless of whether there is congestion. Table 3-21 summarized the syntax of the **priority** and **priority percent** commands.

A packet may experience an additional stage of queuing after the scheduler selects it for transmission. This additional stage controls the delivery of packets to the interface hardware for final transmission. It commonly uses a circular queue that receives the name of transmit ring due to its circular structure. The exact structure, size, and operation of the transmit ring is transparent to the user in most cases. In some exceptional cases, you may need to adjust its size using the **tx-ring-limit** command. A proper size will minimize the introduction of additional latency to the packet while avoiding a negative impact on bandwidth utilization of the output interface. In most cases, nodes select an optimal size automatically based on the interface characteristics and the configured output policy. Consult the platform documentation for details.

In addition, the **queue-limit** command defines the maximum size of a particular queue. When a queue reaches its limits, the enqueuing process drops new arriving packets. The queue limit uses packets at its default configuration unit. You can define different queue limits according to particular packet markings to implement weighted tail dropping. Tables 3-24 and 3-25 list the different forms that the **queue-limit** command can use.

Table 3-24   *Maximum Queue Size*

Syntax	Description
queue-limit [*value*] [**packets**|**bytes**|**cells**|**ms**|**us**]	Maximum queue size

Table 3-25 *Maximum Queue Size for Specific Packet Markings*

Syntax	Weighting Field
queue-limit precedence *value limit-value* [**packets** I **bytes** I **ms**]	IPv4 precedence, IPv6 precedence, or MPLS EXP
queue-limit dscp *value limit-value* [**packets** I **bytes** I **ms**]	IPv4 DSCP, IPv6 DSCP, or MPLS EXP
queue-limit discard-class *value limit-value* [**packets** I **bytes** I **ms**]	Discard class
queue-limit cos *value limit-value* [**packets** I **bytes** I **ms**]	Ethernet 802.1Q user priority
queue-limit clp *value* limit-*value* [**packets** I **bytes** I **ms**]	ATM CLP bit

Example 3-16 illustrates four different queuing policies:

- POLICY1 classifies traffic using the MPLS EXP field. The policy guarantees low latency to CLASS1. An explicit unconditional policer limits the CLASS1 traffic to 20,000,000 bps with a burst size of 25,000 bytes. CLASS2 and the default class, receives a minimum-bandwidth guarantee of 80,000 and 10,000 kbps respectively.

- POLICY2 specifies a queuing policy that requires a three-parameter scheduler. The policy defines all rates and queue limits in relative terms. CLASS2 receives both a minimum and an excess-bandwidth guarantee. The traffic in the default class (class-default) gets only excess-bandwidth allocation.

- POLICY3 illustrates a third example that has two priority classes and allocates bandwidth to two nonpriority classes in the form of excess bandwidth. POLICY4 shows a policy similar to POLICY3. In this case, CLASS3 and CLASS4 have different priority levels and both use explicit policers.

Example 3-16 *Queuing Policies*

```
class-map match-all CLASS1
 match mpls experimental topmost 5
class-map match-all CLASS2
 match mpls experimental topmost 3 4
class-map match-all CLASS3
  match  dscp ef
  match access-group 1
class-map match-all CLASS4
  match  dscp ef
  match access-group 2
class-map match-all CLASS5
  match dscp af11  af12   af13
!
policy-map POLICY1
  class CLASS1
    priority
    police rate 20000000 burst 25000
```

continues

Example 3-16 *Queuing Policies (Continued)*

```
    class CLASS2
      bandwidth 80000
      queue-limit 7500
    class class-default
      bandwidth 10000
      queue-limit 1250
  !
  policy-map POLICY2
    class CLASS1
      priority
      police rate percent 20
    class CLASS2
      bandwidth percent 50
      bandwidth remaining percent 25
      queue-limit 100 ms
    class class-default
      bandwidth remaining percent 75
      queue-limit 200 ms
  !
  policy-map POLICY3
    class CLASS3
      priority percent 5
    class CLASS4
      priority percent 20
    class CLASS5
      bandwidth remaining percent 50
    class class-default
      bandwidth remaining percent 50
  !
  policy-map POLICY4
    class CLASS3
      priority level 1
      police rate percent 5
    class CLASS4
      priority level 2
      police rate percent 20
    class CLASS5
      bandwidth remaining percent 50
    class class-default
      bandwidth remaining percent 50
  !
```

Example 3-17 illustrates the counters available in queuing policies in Cisco IOS. This example shows the output for POLICY3 in Example 3-16. A first set of counters provide the queue depth (packets in the queue) and the number of packet dropped. A second group of counters show the number of packets transmitted from the queue and their byte count. In this example, CLASS3 and CLASS4 share a single priority queue. This queue is currently empty, but shows 104 dropped packets. The individual class counters shows that all dropped priority packets belonged to CLASS3. The queue for CLASS5 is empty and has not experienced any packet drops. The scheduler has serviced 11,667 packets (or

17,337,162 bytes) of this class. If you take a closer look at the default class (class-default), you will notice that queue currently holds 10 packets and has (tail) dropped 222 packets. The queue has processed a total of 32,297 packets (or 47,991,890 bytes). The sum of transmitted and dropped packets matches the classification counter (32,519 packets).

Example 3-17 *Queuing Counters in Cisco IOS*

```
Router#show policy-map interface serial1/0:0

 Serial1/0:0

  Service-policy output: POLICY3

    queue stats for all priority classes:

      queue limit 64 packets
      (queue depth/total drops/no-buffer drops) 0/104/0
      (pkts output/bytes output) 6883/10228138

    Class-map: CLASS3 (match-all)
      320 packets, 475520 bytes
      30 second offered rate 44000 bps, drop rate 15000 bps
      Match: dscp ef (46)
      Match: access-group 1
      Priority: 5% (76 kbps), burst bytes 1900, b/w exceed drops: 104

    Class-map: CLASS4 (match-all)
      6667 packets, 9907162 bytes
      30 second offered rate 187000 bps, drop rate 0 bps
      Match: dscp ef (46)
      Match: access-group 2
      Priority: 20% (307 kbps), burst bytes 7650, b/w exceed drops: 0

    Class-map: CLASS5 (match-all)
      11667 packets, 17337162 bytes
      30 second offered rate 324000 bps, drop rate 0 bps
      Match: dscp af11 (10) af12 (12) af13 (14)
      Queueing
      queue limit 64 packets
      (queue depth/total drops/no-buffer drops) 0/0/0
      (pkts output/bytes output) 11667/17337162
      bandwidth remaining 50% (576 kbps)

    Class-map: class-default (match-any)
      32519 packets, 48321782 bytes
      30 second offered rate 920000 bps, drop rate 26000 bps
      Match: any
         32519 packets, 48321782 bytes
         30 second rate 920000 bps
      Queueing
      queue limit 64 packets
      (queue depth/total drops/no-buffer drops) 10/222/0
      (pkts output/bytes output) 32297/47991890
      bandwidth remaining 50% (576 kbps)
Router#
```

Example 3-18 shows the queuing counters available in Cisco IOS XR. This output corresponds to POLICY1 in Example 3-16. The queuing counters are similar to those that Example 3-15 described. Each queue displays a high watermark, the instant queue length (number of packets in the queue), the average queue length, and the number of packets dropped. CLASS1 shows no current queuing activity as all counters are zero. CLASS2 has a high watermark of 5,120 bytes and one queued packet. In the case of the default class (class-default), the watermark is 232,448 bytes, there are 908 in the queue, the average queue length is 851 packets, and 8220 have been tail dropped.

Example 3-18 *Queuing Counters in Cisco IOS XR*

```
RP/0/4/CPU0:Router#show policy-map interface pos0/3/0/4
POS0/3/0/4 output: POLICY1

Class CLASS1
   Classification statistics          (packets/bytes)      (rate - kbps)
     Matched               :         222054/329972244            5923
     Transmitted           :         222054/329972244            5923
     Total Dropped         :              0/0                      0
   Policing statistics                (packets/bytes)      (rate - kbps)
     Policed(conform)      :         222054/329972244            2080
     Policed(exceed)       :              0/0                      0
     Policed(violate)      :              0/0                      0
     Policed and dropped   :         8220/1221492
   Queueing statistics
     Vital            (packets)         : 0
     Queue ID                           : 18
     High watermark   (bytes)           : 0
     Inst-queue-len   (packets)         : 0
     Avg-queue-len    (packets)         : 0
     Taildropped(packets/bytes)         : 0/0

Class CLASS2
   Classification statistics          (packets/bytes)      (rate - kbps)
     Matched               :        1361878/2023750708          13265
     Transmitted           :        1361878/2023750708          13265
     Total Dropped         :         8220/1221492                 0
   Queueing statistics
     Vital            (packets)         : 0
     Queue ID                           : 16
     High watermark   (bytes)           : 5120
     Inst-queue-len   (packets)         : 1
     Avg-queue-len    (packets)         : 0
     Taildropped(packets/bytes)         : 0/0

Class class-default
   Classification statistics          (packets/bytes)      (rate - kbps)
     Matched               :        1872234/2782139724         18672
     Transmitted           :        1872234/2782139724         18672
     Total Dropped         :              0/0                      0
   Queueing statistics
     Vital            (packets)         : 0
```

Example 3-18 *Queuing Counters in Cisco IOS XR (Continued)*

```
        Queue ID                        : 17
        High watermark   (bytes)        : 232448
        Inst-queue-len   (packets)      : 908
        Avg-queue-len    (packets)      : 851
        Taildropped(packets/bytes)      : 8220/12214920
RP/0/4/CPU0:Router#
```

Active Queue Management

The MQC uses the **random-detect** command to configure *Active Queue Management* (AQM) using the WRED algorithm. This function is part of the queuing component of the Cisco QoS behavioral model. Active queue management is only possible on classes with an underlying queue.

The configuration of WRED defines two main elements: weighting field and thresholds. You need to specify the weighting field first (for example, IP precedence, DSCP, discard class). Then, you can specify the thresholds for a particular marking of the weighting field. Notice that the WRED implementation will use the MPLS EXP markings for MPLS packets when you configure WRED to use IP precedence or DSCP as the weighting field. Table 3-26 summarizes the weighting fields that can control the operation of WRED.

Table 3-26 *WRED Using Different Weighting Fields*

Syntax	Weighting Field
random-detect precedence-based	IPv4 precedence, IPv6 precedence, and MPLS EXP
random-detect dscp-based	IPv4 DSCP, IPv6 DSCP, and MPLS EXP
random-detect discard-class-based	Internal field for packet drop profile
random-detect cos-based	Ethernet 802.1Q user priority
random-detect clp-based	ATM CLP bit

You can define the WRED thresholds for specific packet markings. The underlying implementation provides default thresholds. However, you can override those defaults using the **random-detect** command and specifying the thresholds for a particular marking value (or range of values) of the weighting field. You can define the thresholds in absolute terms (packets or bytes) or in relative time units. The default threshold units correspond to packets. Table 3-27 shows the syntax to define the WRED thresholds. When defining the thresholds for a marking, the last optional parameter is a probability denominator, d. This value determines the maximum drop probability, p_{max}, for a given marking with the following equation:

$$p_{max} = 1 / d$$

See the section "Active Queue Management" in Chapter 1 for a review of the parameters that control the behavior of WRED.

Table 3-27 *WRED Thresholds for Specific Packet Markings*

Syntax	Weighting Field
random-detect precedence *range min-value* [**packets** | **bytes** | **ms**] *max-value* [**packets** | **bytes** | **ms** | **us**] *prob-den-value*]	IPv4 precedence, IPv6 precedence, or MPLS EXP
random-detect dscp *range min-value* [**packets** | **bytes** | **ms**] *max-value* [**packets** | **bytes** | **ms** | **us**] *prob-den-value*	IPv4 DSCP, IPv6 DSCP, or MPLS EXP
random-detect exp *range min-value* [**packet** | **bytes** | **ms** *max-value* [**packet** | **bytes** | **ms** [*prob-den-value*]	MPLS EXP
random-detect discard-class *range min-value* [**packets** | **bytes** | **cells** | **ms**] *max-value* [**packets** | **bytes** | **cells** | **ms**] *prob—den-value*	Discard class
random-detect cos *range min-value* [**packets** | **bytes** | **ms** | **us**] *max-value* [**packets** | **bytes** | **ms**] *prob-den-value*	Ethernet 802.1Q user priority
random-detect clp *value min-value* [**cells** | **ms**] *max-value* [**cells** | **ms** | **us**] *prob-den-value*	ATM CLP bit

NOTE   Some platforms may accept only a single value for the weighting field rather than a range when you define a WRED threshold.

The **random-detect** command also provides control over the computation of the average queue size. The section "Active Queue Management" in Chapter 1 describes the equation that computes the average queue size. You can define an exponential weighting constant, c, to compute the averaging weight in that equation with the following equation:

$$w = 1 / 2^c$$

A high constant value results in a low averaging weight. Low weights make the average queue size less responsive to changes in the instantaneous queue size. A high weight causes the average computation to more closely track the instantaneous queue size. Table 3-28 shows the syntax that you can use to define the exponential weighting constant.

Table 3-28 *Weighting Constant Controlling Queue Size Averaging*

Syntax	Description
random-detect exponential-weighting-constant *value*	Weighting constant to compute the average queue size

You can also configure WRED to perform *explicit congestion notification* (ECN) for IP traffic. ECN affects the operation of WRED between the minimum threshold and maximum threshold. WRED checks the ECN field before deciding the proper action to take on a packet when it has selected that packet for dropping. If the ECN field indicates that the packet endpoints are ECN capable, WRED marks the congestion indication in the ECN field, and the packet enters its respective queue. If the ECN field already contains a congestion indication, WRED also allows the packet to enter its queue. On the other hand, if the ECN field indicates that the endpoints are not ECN capable, WRED proceeds to drop the packet as it normally would. Table 3-29 shows the syntax to enable ECN for IP traffic using WRED.

Table 3-29 *ECN Using WRED*

Syntax	Description
random-detect ecn	Explicit congestion notification for IP traffic based on WRED drop profiles

Example 3-19 includes three policies that perform active queue management with WRED:

- In POLICY1, both CLASS2 and the default class (class-default) make use of precedence-based WRED. They define explicitly the thresholds in terms of number of packets. The policy will apply the thresholds using the MPLS EXP value for CLASS2. For the default class, the policy will use the precedence value for IP packets and the EXP value for MPLS packets to apply the thresholds.

- POLICY2 enables WRED based on the discard class of each packet. The policy specifies explicit thresholds in milliseconds for DSCP values zero, one, and two.

- POLICY3 enables WRED based on the discard class of each packet. The policy specifies explicit thresholds in milliseconds for DSCP values CS1, CS2, and default.

- POLICY4 enables congestion notification for IP traffic using precedence-based WRED and ECN. This policy does not define any threshold explicitly. Therefore, WRED uses default threshold values for the eight different IP precedence values.

Example 3-19 *Queuing Policies with WRED*

```
class-map match-all CLASS1
  match mpls experimental topmost 5
class-map match-all CLASS2
  match mpls experimental topmost 3   4
class-map match-all CLASS3
 match dscp cs1 cs2
!
policy-map POLICY1
  class CLASS1
    priority
    police rate 2000000
  class CLASS2
    bandwidth 10000
    random-detect
```

Example 3-19   *Queuing Policies with WRED (Continued)*

```
       random-detect precedence 3 2000 4000 1
       random-detect precedence 4 4000 6000 1
   class class-default
     random-detect
     random-detect precedence 0 4000 6000 1
  !
policy-map POLICY2
  class class-default
    random-detect discard-class-based
    random-detect discard-class 0 75 ms 150 ms 1
    random-detect discard-class 1 25 ms 150 ms 1
    random-detect discard-class 2 75 ms 150 ms 1
  !
policy-map POLICY3
  class CLASS3
    bandwidth percent 40
    random-detect dscp-based
    random-detect dscp cs1 25 ms 75 ms
    random-detect dscp cs2 50 ms 100 ms
  class class-default
    bandwidth percent 40
    bandwidth remaining percent 60
    random-detect dscp-based
    random-detect dscp default 25 ms 100 ms
  !
policy-map POLICY4
 class class-default
  random-detect
  random-detect ecn
  !
```

NOTE   The WRED configuration and behavior in Cisco IOS XR may differ from the description in this section. First, you may not require defining the weighting field explicitly using one of the commands in Table 3-24. The threshold definitions may define implicitly that field. Also, you may not rely on default thresholds. If a packet arrives with a marking that does not match an explicitly configured WRED threshold, the packet may be subject to tail dropping. Last, DSCP or IP precedence thresholds may not apply to MPLS packets. The definition of WRED thresholds for MPLS packets may always require the use of the **random-detect exp** command. Consult the Cisco IOS XR documentation for details.

Example 3-20 shows the counters that policies maintain for WRED using POLICY2 in Example 3-19. There are transmitted, random drops, and tail drop counters, in packets and bytes, for each of the packet markings that a class can serve. In this example, the default class (class-default) serves all traffic and uses WRED based on the discard class. For packets with a discard class value of zero, the policy has transmitted 14,390 packets (or

21,382,088 bytes) and has randomly dropped 30 packets (or 44,580 bytes). For packets with discard class one, the policy has transmitted 7,059 packets (or 10,489,674 bytes). No packets with this discard class value have experienced a random drop. For a discard class value of two, the policy has transmitted 9398 packets (or 13,965,428 bytes). It has randomly dropped 12 packets (or 17,832 bytes). The policy has not tail dropped any packets. The sum of transmitted packets matches the queue output counter (30,847 packets), and the sum of random and tail drops matches the queue total drops (42 packets).

Example 3-20   *WRED Counters in Cisco IOS*

```
Router#show policy-map interface serial1/0:0

 Serial1/0:0

  Service-policy output: POLICY2

   Class-map: class-default (match-any)
     30889 packets, 45899602 bytes
     30 second offered rate 3000 bps, drop rate 0 bps
     Match: any
       30889 packets, 45899602 bytes
       30 second rate 3000 bps

     queue limit 83 ms/ 16000 bytes
     (queue depth/total drops/no-buffer drops) 0/42/0
     (pkts output/bytes output) 30847/45837190
       Exp-weight-constant: 9 (1/512)
       Mean queue depth: 0 ms/ 0 bytes
     discard-class  Transmitted   Random drop  Tail drop  Minimum   Maximum    Mark
                    pkts/bytes    pkts/bytes   pkts/bytes thresh    thresh     prob
                                                                    ms/bytes ms/bytes
               0   14390/21382088  30/44580     0/0       50/9600   150/28800  1/1
               1   7059/10489674   0/0          0/0       100/19200 150/28800  1/1
               2   9398/13965428   12/17832     0/0       50/9600   150/28800  1/1
               3   0/0             0/0          0/0       20/4000   41/8000    1/10
               4   0/0             0/0          0/0       23/4500   41/8000    1/10
               5   0/0             0/0          0/0       36/7000   41/8000    1/10
               6   0/0             0/0          0/0       31/6000   41/8000    1/10
               7   0/0             0/0          0/0       26/5000   41/8000    1/10
Router#
```

Example 3-21 illustrates the WRED counters in Cisco IOS XR. The example uses POLICY3 in Example 3-19. A set of counters (in packets and bytes) shows the number of WRED drops for each queue. These counters include random drops and drops that happened when the average queue depth reached the maximum threshold. In the case of CLASS3, WRED dropped 3,780 packets (or 5,601,960 bytes) randomly. It also dropped 851 packets (or 1,261,182 bytes) because of the maximum threshold. In addition to these counters, each WRED threshold has a second set of counters. These counters capture the number of packets and bytes that WRED transmitted, dropped randomly, and dropped because of the maximum threshold. For DSCP CS1 (numeric value 8), those counters show

2,311,124 packets (or 3,425,085,768 bytes), 2100 packets (or 3,112,200 bytes), and 515 packets (or 763,230 bytes), respectively. For DSCP CS2 (numeric value 16), the counters are 3,466,687 packets (or 5,137,630,134 bytes), 1,680 packets (or 2489760 bytes), and 336 packets (497,952 bytes) respectively. The default class shows 6,700,982 packets transmitted (or 9,930,855,324 bytes) and 1141 packets (or 1,690,962 bytes) randomly dropped. No packets have been dropped due to the maximum threshold in that class.

Example 3-21 *WRED Counters in Cisco IOS XR*

```
RP/0/4/CPU0:Router#show policy-map interface pos0/3/0/4
POS0/3/0/4 output: POLICY3

Class CLASS3
  Classification statistics          (packets/bytes)     (rate - kbps)
    Matched              :           5782442/8569579044       2952
    Transmitted          :           5777811/8562715902       2952
    Total Dropped        :              4631/6863142             0
  Queueing statistics
    Vital            (packets)       : 0
    Queue ID                         : 16
    High watermark   (bytes)         : 3361176
    Inst-queue-len   (packets)       : 2268
    Avg-queue-len    (packets)       : 2264
    Taildropped(packets/bytes)       : 0/0
    RED random drops(packets/bytes)        : 3780/5601960
    RED maxthreshold drops(packets/bytes): 851/1261182


    WRED profile for DSCP 8
    RED Transmitted (packets/bytes)        : 2311124/3425085768
    RED random drops(packets/bytes)        : 2100/3112200
    RED maxthreshold drops(packets/bytes): 515/763230

    WRED profile for DSCP 16
    RED Transmitted (packets/bytes)        : 3466687/5137630134
    RED random drops(packets/bytes)        : 1680/2489760
    RED maxthreshold drops(packets/bytes): 336/497952


Class class-default
  Classification statistics          (packets/bytes)     (rate - kbps)
    Matched              :           6702123/9932546286       3471
    Transmitted          :           6700982/9930855324       3471
    Total Dropped        :              1141/1690962             0
  Queueing statistics
    Vital            (packets)       : 0
    Queue ID                         : 17
    High watermark   (bytes)         : 1482000
    Inst-queue-len   (packets)       : 960
    Avg-queue-len    (packets)       : 950
    Taildropped(packets/bytes)       : 0/0
    RED random drops(packets/bytes)        : 1141/1690962
    RED maxthreshold drops(packets/bytes): 0/0
```

Example 3-21 *WRED Counters in Cisco IOS XR (Continued)*

```
      WRED profile for DSCP 0
      RED Transmitted (packets/bytes)       : 6700982/9930855324
      RED random drops(packets/bytes)       : 1141/1690962
      RED maxthreshold drops(packets/bytes): 0/0
RP/0/4/CPU0:Router#
```

Link Fragmentation and Interleaving

Cisco IOS supports LFI with Multilink PPP (MLP) and Frame Relay encapsulation. You can use MLP for LFI on serial interfaces, dialer interfaces, ATM PVCs, or Frame Relay PVCs. Cisco Frame Relay also support native fragmentation using FRF.11 and FRF.12.

The configuration of *link fragmentation and interleaving* (LFI) requires the definition of a fragment size. The configuration is specific to the type of fragmentation that you are using (MLP or Frame Relay FRF.12). The **ppp multilink fragment delay** command defines the fragment size (in milliseconds or bytes) for MLP. The **ppp multilink interleave** command enables LFI. In the case of Frame Relay links, the **frame-relay fragment** command defines the fragment size (in bytes). LFI does not require explicit configuration in this case. These commands require the simultaneous use of a policy with a priority class on the interface or PVC where you have enabled fragmentation. Table 3-30 summarizes the LFI commands.

Table 3-30 *LFI with MLP and Frame Relay FRF.12 Fragmentation*

Syntax	Description
ppp multilink interleave	LFI for MLP
ppp multilink fragment {delay *value* | **size** *value*}	Fragment size for LFI with MLP encapsulation
frame-relay fragment *value* **end-to-end**	Fragment size for LFI with Frame Relay encapsulation

NOTE   The definition of a fragment size for LFI is one of the few QoS features that you configure outside of the MQC.

Example 3-22 displays the configuration for LFI using MLP and Frame Relay FRF.12 fragmentation. POLICY1 defines a simple queuing policy with the CLASS1 queue serving priority traffic and the default class (class-default) serving all other traffic. Interface Serial1/0:0 uses MLP for LFI purposes. The interface is part of the multilink group one associated with interface Multilink1. This interface enables interleaving, and defines the fragment size as 480 bytes and serves as the attachment for POLICY1. Similarly, interface Serial1/0:1 implements LFI for a Frame Relay PVC. The interface also serves as the attachment point for POLICY1 and defines a fragment size of 480 bytes (corresponding to 10 milliseconds on a 384 kbps link speed).

Example 3-22 *Policies with LFI*

```
class-map match-all CLASS1
  match  dscp ef
!
policy-map POLICY1
  class CLASS1
    priority
    police rate percent 25 burst 10 ms
!
interface Multilink1
 ip address 192.168.2.1 255.255.255.252
 ppp multilink
 ppp multilink interleave
 ppp multilink group 1
 ppp multilink fragment delay size 480
 service-policy output POLICY1
!
interface Serial1/0:0
 no ip address
 encapsulation ppp
 ppp multilink
 ppp multilink group 1
!
interface Serial1/0:1
 ip address 192.168.2.5 255.255.255.252
 encapsulation frame-relay
 frame-relay interface-dlci 16
 frame-relay fragment 480 end-to-end
 service-policy output POLICY1
!
```

Header Compression

The **compression** command enables header compression in a policy. Header compression is an action of the pre-queuing component of the Cisco QoS behavioral model. You can configure either RTP and TCP header compression for bandwidth efficiency. The policy will perform compression on both protocols if you do not configure one of the two explicitly. Notice that header compression is a point-to-point technology and requires that both ends of a point-to-point link participate in the operation. The underlying encapsulation of the link should be Frame Relay, PPP, or *High-Level Data Link Control* (HLDC). Table 3-31 illustrates the complete syntax of the **compression** command.

Table 3-31 *RTP and TCP Header Compression*

Syntax	Description
compression header ip [rtp | tcp]	Compress RTP/TCP headers

NOTE   Some platforms may use an earlier implementation that relies on the **ip {rtp | tcp} header-compression** interface command.

Example 3-23 illustrates a policy using header compression. CLASS1 uses RTP header compression only. On the other hand, CLASS2 performs both RTP and TCP header compression. Any packet matching the default class (class-default) is not subject to any types of header compression.

Example 3-23 *Policy Using Header Compression*

```
class-map match-all CLASS1
 match  dscp ef
class-map match-all CLASS2
 match  dscp cs4
!
policy-map POLICY1
 class CLASS1
   priority percent 25
   compress header ip rtp
 class CLASS2
   bandwidth percent 50
   compress header ip
!
```

Hierarchical Configurations

You can extend the capabilities of the MQC with hierarchical configurations. These configurations enable you to reference a policy within another policy. Similarly, a class map can reference other existing class maps. Hierarchical policies makes it possible to perform different actions on subclasses of traffic at different levels of granularity. In addition, a hierarchical approach enables you to create configuration modules that you can reuse repeatedly in other policies. Hierarchical policies are useful and popular in actual deployments. The following sections describe how traffic classification and policies operate in hierarchical configurations.

Hierarchical Classification

Hierarchical class map configurations make possible elaborate classification criteria using logical operations between matching criteria. The **match class-map** command in Table 3-7 enables this type of hierarchical configurations. You can define complex logical operations between matching criteria in combination with the **match-any** and **match-all** keywords.

CLASS1 in Example 3-24 has a hierarchical configuration that references CLASS2. In this example, an IP packet will belong to CLASS1 if it has a DSCP value of EF or if it satisfies the classification criteria of CLASS2. A packet belongs to CLASS2 if it has a DSCP value of CS5 and satisfies access list ACL1.

Example 3-24 *Hierarchical Classification*

```
class-map match-any CLASS1
  match  dscp ef
  match class-map CLASS2
class-map match-all CLASS2
  match  dscp cs5
  match access-group name ACL1
  !
```

Hierarchical Policies

The MQC supports the configuration of hierarchical policies where a class within a policy becomes the attachment point for another policy. Many combinations of actions are possible within a hierarchical policy (for example, hierarchical policing, hierarchical queuing, or queuing and shaping).

The implementations of hierarchical policies typically limit the hierarchy to two or three levels. A policy including another policy receives the name of a parent policy. The policy that the parent policy includes receives the name of a child policy.

In a three-level hierarchy, a policy can be a grandparent or a grandchild of another policy. You apply a child policy using the **service-policy** command. The child policy automatically inherits the policy direction from its parent. Figure 3-8 illustrates the class and policy relationships in two hierarchical policies. The diagram on the left represents a two-level hierarchical policy and the diagram on the right shows a three-level hierarchical policy.

Figure 3-8 *Two-Level and Three-Level Hierarchical Policies*

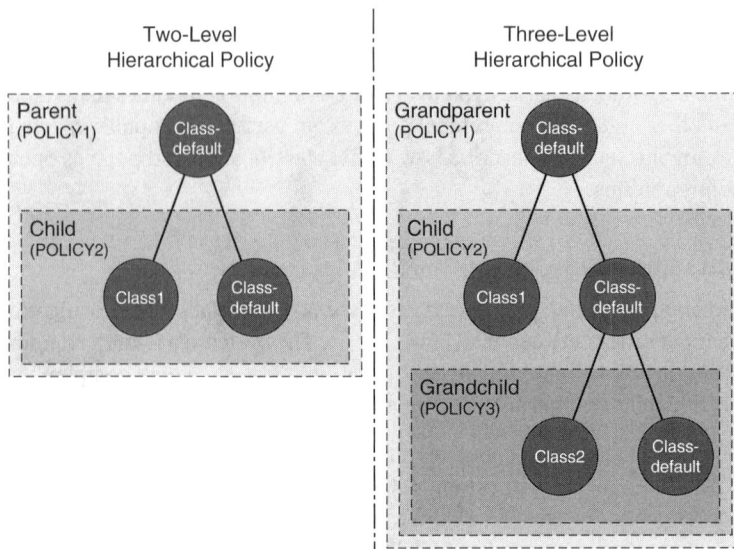

Hierarchical policies use a single classification step. Therefore, the classification of a packet remains unchanged even if an action in a child or grandchild policy re-marks it. The new marking will not result in the reclassification of the packet. However, the new marking will affect the operation of WRED or weighted queue limits.

Actions have a particular order of execution in a hierarchical configuration. After classification, hierarchical policies execute actions in decreasing level of granularity. For example, in a three-level policy, the grandchild policy executes its actions on the packet before the parent policy. Similarly, the latter will execute its actions before the grandparent policy. This ordering applies to all actions with the exception of the **set** command. For example, in a policy that uses this command at all levels, the final marking of the packet will correspond to the value that the grandchild instance of the **set** command indicates.

Example 3-25 and 3-26 show two hierarchical policies. In Example 3-25, POLICY1 defines a two-level hierarchical policy. POLICY1 shapes all traffic to 10,000,000 bps and invokes POLICY2 as the child policy. POLICY2 defines a queuing policy that provides low latency to traffic with a DSCP value of EF and enables WRED on remaining traffic.

Example 3-25 *Two-Level Hierarchical Policy*

```
class-map match-all CLASS1
  match  dscp ef
!
policy-map POLICY1
  class class-default
    shape average 10000000 40000 40000
    service-policy POLICY2
!
policy-map POLICY2
  class CLASS1
    priority percent 20
  class class-default
    random-detect dscp-based
!
```

Example 3-26 expands the hierarchy one level to produce a three-level hierarchical policy. In this example, POLICY2 invokes a POLICY3 as a child policy. POLICY3 marks CLASS2 using a policer and all other traffic with a **set** command. POLICY3 will act only on packets that do not have a DSCP of EF because of its attachment point. POLICY2 uses the new packet marking when performing WRED on the default class (class-default).

Example 3-26 *Three-Level Hierarchical Policy*

```
class-map match-all CLASS1
  match  dscp ef
class-map match-all CLASS2
  match access-group name ACL1
!
policy-map POLICY1
```

Example 3-26   *Three-Level Hierarchical Policy (Continued)*

```
   class class-default
     shape average 10000000 40000 40000
     service-policy POLICY2
 !
 policy-map POLICY2
   class CLASS1
     priority percent 20
   class class-default
     random-detect dscp-based
     service-policy POLICY3
 !
 policy-map POLICY3
   class CLASS2
     police rate percent 50
       conform-action set-dscp-transmit af21
       exceed-action set-dscp-transmit af22
   class class-default
     set dscp af21
 !
```

Percentage-Based Rates

The attachment point of a policy determines the actual rate that the **bandwidth**, **shape**, and **police** commands use when you configure percentage-based rates. The **bandwidth percent** command defines a minimum-bandwidth guarantee relative to the minimum-bandwidth guarantee of the policy attachment point in the parent policy. The **shape** and **police** commands use the maximum rate of the attachment point as a reference. The presence of a **shape** or **police** command in the parent policy defines such maximum rate. In the absence of those commands in the parent policy, the parent policy inherits the maximum from its parent (grandparent policy) and eventually from the interface that serves as attachment point for the hierarchical policy.

NOTE   The **priority percent** command uses the same logic of the **bandwidth percent** command to compute the actual rate of the conditional policer.

Interfaces generally have an implicit bandwidth definition that policies can use as a reference. In some cases, the interface will not have an associated bandwidth amount, and you may need to specify the interface rate. This situation can be particularly common on logical subinterfaces (for example, Ethernet, Frame Relay, or ATM subinterfaces). The **bandwidth qos-reference** command specifies the bandwidth amount that policies should use as a reference on an interface. You apply this command directly under the interface configuration, and any policy that you attach to the interface will use automatically make use of that bandwidth reference. Table 3-30 illustrates the complete syntax of the **bandwidth qos-reference** command.

Table 3-32 *Bandwidth Reference for QoS*

Syntax	Description
bandwidth qos-reference [**input**	**output**] *value*	Maximum queue size

Parameter Units

Tables 3-33 and 3-34 summarize the default parameter units for the MQC commands in this chapter. Both tables include a simplified syntax of the commands. Table 3-33 includes commands that have rates or bursts as parameters. Table 3-34 includes commands that have a queue size as parameters.

Table 3-33 *Default Units for the MQC Commands with Rate or Burst Parameters*

Command	Rate Units	Burst Units
police	Bits per second	Bytes
police cir	Bits per second	Bytes
police rate	Bits per second	Bytes
police cir percent	Not applicable	Milliseconds
police rate percent	Not applicable	Milliseconds
shape average	Bits per second	Bits
shape average	Bits per second	Bits
shape peak	Bits per second	Bits
shape average percent	Not applicable	Milliseconds
shape peak percent	Not applicable	Milliseconds
shape adaptive	Bits per second	Not configurable
shape adaptive percent	Not applicable	Not configurable
bandwidth	Kilobits per second	Not configurable
bandwidth percent	Not applicable	Not configurable
bandwidth remaining percent	Not applicable	Not configurable
priority	Kilobits per second	Bytes
priority percent	Not applicable	Milliseconds

Table 3-34 *Default Units for the MQC Commands with Queue Size Parameters*

Command	Queue Size Units
queue-limit	Packets
random-detect	Packets

Some platforms support the explicit configuration of parameter units in their implementation of the MQC. The flexible definition of units facilitates network operation and contributes to fewer configuration mistakes. Their benefits become more obvious as link speeds increase and the default units for a parameter become less adequate. Table 3-35 lists the different keywords for rate units. These keywords prove useful in the configuration of policers and shapers or when you perform bandwidth allocation for congestion management. Table 3-36 shows the keywords for memory units. These keywords facilitate the configuration of burst sizes for policers and shapers. They also facilitate the definition of the maximum size for a queue or thresholds for active queue management. Finally, Table 3-37 includes time units that help define burst sizes for policers and shapers.

Table 3-35 *Configurable Rate Units in the MQC*

Command Keyword	Units
bps	Bits per second
kbps	Kilobits per second
mbps	Megabits per second
gbps	Gigabits per second
pps	Packets per second
cps	ATM cells per second

Table 3-36 *Configurable Memory Units in the MQC*

Command Keyword	Units
bytes	Bytes
kbytes	Kilobytes
mbytes	Megabytes
gbytes	Gigabytes
packets	Packets per second
cells	ATM cells

Table 3-37 *Configurable Time Units in the MQC*

Command Keyword	Units
ms	Milliseconds
us	Microseconds

Example 3-27 illustrates a policy that relies on explicit configuration of parameter units. CLASS1 uses a policer with a rate in megabits per second and a burst in kilobytes. CLASS2 has a minimum-bandwidth guarantee in megabits per second. Both CLASS2 and the default class (class-default) have a maximum queue size in packets.

Example 3-27   *Policy with Explicit Parameter Units*

```
class-map match-all CLASS1
  match mpls experimental topmost 5
class-map match-all CLASS2
  match mpls experimental topmost 3 4
 !
policy-map POLICY1
  class CLASS1
    priority
    police rate 1 mbps burst 3 kbytes
 class CLASS2
    bandwidth 10 mbps
    queue-limit 1000 packets
  class class-default
    queue-limit 8700 packets
 !
```

Processing of Local Traffic

Processing of local traffic represents a special case in the configuration of QoS. This traffic represents mostly control- and management-plane packets that a node receives and sends. Nodes identify the most crucial control- and management-plane packets with a priority flag. These packets include mainly hello and keepalive messages for Layer 2 and Layer 3 protocols (for example, PPP/HLDC keepalives, ATM OAM cells, *Open Shortest Path First / Intermediate System-to-Intermediate System* [OSPF/IS-IS] Hellos, *Bidirectional Forwarding Detection* [BFD]). Interface QoS policies do not affect these packets. For example, policers or AQM do not drop packets that have a priority flag. Interface policies generally classify and process all other local traffic.

NOTE   In Cisco IOS, you can force the priority flag for all *Label Distribution Protocol* (LDP) packets over TCP sessions using the **mpls ldp tcp pak-priority** command. In addition, IP *service level agreement* (SLA) jitter probes will have the priority flag if you configure the **probe-packet priority high** command. In all other cases, the node automatically decides which packets receive this flag.

Similarly, marking of local IP traffic represents a special case in the configuration of QoS. The node automatically marks some of that traffic. In some cases, you can also preconfigure the marking you want outside of the MQC using protocol or application commands outside of the MQC. Table 3-38 lists the IP local traffic sources that use a non-best-effort marking by default.

Table 3-38 *Default Marking for Locally Generated IP Traffic*

Protocol	Default IP Marking
Bidirectional Forwarding Detection (BFD)	CS6
Border Gateway Protocol (BGP)	CS6
Data-link switching (DLSw)	CS5 (TCP port 2065)
	CS4 (TCP port 1981)
	CS3 (TCP port 1982)
	CS2 (TCP port 1981)
Distance Vector Multicast Routing Protocol (DVMRP)	CS6
Enhanced Interior Gateway Routing Protocol (EIGRP)	CS6
Gateway Load Balancing Protocol (GLBP)	CS6
Generic routing encapsulation (GRE)	CS6 (CDP and GRE keepalives)
Hot Standby Router Protocol (HSRP)	CS6
Internet Control Message Protocol (ICMP)	CS6 (UDP port unreachable, time exceeded, echo reply for LSP ping)
Internet Group Management Protocol (IGMP)	CS6
Layer 2 Tunneling Protocol (L2TP)	CS6 (control messages)
Label Distribution Protocol (LDP)	CS6
Mobile IP (MIP)	CS6
Multicast Source Discovery Protocol (MSDP)	CS6
Next Hop Resolution Protocol (NHRP)	CS6
Network Time Protocol (NTP)	CS6
Open Shortest Path First (OSPF)	CS6
Protocol-Independent Multicast (PIM)	CS6
Rate Based Satellite Control Protocol (RBSCP)	CS6
Router Port Group Management Protocol (RGMP)	CS6
Routing Information Protocol (RIP)	CS6
Resource Reservation Protocol Traffic Engineering (RSVP-TE)	CS6
Stack Group Bidding Protocol (SGBP)	CS6 (keepalive and hello messages)
Secure Shell (SSH)	CS6
Stateful Network Address Translation (NAT)	CS6

Table 3-38   *Default Marking for Locally Generated IP Traffic (Continued)*

Protocol	Default IP Marking
Telnet	CS6
Virtual Router Redundancy Protocol (VRRP)	CS6

NOTE   Cisco IOS XR supports a subset of the protocols listed in the preceding table. For those protocols it supports, the default marking behavior in Cisco IOS and Cisco IOS XR is the same.

NOTE   The details of the processing of local traffic can vary slightly depending on software, hardware, and platform specifics. These differences can be particularly true regarding bandwidth allocation to local traffic in the presence of interface congestion. Consult your platform documentation for details.

Some platforms support the definition of a QoS policy to control local traffic as it flows from and to the route processor. The policies generally classify the traffic and define what packets to transmit, drop, or police. There are two main types of policy: aggregate and distributed. An aggregate control-plane policy acts on the all route processor traffic. Platforms with a distributed architecture can support a set of distributed control-plane policies that act on traffic that flows between line cards and the route processor. Figure 3-9 illustrates the different attachment points for centralized and distributed architectures. The distributed control-plane policies process only traffic that needs to reach the route processor. The line card may process some local traffic (for instance, generating a ping reply) without involving the route processor.

Figure 3-9 *Policies Controlling Local Traffic from and to the Route Processor*

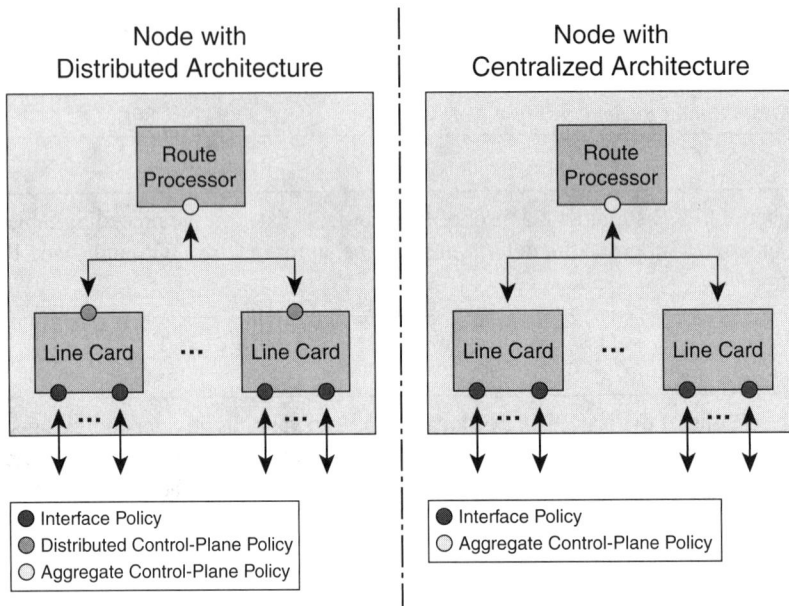

NOTE   The support for control-plane policies can vary significantly depending on the hardware and software specifics. These differences include the type of actions that the policies support and the policy direction (input only, or input and output). Consult your platform documentation for details.

The **control-plane** command defines the attachment points for control-plane policies. In its simplest form, this command enables the attachment point for an aggregate policy. The longer command syntax, **control-plane slot**, defines the attachment point for a distributed control-plane policy on a specific line-card slot. Table 3-39 summarizes the syntax of these two commands.

Table 3-39 *Commands for Control-Plane Policy Attachment*

Syntax	Policy Attachment Description
control-plane	Traffic to/from route processor
control-plane slot *value*	Traffic from/to line card to/from route processor

Example 3-28 illustrates the configuration of aggregate and distributed control-plane policies. Both POLICY1 and POLICY2 police ICMP echo requests and replies associated with the IP ping application. POLICY1 polices ping traffic to 128 kbps with a burst of 16 KBps (1 second) from each line-card slot to the route process. POLICY2 limits the aggregate ping traffic reaching the route processor to a rate of 384 kbps with a burst of 48 KBps (1 second). This configuration is valid on a platform with a distributed architecture. The centralized platform will have only the aggregate control-plane policy.

Example 3-28 *Control-Plane Policies*

```
class-map match-all CLASS1
  match access-group 100
!
policy-map POLICY1
  class CLASS1
    police rate 128000 burst 16000
policy-map POLICY2
  class CLASS1
    police rate 384000 burst 48000
!
access-list 100 permit icmp any any echo
access-list 100 permit icmp any any echo-reply
!
control-plane slot 1
 service-policy input POLICY1
!
control-plane slot 2
 service-policy input POLICY1
!
control-plane slot 3
 service-policy input POLICY1
!
control-plane
 service-policy input POLICY2
!
```

Summary

Cisco QoS uses a behavioral model that abstracts the QoS implementation details. This behavioral model defines the concept of a TMN. This abstraction groups the QoS actions that a device performs at a given point during packet forwarding. The TMN has four components: classification, pre-queuing, queuing, and post-queuing. All components are optional and user configurable. The classification component associates each packet with a class. The pre-queuing component includes policing, marking, dropping, and compression. The queuing component manages queue sizes and packet scheduling. The post-queuing groups any actions that depend on packet sequencing.

The MQC provides the user interface to the QOS behavioral model. Three commands define the configuration components: **class-map**, **policy-map**, and **service-policy**. The

class-map commands control traffic classification and corresponds to the classification component of the TMN. The **policy-map** command defines a policy template that group QoS actions (including marking, policing, shaping, congestion management, active queue management, and so on). These policies may define any of the other three components of the TMN. The **service-policy** command instantiates a previously defined QoS policy and defines its direction. The MQC provides a template-based, hardware-independent configuration model for QoS across different Cisco platforms.

References

Cisco Software Center: http://www.cisco.com/go/software

Cisco Software Advisor: http://tools.cisco.com/Support/Fusion/FusionHome.do

Cisco IOS Quality of Service Solutions Configuration Guide, Release 12.4: http://www.cisco.com/en/US/products/ps6350/ products_configuration_guide_book09186a0080435d50.html

Cisco IOS Software Releases 12.2 S Feature Guides: http://www.cisco.com/en/US/ products/sw/iosswrel/ps1838/products_feature_guides_list.html

Cisco IOS XR Software Configuration Guides: http://www.cisco.com/en/US/partner/ products/ps5845/products_installation_and_configuration_guides_list.html

Traffic Management Specification Version 4.0. The ATM Forum: http://www.atmforum.com/

CHAPTER 4

Cisco MPLS Traffic Engineering

In this chapter, you learn the following topics:

- Basic Operation of MPLS TE
- DiffServ-Aware Traffic Engineering
- Fast Reroute

This chapter provides an overview of *the Multiprotocol Label Switching Protocol Traffic Engineering* (MPLS TE) implementation and configuration in Cisco products. This overview includes details about algorithms and configuration commands. The material includes simple configuration examples to illustrate the use of the commands. The material in this chapter assumes that you are already familiar with the technology aspects of MPLS TE. Chapter 2, "MPLS TE Technology Overview," includes a technology overview that you can use as a reference.

Cisco IOS and IOS XR provide a comprehensive MPLS TE implementation. You can deploy MPLS TE on networks running *Open Shortest Path First* (OSPF) or *Intermediate System-to-Intermediate System* (IS-IS). Various mechanisms are available to forward traffic down a *traffic engineering label switched path* (TE LSP). Cisco MPLS TE also provides support for *Differentiated Services* (DiffServ)-*aware traffic engineering* (DS-TE) and *fast reroute* (FRR). The section "Basic Operation of MPLS TE" describes how to enable MPLS TE, use your *interior gateway protocol* (IGP) to distribute TE link information, perform constraint-based routing, signal TE LSPs, and select the traffic that the TE LSP will carry. The section "DiffServ-Aware Traffic Engineering" describes TE-Classes and bandwidth constraints and discusses the steps to signal DS-TE LSPs and the commands to verify the proper operation. The section "Fast Reroute" presents the configuration of link, node, and bandwidth protection.

For further details about Cisco MPLS TE, see the book *Traffic Engineering with MPLS* (Cisco Press) or consult the software documentation available at Cisco.com.

Basic Operation of MPLS TE

The following sections review the configuration and operation of the most important aspects of Cisco MPLS TE. The section "Enabling MPLS TE" introduces the basic node and interface configuration that enables MPLS TE on a Cisco router. Then, the section

"Defining a TE Tunnel Interface" discusses how you configure a TE LSP on the headend node. The sections "Link Information Distribution," "Signaling of TE LSPs," and "Traffic Selection" explain how to configure the MPLS TE functionality that equivalent sections in Chapter 2 introduced.

Enabling MPLS TE

Cisco MPLS TE requires configuration at the node and interface (link) levels. The configuration involves mainly the definition of MPLS TE and *Resource Reservation Protocol* (RSVP) behavior. In addition, you may want to enable the TE extensions for your IGP to perform constraint-based routing. Cisco IOS uses **mpls traffic-eng** as a command prefix for MPLS TE-related configuration. Similarly, **ip rsvp** is the command prefix for entering RSVP-related configuration. Cisco IOS XR uses a slightly different approach that groups each of those configuration tasks in separate configuration modes that the **mpls traffic-eng** and **rsvp** commands define respectively. The individual command syntax shares significant similarity between Cisco IOS and Cisco IOS XR.

Enabling MPLS TE on a Node

You enable MPLS TE on a node using the **mpls traffic-eng tunnels** command in Cisco IOS. You must configure this global command before you can implement MPLS TE. There are additional global commands. They share the **mpls traffic-eng** prefix. Those commands are all optional with the exception of the **mpls traffic-eng tunnels** command. They configure different aspects of the global behavior of MPLS TE for a node, including timers, automation, and logging. Enabling MPLS TE on a global basis does not result in an operational configuration.

Example 4-1 shows an MPLS TE node configuration in Cisco IOS. In this case, the commands enable MPLS on the node, logging of setup and teardown of TE LSPs, and path reoptimization when a physical interface becomes operational. The sections "Path Computation" and "DiffServ-Aware Traffic Engineering" cover some global commands in more detail. See Appendix A, "Command Reference for Cisco MPLS Traffic Engineering and RSVP," for a list of MPLS TE node commands in Cisco IOS. The Cisco IOS documentation contains additional command details.

Example 4-1 *MPLS TE Node Configuration in Cisco IOS*

```
mpls traffic-eng tunnels
mpls traffic-eng logging lsp setups
mpls traffic-eng logging lsp teardowns
mpls traffic-eng reoptimize events link-up
!
```

You enable MPLS TE on a node using the **mpls traffic-eng** command in Cisco IOS XR. This command defines a separate configuration mode that groups the MPLS TE configuration, with the exception of the TE extensions for the IGP. As the next section describes, you even enable under this configuration mode the physical interfaces that will participate in the MPLS TE network. Most of the global MPLS TE commands in Cisco IOS have an equivalent in Cisco IOS XR. Example 4-2 shows an MPLS TE node configuration under Cisco IOS XR. This configuration enables MPLS TE on two interfaces, defines the maximum number of configurable TE LSPs on the node, and disables *penultimate hop popping* (PHP) on the upstream neighbor when the node acts as ultimate hop.

Example 4-2 *MPLS TE Node Configuration in Cisco IOS XR*

```
mpls traffic-eng
 interface POS0/3/0/0
 !
 interface POS0/3/0/1
 !
 maximum tunnels 500
 signalling advertise explicit-null
 !
```

TIP   You will find the **man** command useful to obtain online help on a command if you are using the EXEC interface to configure a node. The command is available only in Cisco IOS XR.

Enabling MPLS TE on an Interface

You use the **mpls traffic-eng tunnels** command to enable MPLS TE on an interface in Cisco IOS. This command enables MPLS TE on the interface, including the processing of RSVP signaling to set up and tear down TE LSPs. This command, in combination with its global peer, gives the minimal operational configuration. You can configure additional MPLS TE commands under an interface. They share the **mpls traffic-eng** prefix. Those interface commands enable you to specify link attributes, define link flooding thresholds, and control some aspects of FRR behavior. Example 4-3 illustrates interfaces POS0/1/0 and POS1/0/0 configured for MPLS TE. The sections "Link Information Distribution" and "Link and Node Protection" elaborate on the most relevant interface commands.

Example 4-3 *MPLS TE Interface Configuration in Cisco IOS*

```
interface POS0/1/0
 ip address 172.16.0.0 255.255.255.254
 mpls traffic-eng tunnels
 mpls traffic-eng administrative-weight 100
 !
interface POS1/0/0
 ip address 172.16.0.2 255.255.255.254
 mpls traffic-eng tunnels
 mpls traffic-eng srlg 10
 !
```

The **interface** command enables MPLS TE on an interface in Cisco IOS XR. This command resides under the mpls traffic-eng configuration mode. You do not configure any MPLS TE command under the main interface configuration. The **interface** command under the **mpls traffic-eng** mode defines a submode where the interface-specific configuration for MPLS TE resides. Example 4-4 illustrates interfaces POS0/3/0/0 and POS0/3/0/1 with their MPLS TE-specific configuration. As described previously, the sections "Link Information Distribution" and "Link and Node Protection" elaborate on the most relevant interface commands. Contrary to Cisco IOS, enabling MPLS TE on an interface does not enable the processing of RSVP signaling.

Example 4-4 *MPLS TE Interface Configuration in Cisco IOS XR*

```
mpls traffic-eng
 interface POS0/3/0/0
  admin-weight 5
  attribute-flags 0x8
 !
 interface POS0/3/0/1
  attribute-flags 0xf
 !
!
```

NOTE   This approach of enabling interfaces under protocols or technologies is common in Cisco IOS XR. Cisco IOS follows a different approach of enabling protocols or technologies under interfaces.

You can use a rich collection of **show**, **clear**, and **debug** commands to implement and operate an MPLS network. All **show** commands begin with the **show mpls traffic-eng** prefix, **clear** commands with **clear mpls traffic-eng**, and all **debug** commands with **debug mpls traffic-eng**. Appendix A includes a list of these commands. Cisco IOS and Cisco IOS XR use similar command syntax. The upcoming sections in this chapter cover the complete syntax and output of some of the verification commands that you will probably use most frequently.

Defining a TE Tunnel Interface

Nodes in an MPLS TE network use tunnel interfaces to define a new TE LSP. The tunnel interface specifies the characteristics of the TE LSP, including destination, bandwidth, path, protection requirements, and forwarding parameters, among others. At a minimum, you need to specify the destination and path of the TE LSP. You perform the tunnel configuration on the TE LSP headend. The tailend does not require special configuration because TE LSPs are generally unidirectional. In most cases, you want to have TE LSPs in both directions. In that case, you need to configure a second tunnel at the tailend toward the headend.

For all purposes, those will be two separate TE LSPs that happen to have opposite headends and tailends.

Cisco IOS identifies tunnel interfaces with the **tunnel** keyword. These interfaces have multiple uses in Cisco IOS. They can use *Layer 2 Tunnel Protocol* (L2TP), *generic routing encapsulation* (GRE), MPLS, and other protocols as a tunneling mechanism. Therefore, you need to specify the tunnel as an MPLS TE tunnel using the **tunnel mode mpls traffic-eng** command. MPLS TE tunnels also use the existing **tunnel destination** command to define their destination. In general, you configure the behavior that is specific to a TE LSP under the tunnel interface. Those commands use the **tunnel mpls traffic-eng** prefix. Example 4-5 shows how a tunnel configuration looks in Cisco IOS. You will find further details about the most common tunnel commands throughout this chapter.

Example 4-5 *Definition of a TE LSP Headend in Cisco IOS*

```
interface Tunnel1
 ip unnumbered Loopback0
 tunnel destination 172.16.255.3
 tunnel mode mpls traffic-eng
 tunnel mpls traffic-eng path-option 10 dynamic
 !
```

NOTE   Notice that MPLS TE commands that you configure under a tunnel interface have a **tunnel** prefix. MPLS TE commands that you configure under physical interfaces are different and do not have that prefix.

Cisco IOS XR identifies MPLS TE tunnel interfaces with the **tunnel-te** keyword. As the name suggests, you use this type of interface exclusively for MPLS TE tunnels. The tunnel configuration commands available in Cisco IOS XR have an equivalent in Cisco IOS, and their syntaxes resemble each other. However, the Cisco IOS XR syntax is shorter because the **tunnel-te** already provides an MPLS TE context to the configuration. Example 4-6 illustrates how a tunnel configuration looks in Cisco IOS XR. You will find further details about the most common tunnel commands throughout this chapter.

Example 4-6 *Definition of a TE LSP Headend in Cisco IOS XR*

```
interface tunnel-te0
 ipv4 unnumbered Loopback0
 destination 172.16.255.5
 path-option 10 dynamic
 !
```

Link Information Distribution

You can use either IS-IS or OSPF for link information distribution. Both Cisco IOS and Cisco IOS XR support both protocols. The upcoming sections describe how to configure the distribution of link information, how to control the amount of flooding, and how to verify that a node has properly disseminated and received the information.

Using IS-IS for Link Information Distribution

You can use IS-IS to distribute link information relative to MPLS TE in Cisco IOS. You enable the MPLS TE extensions using the **mpls traffic-eng** command under the **router isis** configuration mode. The command must specify the proper IS-IS level (one or two). You also need to enable the wide metric format with the **metric-style wide** command and define an MPLS TE router identifier with the **mpls traffic-eng router-id** command. Example 4-7 shows a sample IS-IS configuration in Cisco IOS that uses the TE extensions of this protocol.

Example 4-7 *MPLS TE Extensions for IS-IS in Cisco IOS*

```
router isis
 net 49.0001.1720.1625.5001.00
 is-type level-2-only
 metric-style wide
 mpls traffic-eng router-id Loopback0
 mpls traffic-eng level-2
 passive-interface Loopback0
 !
```

Cisco IOS XR also supports the distribution of this link information using IS-IS. The commands it uses are nearly identical to those in Cisco IOS. In both cases, the commands that relate to MPLS TE have the mpls traffic-eng prefix. In Cisco IOS XR, you need to enable these TE commands under the **ipv4 unicast** address family in the IS-IS configuration. You can also define the MPLS TE router identifier using the global **router-id** command that applies to all protocols. Example 4-8 shows an IS-IS configuration in Cisco IOS XR using the TE extensions.

Example 4-8 *MPLS TE Extensions for IS-IS in Cisco IOS XR*

```
router isis DEFAULT
 is-type level-2-only
 net 49.0001.1720.1625.5129.00
 address-family ipv4 unicast
  metric-style wide
  mpls traffic-eng level 2
  mpls traffic-eng router-id Loopback0
 !
 interface Loopback0
  passive
  address-family ipv4 unicast
```

Example 4-8 *MPLS TE Extensions for IS-IS in Cisco IOS XR (Continued)*

```
 !
 !
interface POS0/3/0/0
 address-family ipv4 unicast
  !
 !
 !
```

Using OSPF for Link Information Distribution

Cisco IOS and Cisco IOS XR also support MPLS TE extensions for OSPF. You must use the **mpls traffic-eng area** command to specify the OSPF area where you are enabling MPLS TE. You specify the MPLS TE router identifier with the **mpls traffic-eng router-id** command. These two commands use the same syntax in both operating systems. All the OSPF commands that relate to MPLS TE have the **mpls traffic-eng** prefix.

Examples 4-9 and 4-10 show OSPF configurations with MPLS TE extensions for Cisco IOS and Cisco IOS XR, respectively.

Example 4-9 *MPLS TE Extensions for OSPF in Cisco IOS*

```
router ospf 100
 log-adjacency-changes
 mpls traffic-eng router-id Loopback0
 mpls traffic-eng area 0
 passive-interface Loopback0
 network 172.16.0.0 0.0.255.255 area 0
 !
```

Example 4-10 *MPLS TE Extensions for OSPF in Cisco IOS XR*

```
router ospf DEFAULT
 area 0
  interface Loopback0
   passive
  !
  interface POS0/3/0/0
  !
 mpls traffic-eng router-id Loopback0
 mpls traffic-eng area 0
 !
```

Controlling Flooding

Cisco MPLS TE offers granular control on the flooding of link information. You can have changes in available bandwidth trigger flooding of link updates. A node will also send periodic link updates. You tune periodic updates per node using the link management timers and the bandwidth utilization thresholds per interface using the interface flooding threshold. Figure 4-1 shows the default bandwidth utilization thresholds that influence link flooding in both operating systems. In addition, you can manually force the flooding on a node in Cisco IOS XR using the exec **mpls traffic-eng link-management flood** command.

NOTE   "Just because I can" is not a good reason to tune any timer. The timer defaults provide good results for most deployments. Before attempting to modify any timers, make sure you understand what you are trying to achieve and the impact that the change will have on the network.

Figure 4-1 shows the default bandwidth utilization thresholds that influence link flooding in both operating systems. The figure highlights with a circle the changes in bandwidth reservation that trigger the flooding of the link state. Initially, the link has all its bandwidth available. Two TE LSPs reserve 5 percent of the link bandwidth each. Those reservations do not trigger any flooding. The next five reservations cross one of the default thresholds and cause the advertising of the updated link information. At this point, seven reservations have consumed 88 percent of the link bandwidth. After reaching this maximum, five TE LSPs are torn down. All but the fourth TE LSP introduce a change in bandwidth reservation that forces flooding. The link remains with two TE LSPs that hold 10 percent of the link bandwidth.

Configuring Link Attributes

A node will advertise MPLS TE attributes for a link when you configure the IGP with the respective extensions. As described in Chapter 2, those link characteristics include the TE administrative weight, attribute flags, and bandwidth. All links in your MPLS TE network have these three parameters regardless of your IGP choice (IS-IS or OSPF) and regardless of whether you configure them explicitly. This behavior includes all nodes whether they act as TE LSP headends, midpoints, or tailends.

Not all links on a node have to be part of your MPLS TE network. You need to configure at least one link connecting to another MPLS TE node. If you do not configure the link parameters explicitly, a link will use default values as soon as you enable MPLS TE and RSVP on the respective interface.

Figure 4-1 *Bandwidth Utilization Thresholds for Flooding Link Updates*

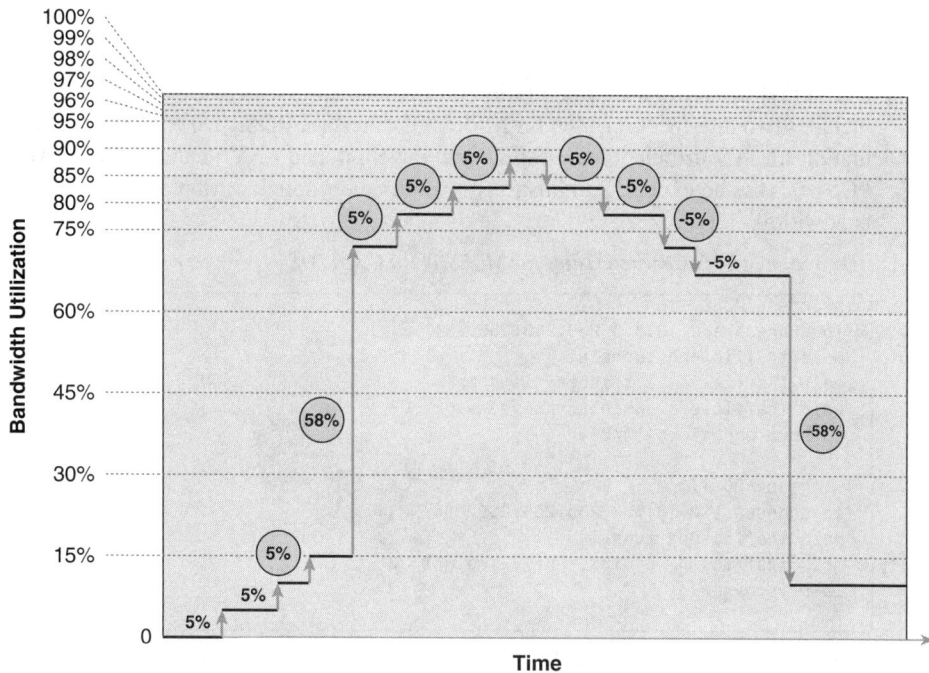

NOTE   When you configure the link characteristics under an interface, you are configuring one end of the link. The node at the other end of the link is responsible for the configuration in the other direction. The configuration on both sides does not necessarily have to match.

Cisco IOS relies on MPLS TE and RSVP interface commands to set the link characteristics. You use the **mpls traffic-eng administrative-weight**, **mpls traffic-eng attribute-flags,** and **ip rsvp bandwidth** commands. As a prerequisite, you must enable MPLS TE on the interface using the **mpls traffic-eng tunnels** command. Unless configured explicitly, the administrative weight defaults to a value of the IGP metric, the attribute flags defaults to 0, and the RSVP bandwidth defaults to 75 percent of the interface bandwidth. If you do not configure the **ip rsvp bandwidth** command, the RVSP bandwidth defaults to 0. You can still signal TE LSPs through that link if those TE LSPs do not try to reserve any bandwidth. You can configure the RSVP bandwidth above or below the actual link capacity. The section "Signaling of TE LSPs" elaborates on the RSVP commands.

Cisco IOS XR uses the **interface** submodes under the **mpls traffic-eng** and **rsvp** configuration modes to define the link characteristics. You use the **admin-weight** and **attribute-**

flags commands within the **mpls traffic-eng** configuration mode. In addition, you configure the **bandwidth** commands within the **rsvp** mode. All three link characteristics have the same defaults as in Cisco IOS.

Example 4-11 shows the configuration of link characteristics in Cisco IOS. The example includes two interfaces enabled for MPLS TE. Interface POS0/1/0 contains explicit configuration for the attribute flags, administrative weight, and RSVP bandwidth. Interface POS1/0/0 has an explicit administrative weight and implicit attribute flags and RSVP bandwidth.

Example 4-11 *Definition of Link Characteristics for MPLS TE in Cisco IOS*

```
interface POS0/1/0
 ip address 172.16.0.0 255.255.255.254
 mpls traffic-eng tunnels
 mpls traffic-eng attribute-flags 0xF
 mpls traffic-eng administrative-weight 20
 ip rsvp bandwidth 100000
 !
interface POS1/0/0
 ip address 172.16.0.2 255.255.255.254
 mpls traffic-eng tunnels
 mpls traffic-eng administrative-weight 30
 ip rsvp bandwidth
 !
```

Example 4-12 shows the configuration of link attributes for two interfaces in Cisco IOS XR. Notice that the interface configuration resides under the **rsvp** and **mpls traffic-eng** configuration modes. Interface POS0/3/0/0 uses an explicit bandwidth, administrative weight, and attribute flags. Interface POS0/3/0/1 only defines the RSVP bandwidth and the attribute flags explicitly.

Example 4-12 *Definition of Link Characteristics for MPLS TE in Cisco IOS XR*

```
rsvp
 interface POS0/3/0/0
  bandwidth 100000
 !
 interface POS0/3/0/1
  bandwidth 155000
 !
!
mpls traffic-eng
 interface POS0/3/0/0
  admin-weight 5
  attribute-flags 0x8
 !
 interface POS0/3/0/1
  attribute-flags 0xf
 !
!
```

Verifying Link Information Distribution

You can examine the link information that a node advertises by using the **show mpls traffic-eng link-management advertisements** command. The output provides details on all the MPLS TE link attributes and the IGP configuration. The same command syntax is available in Cisco IOS and Cisco IOS XR.

Example 4-13 shows the command output in Cisco IOS. The output corresponds to the configuration of interface POS0/1/0 in Example 4-11. Example 4-14 contains the equivalent command output in Cisco IOS XR. The command output corresponds to interface POS0/3/0/0 in Example 4-6. Both Cisco IOS and Cisco IOS XR provide almost identical information with slightly different formats. Both examples highlight the flooding protocol, the MPLS TE router ID, TE metric, the reservable (global) bandwidth, the amount of available bandwidth at each of the eight priority levels, and the link attribute flags.

Example 4-13   *Examining MPLS TE Link Advertisements in Cisco IOS*

```
Router#show mpls traffic-eng link-management advertisements
Flooding Status:        ready
Configured Areas:      1
IGP Area[1] ID:: isis  level-2
  System Information::
    Flooding Protocol:      ISIS
  Header Information::
    IGP System ID:          1720.1625.5001.00
    MPLS TE Router ID:      172.16.255.1
    Flooded Links:          1
  Link ID::  0
    Link Subnet Type:       Point-to-Point
    Link IP Address:        172.16.0.0
    IGP Neighbor:           ID 1720.1625.5129.00, IP 172.16.0.1
    TE metric:              20
    IGP metric:             10
    SRLGs:                  None
    Physical Bandwidth:     155000 kbits/sec
    Res. Global BW:         100000 kbits/sec
    Res. Sub BW:            0 kbits/sec
    Downstream::
                                  Global Pool   Sub Pool
                                  -----------   ----------
          Reservable Bandwidth[0]:      100000              0 kbits/sec
          Reservable Bandwidth[1]:      100000              0 kbits/sec
          Reservable Bandwidth[2]:      100000              0 kbits/sec
          Reservable Bandwidth[3]:      100000              0 kbits/sec
          Reservable Bandwidth[4]:      100000              0 kbits/sec
          Reservable Bandwidth[5]:      100000              0 kbits/sec
          Reservable Bandwidth[6]:      100000              0 kbits/sec
          Reservable Bandwidth[7]:      100000              0 kbits/sec
      Attribute Flags:        0x0000000F
! Output omitted for brevity
```

Example 4-14   *Examining MPLS TE Link Advertisements in Cisco IOS XR*

```
RP/0/4/CPU0:Router[P]#show mpls traffic-eng link-management advertisements

  Flooding Status          : ready
  Last Flooding            : 904 seconds ago
  Last Flooding Trigger    : Link BW changed
  Next Periodic Flooding In : 132 seconds
  Diff-Serv TE Mode        : Not enabled
  Configured Areas         : 1

  IGP Area[1]:: isis DEFAULT level-2
     Flooding Protocol  : ISIS
     IGP System ID      : 1720.1625.5129.00
     MPLS TE Router ID  : 172.16.255.129
     Flooded Links      : 2

     Link ID:: 0 (POS0/3/0/0)
        Link IP Address      : 172.16.0.1
        O/G Intf ID          : 1
        Neighbor             : ID 1720.1625.5001.00, IP 172.16.0.0
        SRLGs                :
        TE Metric            : 5
        IGP Metric           : 10
        Physical BW          : 155520 kbits/sec
        BCID                 : RDM
        Max Reservable BW    : 100000 kbits/sec
        Res Global BW        : 100000 kbits/sec
        Res Sub BW           : 0 kbits/sec

        Downstream::
                               Global Pool   Sub Pool
                               -----------   -----------
           Reservable BW[0]:        100000            0  kbits/sec
           Reservable BW[1]:        100000            0  kbits/sec
           Reservable BW[2]:        100000            0  kbits/sec
           Reservable BW[3]:        100000            0  kbits/sec
           Reservable BW[4]:        100000            0  kbits/sec
           Reservable BW[5]:        100000            0  kbits/sec
           Reservable BW[6]:        100000            0  kbits/sec
           Reservable BW[7]:        100000            0  kbits/sec

        Attribute Flags: 0x00000008

! Output omitted for brevity
```

Examining the MPLS TE topology database is an indispensable task to troubleshoot a vast number of problems. The **show mpls traffic-eng topology** command displays the entire MPLS TE topology database. The output can be rather lengthy, so make sure you get familiar with the command options. They enable you to narrow down the amount of information to display. The topology database includes information about all the links in the MPLS TE network according to the local configuration and the IGP advertisements from other nodes in the same area or level.

Examples 4-15 and 4-16 show an output fragment of this command in Cisco IOS and Cisco IOS XR, respectively. The output highlights the MPLS TE router ID, the TE metric, the attribute flags, the maximum (global) reservable bandwidth, and the amount of available bandwidth at each of the eight priority levels. In both examples, RSVP has not allocated any link bandwidth.

Example 4-15 *Examining the MPLS TE Topology Database in Cisco IOS*

```
Router#show mpls traffic-eng topology
My_System_id: 172.16.255.1 (ospf 100  area 0)

Signalling error holddown: 10 sec Global Link Generation 51

IGP Id: 172.16.255.129, MPLS TE Id:172.16.255.129 Router Node  (ospf 100  area 0)
        link[0]: Point-to-Point, Nbr IGP Id: 172.16.255.1, nbr_node_id:10, gen:51
            frag_id 0, Intf Address:172.16.0.1, Nbr Intf Address:172.16.0.0
            TE metric:1, IGP metric:1, attribute_flags:0x0
            SRLGs: None
            physical_bw: 155520 (kbps), max_reservable_bw_global: 155000 (kbps)
            max_reservable_bw_sub: 0 (kbps)


                                  Global Pool      Sub Pool
                  Total Allocated Reservable       Reservable
                  BW (kbps)       BW (kbps)        BW (kbps)
                  --------------- ----------       ----------
            bw[0]:            0        155000               0
            bw[1]:            0        155000               0
            bw[2]:            0        155000               0
            bw[3]:            0        155000               0
            bw[4]:            0        155000               0
            bw[5]:            0        155000               0
            bw[6]:            0        155000               0
            bw[7]:            0        155000               0

! Output omitted for brevity
```

Example 4-16 *Examining the MPLS TE Topology Database in Cisco IOS XR*

```
RP/0/4/CPU0:Router#show mpls traffic-eng topology
My_System_id: 172.16.255.129 (ospf   area 0)

Signalling error holddown: 10 sec Global Link Generation 173

IGP Id: 172.16.255.129, MPLS TE Id: 172.16.255.129 Router Node  (ospf   area 0)

  Link[0]:Point-to-Point, Nbr IGP Id:172.16.255.1, Nbr Node Id:36, gen:173
        Frag Id:0, Intf Address:172.16.0.1, Intf Id:0
        Nbr Intf Address:172.16.0.0, Nbr Intf Id:0
        TE Metric:1, IGP Metric:1, Attribute Flags:0x0
        Switching Capability:, Encoding:
        Physical BW:155520 (kbps), Max Reservable BW Global:155000 (kbps)
        Max Reservable BW Sub:0 (kbps)
                                Global Pool       Sub Pool
```

continues

Example 4-16 *Examining the MPLS TE Topology Database in Cisco IOS XR (Continued)*

```
                Total Allocated    Reservable       Reservable
                BW (kbps)          BW (kbps)        BW (kbps)
                ---------------    -----------      ----------
        bw[0]:              0         155000                 0
        bw[1]:              0         155000                 0
        bw[2]:              0         155000                 0
        bw[3]:              0         155000                 0
        bw[4]:              0         155000                 0
        bw[5]:              0         155000                 0
        bw[6]:              0         155000                 0
        bw[7]:              0         155000                 0

! Output omitted for brevity
```

TIP   The use of *command-line interface* (CLI) output filtering can be of great help to easily
extract important information from the topology database. You filter the command output
using the pipe operand (I) and the **begin**, **exclude**, or **include** keywords followed by a
regular expression. You can save your most useful filters using the **alias** configuration
command. As an example, the following filter enable you to quickly identify those links that
have an IGP or TE metric of 10 on Cisco IOS or Cisco IOS XR nodes:

show mpls traffic-eng topology | include [Ff]rag | [Mm]etric:10,

Consult the Cisco IOS and Cisco IOS XR configuration guides for further detail about
filtering CLI output.

Path Computation

A headend performs path computation for a TE LSP. The MPLS TE tunnel interface defines
a destination for the TE LSP and a list of path options to reach that destination. These path
options may reference an explicit path or request the computation of a dynamic path to the
destination. Even if you configure a tunnel with an explicit path, the node verifies the path
using the MPLS TE topology database unless you disable this check explicity.

Configuring the TE LSP Path

You can specify multiple path options for a TE LSP. These options can define a complete
or partial (loose) explicit path. In addition, you can configure the node with an option to
compute dynamically the complete path to the destination. As the section "Defining a TE
Tunnel Interface" described, you configure the TE LSP destination with its own command
independent of the path configuration. In Cisco IOS, you configure the TE LSP destination
with the **tunnel destination** command and specify a path option with the **tunnel mpls
traffic-eng path-option** command. Cisco IOS XR uses the **destination** command and the

path-option command. You can configure multiple path options for a tunnel. Each one has a sequence number, and the node evaluates them in increasing order.

You actually define explicit paths outside the scope of the tunnel interface. Both Cisco IOS and Cisco IOS XR use a separate configuration mode to define explicit paths. Cisco IOS uses the **ip explicit-path** command, and Cisco IOS XR uses the **explicit-path** command. Within this configuration mode, you specify the list of hops (in the form of IP addresses) that you want to include or exclude from the path.

Configuring the TE LSP Constraints

The tunnel configuration determines the constraints that the node uses when executing the constraint-based shortest-path first algorithm to signal the TE LSP. The TE LSP bandwidth, affinity (matching attribute flags), priorities, and metric type influence the computation and validation of a path. In Cisco IOS, you can specify these tunnel parameters with the following tunnel commands, respectively:

- **tunnel mpls traffic-eng bandwidth**
- **tunnel mpls traffic-eng affinity**
- **tunnel mpls traffic-eng priority**
- **tunnel mpls traffic-eng path-selection metric**

If you do not configure these parameters explicitly, the bandwidth defaults to 0 kbps, the affinity to links with attribute flags of 0, the priority to 7 (lowest priority), and the use of the TE metric for path selection. You can specify the default path-selection metric using the **mpls traffic-eng path-selection metric** global command.

Cisco IOS also enables you to associate the TE LSP constraints with a path option instead of associating them with the tunnel. You define the tunnel constraints as a template using the **mpls traffic-eng lsp attributes** global command. This command defines a configuration mode where you can use the **bandwidth**, **affinity**, and **priority** commands (among others) to define the behavior you want for a TE LSP. This feature enables you to define multiple path options with progressively less-strict constraints and increase the probability of successfully signaling the tunnel.

Example 4-17 shows a tunnel configuration in Cisco IOS with multiple path options. The tunnel has explicit configuration for setup and hold priority 5, bandwidth reservation of 10,000 kbps, and four different path options. The first three path options are explicit paths with names:

- PATH1 defines a single loose hop.
- PATH2 specifies a particular address that the path computation must exclude.
- PATH3 defines a complete, hop-by-hop path to the destination.

The path computation considers the three paths in that order. If they do not meet all constraints to the tunnel destination, a fourth path option invokes path computation to the destination using LSP attributes LSP-ATTRIB1 to reduce the required bandwidth to 5000 kbps, but limiting the path to links with attribute flags of 0.

Example 4-17 *Path and Tunnel Configuration in Cisco IOS*

```
mpls traffic-eng lsp attributes LSP-ATTRIB1
 affinity 0x0 mask 0xFFFFFFFF
 bandwidth 5000
 !
interface Tunnel1
 description FROM-ROUTER-TO-DST1
 ip unnumbered Loopback0
 no ip directed-broadcast
 tunnel destination 172.16.255.3
 tunnel mode mpls traffic-eng
 tunnel mpls traffic-eng priority 5 5
 tunnel mpls traffic-eng bandwidth  10000
 tunnel mpls traffic-eng path-option 5 explicit name PATH1
 tunnel mpls traffic-eng path-option 10 explicit name PATH2
 tunnel mpls traffic-eng path-option 15 explicit name PATH3
 tunnel mpls traffic-eng path-option 20 dynamic attributes LSP-ATTRIB1
 !
ip explicit-path name PATH1 enable
 next-address loose 172.16.255.5
 !
ip explicit-path name PATH2 enable
 exclude-address 172.16.8.2
 !
ip explicit-path name PATH3 enable
 next-address 172.16.0.1
 next-address 172.16.8.0
 !
```

Cisco IOS XR uses the **signalled-bandwidth**, **affinity**, **priority**, and **path-selection metric** tunnel commands to influence the path computation. These parameters have the same defaults as Cisco IOS if you do not specify them explicitly.

Example 4-18 shows a tunnel configuration in Cisco IOS XR with multiple path options. The tunnel has the following explicit constraints: 100,000 kbps of bandwidth, three path options, and an affinity value of F in hexadecimal notation. The first two paths are explicit paths with names:

- PATH1 defines a complete hop-by-hop path to the tunnel destination.
- PATH2 defines two addresses to exclude from the path computation.

The tunnel considers those two paths in that order. If the path computation cannot satisfy all constraints with those paths, it relies on the third and last path option that enable a dynamic path.

Example 4-18 *Path and Tunnel Configuration in Cisco IOS XR*

```
explicit-path name PATH1
 index 1 next-address ipv4 unicast 172.16.0.4
 index 2 next-address ipv4 unicast 172.16.0.7
 index 3 next-address ipv4 unicast 172.16.4.2
 !
explicit-path name PATH2
 index 1 exclude-address ipv4 unicast 172.16.255.131
 index 2 exclude-address ipv4 unicast 172.16.255.130
 !
interface tunnel-te1
 description FROM-ROUTER-TO-DST1
 ipv4 unnumbered Loopback0
 signalled-bandwidth 100000
 destination 172.16.255.2
 path-option 10 explicit name PATH1
 path-option 20 explicit name PATH2
 path-option 30 dynamic
 affinity f mask f
 !
```

NOTE   A headend always checks the accuracy of a path against the MPLS TE topology database before signaling the TE LSP. This behavior holds true even if you define a hop-by-hop explicit path to the destination. You can omit that path check by using the **verbatim** keyword on the path option.

Path Reoptimization

A headend can reoptimize automatically existing TE LSPs in search of a better path. You can tune a reoptimization timer using the **mpls traffic-eng reoptimize timers frequency** command in Cisco IOS. Cisco IOS XR uses the **reoptimize** command under the **mpls traffic-eng** configuration mode. In both cases, the reoptimization timer defaults to one hour. In addition to the timer-based mechanism, you can have an event-based reoptimization trigger in Cisco IOS using the **mpls traffic-eng reoptimize events link-up** global command. This command forces the reoptimization of TE LSPs when a physical interface in the MPLS TE network becomes operational.

You can also begin the reoptimization process manually. The **mpls traffic-eng reoptimize** EXEC command in Cisco IOS and Cisco IOS XR enables you to request TE LSP reoptimization. The command reoptimizes all eligible TE LSPs by default. Alternatively, you can specify the particular tunnel you want to reoptimize.

A headend will not attempt to reoptimize those TE LSP with a locked down path. You use the **lockdown** keyword as part of the path option or LSP attributes to indicate that the headend must not reoptimize the tunnel after it has established the TE LSP.

Verifying Path Computation

The **show mpls traffic-eng tunnels** command enables you to verify the path selection for a tunnel. Example 4-19 shows the command output in Cisco IOS for the tunnel configuration in Example 4-15. The output begins with the tunnel destination and then specifies the operational status of the path that indicates that there is a valid path. Subsequently, you can see the list of path options. The tunnel is using path option (dynamic) 20 to reach the destination. The path has a weight (or cost) of 3. Further down, you find the tunnel constraints (bandwidth, priorities, and affinity) and then details about the active path option (20 in this case). Finally, you can find details on the signaled path in the RSVP signaling component. In this case, path option 20 resulted in path 172.16.0.1, 172.16.192.1, 172.16.8.2, and 172.16.255.3. This command provides a wealth of information about TE LSPs. You will find the description of additional output fields throughout the chapter.

Example 4-19 *Examining TE LSP Status in Cisco IOS*

```
Router#show mpls traffic-eng tunnels

Name: FROM-ROUTER-TO-DST1                    (Tunnel1) Destination: 172.16.255.3
  Status:
    Admin: up          Oper: up     Path: valid       Signalling: connected
    path option 20, type dynamic (Basis for Setup, path weight 3)
    path option 5, type explicit PATH1
    path option 10, type explicit PATH2
    path option 15, type explicit PATH3

  Config Parameters:
    Bandwidth: 5000      kbps (Global) Priority: 5  5   Affinity: 0x0/0xFFFFFFFF
    Metric Type: TE (default)
    AutoRoute:  disabled LockDown: disabled  Loadshare: 5000      bw-based
    auto-bw: disabled
  Active Path Option Parameters:
    State: dynamic path option 20 is active
    BandwidthOverride: disabled  LockDown: disabled  Verbatim: disabled


  InLabel  :  -
  OutLabel : POS0/1/0, 120
  RSVP Signalling Info:
      Src 172.16.255.1, Dst 172.16.255.3, Tun_Id 1, Tun_Instance 1
    RSVP Path Info:
      My Address: 172.16.0.0
      Explicit Route: 172.16.0.1 172.16.192.1 172.16.8.2 172.16.255.3
      Record   Route:   NONE
      Tspec: ave rate=5000 kbits, burst=1000 bytes, peak rate=5000 kbits
    RSVP Resv Info:
```

Example 4-19 *Examining TE LSP Status in Cisco IOS (Continued)*

```
      Record   Route:   NONE
      Fspec: ave rate=5000 kbits, burst=1000 bytes, peak rate=5000 kbits
    History:
      Tunnel:
        Time since created: 2 minutes, 58 seconds
        Time since path change: 2 minutes, 58 seconds
        Number of LSP IDs (Tun_Instances) used: 1
      Current LSP:
        Uptime: 2 minutes, 58 seconds
  Router#
```

Example 4-20 shows the verification of the path computation result in Cisco IOS XR. As with Cisco IOS, you use the **show mpls traffic-eng tunnels** command for this purpose. This example shows the output for the tunnel configuration in Example 4-18. The tunnel details begin with the tunnel destination. Then, this example shows that the path computation could not find a valid path to the destination with the information available in the MPLS TE topology database. The lack of a path results in a down operational status. The output lists all path options and tunnel constraints plus details regarding the path computation failure in the history component. Using the failure details, you can review the MPLS TE topology database to narrow down the cause of the problem. Examples 4-13 and 4-14 illustrated how to examine the topology database.

Example 4-20 *Examining TE LSP Status in Cisco IOS XR*

```
RP/0/4/CPU0:Router#show mpls traffic-eng tunnels
Signalling Summary:
              LSP Tunnels Process:  running
                    RSVP Process:  running
                      Forwarding:  enabled
           Periodic reoptimization:  every 3600 seconds, next in 3403 seconds
           Periodic FRR Promotion:  every 300 seconds, next in 105 seconds
       Periodic auto-bw collection:  disabled

Name: tunnel-te1  Destination: 172.16.255.2
  Status:
    Admin:    up Oper: down   Path: not valid   Signalling: Down
    path option 10, type explicit PATH1
    path option 20, type explicit PATH2
    path option 30, type dynamic
    G-PID: 0x0800 (internally specified)

  Config Parameters:
    Bandwidth:   100000 kbps (Global) Priority:  7  7 Affinity: 0xf/0xf
    Metric Type: TE (default)
    AutoRoute:  disabled LockDown: disabled   Loadshare:   100000 bw-based
    Auto-bw: disabled(0/0) 0  Bandwidth Requested:   100000
    Direction: unidirectional
    Endpoint switching capability unkown, encoding type: unassigned
    Transit switching capability unkown, encoding type: unassigned
```

continues

Example 4-20 *Examining TE LSP Status in Cisco IOS XR (Continued)*

```
  History:
    Prior LSP:
      ID: path option 10 [3]
      Removal Trigger: path verification failed
      Last Error:
        PCALC:: Can't reach 172.16.0.4 on 172.16.255.4, from node
        172.16.255.129
Displayed 1 (of 1) heads, 0 (of 0) tails
Displayed 0 up, 1 down, 0 recovering, 0 recovered heads
RP/0/4/CPU0:Router#
```

You can manually begin the path computation process from the EXEC prompt. Both Cisco IOS and Cisco IOS XR provide the **show mpls traffic-eng topology path** command for this purpose. You can request the computation of a path for a particular tunnel or you can request a path to a destination with a particular set of constraints (bandwidth, priority, and affinity). The manual execution of path computation might show a path different from the current path. This situation does not trigger the reoptimization of the tunnel.

Example 4-21 and Example 4-22 show the output of the **show mpls traffic-eng topology path** command in Cisco IOS and Cisco IOS XR, respectively. Example 4-21 begins the path computation for Tunnel1 as Example 4-17 defined it. Example 4-22 illustrates the use of the command with an arbitrary choice of constraints. The command output displays the exact constraints that the path computation process used and the hop-by-hop path to the destination if the node found a valid path.

Example 4-21 *Manual Execution of Path Computation in Cisco IOS*

```
Router#show mpls traffic-eng topology path tunnel 1
Query Parameters:
  Destination: 172.16.255.3
  Bandwidth: 10000
  Priorities: 5 (setup), 5 (hold)
  Affinity: 0x0 (value), 0xFFFF (mask)
Query Results:
  Min Bandwidth Along Path: 145000 (kbps)
  Max Bandwidth Along Path: 145000 (kbps)
  Hop  0: 172.16.0.0      : affinity 00000000, bandwidth 145000 (kbps)
  Hop  1: 172.16.8.1      : affinity 00000000, bandwidth 145000 (kbps)
  Hop  2: 172.16.255.3
Router#
```

Example 4-22 *Manual Execution of Path Computation in Cisco IOS XR*

```
RP/0/4/CPU0:Router#show mpls traffic-eng topology path destination 172.16.255.2
bandwidth 1000
Path Setup to 172.16.255.2:
bw 1000 (CT0), min_bw 155000, metric: 2
```

Example 4-22 *Manual Execution of Path Computation in Cisco IOS XR (Continued)*

```
setup_pri 7, hold_pri 7
affinity_bits 0x0, affinity_mask 0xffffffff
Hop0:172.16.192.3
Hop1:172.16.4.2
Hop2:172.16.255.2
RP/0/4/CPU0:Router#
```

Signaling of TE LSPs

You can use node- and interface-level RSVP configuration to influence the signaling of TE LSPs. Cisco IOS XR requires explicit RSVP configuration to enable the signaling of TE LSPs. Cisco IOS enables it when you configured MPLS TE on the interface. In either case, most implementations configure explicitly different aspects of the protocol. At a minimum, you might want to configure the reservable bandwidth on a interface that RSVP will use for admission control. The next two sections discuss how to configure and verify the proper operation of RSVP for the signaling of TE LSPs.

Configuring RSVP

This section examines node configuration commands for RSVP control authentication, graceful restart, refresh behavior, and hello messages. In Cisco IOS, all RSVP node commands start with the **ip rsvp** prefix, and you enter them in global configuration. In Cisco IOS XR, you specify the RSVP node configuration under the **rsvp** configuration mode. All commands are optional in Cisco IOS. In Cisco IOS XR, the **interface** command is mandatory because it enables RSVP processing on individual interfaces. In addition, Cisco IOS XR uses refresh reduction and reliable messages by default, but the behavior is tunable per interface.

RSVP interface commands are optional in Cisco IOS and Cisco IOS XR. In Cisco IOS, all RSVP interface commands have the **ip rsvp** prefix and reside under the physical interface. In Cisco IOS XR, all interface commands reside under the submode that the **interface** command enables under the **rsvp** configuration mode. The nature of the interface commands differs depending on the operating systems. Cisco IOS XR enables you to tune message rate limiting, refresh reduction, and reliable messages per interface. In Cisco IOS, those features are part of the node configuration. In both operating systems, the MPLS TE tunnel does not require any RSVP configuration. The headend automatically signals the TE LSP when it finds a valid path.

Example 4-23 shows an RSVP configuration in Cisco IOS. In this example, the configuration enables the processing of RSVP signaling on interfaces POS0/1/0 and POS1/0/0 with a maximum reservable bandwidth of 155,000 kbps. As part of the global configuration, this node will use the RSVP reliable messaging and refresh reduction extensions. In addition, the node will act as a helper node for neighbors performing RSVP graceful restarts.

Example 4-23 *RSVP TE Configuration in Cisco IOS*

```
interface POS0/1/0
 ip address 172.16.0.0 255.255.255.254
 mpls traffic-eng tunnels
 ip rsvp bandwidth 155000
 !
interface POS1/0/0
 ip address 172.16.0.2 255.255.255.254
 mpls traffic-eng tunnels
 ip rsvp bandwidth 155000
 !
ip rsvp signalling refresh reduction
ip rsvp signalling hello graceful-restart mode help-neighbor
 !
```

Example 4-24 illustrates an RSVP configuration in Cisco IOS XR. The configuration enables RSVP on interfaces POS0/3/0/0 and POS0/3/0/1 with a bandwidth allocation of 155,000 kbps. The message retransmission timer for reliable message deliver will be 5000 ms on interface POS0/3/0/0. Finally, the configuration enables RSVP graceful restart with a refresh interval of 10,000 ms.

Example 4-24 *RSVP TE Configuration in Cisco IOS XR*

```
rsvp
 interface POS0/3/0/0
  bandwidth 155000
  signalling refresh reduction reliable retransmit-time 5000
 !
 interface POS0/3/0/1
  bandwidth 155000
 !
 signalling graceful-restart
 signalling hello graceful-restart refresh interval 10000
 !
```

Verifying RSVP

Many **show**, **clear**, and **debug** commands are available for RSVP in Cisco IOS and Cisco IOS XR. These commands begin with the **show ip rsvp**, **clear ip rsvp**, and **debug ip rsvp** prefixes, respectively. From that group, you can use the **show ip rsvp interface** command in Cisco IOS and the **show rsvp interface** command in Cisco IOS XR to examine the RSVP status on a particular interface. In addition, the **show ip rsvp counters** command in Cisco IOS and the **show rsvp counters** command in Cisco IOS XR will show you detailed counters on RSVP activity. The next section illustrates some additional verification commands for RSVP. The Cisco IOS and Cisco IOS XR documentation completely describes all commands.

Example 4-25 shows the output of the **show ip rsvp interface** command in Cisco IOS. The command shows the detailed status for interface POS0/1/0 with the configuration in Example 4-23. In this case, the interface configuration enabled RSVP. The protocol has allocated 10 Mbps out of the total RSVP bandwidth of 155 Mbps. The interface is not using RSVP authentication or generating RSVP hello messages.

Example 4-25 *Examine RSVP TE Interface Status in Cisco IOS*

```
Router#show ip rsvp interface detail pos0/1/0

PO0/1/0:
  RSVP: Enabled
   Interface State: Up
   Bandwidth:
    Curr allocated: 10M bits/sec
    Max. allowed (total): 155M bits/sec
    Max. allowed (per flow): 155M bits/sec
    Max. allowed for LSP tunnels using sub-pools (pool 1): 0 bits/sec
    Set aside by policy (total): 0 bits/sec
   Traffic Control:
    RSVP Data Packet Classification is ON
   Signalling:
    DSCP value used in RSVP msgs: 0x3F
    Number of refresh intervals to enforce blockade state: 4
  Authentication: disabled
    Key chain:    <none>
    Type:         md5
    Window size: 1
    Challenge:    disabled
  Hello Extension:
    State: Disabled
Router#
```

Example 4-26 illustrates the information that the **show rsvp interface** command provides in Cisco IOS XR. The command provides the detailed output for the interface POS0/3/0/0 with the configuration that Example 4-24 described. In this case, RSVP has not allocated any bandwidth out of the total RSVP bandwidth of 155 Mbps. The interface is using RSVP refresh reduction (supporting both summary refresh and bundle messages). RSVP has one neighbor on this interface, with IP address 172.16.0.0, which is using refresh reduction.

Example 4-26 *Examine RSVP TE Interface Status in Cisco IOS XR*

```
RP/0/4/CPU0:Router#show rsvp interface pos0/3/0/0 detail
INTERFACE: POS0/3/0/0 (ifh=0x4000300).
 VRF ID: 0x60000000 (Default).
 BW (bits/sec): Max=155M. MaxFlow=155M.
               Allocated=0 (0%). MaxSub=0.
 Signalling: No DSCP marking. No rate limiting.
 States in: 1. Max missed msgs: 4.
```

continues

Example 4-26 *Examine RSVP TE Interface Status in Cisco IOS XR (Continued)*

```
Expiry timer: Running (every 30s). Refresh interval: 45s.
Normal Refresh timer: Not running. Summary refresh timer: Running.
Refresh reduction local: Enabled. Summary Refresh: Enabled (4096 bytes max).
Reliable summary refresh: Disabled. Bundling: Enabled. (4096 bytes max).
Ack hold: 400 ms, Ack max size: 4096 bytes. Retransmit: 5000ms.
Neighbor information:
   Neighbor-IP    Nbor-MsgIds States-out  Refresh-Reduction Expiry(min::sec)
   ------------- -------------- ---------- ------------------ ---------------
    172.16.0.0               1          1           Enabled 14::50

RP/0/4/CPU0:Router#
```

Example 4-27 illustrates the output of the **show ip rsvp counters** command in Cisco IOS. The command shows aggregate and per-interface counters for each RSVP message type. In this case, a filter reduces the output to the aggregate counter information. You can verify the number of RSVP messages the node has sent and received. In addition, you find information about disconnect reasons for RSVP sessions.

Example 4-27 *Examining RSVP Counters in Cisco IOS*

```
Router#show ip rsvp counters ¦ begin All
All Interfaces          Recv    Xmit                        Recv      Xmit
      Path                 0       2   Resv                    2         0
      PathError            0       0   ResvError               0         0
      PathTear             0       2   ResvTear                0         0
      ResvConf             0       0   RTearConf               0         0
      Ack                343       3   Srefresh              298       340
      Hello             1112    1111   IntegrityChalle         0         0
      IntegrityRespon      0       0   DSBM_WILLING            0         0
      I_AM_DSBM            0       0   Errors                  0         0

Error Distribution      Recv    Xmit
      Authentication       0       0
      Other                0       0

Recv Msg Queues                 Current     Max
      RSVP                          0         1
      Hello (per-I/F)               0         0
      Awaiting Authentication       0         0

States
   Reason for Teardown                    State torn down
                                          Path    Resv-In   Resv-Out
   PathTear arrival                         0         0         0
   ResvTear arrival                         0         0         0
   Local application requested tear         2         1         0
   Output or Input I/F went down            0         0         0
   Missed refreshes                         0         0         0
   Preemption                               0         0         0
   Backup tunnel failed for FRR Active LSP  0         0         0
   Reroutabilty changed for FRR Active LSP  0         0         0
```

Example 4-27   *Examining RSVP Counters in Cisco IOS (Continued)*

```
          Hello RR Client (HST) requested tear      0        0        0
          Graceful Restart (GR) requested tear      0        0        0
          Downstream neighbor SSO-restarting        0        0        0
          Resource unavailable                      0        0        0
          Policy rejection                          0        0        0
          Policy server sync failed                 0        0        0
          Traffic control error                     0        0        0
          Error in received message                 0        0        0
          Unsupported change in Resv                0        0        0
          Unsupported change in Resv (Label)        0        0        0
          Label programming failed                  0        0        0
          Non RSVP HOP upstream, TE LSP             0        0        0
          Other                                     0        0        0
Router#
```

Example 4-28 shows how to examine the different RSVP counters in Cisco IOS XR using the **show rsvp counters** command. The information is almost identical to the Cisco IOS output, with the exception that this command currently obviates the counters for the disconnect reasons of RSVP sessions.

Example 4-28   *Examining RSVP Counters in Cisco IOS XR*

```
RP/0/4/CPU0:Router#show rsvp counters messages ¦ begin All
 All RSVP Interfaces    Recv    Xmit                      Recv    Xmit
     Path                  8     647   Resv               717       0
     PathError             0       0   ResvError            0       0
     PathTear              9       8   ResvTear             0       0
     ResvConfirm           0       0   Hello             1190    1595
     Ack                   9     362   SRefresh           355     314
     Retransmit                    0   Rate Limited                 0
     OutOfOrder            0
     Bundle                0       8   AckSubmsg            0       7
     PathSubmsg            0       0   ResvSubmsg           0       8
     PathTearSubmsg        0       0   ResvTearSubmsg       0       0
     PathErrorSubmsg       0       0   ResvErrorSubmsg      0       0

RP/0/4/CPU0:Router#
```

Verifying Signaling of TE LSPs

Example 4-29 shows the signaling status of a TE LSP using the **show mpls traffic-eng tunnels** command in Cisco IOS. The successful establishment of a TE LSP results in a signaling status of connected (rather than down). In that case, you will see the output interface and label information for the TE LSP, along with an RSVP section showing the most important Path and Resv details. In this example, you can see that the TE LSP is connected. It uses output interface POS0/1/0 and output label 31. The TE LSP does not show an input label, which evidences that the headend executed the command. The RSVP session has reserved 10 Mbps and signals addresses 172.16.0.1, 172.16.8.0, and 172.16.255.3 in the RSVP *explicit route object* (ERO).

Example 4-29 *Examining TE LSP Signaling Status in Cisco IOS*

```
Router#show mpls traffic-eng tunnels

Name: FROM-ROUTER-TO-DST1                    (Tunnel1) Destination: 172.16.255.3
  Status:
    Admin: up          Oper: up      Path: valid       Signalling: connected
      path option 10, type dynamic (Basis for Setup, path weight 2)

  Config Parameters:
    Bandwidth: 10000    kbps (Global) Priority: 5  5   Affinity: 0x0/0xFFFF
    Metric Type: TE (default)
    AutoRoute:  disabled  LockDown: disabled  Loadshare: 10000    bw-based
    auto-bw: disabled
  Active Path Option Parameters:
    State: dynamic path option 10 is active
    BandwidthOverride: disabled  LockDown: disabled  Verbatim: disabled



    InLabel  :  -
    OutLabel : POS0/1/0, 31
    RSVP Signalling Info:
        Src 172.16.255.1, Dst 172.16.255.3, Tun_Id 1, Tun_Instance 9277
      RSVP Path Info:
        My Address: 172.16.255.1
        Explicit Route: 172.16.0.1 172.16.8.0 172.16.255.3
        Record   Route:   NONE
        Tspec: ave rate=10000 kbits, burst=1000 bytes, peak rate=10000 kbits
      RSVP Resv Info:
        Record   Route:   NONE
        Fspec: ave rate=10000 kbits, burst=1000 bytes, peak rate=10000 kbits
  History:
    Tunnel:
      Time since created: 4 days, 1 hours, 20 minutes
      Time since path change: 7 seconds
      Number of LSP IDs (Tun_Instances) used: 9277
    Current LSP:
      Uptime: 7 seconds
    Prior LSP:
      ID: path option 10 [9274]
      Removal Trigger: tunnel shutdown
Router#
```

Example 4-30 shows the signaling status of a TE LSP using the **show mpls traffic-eng tunnels** command in Cisco IOS XR. The output format differs slightly when you compare it with Cisco IOS. However, you follow the same approach of verifying the signaling status as connected and then consulting the signaling component of the output.

Example 4-30   *Examining TE LSP Signaling Status in Cisco IOS XR*

```
RP/0/4/CPU0:Router#show mpls traffic-eng tunnels detail
Signalling Summary:
              LSP Tunnels Process:  running
                     RSVP Process:  running
                       Forwarding:  enabled
           Periodic reoptimization:  every 3600 seconds, next in 229 seconds
            Periodic FRR Promotion:  every 300 seconds, next in 205 seconds
         Periodic auto-bw collection:  disabled

Name: tunnel-te1  Destination: 172.16.255.2
  Status:
    Admin:    up Oper:   up   Path:  valid   Signalling: connected

    path option 10,  type explicit PATH1 (Basis for Setup, path weight 3)
    G-PID: 0x0800 (derived from egress interface properties)

  Config Parameters:
    Bandwidth:   100000 kbps (CT0) Priority:  7  7 Affinity: 0x0/0xffff
    Metric Type: TE (default)
    AutoRoute:  disabled  LockDown: disabled   Loadshare:   100000 bw-based
    Auto-bw: disabled(0/0) 0  Bandwidth Requested:   100000
    Direction: unidirectional
    Endpoint switching capability: unknown, encoding type: unassigned
    Transit switching capability: unknown, encoding type: unassigned

  History:
    Tunnel has been up for: 05:04:07
    Current LSP:
      Uptime: 05:04:07
    Prior LSP:
      ID: path option 10 [1]
      Removal Trigger: tunnel shutdown
  Current LSP Info:
    Instance: 2, Signaling Area: ospf DEFAULT area 0
    Uptime: 00:04:07
    Incoming Label: -
    Outgoing Interface: POS0/3/0/3, Outgoing Label: 35
    Path Info:
      Explicit Route:
        Strict, 172.16.0.4
        Strict, 172.16.0.7
        Strict, 172.16.4.2
        Strict, 172.16.255.2
      Record Route: None
      Tspec: avg rate=100000 kbits, burst=1000 bytes, peak rate=100000 kbits
    Resv Info:
      Record Route: None
      Fspec: avg rate=100000 kbits, burst=1000 bytes, peak rate=100000 kbits
Displayed 1 (of 1) heads, 0 (of 0) midpoints, 0 (of 0) tails
Displayed 1 up, 0 down, 0 recovering, 0 recovered heads
RP/0/4/CPU0:Router#
Strict, 172.16.255.2
```

continues

Example 4-30 *Examining TE LSP Signaling Status in Cisco IOS XR*

```
Record Route: None
Tspec: avg rate=100000 kbits, burst=1000 bytes, peak rate=100000 kbits
Resv Info: Record Route: None
Fspec: avg rate=100000 kbits, burst=1000 bytes, peak rate=100000 kbits
Displayed 1 (of 1) heads, 0 (of 0) midpoints, 0 (of 0) tails
Displayed 1 up, 0 down, 0 recovering, 0 recovered heads
RP/0/4/CPU0:Router#
```

You can query the session state to review the details of the signaling information that RSVP used to establish a TE LSP. Cisco IOS uses the **show ip rsvp sender detail** and **show ip rsvp reservation detail** commands to generate a complete output of the Path and Resv state information. Cisco IOS XR uses the **show ip rsvp sender detail** and **show ip rsvp reservation detail** commands for the same purpose. Examples 4-31 and 4-32 illustrate the command output in Cisco IOS and Cisco IOS XR, respectively.

Example 4-31 *Examining RSVP Session State in Cisco IOS*

```
Router#show ip rsvp sender detail
PATH:
  Tun Dest:   172.16.255.3  Tun ID: 1  Ext Tun ID: 172.16.255.1
  Tun Sender: 172.16.255.1  LSP ID: 17
  Path refreshes:
    sent:      to   NHOP 172.16.0.1 on POS0/1/0
  Session Attr:
    Setup Prio: 5, Holding Prio: 5
    Flags: (0x4) SE Style
    Session Name: FROM-ROUTER-TO-DST1
  ERO: (incoming)
    172.16.255.1 (Strict IPv4 Prefix, 8 bytes, /32)
    172.16.0.1 (Strict IPv4 Prefix, 8 bytes, /32)
    172.16.8.0 (Strict IPv4 Prefix, 8 bytes, /32)
    172.16.255.3 (Strict IPv4 Prefix, 8 bytes, /32)
  ERO: (outgoing)
    172.16.0.1 (Strict IPv4 Prefix, 8 bytes, /32)
    172.16.8.0 (Strict IPv4 Prefix, 8 bytes, /32)
    172.16.255.3 (Strict IPv4 Prefix, 8 bytes, /32)
  Traffic params - Rate: 10M bits/sec, Max. burst: 1K bytes
    Min Policed Unit: 0 bytes, Max Pkt Size 2147483647 bytes
  Fast-Reroute Backup info:
    Inbound  FRR: Not active
    Outbound FRR: No backup tunnel selected
  Path ID handle: 03000404.
  Incoming policy: Accepted. Policy source(s): MPLS/TE
  Status: Proxied
  Output on POS0/1/0. Policy status: Forwarding. Handle: 2E000407
    Policy source(s): MPLS/TE

Router#
Router#show ip rsvp reservation detail
Reservation:
```

Example 4-31 *Examining RSVP Session State in Cisco IOS (Continued)*

```
      Tun Dest:   172.16.255.3  Tun ID: 1  Ext Tun ID: 172.16.255.1
      Tun Sender: 172.16.255.1  LSP ID: 17
      Next Hop: 172.16.0.1 on POS0/1/0
      Label: 140 (outgoing)
      Reservation Style is Shared-Explicit, QoS Service is Controlled-Load
      Resv ID handle: 03000406.
      Created: 22:11:18 UTC Mon Jul 7 2003
      Average Bitrate is 10M bits/sec, Maximum Burst is 1K bytes
      Min Policed Unit: 0 bytes, Max Pkt Size: 0 bytes
      Status:
      Policy: Accepted. Policy source(s): MPLS/TE
Router#
```

Example 4-32 *Examining RSVP Session State in Cisco IOS XR*

```
RP/0/4/CPU0:Router#show rsvp sender detail
PATH: IPv4-LSP Session addr: 172.16.255.2. TunID: 1. LSPId: 33.
 Source addr: 172.16.255.129. ExtID: 172.16.255.129.
 Prot: Off. Backup tunnel: None.
 Setup Priority: 7, Reservation Priority: 0
 Rate: 100M bits/sec. Burst: 1K bytes. Peak: 100M bits/sec.
 Min unit: 40 bytes, Max unit: 500 bytes
 Flags: Local Sender.
 State expires in 0.000 sec.
 Policy:  Accepted. Policy source(s): Default.
 Header info: RSVP TTL=255. IP TTL=255. Flags: 0x0. TOS=0xff.
 Input interface: None. Previous hop: 0.0.0.0 (lih: 0x0).
 Output on PO0/3/0/3. Policy: Forwarding.
 Class-Type: None.
 Explicit Route (Incoming):
     Strict, 172.16.0.4/32
     Strict, 172.16.0.7/32
     Strict, 172.16.4.2/32
     Strict, 172.16.255.2/32
 Explicit Route (Outgoing):
     Strict, 172.16.0.4/32
     Strict, 172.16.0.7/32
     Strict, 172.16.4.2/32
     Strict, 172.16.255.2/32

RP/0/4/CPU0:Router#
RP/0/4/CPU0:Router#show rsvp reservation detail
RESV: IPv4-LSP Session addr: 172.16.255.2. TunID: 1. LSPId: 33.
 Source addr: 172.16.255.129. ExtID: 172.16.255.129.
 Input adjusted interface: PO0/3/0/3. Input physical interface: PO0/3/0/3.
 Next hop: 172.16.0.4 (lih: 0x59300004).
 Style: Shared-Explicit. Service: Controlled-Load.
 Rate: 100M bits/sec. Burst: 1K bytes. Peak: 100M bits/sec.
 MTU min: 0, max: 0 bytes.
 Flags: None.
 State expires in 231.030 sec.
```

continues

Example 4-32 *Examining RSVP Session State in Cisco IOS XR (Continued)*

```
Policy:  Accepted. Policy source(s): Default.
Header info: RSVP TTL=255. IP TTL=255. Flags: 0x0. TOS=0xc0.
Resource:
 Labels: Outgoing downstream: 34.

RP/0/4/CPU0:Router#
```

Traffic Selection

You can use several mechanisms to select what traffic a tunnel carries. These mechanisms are independent of the establishment of the TE LSP. Traffic selection takes place at the tunnel headend. Any other node along the path of a TE LSP cannot inject traffic into that TE LSP. Cisco IOS and Cisco IOS XR offer multiple alternatives to perform traffic selection. The next two sections provide an overview of these mechanisms.

Traffic-Selection Alternatives

You can use static methods to inject IP traffic into a tunnel. The two static mechanisms available are static routes and policy-based routing. In both cases, you need to specify the tunnel as the output interface for the routing decision. These two mechanisms can be simple, but their static nature can affect their applicability in many MPLS TE implementations.

Autoroute and forwarding adjacencies enable you to route IP traffic dynamically into a tunnel. The autoroute functionality instructs the IGP to use MPLS TE tunnels as the next-hop interface to reach tailends and downstream destinations. The IGP does not need to build adjacencies through the tunnels. You enable this behavior with the **tunnel mpls traffic-eng autoroute** command in Cisco IOS. Cisco IOS XR uses the **autoroute** command. By default, prefixes pointing to tunnel interfaces will have the metric of the shortest physical path. The same commands enable you to tune those metrics. In contrast with autoroute, you can configure a forwarding adjacency between the headend and tailend to instruct the IGP to build a routing adjacency and include the tunnel as another link in their IGP advertisements. In some scenarios, this behavior is desirable. In most cases, autoroute suffices and provides a more scalable solution.

Pseudowire tunnel selection are two additional mechanisms available to inject traffic into a tunnel. The next section covers CBTS, given the importance to use MPLS TE to improve the quality of service of an MPLS network.

Class-Based Tunnel Selection

You can also use MPLS EXP values as tunnel-selection criteria (that is, CBTS). You can use CBTS to discriminate as to which MPLS EXP values a node forwards through specific tunnels. The node must have selected a group of tunnels with the same tailend to reach a particular destination. The selection of the tunnels could be the result of static routes or autoroute configuration. You use the **tunnel mpls traffic-eng exp** command in Cisco IOS to configure CBTS under the tunnel interface. You should configure at least one of the tunnels as a default, or explicitly configure all possible MPLS EXP values among the tunnels that reach the destination.

Figure 4-2 shows node A that uses CBTS to reach two other nodes D and H. Node A has Tunnel1 and Tunnel2 to reach node D. It also has Tunnel3 and Tunnel4 to reach node H. Using CBTS, node A sends packets with destination D down Tunnel1 if they have an MPLS EXP value of 5. It sends all other packets to destination D through Tunnel2. Similarly, node A sends all packets to destination H through Tunnel3 if they have MPLS EXP values 3 or 4. All other packets to destination H follow Tunnel4.

Figure 4-2   *CBTS*

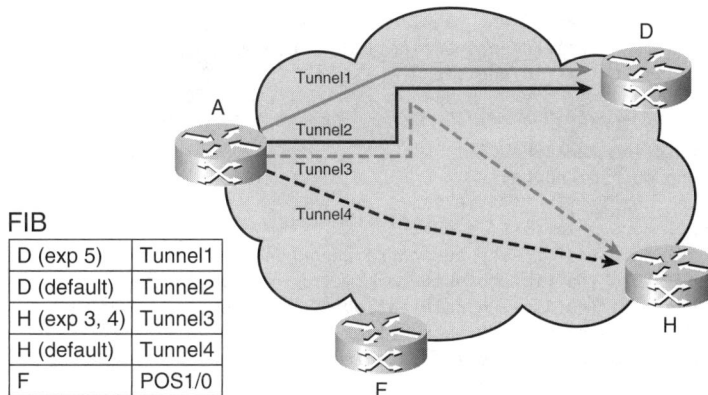

FIB

D (exp 5)	Tunnel1
D (default)	Tunnel2
H (exp 3, 4)	Tunnel3
H (default)	Tunnel4
F	POS1/0

Example 4-33 shows the configuration in node A. Two static routes define Tunnel1 and Tunnel2 as output interfaces for prefix 192.168.0.0/24. Tunnel3 and Tunnel4 select traffic using the autoroute mechanism. Without CBTS, node A would load balance traffic to each destination using the two respective tunnels.

Example 4-33   *CBTS in Cisco IOS Using Autoroute and Static Routes*

```
interface Tunnel1
 description A2D-EF
 ip unnumbered Loopback0
 tunnel destination 172.16.255.3
 tunnel mode mpls traffic-eng
 tunnel mpls traffic-eng priority 5 5
 tunnel mpls traffic-eng bandwidth  10000
```

continues

Example 4-33 *CBTS in Cisco IOS Using Autoroute and Static Routes (Continued)*

```
 tunnel mpls traffic-eng path-option 10 dynamic
 tunnel mpls traffic-eng exp 5
!
interface Tunnel2
 description A2D-DEFAULT
 ip unnumbered Loopback0
 tunnel destination 172.16.255.3
 tunnel mode mpls traffic-eng
 tunnel mpls traffic-eng priority 7 7
 tunnel mpls traffic-eng bandwidth  75000
 tunnel mpls traffic-eng path-option 10 explicit name PATH1
 tunnel mpls traffic-eng exp default
!
interface Tunnel3
 description A2H-3-4
 ip unnumbered Loopback0
 tunnel destination 172.16.255.2
 tunnel mode mpls traffic-eng
 tunnel mpls traffic-eng autoroute announce
 tunnel mpls traffic-eng autoroute metric relative -2
 tunnel mpls traffic-eng priority 7 7
 tunnel mpls traffic-eng bandwidth  50000
 tunnel mpls traffic-eng path-option 10 dynamic
 tunnel mpls traffic-eng exp 3 4
!
interface Tunnel4
 description A2H-DEFAULT
 ip unnumbered Loopback0
 tunnel destination 172.16.255.2
 tunnel mode mpls traffic-eng
 tunnel mpls traffic-eng autoroute announce
 tunnel mpls traffic-eng autoroute metric relative -2
 tunnel mpls traffic-eng path-option 10 dynamic
 tunnel mpls traffic-eng path-selection metric igp
 tunnel mpls traffic-eng exp default
!
ip route 192.168.0.0 255.255.255.0 Tunnel1
ip route 192.168.0.0 255.255.255.0 Tunnel2
!
```

TIP   Using CBTS, you can send some MPLS EXP values through engineered paths and some other values through the IGP shortest path for a specific destination. To use the IGP shortest path, you need to define a tunnel without any constraints and enable autoroute on that tunnel. The path selection should use the IGP metric if you have configured TE metrics explicitly. That is exactly the purpose of Tunnel4 in Example 4-27.

DiffServ-Aware Traffic Engineering (DS-TE)

Cisco IOS and Cisco IOS XR provide support for the DS-TE protocol extensions. You can use either IS-IS or OSPF as your IGP. Both operating systems support the *Russian dolls model* (RDM) and *maximum allocation model* (MAM) for bandwidth constraints. The configuration and verification commands for DS-TE are generally extensions to the original MPLS TE commands. The following section, "Prestandard DS-TE," briefly describes the early DS-TE implementation. The subsequent sections focus on the standard DS-TE implementation.

Prestandard DS-TE

Cisco IOS and Cisco IOS XR support a prestandard and a standard implementation of DS-TE. During the standardization process, the specifications of the protocol extensions evolved since the time that Cisco IOS and Cisco IOS XR introduced support for DS-TE. These implementations are not interoperable because they use different protocol extensions. Moving forward, you can expect this early implementation to support only a subset of the functionality available in the standard implementation. Table 4-1 illustrates the differences between prestandard and standard DS-TE in Cisco IOS and Cisco IOS XR. The following sections focus on the standard DS-TE functionality.

Table 4-1   *Differences Between Prestandard and Standard DS-TE*

Prestandard DS-TE	Standard DS-TE
Enabled by default	Explicitly configured using the **mpls traffic-eng ds-te mode ietf** command in Cisco IOS and the **ds-te mode ietf** command in Cisco IOS XR
Supports RDM	Supports RDM and MAM
No RSVP extensions; subpool signaled as guaranteed service; global pool signaled as controlled-load service.	Uses RSVP extensions (CLASSTYPE object)
Modifies IGP link advertisements to include 2 pools at 8 priority levels each (16 entries per link total)	No modifications to IGP link advertisements (unreserved bandwidth at 8 priority levels), but new semantics
Bandwidth constraints and bandwidth constraint model information *not included* in IGP link advertisement	Bandwidth constraints and bandwidth constraint model information *included* in IGP link advertisement

NOTE   Cisco IOS also supports a migration mode for DS-TE deployments that used the initial DS-TE implementation. In this migration mode, a node uses prestandard link flooding and TE LSP signaling but can process prestandard and standard link flooding and TE LSP signaling. You can enable this migration mode with the **mpls traffic-eng ds-te mode migration** command.

Class-Types and TE-Class

A DS-TE deployment requires the definition of TE-Classes, Class-Types for MPLS TE tunnels, and bandwidth constraints that links will enforce. DS-TE reuses the MPLS TE mechanisms and commands. In Cisco IOS, you enable DS-TE on a node using the **mpls traffic-eng ds-te mode ietf** command and enter the configuration mode where you define any TE-Class with the **mpls traffic-eng ds-te te-classes** command. Cisco IOS XR uses the **ds-te mode ietf** command to enable DS-TE and the **ds-te te-classes** command to enter the configuration mode for TE-Class definition. These two commands reside under the **mpls traffic-eng** configuration mode. The **te-class** command allows you to define individual classes under the TE-Class configuration. Table 4-2 shows the default TE-Class definitions in both operating systems.

Table 4-2   *Default TE-Class Definition in Cisco IOS and Cisco IOS XR*

TE-Class	Class-Type	Priority
0	0	7
1	1	7
2	Unused	Unused
3	Unused	Unused
4	0	0
5	1	0
6	Unused	Unused
7	Unused	Unused

Examples 4-34 and 4-35 show a TE-Class configuration in Cisco IOS and Cisco IOS XR, respectively.

In Example 4-34, a CT1 TE LSP can preempt a CT0 TE LSP but not vice versa. A CT0 TE LSP with a better priority (for instance, those corresponding to TE-Class 4) could still preempt a CT0 TE LSP with worse priority (TE-Class 5 through 7).

Example 4-34 *TE-Class Definition in Cisco IOS*

```
mpls traffic-eng tunnels
mpls traffic-eng ds-te te-classes
 te-class 0 class-type 1 priority 0
 te-class 1 class-type 1 priority 1
 te-class 2 class-type 1 priority 2
 te-class 3 class-type 1 priority 3
 te-class 4 class-type 0 priority 4
 te-class 5 class-type 0 priority 5
 te-class 6 class-type 0 priority 6
 te-class 7 class-type 0 priority 7
mpls traffic-eng ds-te mode ietf
 !
```

Example 4-35 shows a different TE-Class definition using Cisco IOS XR. In this case, a CT1 TE LSP can preempt some CT0 TE LSPs and vice versa. However, Other TE LSPs cannot preempt CT1 TE LSPs corresponding to TE-Class 0. This configuration defines only a subset of the eight maximum TE-Classes you can specify.

Example 4-35 *TE-Class Definition in Cisco IOS XR*

```
mpls traffic-eng
 interface POS0/3/0/0
 !
 interface POS0/3/0/1
 !
 ds-te mode ietf
 ds-te te-classes
  te-class 0 class-type 1 priority 0
  te-class 1 class-type 0 priority 1
  te-class 2 class-type 1 priority 2
  te-class 3 class-type 0 priority 3
  te-class 4 unused
  te-class 5 unused
  te-class 6 unused
  te-class 7 unused
 !
 !
```

Defining a DS-TE Tunnel Interface

Example 4-36 shows the configuration of two DS-TE tunnels in Cisco IOS. Tunnel1 signals CT1 with setup priority 0. The **class-type** keyword in the **tunnel mpls traffic-eng bandwidth** command instructs the node to use CT1. Tunnel2 signals Class-Type 0 with priority 7. These two tunnels correspond to TE-Class 0 and 7 in Example 4-34, respectively. The **tunnel mpls traffic-eng bandwidth** command defines CT0 TE LSPs by default if you do not specify the **class-type** (or **sub-pool**) keyword. The class type and priority that you configure for a tunnel must be consistent with your TE-Class definitions, and those definitions must be consistent throughout your DS-TE network.

Example 4-36 *MPLS TE Tunnels Using DS-TE in Cisco IOS*

```
interface Tunnel1
 description FROM-ROUTER-TO-DST1-CT1
 ip unnumbered Loopback0
 tunnel destination 172.16.255.131
 tunnel mode mpls traffic-eng
 tunnel mpls traffic-eng priority 0 0
 tunnel mpls traffic-eng bandwidth class-type 1 5000
 tunnel mpls traffic-eng path-option 20 dynamic
 !
interface Tunnel2
 description FROM-ROUTER-TO-DST1-CT0
 ip unnumbered Loopback0
 tunnel destination 172.16.255.131
 tunnel mode mpls traffic-eng
 tunnel mpls traffic-eng priority 7 7
 tunnel mpls traffic-eng bandwidth  100000
 tunnel mpls traffic-eng path-option 20 dynamic
 !
```

Example 4-37 shows the configuration of two DS-TE tunnels in Cisco IOS XR. The **class-type** keyword in the **signalled-bandwidth** command specifies the Class-Type to 1. If you do not use the **sub-pool** keyword, the node signals CT0 for the TE LSP. In this case, tunnel-te1 uses CT1 with priority 2, and tunnel-te2 uses CT0 with priority 3. Those combinations correspond to TE-Class 2 and 3 in Example 4-35, respectively. Again, the Class-Type and priorities that you configure for a tunnel must match a valid TE-Class, and your TE-Class definitions must be consistent throughout your DS-TE network.

Example 4-37 *MPLS TE Tunnels Using DS-TE in Cisco IOS XR*

```
interface tunnel-te1
 description FROM-ROUTER-TO-DST1-CT1
 ipv4 unnumbered Loopback0
 priority 2 2
 signalled-bandwidth class-type 1 5000
 destination 172.16.255.130
 path-option 30 dynamic
 !
interface tunnel-te2
 description FROM-ROUTER-TO-DST1-CT0
 ipv4 unnumbered Loopback0
 priority 3 3
 signalled-bandwidth 50000
 destination 172.16.255.130
 path-option 30 dynamic
 !
```

Configuring Bandwidth Constraints

You need to define the per-link bandwidth constraints throughout your DS-TE network. Cisco IOS supports the RDM and MAM. RDM is the default bandwidth constraints mode. You use the **mpls traffic-eng ds-te bc-model mam** command to enable MAM. The **ip rsvp bandwidth** interface command specifies the bandwidth constraints for a link. The command uses the **rdm** and **mam** keywords to associate the constraints to a particular model. For RDM, the first bandwidth amount in the command specifies **BC0**. A second bandwidth amount following the **sub-pool** keyword specifies **BC1**. For MAM, you use the **max-reservable-bw** keyword to define the maximum reservable bandwidth. The **bc0** and **bc1** keywords enable you to specify **BC0** and **BC1**, respectively. You can also specify BC1 with the **sub-pool** keyword.

Example 4-38 shows the configuration of the RDM bandwidth constraints that two interfaces will enforce. In this case, interface POS0/1/0 has a BC0 of 100,000 kbps and a BC1 of 0. Interface POS1/0/0 has a BC0 of 155,000 kbps and a BC1 of 55,000 kbps.

Example 4-38   *Interfaces Using DS-TE with RDM in Cisco IOS*

```
interface POS0/1/0
 ip address 172.16.0.0 255.255.255.254
 mpls traffic-eng tunnels
 ip rsvp bandwidth rdm bc0 100000
!
interface POS1/0/0
 ip address 172.16.0.2 255.255.255.254
 mpls traffic-eng tunnels
 ip rsvp bandwidth rdm bc0 155000 bc1 55000
!
```

Example 4-39 illustrates the configuration of MAM in Cisco IOS. In this case, both interfaces POS0/1/0 and POS1/0/0 have a maximum reservable bandwidth of 155,000 kbps. Interface POS0/1/0 divides the maximum reservable bandwidth in 100,000 kbps for BC0 and 55,000 for BC1. Interface POS1/0/0 uses a different approach where both BC0 and BC1 are 90,000 kbps and their sum exceeds the maximum reservable bandwidth. These constraints facilitate bandwidth sharing between CT0 and CT1 on this interface.

Example 4-39   *Interfaces Using DS-TE with MAM in Cisco IOS*

```
mpls traffic-eng ds-te bc-model mam
!
interface POS0/1/0
 ip address 172.16.0.0 255.255.255.254
 mpls traffic-eng tunnels
 ip rsvp bandwidth mam max-reservable-bw 155000 bc0 100000 bc1 55000
!
interface POS1/0/0
 ip address 172.16.0.2 255.255.255.254
 mpls traffic-eng tunnels
 ip rsvp bandwidth mam max-reservable-bw 155000 bc0 90000 bc1 90000
!
```

Cisco IOS XR also supports both RDM and MAM. You select the bandwidth constraint model using the **ds-te bc-model** command, with RDM being the default model. You specify BC0 with the **bc0** keyword in the **bandwidth** interface command under the **rsvp** configuration mode. The **bc1** keyword defines BC1. The same **bandwidth** command specifies the model the bandwidth constraints apply to with the **rdm** and **mam** keywords. The model you configure on the node must match the model you configure with the **bandwidth** command. When you define MAM constraints, the **max-reservable-bw** keyword defines the maximum reservable bandwidth on the interface.

NOTE   Consult the software documentation for the most updated information on the number of bandwidth constraints that a particular device can support.

Example 4-40 shows the configuration of RDM in Cisco IOS XR. In this case, interface POS0/3/0/0 has a BC0 of 155,000 kbps and a BC1 value of 55,000 kbps. Interface POS0/3/0/1 has a slightly different configuration with a BC0 of 100,000 kbps and a BC1 of 55,000 kbps.

Example 4-40 *Interfaces Using DS-TE with RDM in Cisco IOS XR*

```
rsvp
 interface POS0/3/0/0
  bandwidth rdm bc0 155000 bc1 55000
 !
 interface POS0/3/0/1
  bandwidth rdm bc0 100000 bc1 55000
 !
!
```

Example 4-41 illustrates the configuration of MAM in Cisco IOS XR. Interface POS0/3/0/0 has a maximum reservable bandwidth of 155,000 kbps, a BC0 of 100,000 kbps, and a BC1 of 100,000 kbps. Interface POS0/3/0/1 has a maximum reservable bandwidth of 155,000 kbps, a BC0 of 100,000 kbps, and a BC1 of 55,000 kbps. Notice that for interface POS0/3/0/0, the sum of the two bandwidth constraints is higher than the maximum reservable bandwidth to improve bandwidth sharing acess CTs with this model.

Example 4-41 *Interfaces Using DS-TE with MAM in Cisco IOS XR*

```
rsvp
 interface POS0/3/0/0
  bandwidth mam max-reservable-bw 155000 bc0 100000 bc1 100000
 !
 interface POS0/3/0/1
  bandwidth mam max-reservable-bw 155000 bc0 100000 bc1 55000
 !
!
```

Example 4-41 *Interfaces Using DS-TE with MAM in Cisco IOS XR (Continued)*

```
mpls traffic-eng
 interface POS0/3/0/0
 !
 interface POS0/3/0/1
 !
 ds-te mode ietf
 ds-te bc-model mam
 !
```

Verifying DS-TE Link Information Distribution

DS-TE slightly modifies existing verification and **debug** commands instead of introducing new ones. Therefore, you continue to use the troubleshooting commands that previous verification sections discussed, primarily **show mpls traffic-eng link-management advertisements**, **show mpls traffic-eng topology**, and **show mpls traffic-eng tunnels**.

Example 4-42 illustrates the modification that DS-TE introduces to the output of the **show mpls traffic-eng topology** command in Cisco IOS. Similarly, Example 4-43 illustrates the output of the **show mpls traffic-eng topology** command in Cisco IOS XR when you enable DS-TE. Notice that both outputs highlight the bandwidth constraint model, the bandwidth constraint values, and the bandwidth available for each of the TE-Classes for each link.

Example 4-42 *Examining the MPLS TE Topology Database with DS-TE Enabled in Cisco IOS*

```
Router#show mpls traffic-eng topology 172.16.255.1

IGP Id: 172.16.255.1, MPLS TE Id:172.16.255.1 Router Node  (ospf 100  area 0) id 1
      link[0]: Point-to-Point, Nbr IGP Id: 172.16.255.131, nbr_node_id:2, gen:121
            frag_id 0, Intf Address:172.16.0.2, Nbr Intf Address:172.16.0.3
            TE metric:1, IGP metric:1, attribute flags:0x0
            SRLGs: None
            physical_bw: 155000 (kbps),

            BC Model Id: RDM
            BC0 (max_reservable): 155000 (kbps)
            BC0 (max_reservable_bw_global): 155000 (kbps)
            BC1 (max_reservable_bw_sub): 55000 (kbps)

                            Total Allocated   Reservable
                            BW (kbps)         BW (kbps)
                            ---------------   -----------
            TE-Class[0]:          5000              50000
            TE-Class[1]:          5000              50000
            TE-Class[2]:          5000              50000
            TE-Class[3]:          5000              50000
            TE-Class[4]:          5000             150000
            TE-Class[5]:          5000             150000
            TE-Class[6]:          5000             150000
            TE-Class[7]:        105000              50000

! Output omitted for brevity
```

Example 4-43 *Examining the MPLS TE Topology Database with DS-TE Enabled in Cisco IOS XR*

```
RP/0/4/CPU0:Router#show mpls traffic-eng topology 172.16.255.129
My_System_id: 172.16.255.129 (ospf DEFAULT area 0)
My_BC_Model_Type: RDM

Signalling error holddown: 10 sec Global Link Generation 481

IGP Id: 172.16.255.129, MPLS TE Id: 172.16.255.129 Router Node  (ospf DEFAULT area 0)

  Link[0]:Point-to-Point, Nbr IGP Id:172.16.255.130, Nbr Node Id:28, gen:481
      Frag Id:0, Intf Address:172.16.192.0, Intf Id:0
       Nbr Intf Address:172.16.192.1, Nbr Intf Id:0
      TE Metric:1, IGP Metric:1, Attribute Flags:0x0
      Switching Capability:, Encoding:
      BC Model ID:RDM
      Physical BW:155520 (kbps), Max Reservable BW:100000 (kbps)
      BC0:100000 (kbps) BC1:55000 (kbps)
                      Total Allocated    Reservable
                      BW (kbps)          BW (kbps)
                      ---------------    -----------
          TE-class[0]:             0           55000
          TE-class[1]:             0          100000
          TE-class[2]:          5000           50000
          TE-class[3]:         55000           45000
          TE-class[4]:             0               0
          TE-class[5]:             0               0
          TE-class[6]:             0               0
          TE-class[7]:             0               0

! Output omitted for brevity
```

Verifying Signaling of DS-TE LSPs

DS-TE does not define new commands to verify the signaling of TE LSPs. As described in section "Verifying Signaling of TE LSPs," the **show mpls traffic-eng tunnels, show ip rsvp sender detail**, and **show ip rsvp reservation detail** commands provide all the signaling details for a TE LSP in Cisco IOS. Cisco IOS XR provides the equivalent **show mpls traffic-eng tunnels**, **show rsvp sender detail**, and **show rsvp reservation detail** commands. When you use DS-TE, those commands provide similar output and specify the CT that the TE LSP uses.

Fast Reroute (FRR)

Cisco IOS and Cisco IOS XR provide FRR for link and node protection. Both operating systems use the facility technique because of its superior scalability. You can use FRR with regular TE LSPs or DS-TE LSPs. In addition, you can configure your network to provide connectivity protection or bandwidth protection to make sure that backup tunnels have sufficient capacity before the *point of local repair* (PLR) selects them to protect a primary TE LSP. To deploy FRR, you must configure the headend of the primary tunnel to request protection-and you must configure at least one midpoint with a backup tunnel to reroute the primary TE LSPs. The backup tunnel must be a *next hop* (NHOP) or *next-next hop* (NNHOP) tunnel that bypasses the failure and intersects the primary TE LSP.

You need to configure which TE LSPs require protection with FRR. Cisco IOS uses the **tunnel mpls traffic-eng fast-reroute** command that you need to apply on the MPLS TE tunnel interface at the headend. The **node-protect** and **bw-protect** keywords are optional and set the corresponding node protection desired and bandwidth protection desired flags in the signaling of the primary TE LSP. Cisco PLRs attempt to provide the best protection possible to a primary TE LSP even if you do not set these flags. Cisco IOS XR uses the **fast-reroute** command on the MPLS TE tunnel to signal that the TE LSP desires protection. Examples 4-44 and 4-45 show MPLS TE tunnels in Cisco IOS and Cisco IOS XR that request FRR protection.

Example 4-44   *Tunnel Requesting FRR with Node and Bandwidth Protection in Cisco IOS*

```
interface Tunnel1
 description FROM-ROUTER-TO-DST1-FRR-NODEP-BWP
 ip unnumbered Loopback0
 tunnel destination 172.16.255.2
 tunnel mode mpls traffic-eng
 tunnel mpls traffic-eng priority 7 7
 tunnel mpls traffic-eng bandwidth  20000
 tunnel mpls traffic-eng path-option 10 explicit name PATH2
 tunnel mpls traffic-eng fast-reroute bw-protect node-protect
 !
```

Example 4-45   *Tunnel Requesting FRR Protection in Cisco IOS XR*

```
interface tunnel-te1
 description FROM-ROUTER-TO-DST1-FRR
 ipv4 unnumbered Loopback0
 priority 3 3
 signalled-bandwidth 30000 class-type 1
 destination 172.16.255.2
 fast-reroute
 path-option 10 explicit name PATH1
 !
```

Link and Node Protection

You need to pre-establish a backup TE LSP to implement link and node protection. You can configure this backup with an MPLS TE tunnel interface using the same commands that you use to configure the primary tunnel. The headend of the backup tunnel will always reside on the PLR. Conversely, the tailend will always be the *merge point* (MP). The backup tunnel can rely on a dynamically computed path or an explicit path. The only obvious restriction is that the path options for the backup tunnel must not use the facility (link, node, or *shared-risk link group* [SRLG]) whose failure you are trying to protect against. Backup tunnels commonly do not use an explicit bandwidth reservation. Remember that backup tunnels remain unused most of the time, and an explicit reservation limits your ability to share bandwidth.

The tunnel destination determines the type of protection a backup tunnel provides. An NHOP (adjacent neighbor) destination defines a backup tunnel that can protect against the failure of the link that connects to that neighbor. An NNHOP (a neighbor's neighbor) destination protects against the adjacent neighbor failure for those TE LSPs also traversing that second neighbor. Depending on your topology, you may need multiple backup tunnels to fully protect against the failure of an adjacent neighbor. A PLR may also have multiple backup tunnels to the same destination and protect against the same failure. This allows you to provide redundancy in case a backup tunnel fails and to distribute the primary TE LSPs across several backup tunnels.

You need to associate the backup tunnel with a physical interface that will detect the failure. Cisco IOS uses the **mpls traffic-eng backup-path** interface command for that purpose. Cisco IOS XR uses the **backup-path** command under a particular interface in the **mpls traffic-eng** configuration mode. You use the same command regardless of the type of protection you are trying to implement. To accelerate the detection of some node failures, you might need to enable RSVP hello messages or *Bidirectional Forwarding Detection* (BFD) between the PLR and the adjacent neighbor. In many cases, the PLR will detect the node failure as a link failure.

Examples 4-39 and 4-40 illustrate the configuration of backup tunnels in Cisco IOS and Cisco IOS XR, respectively. In both examples, one of the tunnels provides link protection; the other tunnel provides node protection. All tunnels use dynamic path computation that excludes the appropriate node or link. Figure 4-3 shows the details of the network topology and the tunnel paths.

In Example 4-46, node A has an NHOP tunnel, Tunnel1, and NNHOP tunnel, Tunnel2. Tunnel1 provides link protection, with interface POS0/1/1 acting as the failure-detection point. Tunnel2 provides node protection, with interface POS1/0/0 as failure-detection point. Similarly, Example 4-47 shows an NHOP tunnel, tunnel-te1, and an NNHOP tunnel, tunnel-te2, on node B. In this example, tunnel-te1 provides link protection and uses interface POS0/3/0/1 as the failure-detection point. Similarly, tunnel-te2 provides node protection and uses interface POS0/3/0/2 for the same purpose.

Figure 4-3 *Sample Network Topology with Link and Node Protection*

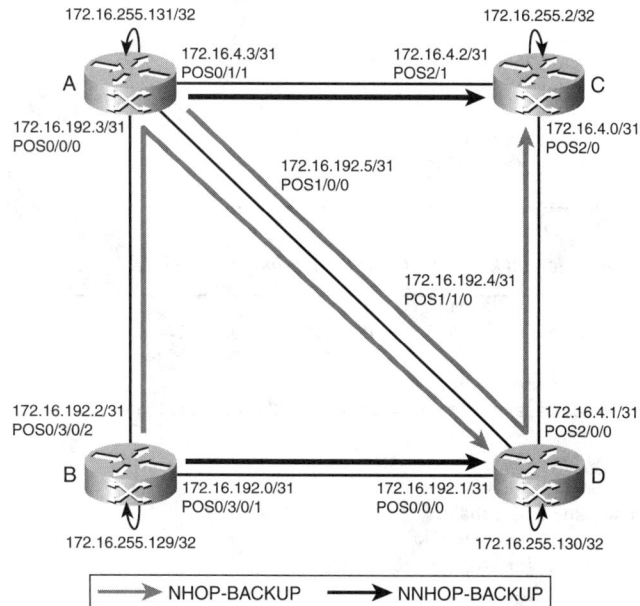

Example 4-46 *Backup Tunnels for Link and Node Protection in Cisco IOS*

```
interface Tunnel1
 description NHOP-BACKUP
 ip unnumbered Loopback0
 tunnel destination 172.16.255.2
 tunnel mode mpls traffic-eng
 tunnel mpls traffic-eng path-option 10 explicit name PATH1
!
interface Tunnel2
 description NNHOP-BACKUP
 ip unnumbered Loopback0
 tunnel destination 172.16.255.2
 tunnel mode mpls traffic-eng
 tunnel mpls traffic-eng path-option 10 explicit name PATH2
!
interface POS0/1/1
 ip address 172.16.4.3 255.255.255.254
 mpls traffic-eng tunnels
 mpls traffic-eng backup-path Tunnel1
 ip rsvp bandwidth 155000
!
interface POS1/0/0
 ip address 172.16.192.5 255.255.255.254
 mpls traffic-eng tunnels
 mpls traffic-eng backup-path Tunnel2
```

continues

Example 4-46 *Backup Tunnels for Link and Node Protection in Cisco IOS (Continued)*

```
 ip rsvp bandwidth 155000
 !
ip explicit-path name PATH1 enable
 exclude-address 172.16.4.2
 !
ip explicit-path name PATH2 enable
 exclude-address 172.16.255.130
 !
```

Example 4-47 *Backup Tunnels for Link and Node Protection in Cisco IOS XR*

```
explicit-path name PATH1
 index 1 exclude-address ipv4 unicast 172.16.192.1
 !
explicit-path name PATH2
 index 1 exclude-address ipv4 unicast 172.16.255.131
 !
interface tunnel-te1
 description NHOP-BACKUP
 ipv4 unnumbered Loopback0
 destination 172.16.255.130
 path-option 10 explicit name PATH1
 !
interface tunnel-te2
 description NNHOP-BACKUP
 ipv4 unnumbered Loopback0
 destination 172.16.255.130
 path-option 10 explicit name PATH2
 !
mpls traffic-eng
 interface POS0/3/0/1
  backup-path tunnel-te 1
  !
 interface POS0/3/0/2
  backup-path tunnel-te 2
  !
 !
```

NOTE   Cisco IOS provides the automatic creation of backup TE LSPs. You enable this behavior
with the **mpls traffic-eng auto-tunnel backup** command. A detailed discussion of this
functionality is beyond the scope of this book. Consult the Cisco IOS documentation for
further details.

Bandwidth Protection

The PLR can manage the capacity of backup tunnels to provide bandwidth protection. You can use the **tunnel mpls traffic-eng backup-bw** command and the **backup-bw** command to explicitly configure the backup tunnel capacity in Cisco IOS and Cisco IOS XR, respectively. They provide local knowledge of the capacity of the backup tunnels and do not instruct the PLR to signal a bandwidth reservation. With proper design, a PLR can provide bandwidth protection even if the backup tunnel does not reserve bandwidth. A PLR provides bandwidth protection for any primary TE LSP that requests protection if possible. However, it gives precedence to TE LSPs with nonzero bandwidth that request bandwidth protection.

You configure the capacity of a backup tunnel in terms of a bandwidth amount and the Class-Types they can protect. With respect to the bandwidth amount, you can configure the backup with an explicit (limited) bandwidth amount or as a backup with unlimited bandwidth. With respect to Class-Types, you can configure a backup tunnel to protect TE LSPs using the global pool (CT0), the subpool (CT1), or any bandwidth pool (CT0 or CT1). Bandwidth protection enables you to define multiple backup tunnels with different capacity configuration to protect against the same failure. When the PLR detects a TE LSP that requires protection, it evaluates which backup tunnel can provide the best level of bandwidth protection.

Table 4-3 shows the criteria that the PLR uses to select from among multiple backup tunnels to protect a primary TE LSP. In general, the PLR prefers NNHOP over NHOP tunnels because they can protect against both a node and a link failure. It prefers backup tunnels with an explicit (limited) bandwidth amount. Finally, it prefers an exact Class-Type match over backup tunnels that protect any Class-Type. The most preferable backup tunnel will be an NNHOP tunnel with a limited bandwidth amount and an exact class match. In contrast, the least desirable backup tunnel will be an NHOP tunnel with unlimited bandwidth for any Class-Type. This tunnel provides the lowest certain of bandwidth guarantee.

Table 4-3   *Priorities for Backup Tunnel Selection in Cisco IOS and Cisco IOS XR*

Preference	Backup Tunnel Destination	Bandwidth Amount	Bandwidth Pool
0 (best)	NNHOP	Limited	Exact match
1	NNHOP	Limited	Any
2	NNHOP	Unlimited	Exact match
3	NNHOP	Unlimited	Any
4	NHOP	Limited	Exact match
5	NHOP	Limited	Any
6	NHOP	Unlimited	Exact match
7 (worst)	NHOP	Unlimited	Any

Example 4-48 shows the bandwidth protection configuration on a PLR in Cisco IOS and Cisco IOS XR, respectively. Examine Figure 4-4.

Figure 4-4   *Sample Network Topology with Cisco IOS PLR Providing Bandwidth Protection*

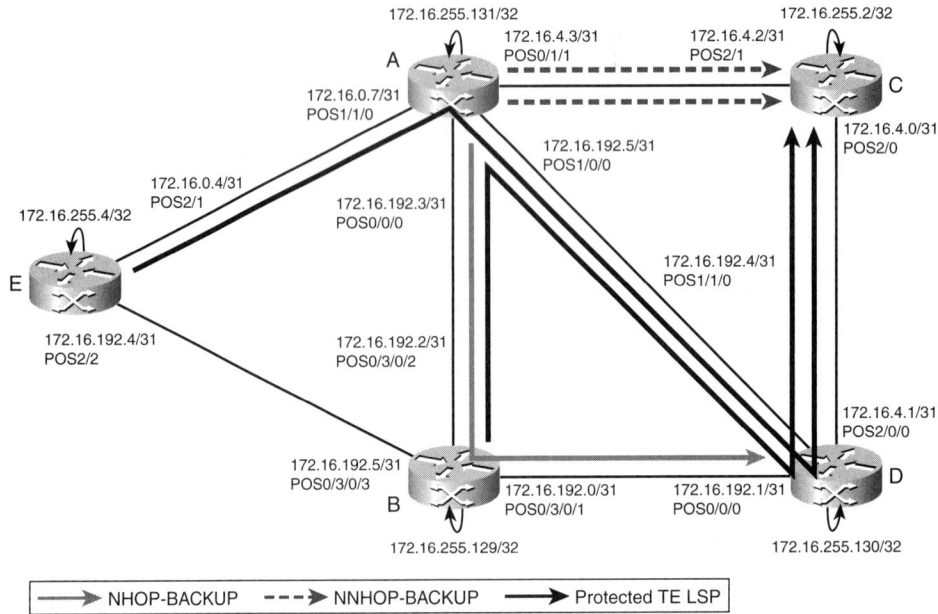

In Example 4-48, interface POS1/0/0 can trigger three backup tunnels:

- Tunnel1 is an NNHOP backup tunnel protecting 40,000 kbps for CT TE LSPs.
- Tunnel2 is an NNHOP tunnel that can protect 90,000 kbps for CT0 LSPs.

Tunnel3 is an NHOP tunnel that can protect 90,000 kbps for TE LSPs of any CT.

Example 4-48   *Backup Tunnels for Bandwidth Protection in Cisco IOS*

```
interface Tunnel1
 description NNHOP-BACKUP-40M-CT1
 ip unnumbered Loopback0
 tunnel destination 172.16.255.2
 tunnel mode mpls traffic-eng
 tunnel mpls traffic-eng backup-bw 40000 class-type 1
 tunnel mpls traffic-eng path-option 10 explicit name PATH1
!
interface Tunnel2
 description NNHOP-BACKUP-90M-CT0
 ip unnumbered Loopback0
 tunnel destination 172.16.255.2
 tunnel mode mpls traffic-eng
 tunnel mpls traffic-eng backup-bw 90000 class-type 0
```

Example 4-48   *Backup Tunnels for Bandwidth Protection in Cisco IOS (Continued)*

```
 tunnel mpls traffic-eng path-option 10 explicit name PATH2
 !
interface Tunnel3
 description NHOP-BACKUP-90M-ANY-CT
 ip unnumbered Loopback0
 tunnel destination 172.16.255.130
 tunnel mode mpls traffic-eng
 tunnel mpls traffic-eng backup-bw 90000
 tunnel mpls traffic-eng path-option 10 explicit name PATH3
 !
interface POS1/0/0
 ip address 172.16.192.5 255.255.255.254
 mpls traffic-eng tunnels
 mpls traffic-eng backup-path Tunnel1
 mpls traffic-eng backup-path Tunnel2
 mpls traffic-eng backup-path Tunnel3
 ip rsvp bandwidth rdm 155000 sub-pool 55000
 !
ip explicit-path name PATH1 enable
 exclude-address 172.16.255.130
 !
ip explicit-path name PATH3 enable
 next-address 172.16.192.2
 next-address 172.16.192.1
 !
ip explicit-path name PATH2 enable
 next-address 172.16.4.2
 !
```

Examine Figure 4-5.

Example 4-49 shows three backup tunnels that could re-reroute traffic in case of a failure on interface POS0/3/0/1:

- tunnel-te1 is an NHOP tunnel protecting 55,000 kbps for CT0 TE LSPs.
- tunnel-te2 is an NNHOP tunnel that supports a protection capacity of 20,000 for CT0 TE LSPs.

tunnel-te3 is an NHOP tunnel that protects 25,000 kbps for CT1 TE LSPs.

Figure 4-5 *Sample Network Topology with Cisco IOS XR PLR Providing Bandwidth Protection*

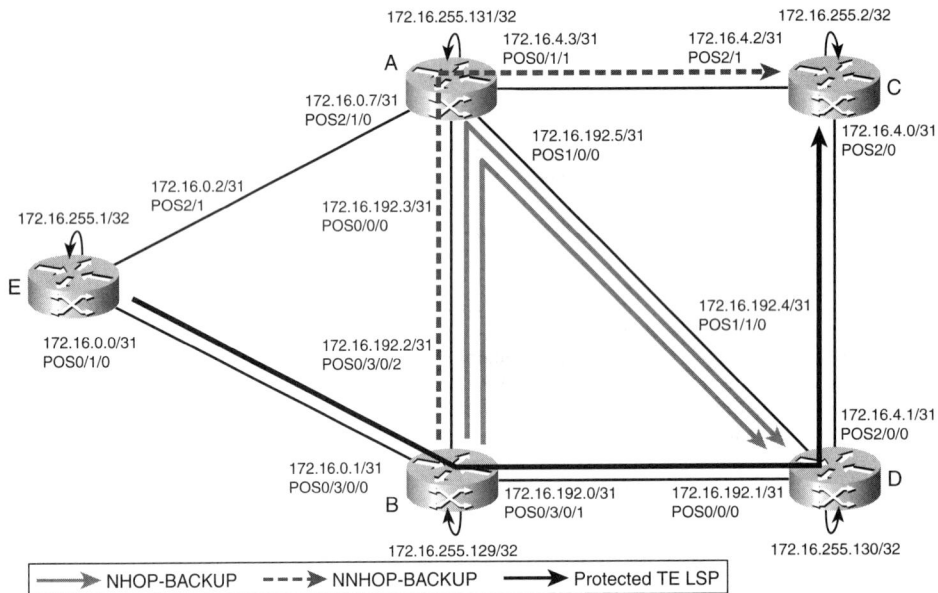

Example 4-49 *Bandwidth Protection in Cisco IOS XR*

```
interface tunnel-te1
 description NHOP-BACKUP-55M-CTO
 ipv4 unnumbered Loopback0
 backup-bw 55000 class-type 0
 destination 172.16.255.130
 path-option 10 explicit name PATH1
!
interface tunnel-te2
 description NNHOP-BACKUP-20M-CTO
 ipv4 unnumbered Loopback0
 backup-bw 20000 class-type 0
 destination 172.16.255.2
 path-option 10 explicit name PATH2
!
interface tunnel-te3
 description NHOP-BACKUP-25M-ANY-CT
 ipv4 unnumbered Loopback0
 backup-bw 25000 class-type 1
 destination 172.16.255.130
 path-option 10 explicit name PATH1
!
mpls traffic-eng
 interface POS0/3/0/1
  backup-path tunnel-te 1
  backup-path tunnel-te 2
  backup-path tunnel-te 3
 !
!
```

Verifying FRR on the Headend

In Cisco IOS, you can verify the operation of FRR on a headend by examining the Path and Resv state of the primary TE LSP. The **show ip rsvp sender detail** command provides the most detail about the Path state of a TE LSP. This command enables you to verify whether the node is signaling the TE LSP with any of the FRR flags (local protection desired, node protection desired, or bandwidth protection desired). Similarly, the **show ip rsvp reservation detail** command provides the details of the Resv state. This command displays the hop-by-hop route information that the signaling packets collected. In Example 4-50, you see that the first node in the path is providing bandwidth protection for an LSP with an NNHOP backup tunnel.

Example 4-50 *Examining Primary TE LSP Protection at the Headend in Cisco IOS*

```
Router#show ip rsvp reservation detail
Reservation:
  Tun Dest:   172.16.255.2  Tun ID: 1  Ext Tun ID: 172.16.255.1
  Tun Sender: 172.16.255.1  LSP ID: 6
  Next Hop: 172.16.0.3 on POS1/0/0
  Label: 30 (outgoing)
  Reservation Style is Shared-Explicit, QoS Service is Controlled-Load
  Resv ID handle: 06000410.
  Created: 16:25:39 UTC Tue Jul 29 2003
  Average Bitrate is 20M bits/sec, Maximum Burst is 1K bytes
  Min Policed Unit: 0 bytes, Max Pkt Size: 0 bytes
  RRO:
    172.16.255.131/32, Flags:0x2D (Local Prot Avail/Has BW/to NNHOP, Node-id)
      Label subobject: Flags 0x1, C-Type 1, Label 30
    172.16.255.130/32, Flags:0x20 (No Local Protection, Node-id)
      Label subobject: Flags 0x1, C-Type 1, Label 33
    172.16.255.2/32, Flags:0x20 (No Local Protection, Node-id)
      Label subobject: Flags 0x1, C-Type 1, Label 0
  Status:
  Policy: Accepted. Policy source(s): MPLS/TE
Router#
```

Example 4-51 shows how to verify the operation of FRR on a headend in Cisco IOS XR. In this case, the **show mpls traffic-eng tunnels** command provides enough detail about the RSVP state of the TE LSP. In particular, the decoded *route record object* (RRO) will show you, for every hop in the path, whether the TE LSP has local protection, whether protection is active (the node is rerouting the TE LSP through a backup), and whether bandwidth or node protection is available. The flags in the IPv4/IPv6 subobject contain that information. In this example, the first hop (node ID 172.16.255.131) provides local protection with node and bandwidth protection (flags 0x2d).

Example 4-51 *Examining Primary TE LSP Protection at the Headend in Cisco IOS XR*

```
RP/0/4/CPU0:Router#show mpls traffic-eng tunnels role head detail
Signalling Summary:
          LSP Tunnels Process:  running
```

continues

Example 4-51 *Examining Primary TE LSP Protection at the Headend in Cisco IOS XR (Continued)*

```
                          RSVP Process:  running
                            Forwarding:  enabled
                 Periodic reoptimization:  every 3600 seconds, next in 1244 seconds
                  Periodic FRR Promotion:  every 300 seconds, next in 173 seconds
              Periodic auto-bw collection:  disabled


Name: tunnel-te1  Destination: 172.16.255.2
  Status:
    Admin:    up Oper:   up   Path:  valid  Signalling: connected

    path option 10,  type explicit PATH1 (Basis for Setup, path weight 3)
    G-PID: 0x0800 (derived from egress interface properties)

  Config Parameters:
    Bandwidth:    30000 kbps (CT1) Priority:  3  3 Affinity: 0x0/0xffff
    Metric Type: TE (default)
    AutoRoute:  disabled  LockDown: disabled    Loadshare:    30000 bw-based
    Auto-bw: disabled(0/0) 0  Bandwidth Requested:    30000
    Direction: unidirectional
    Endpoint switching capability: unknown, encoding type: unassigned
    Transit switching capability: unknown, encoding type: unassigned

  History:
    Tunnel has been up for: 02:01:00
    Current LSP:
      Uptime: 02:01:00
  Current LSP Info:
    Instance: 9, Signaling Area: ospf DEFAULT area 0
    Uptime: 02:01:00
    Incoming Label: explicit-null
    Outgoing Interface: POS0/3/0/2, Outgoing Label: 33
    Path Info:
      Explicit Route:
        Strict, 172.16.192.3
        Strict, 172.16.192.4
        Strict, 172.16.4.0
        Strict, 172.16.255.2
      Record Route: None
      Tspec: avg rate=30000 kbits, burst=1000 bytes, peak rate=30000 kbits
    Resv Info:
      Record Route:
        IPv4 172.16.255.131, flags 0x2d
        Label 33, flags 0x1
        IPv4 172.16.255.130, flags 0x20
        Label 32, flags 0x1
        IPv4 172.16.255.2, flags 0x20
        Label 0, flags 0x1
      Fspec: avg rate=30000 kbits, burst=1000 bytes, peak rate=30000 kbits
Displayed 1 (of 1) heads, 0 (of 1) midpoints, 0 (of 0) tails
Displayed 1 up, 0 down, 0 recovering, 0 recovered heads
RP/0/4/CPU0:Router#
```

Examine the information in Table 4-4.

Table 4-4   *Flags in the RRO IPv4/IPv6 Subobject*

Value (Hexadecimal)	Flag	Description
0x01	Local protection available	Node can protect TE LSP.
0x02	Local protection in use	Node is rerouting the TE LSP through the backup tunnel.
0x04	Bandwidth protection	Node can provide bandwidth protection for the TE LSP.
0x08	Node protection	Node can provide protection against downstream node failure.
0x10	Preemption pending	TE LSP preemption pending. Headend should reroute the TE LSP.
0x20	Node ID	Address represents node ID rather than a link address.

Verifying FRR on the PLR

A PLR will provide the details of the primary TE LSPs it is protecting and what backup tunnel it uses for that purpose.

Example 4-52 shows the output of the **show mpls traffic-eng fast-reroute database** command in Cisco IOS. If the PLR has selected a backup for a primary TE LSP, the command displays the TE LSP, the input label, the output interface, the output label, the output backup tunnel, and the backup label. The protection status can be *ready* when a failure has not occurred or *active* when the node is rerouting the primary TE LSP through the backup.

Example 4-52   *Examining the FRR Database on the PLR in Cisco IOS*

```
Router#show mpls traffic-eng fast-reroute database
Headend frr information:
Protected tunnel            In-label Out intf/label  FRR intf/label   Status

LSP midpoint frr information:
LSP identifier              In-label Out intf/label  FRR intf/label   Status
172.16.255.1 1 [6]          30       PO1/0/0:33      Tu2:implicit-nul ready
172.16.255.129 1 [9]        33       PO1/0/0:32      Tu1:implicit-nul ready
Router#
*Nov 10 16:32:52.852: %LINK-3-UPDOWN: Interface POS1/0/0, changed state to down
*Nov 10 16:32:52.856: %OSPF-5-ADJCHG: Process 100, Nbr 172.16.255.130 on POS1/0/0
from FULL to DOWN, Neighbor Down: Interface down or detached
*Nov 10 16:32:53.852: %LINEPROTO-5-UPDOWN: Line protocol on Interface POS1/0/0,
changed state to down
Router#
Router#show mpls traffic-eng fast-reroute database
Headend frr information:
```

continues

Example 4-52 *Examining the FRR Database on the PLR in Cisco IOS*

```
Protected tunnel              In-label Out intf/label   FRR intf/label   Status

LSP midpoint frr information:
LSP identifier                In-label Out intf/label   FRR intf/label   Status
172.16.255.1 1 [6]               30     PO1/0/0:33       Tu2:implicit-nul active
172.16.255.129 1 [9]             33     PO1/0/0:32       Tu1:implicit-nul active
Router#
```

Cisco IOS XR supports the same command with equivalent information. Example 4-53 shows the command output in Cisco IOS XR. Both examples show the command output before and while the node reroutes the TE LSPs.

Example 4-53 *Examining the FRR Database on the PLR in Cisco IOS XR*

```
RP/0/4/CPU0:Router#show mpls traffic-eng fast-reroute database
LSP midpoint FRR information:
LSP Identifier                Local  Out Intf/        FRR Intf/        Status
                              Label  Label            Label
----------------------------- ------ ---------------- ---------------- -------
172.16.255.1 1 [677]             83    PO0/3/0/1:31    tt2:ExpNull4      Ready
RP/0/4/CPU0:Router#
RP/0/4/CPU0:Router#LC/0/3/CPU0:May  2 01:23:29.614 : ifmgr[154]: %PKT_INFRA-LINK-3-
UPDOWN : Interface POS0/3/0/1, changed state to Down
LC/0/3/CPU0:May  2 01:23:29.615 : ifmgr[154]: %PKT_INFRA-LINEPROTO-5-UPDOWN : Line
protocol on Interface POS0/3/0/1, changed state to Down
RP/0/4/CPU0:May  2 01:23:29.643 : ospf[269]: %ROUTING-OSPF-5-ADJCHG : Process
DEFAULT, Nbr 172.16.255.130 on POS0/3/0/1 from FULL to DOWN, Neighbor Down:
interface down or detached

RP/0/4/CPU0:Router#
RP/0/4/CPU0:Router#show mpls traffic-eng fast-reroute database
LSP midpoint FRR information:
LSP Identifier                Local  Out Intf/        FRR Intf/        Status
                              Label  Label            Label
----------------------------- ------ ---------------- ---------------- -------
172.16.255.1 1 [677]             83    tt2:ExpNull4                      Active
RP/0/4/CPU0:Router#
```

You can use the **show mpls traffic-eng tunnels protection** command to examine the details of a protected TE LSP on a PLR. You can use the command in Cisco IOS and Cisco IOS XR. Example 4-54 shows a protected TE LSP traversing interface POS1/0/0. The backup selection process has chosen Tunnel2 to protect this TE LSP. See Example 4-41 for the backup tunnel configuration. Example 4-55 shows the equivalent command output in Cisco IOS XR. In that example, the PLR has selected tunnel-te2 to reroute the protected TE LSP. See Example 4-42 for the backup tunnel configuration

Example 4-54 *Examining Protected TE LSPs on the PLR in Cisco IOS*

```
Router#show mpls traffic-eng tunnels protection
NNHOP-BACKUP-40M-CT1
  LSP Head, Tunnel1, Admin: up, Oper: up
  Src 172.16.255.131, Dest 172.16.255.2, Instance 4
  Fast Reroute Protection: None
  Path Protection: None
NNHOP-BACKUP-90M-CT0
  LSP Head, Tunnel2, Admin: up, Oper: up
  Src 172.16.255.131, Dest 172.16.255.2, Instance 1
  Fast Reroute Protection: None
  Path Protection: None
NHOP-BACKUP-90M-ANY-CT
  LSP Head, Tunnel3, Admin: up, Oper: up
  Src 172.16.255.131, Dest 172.16.255.130, Instance 1
  Fast Reroute Protection: None
  Path Protection: None

LSP Tunnel FROM-ROUTER-TO-DST1-FRR-NODEP-BWP is signalled, connection is up
  InLabel  : POS2/0/0, 30
  OutLabel : POS1/0/0, 33
  FRR OutLabel : Tunnel2, explicit-null
  RSVP Signalling Info:
      Src 172.16.255.1, Dst 172.16.255.2, Tun_Id 1, Tun_Instance 6
    RSVP Path Info:
     My Address: 172.16.192.5
     Explicit Route: 172.16.192.4 172.16.4.0 172.16.255.2
     Record   Route:   NONE
     Tspec: ave rate=20000 kbits, burst=1000 bytes, peak rate=20000 kbits
    RSVP Resv Info:
     Record   Route:  172.16.255.130(33) 172.16.255.2(0)
     Fspec: ave rate=20000 kbits, burst=1000 bytes, peak rate=20000 kbits

LSP Tunnel FROM-ROUTER-TO-DST1-FRR is signalled, connection is up
  InLabel  : POS0/0/0, 33
  OutLabel : POS1/0/0, 32
  FRR OutLabel : Tunnel1, explicit-null
  RSVP Signalling Info:
      Src 172.16.255.129, Dst 172.16.255.2, Tun_Id 1, Tun_Instance 9
    RSVP Path Info:
     My Address: 172.16.192.5
     Explicit Route: 172.16.192.4 172.16.4.0 172.16.255.2
     Record   Route:   NONE
     Tspec: ave rate=30000 kbits, burst=1000 bytes, peak rate=30000 kbits
    RSVP Resv Info:
     Record   Route:  172.16.255.130(32) 172.16.255.2(0)
     Fspec: ave rate=30000 kbits, burst=1000 bytes, peak rate=30000 kbits
Router#
```

Example 4-55 *Examining Protected TE LSPs on the PLR in Cisco IOS XR*

```
RP/0/4/CPU0:Router#show mpls traffic-eng tunnels protection
NHOP-BACKUP-90M-ANY-CT
  LSP Midpoint, signaled, connection up
  Src: 172.16.255.131, Dest: 172.16.255.130, Instance: 1
  Fast Reroute Protection: None

NHOP-BACKUP-55M-CT0
  LSP Head, Admin: up, Oper: up
  Src: 172.16.255.129, Dest: 172.16.255.130, Instance: 1
  Fast Reroute Protection: None

NNHOP-BACKUP-20M-CT0
  LSP Head, Admin: up, Oper: up
  Src: 172.16.255.129, Dest: 172.16.255.2, Instance: 1
  Fast Reroute Protection: None

NHOP-BACKUP-25M-ANY-CT
  LSP Head, Admin: up, Oper: up
  Src: 172.16.255.129, Dest: 172.16.255.130, Instance: 1
  Fast Reroute Protection: None

FROM-ROUTER-TO-DST1-FRR-NODEP-BWP
  LSP Midpoint, signaled, connection up
  Src: 172.16.255.1, Dest: 172.16.255.2, Instance: 677
  Fast Reroute Protection: Requested
    Inbound: FRR Inactive
    LSP signalling info:
      Original: in i/f: POS0_3_0_0, label:  83, phop: 172.16.0.0
    Outbound: FRR Ready
    Backup tunnel-te2 to LSP nnhop
    tunnel-te2: out i/f: POS0/3/0/2
    LSP signalling info:
      Original: out i/f: POS0/3/0/1, label:  31, nhop: 172.16.192.1
      With FRR: out i/f: tunnel-te2, label:  0
    LSP bw: 20000 kbps, Backup level: CT0 limited, type: CT0

RP/0/4/CPU0:Router#
```

The **show mpls traffic-eng tunnels backup** command enables you to obtain details about the backup tunnels on the PLR. The output shows you how many TE LSPs the backup tunnel is protecting. It also shows you the current allocation of backup bandwidth. Example 4-56 illustrates the command output in Cisco IOS. In this case, Tunnel2 is protecting one TE LSP and has allocated 10,000 kbps of the total 90,000 kbps of backup bandwidth. Example 4-57 shows the equivalent command output in Cisco IOS XR. In that example, te-tunnel2 is protecting one TE LSP and has allocated all its backup bandwidth (20,000 kbps).

Example 4-56 *Examining Backup Tunnels on the PLR in Cisco IOS*

```
Router#show mpls traffic-eng tunnels backup
NNHOP-BACKUP-40M-CT1
  LSP Head, Tunnel1, Admin: up, Oper: up
  Src 172.16.255.131, Dest 172.16.255.2, Instance 4
  Fast Reroute Backup Provided:
    Protected i/fs: PO1/0/0
    Protected lsps: 1
    Backup BW: sub-pool; limit: 40000 kbps, inuse: 30000 kbps (BWP inuse: 0 kbps)
NNHOP-BACKUP-90M-CT0
  LSP Head, Tunnel2, Admin: up, Oper: up
  Src 172.16.255.131, Dest 172.16.255.2, Instance 1
  Fast Reroute Backup Provided:
    Protected i/fs: PO1/0/0
    Protected lsps: 1
    Backup BW: global pool; limit 90000 kbps, inuse: 20000 kbps (BWP inuse: 20000
    kbps)
NHOP-BACKUP-90M-ANY-CT
  LSP Head, Tunnel3, Admin: up, Oper: up
  Src 172.16.255.131, Dest 172.16.255.130, Instance 1
  Fast Reroute Backup Provided:
    Protected i/fs: PO1/0/0
    Protected lsps: 0
    Backup BW: any pool; limit: 90000 kbps, inuse: 0 kbps (BWP inuse: 0 kbps)
Router#
```

Example 4-57 *Examining Backup Tunnels on the PLR in Cisco IOS XR*

```
RP/0/4/CPU0:Router#show mpls traffic-eng tunnels backup

tunnel-te1
 Admin: up, Oper: up
 Src: 172.16.255.129, Dest: 172.16.255.130, Instance: 1
 Fast Reroute Backup Provided:
  Protected LSPs: 0
  Backup BW: CT0; limit: 55000 kbps, Inuse: 0 kbps
  Protected i/fs: POS0/3/0/1
tunnel-te2
 Admin: up, Oper: up
 Src: 172.16.255.129, Dest: 172.16.255.2, Instance: 1
 Fast Reroute Backup Provided:
  Protected LSPs: 1
  Backup BW: CT0; limit: 20000 kbps, Inuse: 20000 kbps
  Protected i/fs: POS0/3/0/1
tunnel-te3
 Admin: up, Oper: up
 Src: 172.16.255.129, Dest: 172.16.255.130, Instance: 1
 Fast Reroute Backup Provided:
  Protected LSPs: 0
  Backup BW: any-class; limit: 25000 kbps, Inuse: 0 kbps
  Protected i/fs: POS0/3/0/1
RP/0/4/CPU0:Router#
```

Summary

Cisco IOS and Cisco IOS XR provide a comprehensive implementation of MPLS TE. They use tunnel interfaces as an abstraction of TE LSPs. You can perform constraint-based routing using IS-IS or OSPF. RSVP performs the signaling of TE LSPs. You can configure different aspects of the protocol (for instance, graceful restart, reliable messages, authentication) that can influence the scalability and reliability of an MPLS TE implementation. You can use multiple traffic-selection mechanisms to inject traffic into a TE LSP. CBTS enables you to use the MPLS EXP value for this purpose.

DS-TE and FRR extend the basic functionality in Cisco MPLS TE. You can implement DS-TE using the RDM or MAM models. Cisco FRR TE supports link, node, SRLG, bandwidth, and path protection.

References

Osborne, E., and A. Simha. *Traffic Engineering with MPLS*. Cisco Press; 2003.

Cisco Software Center
http://www.cisco.com/go/software

Cisco Software Advisor
http://tools.cisco.com/Support/Fusion/FusionHome.do

Cisco IOS Quality of Service Solutions Configuration Guide, Release 12.4
http://www.cisco.com/en/US/products/ps6350/products_configuration_guide_
book09186a0080435d50.html

Cisco IOS Software Releases 12.2 S Feature Guides http://www.cisco.com/en/US/
products/sw/iosswrel/ps1838/products_feature_guides_list.htmlCisco IOS XR Software
Configuration Guides http://www.cisco.com/en/US/partner/products/ps5845/
products_installation_and_configuration_guides_list.html

CHAPTER 5

Backbone Infrastructure

In this chapter, you learn the following topics:

- Backbone Performance
- Latency Versus Link Utilization
- Reference Network
- QoS Design Alternatives

This chapter discusses the implementation of *quality of service* (QoS) in a *Multiprotocol Label Switching Protocol* (MPLS) backbone. You will find several design options with different levels of granularity and complexity. Most designs use *Differentiated Services* (DiffServ) as a base technology and equally apply to pure IP backbones. Some designs incorporate *MPLS Traffic Engineering* (MPLS TE) to improve the performance characteristics of the network and are specific to MPLS backbones. Many factors influence the selection of the most appropriate design for a particular network. Although the services the network provides are of prime importance, bandwidth and operational costs can play an important role in the design selection. Overall, the backbone uses a simpler QoS model when you compare it with the designs that network services require. This chapter focuses exclusively on the implementation of QoS in the backbone to support multiple services. In most cases, those services have their own QoS implementations that you need to integrate with your backbone design.

Backbone Performance

This section discusses multiple aspects of the performance of a network backbone. The section "Performance Requirements for Different Applications" explains how applications determine the performance requirements for the backbone. Identifying these requirements is crucial before discussing QoS design alternatives. The section "Segmentation of Performance Targets" covers how you can divide performance targets to facilitate their implementation. Finally, the section "Factors Affecting Performance Targets" discusses the different components that contribute to latency, jitter, and loss.

Performance Requirements for Different Applications

A network backbone needs a scalable and flexible QoS design that can satisfy a wide range of services. Some of these services can transport a range of different application themselves. Most networks have the short- or long-term goal of transporting a varied mix of traffic. Think of voice, video, and data as the three main components. However, these applications can have different requirements depending on the nature of the service. From a QoS perspective, latency, jitter, and packet loss are the main performance metrics. They constitute the main criteria to specify the requirements of a specific type of traffic.

Table 5-1 illustrates the traffic classification that the Transport Area working group at the *Internet Engineering Task Force* (IETF) is currently discussing. This list proposes a comprehensive enumeration of different types of traffic. Packet size, burstiness, elasticity, bandwidth consumption, and flow duration are the main criteria to classify all traffic. This list is useful to understand the different nature of the traffic that the network is likely to transport. The original document details how to treat these categories as individual classes. However, deployment experience shows that, with some assumptions, your backbone QoS design can abstract this level of detail and still meet the application requirements.

NOTE   Elastic traffic (for example, a file transfer) experiences increasing or decreasing levels of performance according to bandwidth access. On the other hand, nonelastic traffic (for example, a voice call) has hard requirements. Performance remains constant while the requirements are met (regardless of bandwidth access), and it drops drastically otherwise.

This traffic classification also describes the packet latency, jitter, and loss tolerance for each class. The original specification only provides a relative performance characterization (high, medium, low). For packet jitter in particular, the classification identifies some classes as jitter tolerant. This characterization implies that a moderate level of jitter does not affect the application performance. Those applications use buffering at the application endpoint that allows them to adapt to latency variation. In many cases, TCP provides such buffering.

Table 5-1   *Service Class Characteristics Proposal at the IETF Transport Area Working Group*

Traffic	Characteristics	Latency Tolerance	Jitter Tolerance	Loss Tolerance
Network control	Variable-size packets, mostly inelastic short messages, but traffic can also burst (BGP[*])	Low	Yes	Low
Telephony	Fixed-size small packets, constant emission rate, inelastic and low rate flows	Very low	Very low	Very low

Table 5-1   *Service Class Characteristics Proposal at the IETF Transport Area Working Group (Continued)*

Traffic	Characteristics	Latency Tolerance	Jitter Tolerance	Loss Tolerance
Signaling	Variable-size packets, somewhat bursty short-lived flows	Low	Yes	Low
Multimedia conferencing	Variable-size packets, constant send interval, rate adaptive, reacts to loss	Very low	Low	Low to medium
Real-time interactive	RTP/UDP streams, inelastic, mostly variable rate	Very low	Low	Low
Multimedia streaming	Variable-size packets, elastic with variable rate	Medium	Yes	Low to medium
Broadcast video	Constant and variable rate, inelastic, nonbursty flows	Medium	Low	Very low
Low-latency data	Variable rate, bursty short-lived elastic flows	Low to medium	Yes	Low
OAM*	Variable-size packets, elastic and inelastic flows	Medium	Yes	Low
High-throughput data	Variable rate, bursty long-lived elastic flows	Medium to high	Yes	Low
Standard	A bit of everything	Not Specified	Not Specified	Not Specified
Low-priority data	Non-real-time and elastic	High	Yes	High

* BGP = Border Gateway Protocol

OAM = Operations and maintenance

ITU-T Recommendation G.1010 includes a definition of traffic types with general delay targets from a user perspective. Table 5-2 lists the different traffic categories. This classification uses error tolerance and latency requirements (interactive, responsive, timely, and noncritical) as main criteria. The delay targets represent the broad end-to-end user requirements. Table 5-3 provides a summarized version of more-specific performance targets that the same ITU-T recommendation provides. These targets represent the end-to-end application requirements regardless of particular network technologies or designs. This table focuses on those applications with subsecond latency targets. You can use these values as a guideline to define your own targets.

Table 5-2   *ITU-T Rec. G.1010 Model for User-Centric QoS Categories*

Traffic	Characteristics	Delay Target
Conversational voice and video	Interactive, error tolerant	<< 1 s
Command/control (for example, Telnet, interactive games)	Interactive, error intolerant	<< 1 s
Voice/video messaging	Responsive, error tolerant	~2 s
Transactions (for example, e-commerce, Internet browsing, e-mail access)	Responsive, error intolerant	~2 s
Streaming audio and video	Timely, error tolerant	~10 s
Messaging, downloads (for example, FTP, still image)	Timely, error intolerant	~10 s
Fax	Noncritical, error tolerant	>>10 s
Background (for example, Usenet)	Noncritical, error intolerant	>>10 s

Table 5-3   *ITU-T Rec. G.1010 Performance Targets for Sensitive Audio, Video, and Data Applications*

Application	Latency	Jitter	Loss
Conversational voice	<150 ms preferred, <400 ms limit	<1 ms	<3%
Videophone	<150 ms preferred, <400 ms limit	—	<1%
Command/control	<250 ms	—	0%
Interactive games	<200 ms	—	0%
Telnet	<200 ms	—	0%

NOTE   Remember that the performance targets in Table 5-3 represent the end-to-end application requirements. A network does not necessarily require meeting all those targets. For instance, buffering at the application endpoint can help reduce jitter at the expense of additional latency. Also, the application may use error-correcting mechanisms to compensate for packet loss.

Segmentation of Performance Targets

In most cases, several network segments contribute to the final delay, jitter, and packet loss that an application experiences. Figure 5-1 illustrates an example where you can easily identify five network segments between application endpoints. In this case, the network backbone is only one of them.

Figure 5-1   *Segmentation of End-to-End Performance Targets*

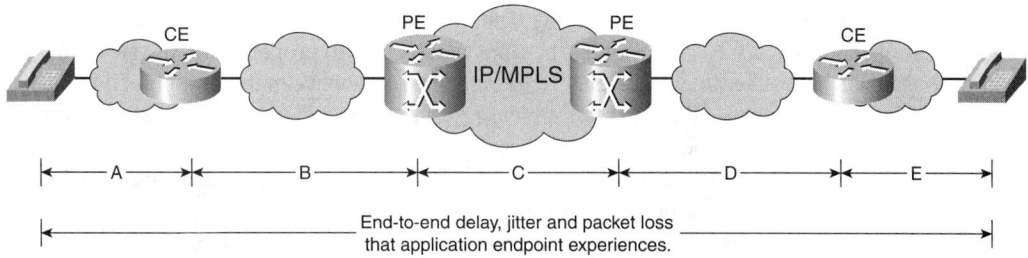

Figure 5-1   *Segmentation of End-to-End Performance Targets*

The specific targets for latency jitter and packet loss in the backbone should factor the impact of other components. Therefore, the backbone targets will ultimately be significantly lower than those in Table 5-3. By the end of the book, it should be obvious that, under normal operation and with proper engineering, the backbone should have a relatively low contribution to the total end-to-end latency, jitter, and packet loss.

You can further segment your performance targets within your backbone. A simple approach divides the target equally at each hop (see Figure 5-2). If you focus on latency for a moment, you can define your latency target per hop as the edge-to-edge latency target divided by the number of hops. This calculation should yield a conservative result. A packet should be more likely to face congestion on one hop than in multiple hops. When following the same approach for jitter, be aware of the nonadditive nature of this metric. Amendment 2 of the ITU-T Recommendation Y.1541 provides details about how to concatenate performance parameters.

Figure 5-2   *Segmentation of Backbone Performance Targets*

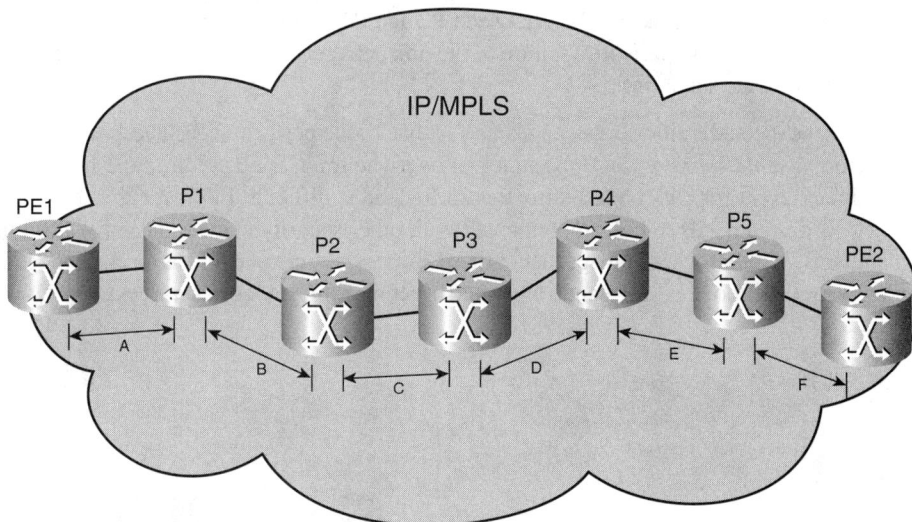

Factors Affecting Performance Targets

Propagation, serialization, processing, and queuing are sources of latency in a network. Propagation delay is a function of the time signals take to propagate on physical links and their distances. Serialization delay represents the time between the first bit and the last bit of a packet entering a link. As rates increase, serialization becomes less significant. Processing delay represents the time a node takes to process a packet since its arrival until it is ready for transmission. It is also called switching delay. The last component is queuing delay, which results from any buffering attributable to congestion. This congestion may happen mainly on the output interface, but some nodes may have other congestion points (for instance, switch fabrics). Queuing can be the main delay source, but you can control it through careful network design. Fluctuations on these delay sources produce jitter.

Physical link errors, routing failures, node processing errors, and queue drops are the main source of packet loss in a network. In the first place, nodes discard packets when they detect bit errors. In addition, packet loss can result from transient routing failures during topology changes. Nodes also drop packets because of malfunctioning hardware or improper configuration. Queue drops (being the result of tail dropping or *active queue management* [AQM]) can introduce packet loss in the presence of congestion. As with latency and jitter, careful network design enables you to control the negative impact that congestion can cause in the network.

Network failures can also significantly impact the latency, jitter, and packet loss that a packet may experience at a particular point in the network. A link or node failure will obviously have an impact on traffic while routing converges. However, the performance impact can be significant after convergence because some links will receive higher traffic loads. The exact impact of a link or node failure is highly dependent on the topology of the network. Figure 5-3 shows an example of how a link failure (the link between P1 and P3) results in another link (the link between P2 and P4) potentially receiving twice as much traffic load. In comparison, a failure of the link between PE1 and P1 is likely to have a lesser impact on the same link.

An unexpected traffic surge can also affect backbone performance. These surges can result from a *denial-of-service* (DoS) attack or overwhelming application traffic from an extraordinary event for which predicting the traffic load is difficult. In most cases, the backbone QoS design needs to be complemented with other security and admission-control mechanisms. Without a holistic approach, these sources of unexpected traffic could negatively impact backbone performance and thus affect multiple network services.

Figure 5-3   *Impact of Network Failures on Traffic Load Distribution*

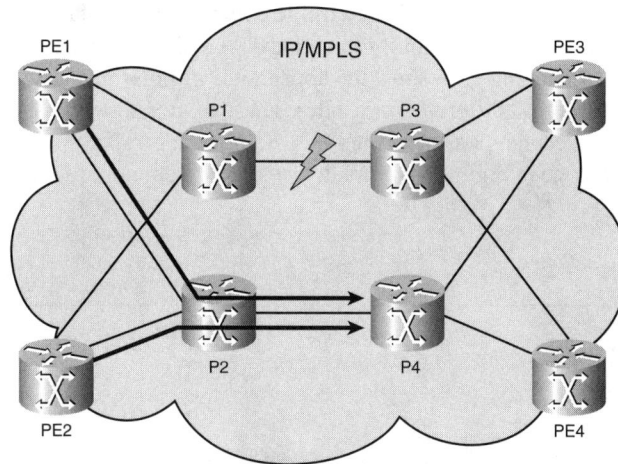

Latency Versus Link Utilization

Queuing delay increases rapidly as the link utilization gets closer to 100 percent. Intuitively, congestion should not arise as long as the link utilization remains below 100 percent. In reality, the rate at which packets reach an output interface varies significantly over time, and some level of congestion will take place even when the average utilization is well below 100 percent. Figure 5-4 illustrates this relationship. This figure uses normalized latency time units and assumes random packet arrivals according to a Poisson distribution. The exact shape of the curve depends on the exact statistical nature of the arrivals and the distribution of packet sizes; however, it illustrates the rapid growth of latency as utilization of a link inceases.

Figure 5-4   *Congestion Latency as a Function of Link Utilization*

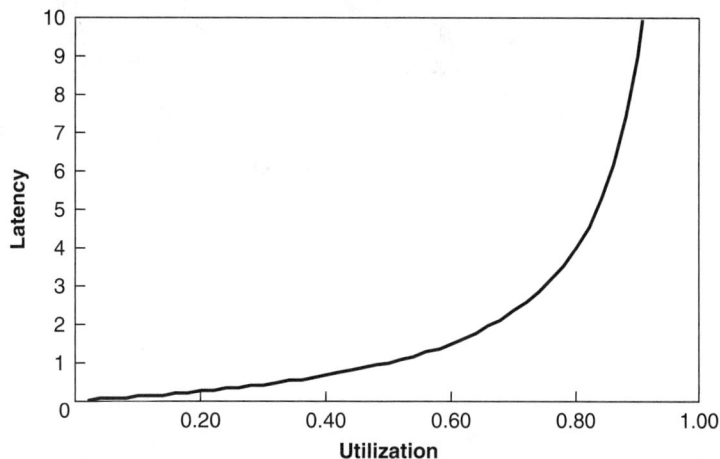

In the past decade, many studies have questioned the validity of the Poisson assumption and have suggested that packet-switched traffic exhibits self-similar behavior. This finding suggests that the traffic variability (burstiness) remains the same at different measuring intervals. Figures 5-5 and 5-6 show the appearance of Poisson and self-similar traffic when you measure them at different time scales. These figures show the same traffic pattern at 10-second and 1-second measuring intervals. Self-similar traffic results in a latency behavior similar to the one in Figure 5-4, but latency grows even more rapidly as the link utilization increases.

Figure 5-5   *Poisson Traffic Pattern*

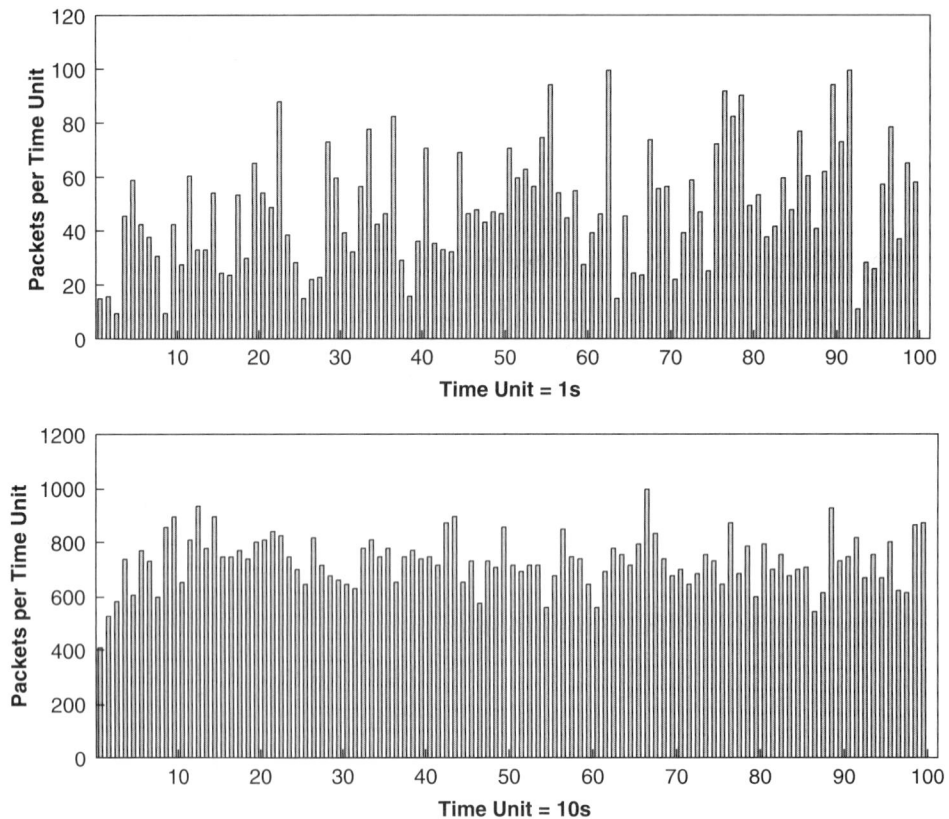

Figure 5-6   *Self-Similar Traffic Pattern*

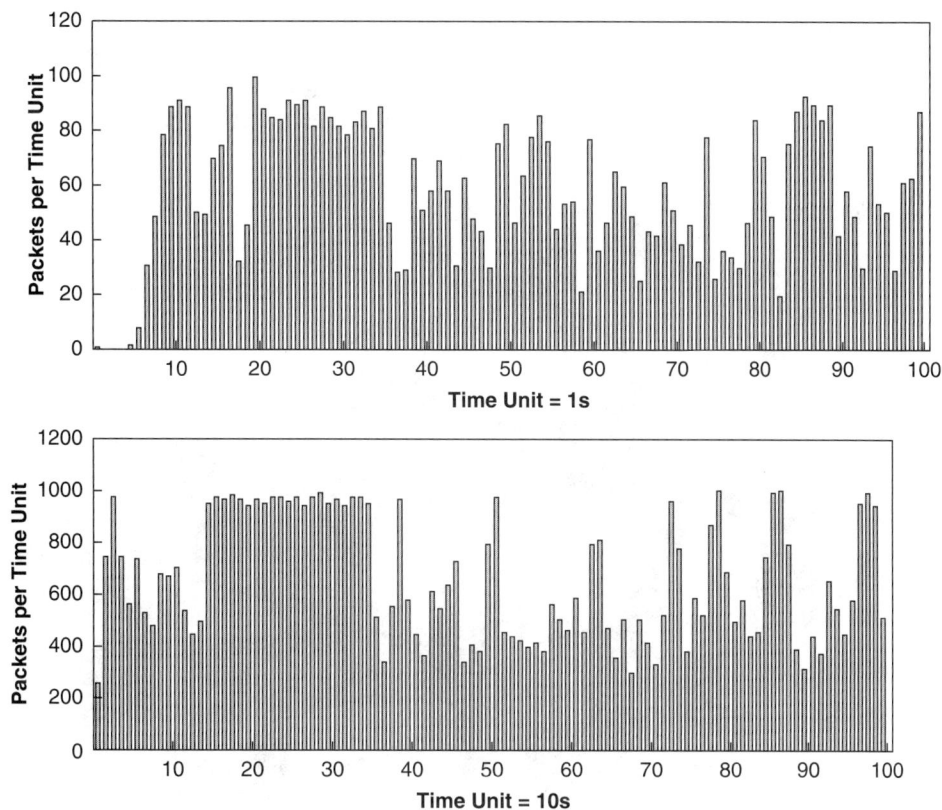

NOTE   A detailed discussion about traffic patterns is beyond the scope of this book. The "References" section at the end of this chapter lists additional sources of information on the subject.

Minimizing latency and maximizing link utilization poses two opposite goals. On one hand, bandwidth has a significant cost and should not be idle. On the other hand, maximizing its use can lead to congestion and a negative impact on latency, jitter, and packet loss. You can manage utilization with adjustments to traffic load, traffic capacity, or both. You can make these adjustments at the link or class level with the different designs that this chapter describes. The upcoming sections show you multiple alternatives to achieve your latency, jitter, and loss targets. Risk tolerance, operational costs, and bandwidth costs, among other factors, will determine what approach is more appropriate in a particular network.

Reference Network

Figure 5-7 shows the reference network that this chapter uses to illustrate different design options for an MPLS backbone. The network includes five *provider edge* (PE) and three *provider* (P) devices. Each hostname indicates which role the node plays in the network. The network uses the 172.16.0.0/24 block for all addressing. All nodes run Cisco IOS with the exception of Yosemite[P], which runs Cisco IOS XR.

Figure 5-7   *Reference IP/MPLS Network for Later Examples*

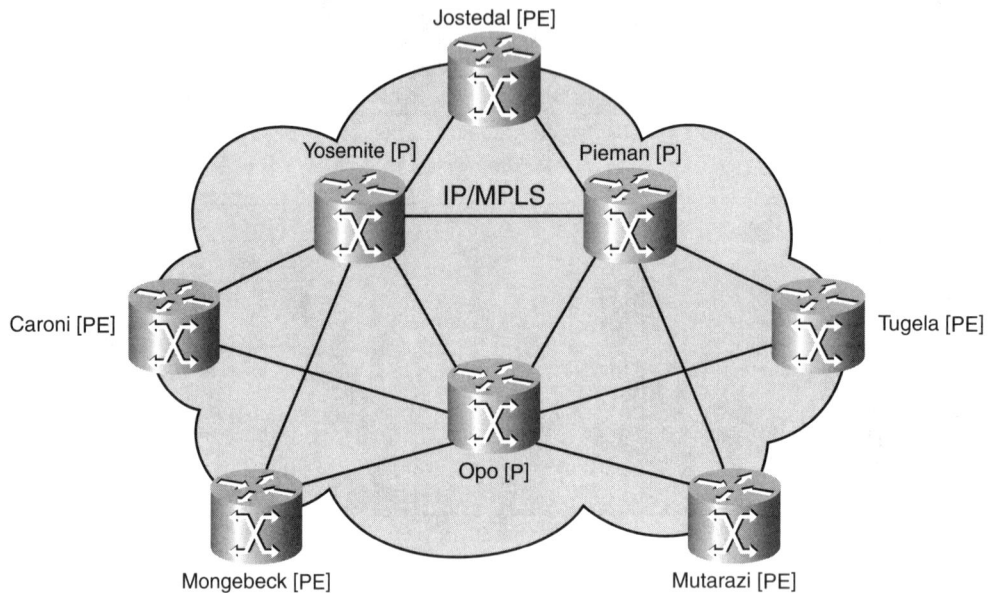

Edge Nodes

Tables 5-4 through 5-11 list the addresses and neighbors for each of the interfaces on all PE and P devices. You might find this information useful, along with the network topology, to follow some of the configuration examples in later sections.

Table 5-4   *Interface Information for Node Caroni[PE]*

Interface	IP Address	Neighbor
Loopback0	172.16.255.1/32	Caroni[PE]
POS0/1/0	172.16.0.0/31	Yosemite[P]
POS1/0/0	172.16.0.2/31	Opo[P]

Table 5-5 *Interface Information for Node Tugela[PE]*

Interface	IP Address	Neighbor
Loopback0	172.16.255.2/32	Tugela[PE]
POS2/0	172.16.4.0/31	Pieman[P]
POS2/1	172.16.4.2/31	Opo[P]

Table 5-6 *Interface Information for Node Jostedal[PE]*

Interface	IP Address	Neighbor
Loopback0	172.16.255.3/32	Jostedal[PE]
POS1/0	172.16.8.0/31	Yosemite[P]
POS1/1	172.16.8.2/31	Pieman[P]

Table 5-7 *Interface Information for Node Mongebeck[PE]*

Interface	IP Address	Neighbor
Loopback0	172.16.255.4/32	Mongebeck[PE]
POS2/1	172.16.0.6/31	Opo[P]
POS2/2	172.16.0.4/31	Yosemite[P]

Table 5-8 *Interface Information for Node Mutarazi[PE]*

Interface	IP Address	Neighbor
Loopback0	172.16.255.5/32	Mutarazi[PE]
POS2/1	172.16.4.6/31	Opo[P]
POS2/2	172.16.4.4/31	Pieman[P]

Table 5-9 *Interface Information for Node Yosemite[P]*

Interface	IP Address	Neighbor
Loopback0	172.16.255.129/32	Yosemite[P]
POS0/3/0/0	172.16.0.1/31	Caroni[PE]
POS0/3/0/1	172.16.192.0/31	Pieman[P]
POS0/3/0/2	172.16.192.2/31	Opo[P]
POS0/3/0/3	172.16.0.5/31	Mongebeck[P]
POS0/3/0/4	172.16.8.1/31	Jostedal[PE]

Table 5-10   *Interface Information for Node Pieman[P]*

Interface	IP Address	Neighbor
Loopback0	172.16.255.130/32	Pieman[P]
POS0/0/0	172.16.192.1/31	Yosemite[P]
POS0/1/0	172.16.4.5/31	Mutarazi[PE]
POS1/0/0	172.16.8.3/31	Jostedal[PE]
POS1/1/0	172.16.192.4/31	Opo[P]
POS2/0/0	172.16.4.1/31	Tugela[PE]

Table 5-11   *Interface Information for Node Opo[P]*

Interface	IP Address	Neighbor
Loopback0	172.16.255.131/32	Opo[P]
POS0/0/0	172.16.192.3/31	Yosemite[P]
POS0/1/0	172.16.4.7/31	Mutarazi[P]
POS0/1/1	172.16.4.3/31	Tugela[PE]
POS1/0/0	172.16.192.5/31	Pieman[P]
POS1/1/0	172.16.0.7/31	Mongebeck[PE]
POS2/0/0	172.16.0.3/31	Caroni[PE]

Later sections include configuration examples to help you understand the important concepts behind a particular design. Do *not* consider those as complete configurations. There are security, scalability, and platform-specific functionality you would need to consider to come up with a detailed design. Remember that some hardware and software you use might not support some of the commands or options in the examples. Furthermore, some of the configuration parameters that the configuration examples use are specific to the link speeds that this reference network uses. However, you should be able to use these configurations as starting points for your deployments.

QoS Design Alternatives

This section reviews several design alternatives that you can use to meet your backbone QoS targets. You will find that the first design is the simplest one; subsequent designs are progressively more elaborate. Each design explains whether it relies on controlling traffic load, capacity planning, or both. You will also find a comparison with respect to the differentiation and optimization that each alternative provides. In general, you can make any of these approaches provide your backbone performance targets. However, some will be more cost-effective than others depending on the specifics of your network, including the services it provides and the markets it serves.

Best-Effort Backbone

The simplest backbone approach to QoS is a best-effort backbone. This type of backbone offers no traffic differentiation. You must engineer your network for the tightest *service level agreement* (SLA) it must provide. All traffic will receive that SLA whether it needs it or not. The benefit of this approach might become questionable as the percentage of traffic needing the tightest SLA on a link decreases. As Figure 5-8 shows, you need to rely on capacity planning to guarantee the proper utilization level. A common approach is to make sure the link capacity is more than twice the average load on the traffic. Therefore, the maximum average utilization will be 50 percent.

Figure 5-8 *Control of Link Capacity Using a Best-Effort Backbone*

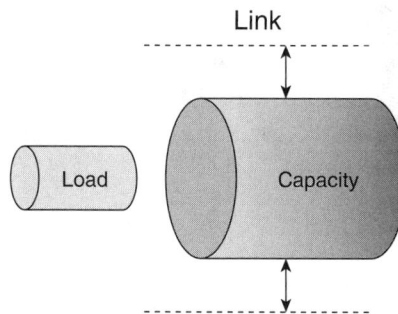

You should still engineer a best-effort backbone to handle the rare occurrence of congestion. Interfaces will not have to make any sophisticated packet-scheduling decisions in the presence of congestion, but you should specify a policy to manage the queue size. Numerous studies document the positive impact that *weighted random early detection* (WRED) has on TCP sessions. RFC 2309 provides a summary of those benefits and provides some useful references. TCP should contribute most of the traffic load on a backbone link, and WRED (as an AQM mechanism) should provide the best performance experience for those TCP sessions and for the network. You can do little to protect non-TCP traffic, and other traffic with strict performance requirements with this design. These considerations also apply to a best-effort network using IP exclusively.

You can use the *delay-bandwidth product* (DBP) as a guideline for your WRED configuration. The DBP equals the *round-trip time* (RTT) times the link bandwidth. This parameter determines the number of bytes that a sender can send before receiving feedback from the receiver. The DBP is an important parameter for window-based protocols such as TCP. A link that does not have enough queuing capacity will affect TCP throughput and link utilization. On the other hand, a link that queues an excessive amount of traffic will affect TCP latency. The maximum WRED threshold does not need to exceed the DBP, and the minimum threshold should be a scaled-down value of the maximum threshold. Figure 5-9 shows the DBP for different RTT values and different link rates. Tables 5-12 and 5-13 show the DBP for specific link types in bytes and 1500-byte packets, respectively.

Figure 5-9 *DBP for Different RTTs and Link Bandwidth Rates*

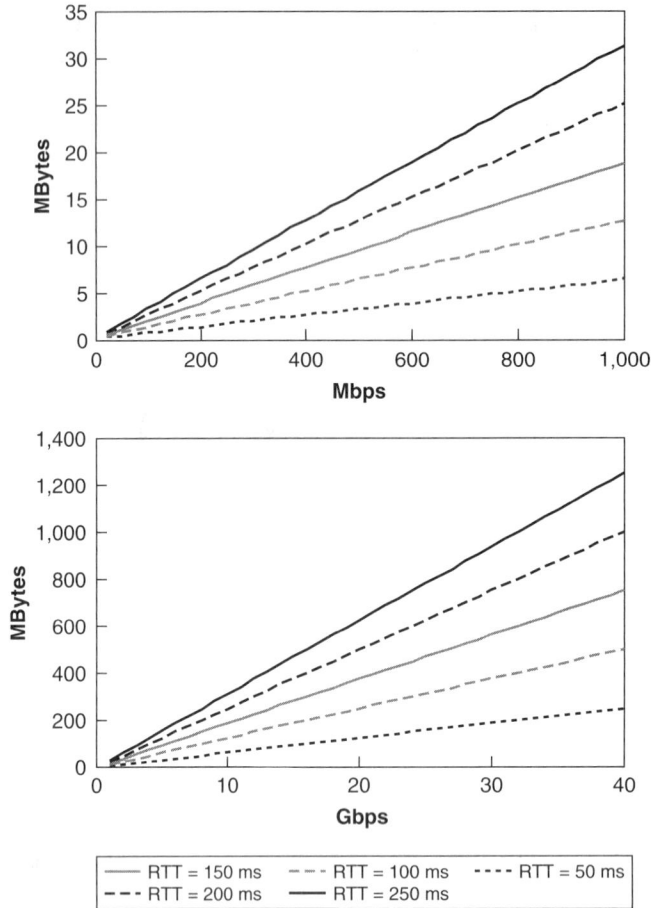

Table 5-12 *DBP in Bytes for Different RTTs and Selected Link Bandwidth Rates*

Link	RTT = 50 ms	RTT = 100 ms	RTT = 150 ms	RTT = 200 ms	RTT = 250 ms
Ethernet	62.5 KB	125 KB	187.5 KB	250 KB	312.5 KB
Fast Ethernet	0.625 MB	1.250 MB	1.875 MB	2.5 MB	3.125 MB
Gigabit Ethernet	6.25 MB	12.5 MB	18.75 MB	25 MB	31.25 MB
OC-3/STM-1	0.972 MB	1.944 MB	2.916 MB	3.888 MB	4.86 MB
OC-12/STM-4	3.888 MB	7.776 MB	11.664 MB	15.552 MB	19.440 MB
OC-48/STM-16	15.552 MB	31.104 MB	46.656 MB	62.208 MB	77.760 MB

Table 5-12 *DBP in Bytes for Different RTTs and Selected Link Bandwidth Rates (Continued)*

Link	RTT = 50 ms	RTT = 100 ms	RTT = 150 ms	RTT = 200 ms	RTT = 250 ms
OC-192/STM-64	62.208 MB	124.416 MB	186.624 MB	248.832 MB	311.04 MB
OC-768/STM-256	248.832 MB	497.664 MB	746.496 MB	995.328 MB	1244.16 MB

Table 5-13 *DBP in 1500-Byte Packets for Different RTTs and Selected Link Bandwidth Rates*

Link	RTT = 50 ms	RTT = 100 ms	RTT = 150 ms	RTT = 200 ms	RTT = 250 ms
Ethernet	42	83	125	167	208
Fast Ethernet	417	833	1250	1667	2083
Gigabit Ethernet	4167	8333	12,500	16,667	20,833
OC-3/STM-1	648	1296	1944	2592	3240
OC-12/STM-4	2592	5184	7776	10,368	12,960
OC-48/STM-16	10,368	20,736	31,104	41,472	51,840
OC-192/STM-64	41,472	82,944	124,416	165,888	207,360
OC-768/STM-256	165,888	331,776	497,664	663,552	829,440

Buffering requirements actually fall below the DBP for aggregated TCP flows. For a given link rate, the maximum queue size that a link requires to avoid affecting TCP performance decreases as the number of TCP flows increases. Links with higher rates carry more TCP flows. The DBP increases linearly with the link rate, but the buffering requirements do not grow at the same rate (because of the higher number of flows). This relationship implies that backbone links can use more-aggressive WRED thresholds than customer-facing links, which typically have lower speeds and, consequently, fewer TCP flows. See the "References" section sources for more information about sizing router buffers.

Example 5-1 shows the configuration of a Cisco IOS node for a best-effort design using WRED. The policy OUT-POLICY enables precedence-based WRED. This syntax has the effect of acting on the Precedence field for IP (unlabeled) packets and the MPLS EXP field for MPLS (labeled) packets. Values zero through five use the same minimum and maximum thresholds (33 ms and 100 ms, respectively). You could adjust these thresholds for specific values depending on the traffic type. In addition, the policy defines the maximum queue size as 150 ms. Values six and seven use the same minimum and maximum thresholds as these values should carry control-plane traffic. You could simplify the policy if the edge of the network marks all MPLS packets with the same value (for example, zero) or if you decide not to use WRED. The policy in this example would be equally appropriate for a pure IP network.

Example 5-1 *Node with Best-Effort Configuration Using WRED in Cisco IOS*

```
hostname Pieman[P]
!
policy-map OUT-POLICY
  class class-default
    random-detect
    random-detect precedence 0 33 ms 100 ms 1
    random-detect precedence 1 33 ms 100 ms 1
    random-detect precedence 2 33 ms 100 ms 1
    random-detect precedence 3 33 ms 100 ms 1
    random-detect precedence 4 33 ms 100 ms 1
    random-detect precedence 5 33 ms 100 ms 1
    random-detect precedence 6 100 ms 100 ms 1
    random-detect precedence 7 100 ms 100 ms 1
    queue-limit 150 ms
!
mpls label protocol ldp
!
interface Loopback0
 ip address 172.16.255.130 255.255.255.255
!
interface POS0/0/0
 description CONNECTS TO Yosemite[P]
 ip address 172.16.192.1 255.255.255.254
 encapsulation ppp
 mpls ip
 service-policy output OUT-POLICY
!
interface POS0/1/0
 description CONNECTS TO Mutarazi[PE]
 ip address 172.16.4.5 255.255.255.254
 encapsulation ppp
 mpls ip
 service-policy output OUT-POLICY
!
interface POS1/0/0
 description CONNECTS TO Jostedal[PE]
 ip address 172.16.8.3 255.255.255.254
 encapsulation ppp
 mpls ip
 service-policy output OUT-POLICY
!
interface POS1/1/0
 description CONNECTS TO Opo[P]
 ip address 172.16.192.4 255.255.255.254
 encapsulation ppp
 mpls ip
 service-policy output OUT-POLICY
!
interface POS2/0/0
 description CONNECTS TO Tugela[PE]
 ip address 172.16.4.1 255.255.255.254
 encapsulation ppp
```

Example 5-1 *Node with Best-Effort Configuration Using WRED in Cisco IOS (Continued)*

```
 mpls ip
 service-policy output OUT-POLICY
 !
router ospf 100
 log-adjacency-changes
 passive-interface Loopback0
 network 172.16.0.0 0.0.255.255 area 0
 !
```

Example 5-2 shows the configuration of a Cisco IOS XR node for a best-effort backbone that uses WRED. The definition of the WRED thresholds uses a slightly different syntax. You can define explicitly thresholds for specific MPLS packets. An exception is locally generated traffic that routers direct to adjacent neighbors. That traffic is typically control-plane traffic that includes Layer 2 packets and IP packets automatically generated with IP precedence 6. If your network carries some traffic as label packets and other traffic as un-labeled, make sure that the policy defines appropriate thresholds for both types of traffic.

Example 5-2 *Node with Best-Effort Configuration Using WRED in Cisco IOS XR*

```
hostname Yosemite[P]
router-id Loopback0
policy-map OUT-POLICY
 class class-default
  queue-limit 150 ms
  random-detect exp 0 33 ms 100 ms
  random-detect exp 1 33 ms 100 ms
  random-detect exp 2 33 ms 100 ms
  random-detect exp 3 33 ms 100 ms
  random-detect exp 4 33 ms 100 ms
  random-detect exp 5 33 ms 100 ms
  random-detect exp 6 100 ms 100 ms
  random-detect exp 7 100 ms 100 ms
 !
!
interface Loopback0
 ipv4 address 172.16.255.129 255.255.255.255
!
interface POS0/3/0/0
 description CONNECTS TO Caroni[PE]
 service-policy output OUT-POLICY
 ipv4 address 172.16.0.1 255.255.255.254
 encapsulation ppp
!
interface POS0/3/0/1
 description CONNECTS TO Pieman[P]
 service-policy output OUT-POLICY
 ipv4 address 172.16.192.0 255.255.255.254
 encapsulation ppp
!
interface POS0/3/0/2
```

continues

Example 5-2 *Node with Best-Effort Configuration Using WRED in Cisco IOS XR (Continued)*

```
  description CONNECTS TO Opo[P]
  service-policy output OUT-POLICY
  ipv4 address 172.16.192.2 255.255.255.254
  encapsulation ppp
 !
 interface POS0/3/0/3
  description CONNECTS TO Mongebeck[PE]
  service-policy output OUT-POLICY
  ipv4 address 172.16.0.5 255.255.255.254
  encapsulation ppp
 !
 interface POS0/3/0/4
  description CONNECTS TO Jostedal[PE]
  service-policy output OUT-POLICY
  ipv4 address 172.16.8.1 255.255.255.254
  encapsulation ppp
 !
 router ospf DEFAULT
  area 0
   interface Loopback0
    passive
    !
   interface POS0/3/0/0
   !
   interface POS0/3/0/1
   !
   interface POS0/3/0/2
   !
   interface POS0/3/0/3
   !
   interface POS0/3/0/4
   !
  !
 !
 mpls ldp
  interface POS0/3/0/0
  !
  interface POS0/3/0/1
  !
  interface POS0/3/0/2
  !
  interface POS0/3/0/3
  !
  interface POS0/3/0/4
  !
 !
```

Best-Effort Backbone with MPLS TE

You can enhance a best-effort backbone with the deployment of MPLS TE to improve control over link utilization and to achieve better bandwidth optimization. MPLS TE provides admission control, enabling you to manage how much traffic load you put on a link. As Figure 5-10 shows, you can achieve a target link utilization level by controlling the traffic load using MPLS TE. Furthermore, MPLS TE enables you to perform constraint-based routing that can factor bandwidth availability. This routing enhancement allows traffic to take advantage of underused links and thus avoid backbone congestion. This design contrasts with a simple best-effort backbone that does not have much control on traffic load and relies exclusively on capacity planning to achieve a particular utilization target.

Figure 5-10 *Control of Link Load Using a Best-Effort Backbone and MPLS TE*

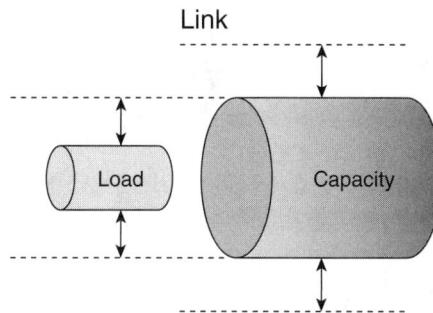

The use of MPLS TE still requires control over how traffic enters the backbone. The network needs to use TE *link switched paths* (LSPs) to forward all traffic if you want admission control to be functional as a mechanism to control traffic load. If the network forwards significant amounts of traffic outside of TE LSPs, the bandwidth that MPLS TE considers available when performing path computation and admission control might differ from the actual bandwidth availability. Given that the network does not perform any traffic differentiation in the forwarding plane (remember this scenario assumes a best-effort network), this difference can result in unexpected congestion. As Figure 5-11 shows, you want to build a full mesh of TE LSPs that you size according to the traffic matrix between headends and tailends.

Figure 5-11 *Full Mesh of TE LSPs Between PE Devices*

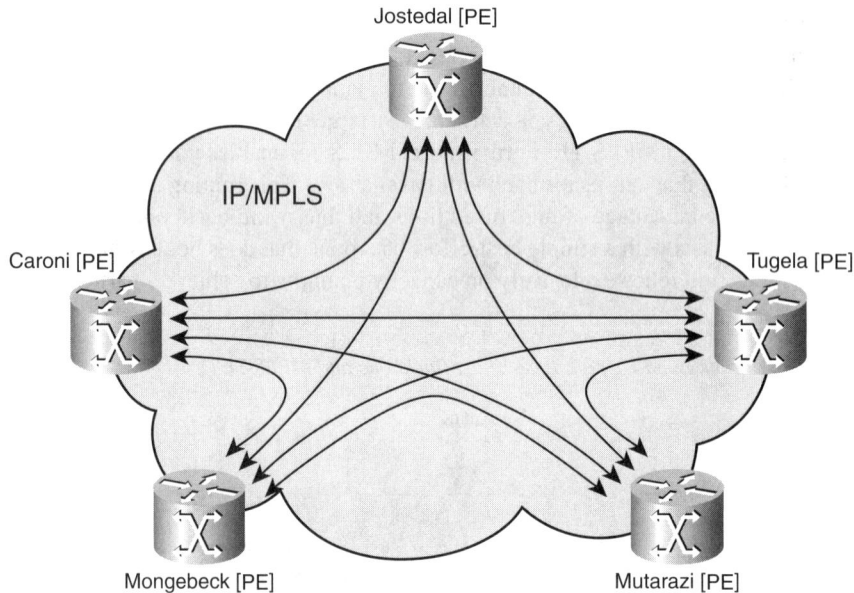

NOTE	The deployment of LDP is common in this design despite the presence of a full mesh of TE LSPs. LDP provides a safety net to guarantee the correct operation of several network services in case a TE LSP fails. The deployment of high-availability mechanisms and *fast reroute* (FRR) can significantly reduce the chances of TE LSP failure.

You can build your TE LSP mesh between nonedge devices to reduce complexity and increase scalability. For example, you could use the P devices that aggregate the traffic of a *point of presence* (POP) as tailends and headends instead of using your PE devices. This approach results in a smaller mesh of TE LSPs (because of the lower number of endpoints). Many network services require an LSP between PE devices. Therefore, you need to enable LDP on those interfaces that are not part of the MPLS TE network and the tunnel interfaces of the TE LSP headends. Figure 5-12 shows the full mesh that will result from the reference network. When you compare it with Figure 5-11, you easily notice the lower number of endpoints and TE LSPs.

Figure 5-12 *Full Mesh of TE LSPs Between P Devices*

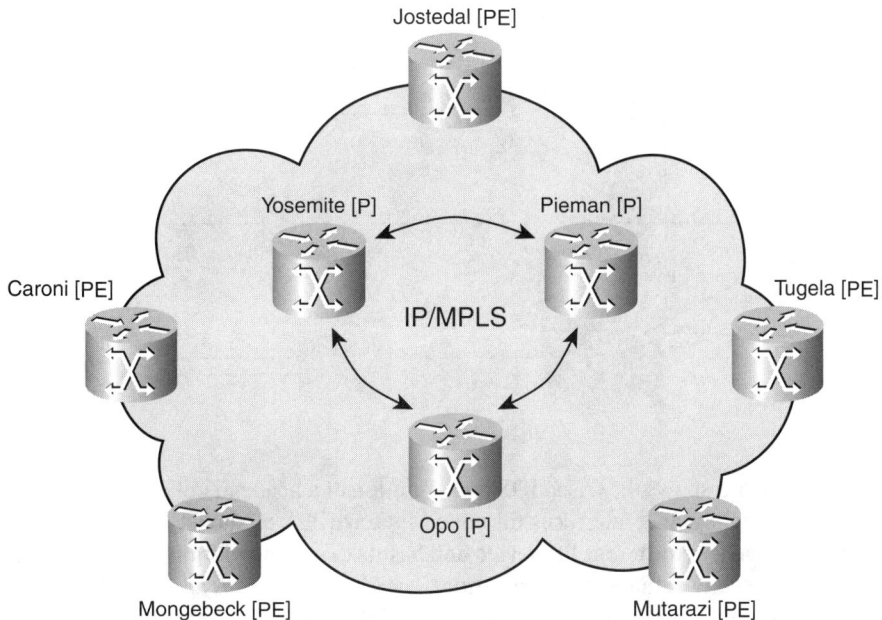

MPLS TE also requires control over the amount of traffic that enters a TE LSP that made a bandwidth reservation. The TE LSP does not enforce automatically the bandwidth reservation while forwarding traffic. That is, the fact that you signal a TE LSP successfully for 100 Mbps does not imply that the network will ensure automatically that the LSP only forwards 100 Mbps worth of traffic. You must perform capacity planning on the TE LSP at the headend and proper traffic conditioning (shaping or policing) upstream. Figure 5-13 shows how a PE device can police traffic before it reaches the TE LSP. Traffic conditioning may even take place further upstream on a *customer e*dge (CE) device if you have administrative control over such device.

This design still relies on a best-effort backbone and does not offer traffic differentiation. You must engineer your network for the tightest SLA that the network must provide. All traffic will receive that SLA whether it requires it or not. As the previous section discussed, you might still want to engineer the network to handle the rare occurrence of congestion despite the fact that the use of MPLS TE makes the presence of congestion on an interface less likely. This requirement implies the use of AQM. The previous section already provided some guidelines regarding the configuration of AQM on a best-effort backbone. Such configuration enables a rudimentary form of traffic differentiation.

Figure 5-13 *Policing Traffic That a TE LSP Transports*

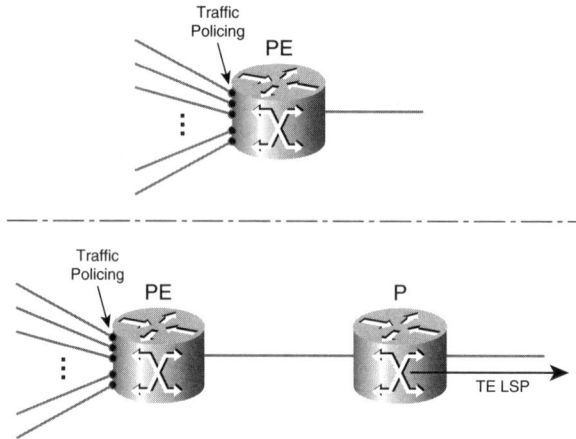

Example 5-3 shows the Cisco IOS configuration of a headend node. This example includes four different tunnel interfaces for node Mutarazi[PE], as shown in Figure 5-11. Each tunnel reaches a different PE device and has its own bandwidth reservation to meet traffic requirements. All tunnels use *constraint-based, shortest path first* (CSPF) to compute the TE LSPs and autoroute for traffic selection. Interfaces facing other P devices make use of WRED for AQM. This example does not illustrate the conditioning of the traffic that the tunnel will eventually forward.

Example 5-3 *Node with MPLS TE and Best-Effort Configuration Using WRED in Cisco IOS*

```
hostname Mutarazi[PE]
!
mpls label protocol ldp
mpls traffic-eng tunnels
!
policy-map OUT-POLICY
  class class-default
    random-detect
    random-detect precedence 0 2498 7568
    random-detect precedence 1 2498 7568
    random-detect precedence 2 2498 7568
    random-detect precedence 3 2498 7568
    random-detect precedence 4 2498 7568
    random-detect precedence 5 2498 7568
    random-detect precedence 6 7568 7568
    random-detect precedence 7 7568 7568
    queue-limit 11353
!
interface Loopback0
 ip address 172.16.255.5 255.255.255.255
!
interface Tunnel1
 description Mutarazi[PE]->Caroni[PE]
```

Example 5-3 *Node with MPLS TE and Best-Effort Configuration Using WRED in Cisco IOS (Continued)*

```
 ip unnumbered Loopback0
 tunnel destination 172.16.255.1
 tunnel mode mpls traffic-eng
 tunnel mpls traffic-eng autoroute announce
 tunnel mpls traffic-eng priority 7 7
 tunnel mpls traffic-eng bandwidth  30000
 tunnel mpls traffic-eng path-option 10 dynamic
!
interface Tunnel2
 description Mutarazi[PE]->Tugela[PE]
 ip unnumbered Loopback0
 tunnel destination 172.16.255.2
 tunnel mode mpls traffic-eng
 tunnel mpls traffic-eng autoroute announce
 tunnel mpls traffic-eng priority 7 7
 tunnel mpls traffic-eng bandwidth  10000
 tunnel mpls traffic-eng path-option 10 dynamic
!
interface Tunnel3
 description Mutarazi[PE]->Jostedal[PE]
 ip unnumbered Loopback0
 tunnel destination 172.16.255.3
 tunnel mode mpls traffic-eng
 tunnel mpls traffic-eng autoroute announce
 tunnel mpls traffic-eng priority 7 7
 tunnel mpls traffic-eng bandwidth  20000
 tunnel mpls traffic-eng path-option 10 dynamic
!
interface Tunnel4
 description Mutarazi[PE]->Mongebeck[PE]
 ip unnumbered Loopback0
 tunnel destination 172.16.255.4
 tunnel mode mpls traffic-eng
 tunnel mpls traffic-eng autoroute announce
 tunnel mpls traffic-eng priority 7 7
 tunnel mpls traffic-eng bandwidth  30000
 tunnel mpls traffic-eng path-option 10 dynamic
!
interface POS2/1
 description CONNECTS TO Opo[P]
 ip address 172.16.4.6 255.255.255.254
 encapsulation ppp
 mpls traffic-eng tunnels
 mpls ip
 service-policy output OUT-POLICY
 ip rsvp bandwidth 155000
!
interface POS2/2
 description CONNECTS TO Pieman[P]
 ip address 172.16.4.4 255.255.255.254
 encapsulation ppp
 mpls traffic-eng tunnels
```

continues

Example 5-3 *Node with MPLS TE and Best-Effort Configuration Using WRED in Cisco IOS (Continued)*

```
 mpls ip
 service-policy output OUT-POLICY
 ip rsvp bandwidth 155000
 !
router ospf 100
 mpls traffic-eng router-id Loopback0
 mpls traffic-eng area 0
 log-adjacency-changes
 redistribute connected
 passive-interface Loopback0
 network 172.16.0.0 0.0.255.255 area 0
 !
```

Example 5-4 shows the Cisco IOS XR configuration of a headend node residing inside the MPLS network. This example includes two different tunnel interfaces for node Yosemite[P] (as shown in Figure 5-12) and represents a different design compared to that in Example 5-3. In this case, the tunnels also use CSPF for path computation and autoroute for traffic forwarding. The tunnels run LDP sessions to signal LSPs between PE devices. All physical interfaces use WRED for AQM. This example shows how the deployment of TE LSPs between P devices simplifies the implementation of a full mesh. However, the control over the PE-to-P links decreases because those links are not part of the MPLS TE network. Furthermore, you have less control over the amount of traffic that the TE LSP will carry. Controlling these links might not be critical because they generally connect devices within the same facility, and you can engineer them with ample capacity. You can also enable LDP sessions over a tunnel in Cisco IOS.

Example 5-4 *Node with MPLS TE and Best-Effort Configuration Using WRED in Cisco IOS XR*

```
hostname Yosemite[P]
router-id Loopback0
policy-map OUT-POLICY
 class class-default
  queue-limit 11353
  random-detect exp 0 2498 7568
  random-detect exp 1 2498 7568
  random-detect exp 2 2498 7568
  random-detect exp 3 2498 7568
  random-detect exp 4 2498 7568
  random-detect exp 5 2498 7568
  random-detect exp 6 7568 7568
  random-detect exp 7 7568 7568
 !
!
interface Loopback0
 ipv4 address 172.16.255.129 255.255.255.255
 !
interface tunnel-te1
 description Yosemite[P]->Pieman[P]
 ipv4 unnumbered Loopback0
 signalled bandwidth 100000
 autoroute announce
```

Example 5-4 *Node with MPLS TE and Best-Effort Configuration Using WRED in Cisco IOS XR (Continued)*

```
 destination 172.16.255.130
 path-option 10 dynamic
!
interface tunnel-te2
 description Yosemite[P]->Opo[P]
 ipv4 unnumbered Loopback0
 signalled-bandwidth 75000
 autoroute announce
 destination 172.16.255.131
 path-option 10 dynamic
!
interface POS0/3/0/0
 description CONNECTS TO Caroni[PE]
 service-policy output OUT-POLICY
 ipv4 address 172.16.0.1 255.255.255.254
 encapsulation ppp
!
interface POS0/3/0/1
 description CONNECTS TO Pieman[P]
 service-policy output OUT-POLICY
 ipv4 address 172.16.192.0 255.255.255.254
 encapsulation ppp
!
interface POS0/3/0/2
 description CONNECTS TO Opo[P]
 service-policy output OUT-POLICY
 ipv4 address 172.16.192.2 255.255.255.254
 encapsulation ppp
!
interface POS0/3/0/3
 description CONNECTS TO Mongebeck[PE]
 service-policy output OUT-POLICY
 ipv4 address 172.16.0.5 255.255.255.254
 encapsulation ppp
!
interface POS0/3/0/4
 description CONNECTS TO Jostedal[PE]
 service-policy output OUT-POLICY
 ipv4 address 172.16.8.1 255.255.255.254
 encapsulation ppp
!
router ospf DEFAULT
 area 0
  interface Loopback0
   passive
   !
  interface POS0/3/0/0
   !
  interface POS0/3/0/1
   !
  interface POS0/3/0/2
   !
```

continues

Example 5-4 *Node with MPLS TE and Best-Effort Configuration Using WRED in Cisco IOS XR (Continued)*

```
 interface POS0/3/0/3
 !
 interface POS0/3/0/4
 !
!
mpls traffic-eng area 0
!
rsvp
 interface POS0/3/0/1
  bandwidth 155000
 !
 interface POS0/3/0/2
  bandwidth 155000
 !
!
mpls traffic-eng
 interface POS0/3/0/1
 !
 interface POS0/3/0/2
 !
!
mpls ldp
 interface POS0/3/0/0
 !
 interface POS0/3/0/1
 !
 interface POS0/3/0/2
 !
 interface POS0/3/0/3
 !
 interface POS0/3/0/4
 !
 interface tunnel-te1
 !
 interface tunnel-te2
 !
!
```

DiffServ Backbone

DiffServ introduces traffic differentiation to the backbone. As Figure 5-14 shows, you now perform capacity planning per class and use different utilization targets for the different classes according to their performance requirements. This per-class control brings some level of resource optimization because you do not need to engineer the entire link capacity to meet the tightest SLA. The benefit of deploying DiffServ increases as the percentage of traffic needing the tightest SLA on a link decreases. In a way, the deployment of DiffServ creates multiple virtual networks, where you perform capacity planning independently.

Figure 5-14 *Control of Class Capacity Using DiffServ*

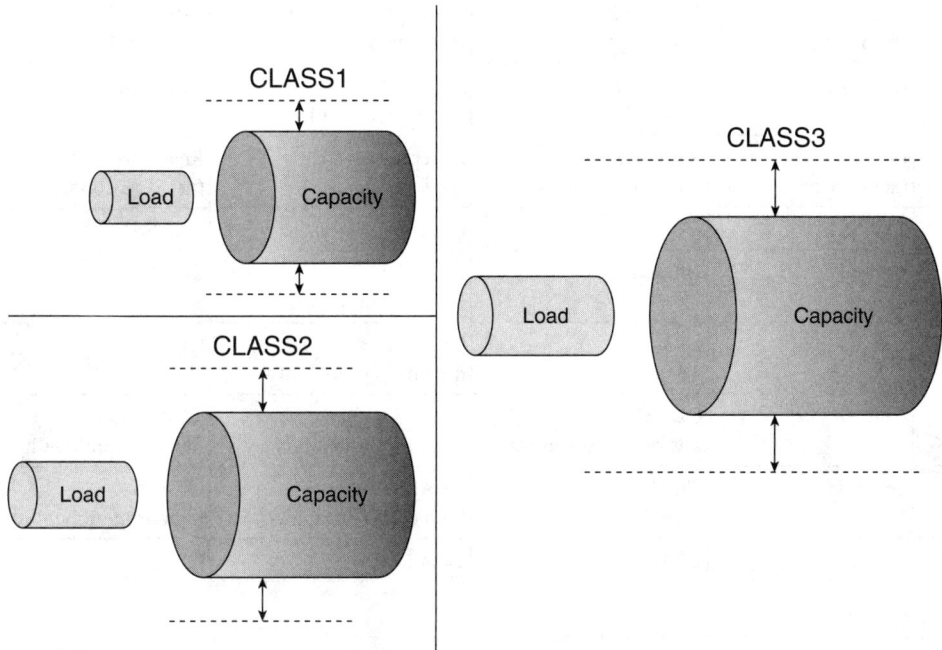

You need to define the different classes and their respective packet markings to implement DiffServ in an MPLS network. *EXP-inferred LSPs* (E-LSPs) are the preferred approach for the implementation of DiffServ on MPLS networks. The MPLS EXP field provides enough values to satisfy the requirements of most current deployments. Table 5-14 illustrates four designs with different uses of the MPLS EXP field. In general, network control traffic should make use of MPLS EXP values six and seven. You should use the MPLS EXP value of five for *Expedited Forwarding* (EF) traffic and the MPLS EXP value of zero for default or best-effort traffic. You can use values one through four to define other classes, including those offering *Assured Forwarding* (AF) behaviors. These are obviously not the only designs possible, but they follow common best practices. A pure IP network should use the recommended DSCP values.

Table 5-14 *Sample Alternatives for the Allocation of MPLS EXP Values*

MPLS EXP	Design 1 (EF and DF)	Design 2 (EF, AF, and DF)	Design 3 (EF, AF1, AF2, and DF)	Design 4 (EF, CS4, CS3, AF, and DF)
7	Reserved (network control)	Reserved (network control)	Reserved (network control)	Reserved (network control)
6	Reserved (network control)	Reserved (network control)	Reserved (network control)	Reserved (network control)
5	CLASS1	CLASS1	CLASS1	CLASS1
4	Unused	Unused	CLASS2; low drop probability	CLASS2
3	Unused	Unused	CLASS2; high drop probability	CLASS3
2	Unused	CLASS2; low drop probability	CLASS3; low drop probability	CLASS4; low drop probability
1	Unused	CLASS2; high drop probability	CLASS3; high drop probability	CLASS4; high drop probability
0	CLASS2	CLASS3	CLASS4	CLASS5

NOTE The recommendation to reserve MPLS EXP values 6 and 7 for network control relates to the historical definition of the IP Precedence field in RFC 1349. By default, Cisco routers make use of only IP precedence 6 and, therefore, MPLS EXP 6 for control-plane traffic.

Most DiffServ deployments use a relatively small number of queues in the backbone. They typically use between two and four queues. This simplification facilitates the operation and management of the network but requires proper design to guarantee that the network meets all performance requirements.

Table 5-15 illustrates three common designs for the implementation of DiffServ. All of them use a dedicated queue for real-time traffic and a separate queue that does not provide any performance guarantees. Designs 2 and 3 make use of additional queues that have special low-loss targets. You can map classes with similar performance requirements to the same queue. In general, the number of queues is equal or lower than the number of classes. Most deployments resemble one of these designs.

Table 5-15 *Sample Alternatives for DiffServ Implementation*

Performance Guarantees	Design 1	Design 2	Design 3
Low latency, low jitter, and low loss (no AQM)	Queue1	Queue1	Queue1
Low loss (no AQM)	—	—	Queue2

Table 5-15 *Sample Alternatives for DiffServ Implementation (Continued)*

Performance Guarantees	Design 1	Design 2	Design 3
Low loss (AQM)	—	Queue2	Queue3
No guarantees (AQM)	Queue2	Queue3	Queue4

You must carefully select and test the configuration parameters of your DiffServ configuration. You need to identify the expected load for each class and determine the overprovisioning or oversubscription factor. You can police the real-time traffic to avoid unexpected starvation of other classes. If you decide to use a policer, you need to identify the proper traffic profile to use. Adjusting the burst size allows you to control the trade-off between delay, jitter, and packet loss. For other queues, the maximum queue size determines the worst-case delay. The DBP will provide you with an upper bound. Those queues carrying classes with a drop priority should use WRED thresholds that discard first the packets with higher drop priority.

You need to completely understand the marking and encapsulation of all traffic in an MPLS network that uses DiffServ. Not all packets in an MPLS network will receive a label. The network may forward some traffic as IP packets. You need to verify that all nodes will classify and process packets according to their encapsulation. In addition, all traffic coming into the network must receive a marking corresponding to its appropriate performance level. All edge devices should mark all incoming packets as traffic without any guarantees after they carefully classify and mark the packets that should receive a differentiated service. In addition, all backbone devices should treat all packets as traffic without any guarantees after they select the traffic to differentiate.

Example 5-5 shows an MPLS DiffServ implementation with a two-parameter scheduler and four queues using Cisco IOS. CLASS1 groups packets with an MPLS EXP value of five. The policy provides EF treatment to CLASS1. CLASS2 includes IP packets with a DSCP value of CS6 and MPLS packets with EXP values of four and six. It serves control traffic and interactive data without a need for TCP optimization and with a lower delay and loss target. Packets with MPLS EXP values of one or two are part of CLASS3, which provides AF treatment for high-throughput data traffic and uses WRED for AQM to provide differentiated packet dropping and TCP optimization. Finally, class-default serves all other traffic (MPLS EXP value of zero) without a particular performance target other than TCP optimization.

Example 5-5 *MPLS Node with DiffServ Configuration Using Cisco IOS*

```
hostname Mutarazi[PE]
!
mpls label protocol ldp
!
class-map match-all CLASS1
  match mpls experimental topmost 5
class-map match-any CLASS2
  match mpls experimental topmost 4  6
  match  dscp cs6
```

continues

Example 5-5 *MPLS Node with DiffServ Configuration Using Cisco IOS (Continued)*

```
class-map match-all CLASS3
  match mpls experimental topmost 1  2
!
policy-map OUT-POLICY
  class CLASS1
    priority
    police rate 50 burst 20 ms
  class CLASS2
    bandwidth percent 20
    queue-limit 757
  class CLASS3
    bandwidth percent 20
    random-detect
    random-detect precedence 1 151 500 1
    random-detect precedence 2 86 1514 1
    queue-limit 387
  class class-default
    random-detect
    random-detect precedence 0 378 1135 1
    queue-limit 1514
    bandwidth percent 10
!
interface Loopback0
 ip address 172.16.255.5 255.255.255.255
!
interface POS2/1
 description CONNECTS TO Opo[P]
 ip address 172.16.4.6 255.255.255.254
 encapsulation ppp
 mpls ip
 service-policy output OUT-POLICY
!
interface POS2/2
 description CONNECTS TO Pieman[P]
 ip address 172.16.4.4 255.255.255.254
 encapsulation ppp
 mpls ip
 service-policy output OUT-POLICY
!
router ospf 100
 log-adjacency-changes
 passive-interface Loopback0
 network 172.16.0.0 0.0.255.255 area 0
!
```

The QoS policy in Example 5-5 uses parameters with the appropriate scale for an OC-3/STM-1 interface. CLASS1 receives low-latency service, and a policer limits it to 50 percent of the total bandwidth (77.5 Mbps) with a burst of 20 ms (193,750 bytes). CLASS2 has a minimum-bandwidth guarantee of 20 percent and a maximum queue size of 757 packets (50 ms for 256-bytes packets). CLASS3 has the same bandwidth guarantee but uses WRED to implement differentiated drop behavior. Packets with an MPLS EXP value of one have a higher drop probability and experience more aggressive thresholds (151 and 500 packets, or 10 ms and 33 ms, respectively). A value of two indicates a lower drop probability and experiences less-aggressive thresholds (100 and 1514 packets, or 33 ms and 100 ms, respectively). The maximum queue size for CLASS3 is 2271 packets (150 ms). Finally, class-default receives a ten percent bandwidth guarantee, uses WRED for TCP optimization (378 and 1135 packets, or 50 ms and 150 ms, respectively), and has a maximum queue size of 1514 packets (200 ms).

NOTE	Tuning your DiffServ policies is a complex task that requires a good understanding of traffic patterns and target utilization levels (among other variables). You should not assume that the examples in this section are appropriate for an arbitrary network environment.

Example 5-6 shows an MPLS DiffServ implementation with four queues and a three-parameter scheduler using Cisco IOS XR. The QoS policy uses the same number of classes with the same performance characteristics. The main difference is the use of a three-parameter scheduler. In this case, CLASS2, CLASS3, and class-default have minimum- and excess-bandwidth guarantees. CLASS2 has more access to excess bandwidth followed by CLASS3 and then followed by class-default. This policy should result in slightly better performance characteristics for CLASS2 and CLASS3 when you compare it with the policy in Example 5-5. This policy uses the same parameters for the maximum queue sizes and WRED threshold that the previous example used.

Example 5-6 *MPLS Node with DiffServ Configuration Using Cisco IOS XR*

```
hostname Yosemite[P]
router-id Loopback0
class-map match-any CLASS1
 match mpls experimental topmost 5
!
class-map match-any CLASS2
 match mpls experimental topmost 4 6
 match dscp ipv4 cs6
!
class-map match-any CLASS3
 match mpls experimental topmost 1 2
!
policy-map OUT-POLICY
 class CLASS1
  police rate percent 50 burst 20 ms
  priority
 !
 class CLASS2
  queue-limit 757
```

continues

Example 5-6 *MPLS Node with DiffServ Configuration Using Cisco IOS XR (Continued)*

```
   bandwidth percent 20
   bandwidth remaining percent 60
  !
 class CLASS3
  queue-limit 2271
  random-detect exp 1 151 500
  random-detect exp 2 500 1514
  bandwidth percent 20
  bandwidth remaining percent 30
  !
 class class-default
  queue-limit 1514
  random-detect exp 0 378 1135
  bandwidth percent 10
  bandwidth remaining percent 10
  !
 !
interface Loopback0
 ipv4 address 172.16.255.129 255.255.255.255
 !
interface POS0/3/0/0
 description CONNECTS TO Caroni[PE]
 service-policy output OUT-POLICY
 ipv4 address 172.16.0.1 255.255.255.254
 encapsulation ppp
 !
interface POS0/3/0/1
 description CONNECTS TO Pieman[P]
 service-policy output OUT-POLICY
 ipv4 address 172.16.192.0 255.255.255.254
 encapsulation ppp
 !
interface POS0/3/0/2
 description CONNECTS TO Opo[P]
 service-policy output OUT-POLICY
 ipv4 address 172.16.192.2 255.255.255.254
 encapsulation ppp
 !
interface POS0/3/0/3
 description CONNECTS TO Mongebeck[PE]
 service-policy output OUT-POLICY
 ipv4 address 172.16.0.5 255.255.255.254
 encapsulation ppp
 !
interface POS0/3/0/4
 description CONNECTS TO Jostedal[PE]
 service-policy output OUT-POLICY
 ipv4 address 172.16.8.1 255.255.255.254
 encapsulation ppp
 !
router ospf DEFAULT
 area 0
```

Example 5-6 *MPLS Node with DiffServ Configuration Using Cisco IOS XR (Continued)*

```
     interface Loopback0
      passive
     !
     interface POS0/3/0/0
     !
     interface POS0/3/0/1
     !
     interface POS0/3/0/2
     !
     interface POS0/3/0/3
     !
     interface POS0/3/0/4
      !
     !
    !
   mpls ldp
    interface POS0/3/0/0
    !
    interface POS0/3/0/1
    !
    interface POS0/3/0/2
    !
    interface POS0/3/0/3
    !
    interface POS0/3/0/4
    !
    !
```

NOTE   Some Cisco platforms have internal points of congestion. This is particularly true for platforms with distributed architectures that provide queuing capabilities for traffic entering the switching fabric. A complete DiffServ implementation must also define proper policies to perform traffic differentiation at those congestion points.

DiffServ Backbone with MPLS TE

You can combine DiffServ and MPLS TE to achieve traffic differentiation and some degree of optimization. In this case, MPLS TE can provide control over link utilization and help obtain better bandwidth utilization while DiffServ provides traffic differentiation in the forwarding plane. You can use MPLS TE to achieve a target link utilization and avoid congestion, while your DiffServ configuration acts as a safety net in case a link experiences congestion (for example, because of link or node failure in the network). The headend does not require taking MPLS EXP values into consideration when forwarding traffic through the TE LSPs. Figures 5-10 and 5-14 illustrate how this design controls link utilization using MPLS TE and the capacity of individual traffic classes using DiffServ.

Alternatively, you can use MPLS TE to control the load of a DiffServ class. In this approach, the maximum reservable bandwidth of each link relates to the bandwidth allocation of one of your DiffServ classes. You can control the link capacity for each class using your DiffServ configuration and control the load of one of them using MPLS TE. Figure 5-15 illustrates this design where MPLS TE controls the load of CLASS1. An obvious implementation is to use MPLS TE to control the load for your real-time traffic. MPLS TE would provide admission control for your priority queue. TE LSPs would carry real-time traffic exclusively, and the network would transport only real-time traffic using TE LSPs. You need to make sure that the headend switches packets only of the appropriate class into the TE LSP.

Figure 5-15 *Control of Class Capacity Using DiffServ and Load on a Single Class Using MPLS TE*

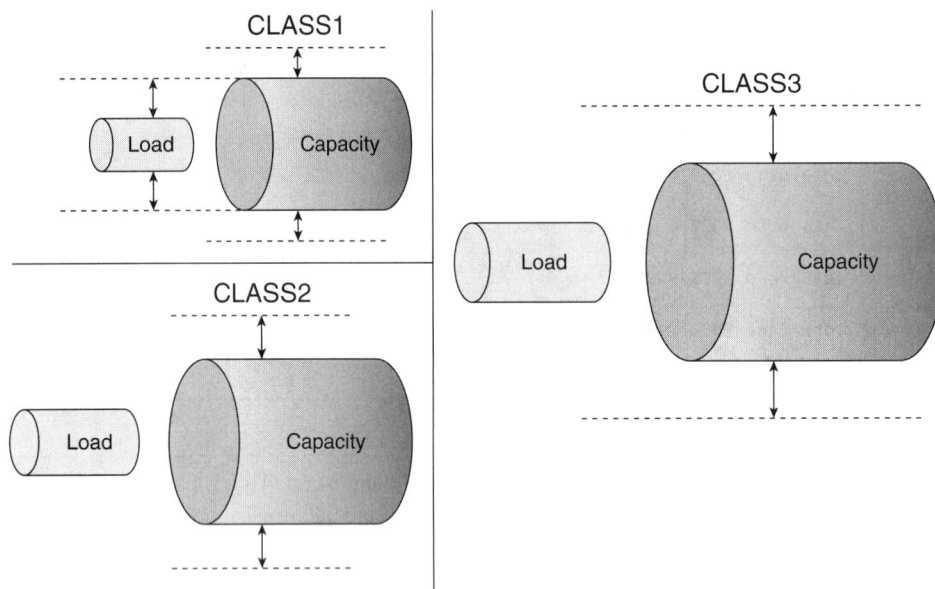

Example 5-7 shows how you can use MPLS TE to perform admission control for a DiffServ class in Cisco IOS. This node has a QoS policy that resembles previous examples. MPLS TE will control the load of CLASS1 that corresponds to the priority (EF) traffic. The policy limits the priority traffic to 40 percent (62 Mbps) of the total link capacity (155 Mbps) on interfaces POS2/1 and POS2/0. Simultaneously, MPLS TE limits the maximum reservable bandwidth on those two interfaces to 20 percent (31 Mbps) of the total link capacity. This example illustrates a design that overprovisions the priority capacity on these links by a factor of two. Overprovisioning makes the performance guarantees of the priority traffic more resilient to network failures.

Example 5-7 *Node with DiffServ and MPLS TE Configuration in Cisco IOS*

```
hostname Tugela[PE]
!
class-map match-all CLASS1
  match mpls experimental  5
class-map match-any CLASS2
  match mpls experimental  4  6
  match  dscp cs6
class-map match-all CLASS3
  match mpls experimental  1  2
!
policy-map OUT-POLICY
  class CLASS1
    priority
    police rate percent 40 burst 20 ms
  class CLASS2
    bandwidth remaining percent 30
    queue-limit 50 ms
  class CLASS3
    bandwidth remaining percent 60
    random-detect
    random-detect precedence 1 15 ms 44 ms 1
    random-detect precedence 2 44 ms 132 ms 1
    queue-limit 200 ms
  class class-default
    bandwidth remaining percent 10
    random-detect
    random-detect precedence 0 44 ms 132 ms 1
    queue-limit 200 ms
!
mpls label protocol ldp
mpls traffic-eng tunnels
!
interface Loopback0
 ip address 172.16.255.2 255.255.255.255
!
interface Tunnel1
 description Tugela[PE]->Caroni[PE]-1
 ip unnumbered Loopback0
 tunnel destination 172.16.255.1
 tunnel mode mpls traffic-eng
 tunnel mpls traffic-eng autoroute announce
 tunnel mpls traffic-eng priority 7 7
 tunnel mpls traffic-eng bandwidth  15000
 tunnel mpls traffic-eng path-option 10 dynamic
 tunnel mpls traffic-eng exp 5
!
interface Tunnel2
 description Tugela[PE]->Caroni[PE]-2
 ip unnumbered Loopback0
 tunnel destination 172.16.255.1
 tunnel mode mpls traffic-eng
 tunnel mpls traffic-eng autoroute announce
```

continues

Example 5-7 *Node with DiffServ and MPLS TE Configuration in Cisco IOS (Continued)*

```
 tunnel mpls traffic-eng path-option 10 dynamic
 tunnel mpls traffic-eng exp default
!
interface POS2/0
 description CONNECTS TO Pieman[P]
 ip address 172.16.4.0 255.255.255.254
 encapsulation ppp
 mpls traffic-eng tunnels
 mpls ip
 service-policy output OUT-POLICY
 ip rsvp bandwidth 31000
!
interface POS2/1
 description CONNECTS TO Opo[P]
 ip address 172.16.4.2 255.255.255.254
 encapsulation ppp
 mpls traffic-eng tunnels
 mpls ip
 service-policy output OUT-POLICY
 ip rsvp bandwidth 31000
!
router ospf 100
 mpls traffic-eng area 0
 log-adjecency-changes
 mpls traffic-eng level-2
 passive-interface Loopback0
 network 172.16.0.0.0.0.255.255 area 0
!
```

Example 5-7 uses CBTS to control traffic forwarding at the tunnel headend. The goal of this configuration is to guarantee that only packets with an MPLS EXP value of five use the priority queue and that all those packets make use of a TE tunnel. To guarantee the proper functioning of CBTS, the node uses a second tunnel (Tunnel2) to carry other traffic (packets with MPLS EXP values different from five). The tunnel uses a dynamic path without any constraints (for example, bandwidth or affinity bits). The CBTS configuration guarantees that nonpriority traffic will follow the shortest path that the *interior gateway protocol* (IGP) would use. Furthermore, the QoS policy guarantees that nonpriority queues serve nonpriority traffic.

NOTE   CTBS will act on MPLS-switched packets and IP-routed packets that have just received a label. If your tunnel headend is providing Layer 2 services, you need to verify in the equipment you are configuring whether CBTS will act on Layer 2 (*Layer 2 virtual private network* [L2VPN]) packets that have just received a label. You might need to use complementary mechanisms to make sure that those MPLS packets follow the same forwarding behavior that CBTS implements.

You do not require a full mesh of TE LSPs when using MPLS TE to control a DiffServ class. As you probably noticed in Example 5-7, the node only uses two tunnels. Traffic toward other PEs uses the IGP shortest path. Basically, you need to configure a tunnel to those peers that will receive traffic of the class that you are controlling with MPLS TE. Example 5-7 illustrated a design where tunnels run between PE devices to control real-time traffic. The current configuration evidences that the Tugela[PE] node only requires to forward real-time traffic toward Caroni[PE]. If Tugela[PE] later required to forward real-time traffic to other PE devices (for instance, Jostedal[PE] and Mutarazi[PE]), you would need to define additional tunnels to those destinations.

Example 5-8 shows a combination of DiffServ and aggregate MPLS TE using Cisco IOS XR. This example illustrates a design different from that in Example 5-7. In this case, the node maintains a full mesh of tunnels between P devices to perform bandwidth optimization in the network. The maximum reservable bandwidth represents the actual link capacity and the TE LSPs transport traffic of all types. The DiffServ configuration provides traffic differentiation in case of congestion. The occurrence of congestion should be unusual because of the use of MPLS TE to control the utilization of backbone links. Unexpected events such as operational mistakes or network failures could generate some periods of congestion for which DiffServ will guarantee that the network can still meet performance targets.

Example 5-8 *Node with DiffServ and MPLS TE Configuration in Cisco IOS XR*

```
hostname Yosemite[P]
router-id Loopback0
class-map match-any CLASS1
 match mpls experimental topmost 5
!
class-map match-any CLASS2
 match mpls experimental topmost 4 6
 match dscp ipv4 cs6
!
class-map match-any CLASS3
 match mpls experimental topmost 1 2
!
policy-map OUT-POLICY
 class CLASS1
  police rate percent 40 burst 20 ms
  priority
 !
 class CLASS2
  queue-limit 50 ms
  bandwidth remaining percent 30
 !
 class CLASS3
  queue-limit 200 ms
  random-detect exp 1 15 ms 44 ms
  random-detect exp 2 44 ms 132 ms
  bandwidth remaining percent 60
```

continues

Example 5-8 *Node with DiffServ and MPLS TE Configuration in Cisco IOS XR (Continued)*

```
 !
 class class-default
  queue-limit 200 ms
  random-detect exp 0 44 ms 132 ms
  bandwidth remaining percent 10
  !
 !
interface Loopback0
 ipv4 address 172.16.255.129 255.255.255.255
 !
interface tunnel-te1
 description Yosemite[P]->Pieman[P]
 ipv4 unnumbered Loopback0
 priority 0 0
 signalled-bandwidth 80000
 autoroute announce
 destination 172.16.255.130
 path-option 10 dynamic
 !
interface tunnel-te2
 description Yosemite[P]->Opo[P]
 ipv4 unnumbered Loopback0
 priority 0 0
 signalled-bandwidth 90000
 autoroute announce
 destination 172.16.255.131
 path-option 10 dynamic
 !
interface POS0/3/0/0
 description CONNECTS TO Caroni[PE]
 service-policy output OUT-POLICY
 ipv4 address 172.16.0.1 255.255.255.254
 encapsulation ppp
 !
interface POS0/3/0/1
 description CONNECTS TO Pieman[P]
 service-policy output OUT-POLICY
 ipv4 address 172.16.192.0 255.255.255.254
 encapsulation ppp
 !
interface POS0/3/0/2
 description CONNECTS TO Opo[P]
 service-policy output OUT-POLICY
 ipv4 address 172.16.192.2 255.255.255.254
 encapsulation ppp
 !
interface POS0/3/0/3
 description CONNECTS TO Mongebeck[PE]
 service-policy output OUT-POLICY
 ipv4 address 172.16.0.5 255.255.255.254
 encapsulation ppp
 !
interface POS0/3/0/4
```

Example 5-8 *Node with DiffServ and MPLS TE Configuration in Cisco IOS XR (Continued)*

```
 description CONNECTS TO Jostedal[PE]
 service-policy output OUT-POLICY
 ipv4 address 172.16.8.1 255.255.255.254
 encapsulation ppp
!
router ospf DEFAULT
 area 0
  interface Loopback0
   passive
  !
  interface POS0/3/0/0
  !
  interface POS0/3/0/1
  !
  interface POS0/3/0/2
  !
  interface POS0/3/0/3
  !
  interface POS0/3/0/4
  !
 !
 mpls traffic-eng area 0
!
rsvp
 interface POS0/3/0/1
  bandwidth 155000
 !
 interface POS0/3/0/2
  bandwidth 155000
 !
!
mpls traffic-eng
 interface POS0/3/0/1
 !
 interface POS0/3/0/2
 !
!
mpls ldp
 interface POS0/3/0/0
 !
 interface POS0/3/0/1
 !
 interface POS0/3/0/2
 !
 interface POS0/3/0/3
 !
 interface POS0/3/0/4
 !
 interface tunnel-te1
 !
 interface tunnel-te2
 !
!
```

NOTE   Previous examples in this chapter have used *Open Shortest Path First* (OSPF) as the IGP. Most of the examples in the rest of this chapter use *Intermediate System-to-Intermediate System* (IS-IS). The intent is to show configurations with both protocols. The choice of IGP in each section is random and does not imply that one protocol is more appropriate than the other for the design that the section describes.

DiffServ Backbone with DiffServ-Aware Traffic Engineering

The combination of DiffServ and MPLS *DiffServ-aware TE* (DS-TE) provides the highest level of traffic differentiation and optimization. You can control class load using DS-TE while controlling class capacity using DiffServ, as Figure 5-16 illustrates. The control of class load depends on the bandwidth constraint model you deploy (*maximum allocation model* [MAM] versus *Russian dolls model* [RDM]). Even though both DS-TE and DiffServ have the concept of classes, there is not a necessarily one-to-one mapping between these classes. However, the DiffServ bandwidth allocation on a particular link should have a clear relationship with the bandwidth constraints that DS-TE enforces on that link. You need to carefully design this relationship because nodes do not synchronize such configuration by default.

Figure 5-16 *Control of Class Capacity and Class Load Using DiffServ and DS-TE*

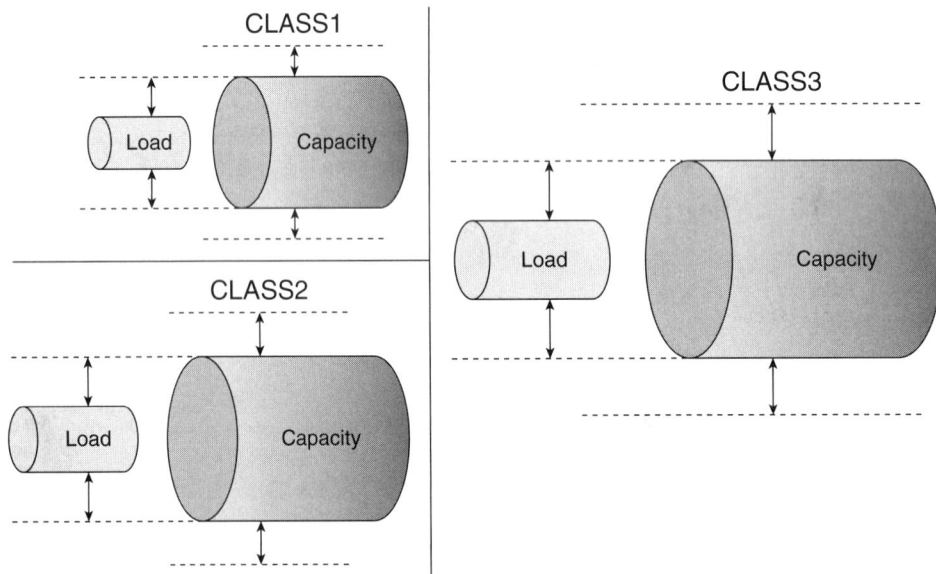

Table 5-16 illustrates a design where all DiffServ classes map to a unique DS-TE Class-Type. The DiffServ configuration defines CLASS1 with unlimited priority access to bandwidth and class-default as all other traffic that will have access to all excess (remaining) bandwidth. There are four TE-Class values with two preemption priorities for each Class-Type. CT1 TE LSPs will transport the priority packets that CLASS1 serves; CT0 will carry class-default packets and cannot preempt CT1 TE LSPs. DS-TE will enforce a limit (BC1) of 20 percent of the link bandwidth for CT1 and a limit (BC0) of 100 percent for CT0. The maximum reservable bandwidth will be 100 percent regardless of the Class-Type. This design uses DS-TE to limit the amount of priority traffic on the link.

Table 5-16 *DiffServ and DS-TE Design Where MAM max-reservable-bw = 100%, BC0 = 100%, and BC1 = 20%*

Class	DiffServ	DS-TE
CLASS1	Unlimited priority	TE-Class0 (CT1, priority 0)
		TE-Class1 (CT1, priority 1)
Class-default	Excess = 100%	TE-Class2 (CT0, priority 2)
		TE-Class3 (CT0, priority 3)

Table 5-17 shows a design using RDM bandwidth constraints that is similar to Table 5-16. Again, all DiffServ classes have a unique correspondence with a DS-TE Class-Type. The DiffServ and TE-Class definitions remain the same. As before, preemption is possible within a given Class-Type, and CT1 TE LSPs can preempt CT0 TE LSPs. DS-TE will enforce a limit (BC1) of 20 percent of the link capacity for CT1 and a limit (BC0) of 100 percent for CT0+CT1. This design allows CT0 to use any bandwidth that CT1 is not using, similar to how the scheduler allows class-default packets to use the bandwidth that CLASS1 is not using. CT1 TE LSPs may need to use preemption to reclaim bandwidth if CT0 LSPs are consuming more than 80 percent of the link capacity. CT1 TE LSPs could also preempt CT0 LSPs with the design in Table 5-16.

Table 5-17 *DiffServ and DS-TE Design with RDM BC0 = 100%, BC1 = 20%*

Class	DiffServ	DS-TE
CLASS1	Unlimited priority	TE-Class0 (CT1, priority 0)
		TE-Class1 (CT1, priority 1)
Class-default	Excess = 100%	TE-Class2 (CT0, priority 2)
		TE-Class3 (CT0, priority 3)

Table 5-18 shows a design using DS-TE with RDM constraints to control a subset of the DiffServ classes. This design makes use of eight TE-Class values with two CTs (CT0 and CT1) and four preemption priorities each. The DiffServ configuration defines four classes: CLASS1, CLASS2, CLASS3, and class-default. The network will perform only TE on CLASS1 and CLASS2 using CT1 and CT0, respectively. CT1 TE LSPs will transport the priority packets that CLASS1 serves; CT0 will transport CLASS2 packets. DS-TE will enforce a limit (BC1) of 20 percent of the link capacity for CT1 and a limit (BC0) of 40 percent for CT0+CT1. CLASS1 has an overprovisioning factor of two with respect to CT1.

Table 5-18 *DiffServ and DS-TE Design with RDM BC0 = 40%, BC1 = 20%*

Class	DiffServ	DS-TE
CLASS1	Priority 40%	TE-Class0 (CT1, priority 0)
		TE-Class1 (CT1, priority 1)
		TE-Class2 (CT1, priority 2)
		TE-Class3 (CT1, priority 3)
CLASS2	Minimum = 20%	TE-Class4 (CT0, priority 0)
		TE-Class5 (CT0, priority 1)
		TE-Class6 (CT0, priority 2)
		TE-Class7 (CT0, priority 3)
CLASS3	Minimum = 30	Not used
Class-default	Minimum = 10%	Not used

Table 5-19 shows a design using DS-TE with RDM constraints to control all DiffServ classes using different levels of granularity. The DiffServ configuration defines four classes: CLASS1, CLASS2, CLASS3, and class-default. CLASS1 and CLASS2 map to a separate Class-Type each. The third Class-Type, CT0, performs aggregate TE for CLASS3 and class-default. Therefore, CT2 TE LSPs will transport the priority packets that CLASS1 serves; CT1 will transport CLASS2 packets. CT0 LSPs aggregate CLASS3 and class-default traffic. DS-TE will enforce a limit (BC2) of 25 percent of the link capacity for CT1 and a limit (BC1) of 35 percent for CT1+CT2. CLASS1 has an overprovisioning factor of two with respect to CT2.

Table 5-19 *DiffServ and DS-TE Design with RDM BC0 = 100%, BC1 = 35%, and BC2 = 25%*

Class	DiffServ	DS-TE
CLASS1	Priority 50%	TE-Class0 (CT2, priority 0)
		TE-Class1 (CT2, priority 1)
CLASS2	Minimum = 20%	TE-Class2 (CT1, priority 0)
		TE-Class3 (CT1, priority 1)
CLASS3	Minimum = 20%	TE-Class4 (CT0, priority 2)
Class-default	Minimum = 5%	TE-Class5 (CT0, priority 3)
		TE-Class6 (CT0, priority 4)
		TE-Class7 (CT0, priority 5)

CAUTION	All nodes in a DS-TE network must have the same TE-Class definition to operate correctly. A mismatch can lead a node to compute paths and signal LSPs that fail or have unexpected effects.

RDM provides greater bandwidth sharing among different Class-Types. For the design in Table 5-19, CT0 TE LSPs can reserve a maximum ranging from 65 percent to 100 percent of the total bandwidth depending on what CT2 and CT1 TE LSPs consume. Similarly, CT1 TE LSPs can reserve a maximum ranging from 10 percent to 35 percent, subject to how much bandwidth CT2 reserves. On the other hand, CT2 can reserve up to 25 percent, independent of other Class-Types. However, CT2 might require using preemption to secure access to that 25 percent of the link bandwidth because CT2, CT1, and CT0 share that bandwidth. Similarly, CT1 might need to use preemption to secure access to at least 10 percent of the bandwidth because CT1 and CT0 share that bandwidth. MAM provides limited bandwidth sharing. This limitation is more evident as the number of Class-Types increases. RFC 4128 presents a performance evaluation of MAM and RDM.

Example 5-9 shows a configuration with DiffServ and DS-TE using Cisco IOS. The DiffServ policy has three classes, and the DS-TE configuration uses two (CT0 and CT1). Table 5-20 summarizes the DiffServ class and DS-TE TE-Class definitions.

Table 5-20   *DiffServ and DS-TE Design where RDM BC0 = 100%, BC1 = 25% for Examples 5-9 and 5-10*

Class	DiffServ	DS-TE
CLASS1	Priority 50%	TE-Class0 (CT1, priority 0)
		TE-Class1 (CT1, priority 1)
		TE-Class2 (CT1, priority 2)
		TE-Class3 (CT1, priority 3)
CLASS2	Excess = 80%	TE-Class4 (CT0, priority 0)
Class-default	Excess = 20%	TE-Class5 (CT0, priority 1)
		TE-Class6 (CT0, priority 2)
		TE-Class7 (CT0, priority 3)

In this design, P devices act as headends and tailends for the TE LSPs. Therefore, the node establishes targeted LDP sessions to the tailends to set up the LSPs between PE devices. Interfaces facing PE devices are not part of the MPLS TE network. Tunnel1 and Tunnel3 form a full mesh of CT0 TE LSPs to the other two P devices. Tunnel2 establishes a CT1 TE LSP to node Opo[P]. Notice that, in this case, this node does not establish a full mesh of CT1 TE LSPs. This implies that it does not require transporting CT1 (CLASS1) traffic toward all destinations.

Example 5-9 *Node with DiffServ and DS-TE Configuration in Cisco IOS*

```
hostname Pieman[P]
!
mpls traffic-eng tunnels
mpls traffic-eng ds-te te-classes
 te-class 0 class-type 0 priority 0
 te-class 1 class-type 0 priority 1
 te-class 2 class-type 0 priority 2
 te-class 3 class-type 0 priority 3
 te-class 4 class-type 1 priority 0
 te-class 5 class-type 1 priority 1
 te-class 6 class-type 1 priority 2
 te-class 7 class-type 1 priority 3
mpls traffic-eng ds-te mode ietf
mpls label protocol ldp
!
class-map match-all CLASS1
  match mpls experimental topmost 5
class-map match-any CLASS2
  match mpls experimental topmost 1  2  6
  match  dscp cs6
!
policy-map OUT-POLICY
  class CLASS1
    priority
    police rate percent 50 burst 20 ms
  class CLASS2
    bandwidth remaining percent 80
    queue-limit 200 ms
    random-detect
    random-detect precedence 1 15 ms 44 ms 1
    random-detect precedence 2 44 ms 132 ms 1
    random-detect precedence 6 132 ms 132 ms 1
   class class-default
    queue-limit 200 ms
    random-detect
    random-detect precedence 0 44 ms 132 ms
    bandwidth remaining percent 20
 !
interface Tunnel1
 description Pieman[P]->Opo[P]-1
 ip unnumbered Loopback0
 mpls ip
 tunnel destination 172.16.255.131
 tunnel mode mpls traffic-eng
 tunnel mpls traffic-eng autoroute announce
 tunnel mpls traffic-eng priority 3 3
 tunnel mpls traffic-eng bandwidth  4000000
 tunnel mpls traffic-eng affinity 0x0 mask 0x0
 tunnel mpls traffic-eng path-option 10 dynamic
 tunnel mpls traffic-eng path-selection metric igp
 tunnel mpls traffic-eng exp default
 !
```

Example 5-9   *Node with DiffServ and DS-TE Configuration in Cisco IOS (Continued)*

```
interface Tunnel2
 description Pieman[P]->Opo[P]-2
 ip unnumbered Loopback0
 mpls ip
 tunnel destination 172.16.255.131
 tunnel mode mpls traffic-eng
 tunnel mpls traffic-eng autoroute announce
 tunnel mpls traffic-eng priority 0 0
 tunnel mpls traffic-eng bandwidth 500000 class type 1
 tunnel mpls traffic-eng affinity 0x1 mask 0x1
 tunnel mpls traffic-eng path-option 10 dynamic
 tunnel mpls traffic-eng exp 5
!
interface Tunnel3
 description Pieman[P]->Yosemite[P]
 ip unnumbered Loopback0
 mpls ip
 tunnel destination 172.16.255.129
 tunnel mode mpls traffic-eng
 tunnel mpls traffic-eng autoroute announce
 tunnel mpls traffic-eng priority 3 3
 tunnel mpls traffic-eng bandwidth  4000000
 tunnel mpls traffic-eng path-option 10 dynamic
 tunnel mpls traffic-eng path-selection metric igp
!
interface Loopback0
 ip address 172.16.255.130 255.255.255.255
!
interface POS0/0/0
 description CONNECTS TO Yosemite[P]
 ip address 172.16.192.1 255.255.255.254
 ip router isis
 encapsulation ppp
 mpls traffic-eng tunnels
 mpls traffic-eng administrative-weight 200
 mpls ip
 isis metric 64
 service-policy output OUT-POLICY
 ip rsvp bandwidth rdm bc0 10000000 bc1 2500000
!
interface POS0/1/0
 description CONNECTS TO Mutarazi[PE]
 ip address 172.16.4.5 255.255.255.254
 ip router isis
 encapsulation ppp
 mpls ip
 isis metric 1024
 service-policy output OUT-POLICY
!
interface POS1/0/0
 description CONNECTS TO Jostedal[PE]
 ip address 172.16.8.3 255.255.255.254
```

continues

Example 5-9 *Node with DiffServ and DS-TE Configuration in Cisco IOS (Continued)*

```
 ip router isis
 encapsulation ppp
 mpls ip
 isis metric 1024
 service-policy output OUT-POLICY
 !
interface POS1/1/0
 description CONNECTS TO Opo[P]
 ip address 172.16.192.4 255.255.255.254
 ip router isis
 encapsulation ppp
 mpls traffic-eng tunnels
 mpls traffic-eng attribute-flags 0xF
 mpls traffic-eng administrative-weight 50
 mpls ip
 isis metric 64
 service-policy output OUT-POLICY
 ip rsvp bandwidth rdm bc0 10000000 bc1 2500000
 !
interface POS2/0/0
 description CONNECTS TO Tugela[PE]
 ip address 172.16.4.1 255.255.255.254
 ip router isis
 encapsulation ppp
 mpls ip
 isis metric 1024
 service-policy output OUT-POLICY
 !
router isis
 net 49.0001.1720.1625.5130.00
 is-type level-2-only
 metric-style wide
 passive-interface Loopback0
 mpls traffic-eng router-id Loopback0
 mpls traffic-eng level-2
 !
```

CBTS directs packets down the appropriate tunnel to Opo[P] using the MPLS EXP value of the packets. Packets with an MPLS EXP value of five (CLASS1) follow Tunnel2; all other packets (CLASS2 and class-default) follow Tunnel1. In this manner, CBTS ties the DiffServ class definition with the DS-TE Class-Types, making sure that each tunnel carries the correct traffic. Notice that Tunnel3 does not use CBTS. As the previous paragraph described, the absence of a CT1 TE LSP toward Yosemite[P] evidences that there is not a requirement for transporting CLASS1 traffic toward that destination. Therefore, all packets should belong to CLASS2 or class-default, which Tunnel3 will transport.

This node uses different path metrics to enhance path computation for the two DS-TE Class-Types. Tunnel1 and Tunnel3, which signal CT0 TE LSPs, use the IGP metric to perform constrain-based routing. Conversely, Tunnel2 uses the default TE metric. The IGP metric is typically inversely proportional to the link bandwidth; so the faster the link, the lower the metric. You can configure the TE metric separately to represent other link feature. For example, the TE metric can represent the link propagation delay or a combination of link bandwidth and propagation delay. In that case, Tunnel2 will use the shortest path with respect to link bandwidth and propagation delay. Table 5-21 lists the interfaces in Example 5-9 and their different metric values.

This example also uses tunnel affinities to enhance the path computation. Tunnel2 uses an affinity of 0x1/0x1, which means the path computation process for this tunnel only considers links with administrative flags that have the last bit set. In this example, that last bit indicates that the link is suitable for CT1 LSPs. Tunnel3 uses the default affinity 0x0/0xFFFF (all administrative flags must be 0), which matches the default link flags. Finally, Tunnel1 has the affinity 0x0/0x0 (ignore administrative flags). Given this configuration, this node will signal a TE LSP for Tunnel2 through interface POS1/1/0 only. Similarly, it will signal a TE LSP for Tunnel3 through POS0/0/0 only. Tunnel1, in contrast, can use any of the two interfaces.

Table 5-21 *Link Characteristics for Example 5-9*

Interface	Link BW	IGP Metric	TE Metric	BC1 (Subpool)	BC0 (Global Pool)	Attribute
POS0/0/0	10 Gbps	64	200	2.5 Gbps	10 Gbps	0x0 (default)
POS0/1/0	622 Mbps	1024	–	–	–	–
POS1/0/0	622 Mbps	1024	–	–	–	–
POS1/1/0	10 Gbps	64	50	2.5 Gbps	10 Gbps	0xF
POS2/0/0	622 Mbps	1024	–	–	–	–

Example 5-10 shows a Cisco IOS XR configuration for the DiffServ and DS-TE design that the previous example described. As before, Table 5-20 summarizes the DiffServ class and DS-TE TE-Class definitions. Table 5-22 lists the relevant interface parameters for this example.

Table 5-22 *Link Characteristics for Example 5-10*

Interface	Link BW	IGP Metric	TE Metric	BC1 (Subpool)	BC0 (Global Pool)	Attribute
POS0/3/0/0	622 Mbps	1024	–	–	–	–
POS0/3/0/1	10 Gbps	64	200	2.5 Gbps	10 Gbps	0x0 (default)
POS0/3/0/2	10 Gbps	64	50	2.5 Gbps	10 Gbps	0x3
POS0/3/0/3	622 Mbps	1024	–	–	–	–
POS0/3/0/4	622 Mbps	1024	–	–	–	–

The node configuration in Example 5-10 uses a CT0 tunnel (tunnel-te2) and a CT1 tunnel (tunnel-te3) toward the node Opo[P]. Two static routes control traffic forwarding into these two tunnels. Packets to 172.16.255.2/32 travel through tunnel-te2; packets to 172.16.255.102/32 travel through tunnel-te3. These routes represent two loopback addresses at a remote PE. That node defines multiple loopbacks to control the manner in which the network forwards traffic of different services.

Example 5-10 *Node with DiffServ and DS-TE Configuration in Cisco IOS XR*

```
hostname Yosemite[P]
router-id Loopback0
class-map match-any CLASS1
 match mpls experimental topmost 5
 !
class-map match-any CLASS2
 match mpls experimental topmost 1 2 6
 match dscp ipv4 cs6
 !
policy-map OUT-POLICY
 class CLASS1
  police rate percent 50 burst 20 ms
  priority
  !
 class CLASS2
  queue-limit 200 ms
  bandwidth remaining percent 80
  random-detect exp 1 15 ms 44 ms
  random-detect exp 2 44 ms 132 ms
  random-detect exp 6 132 ms 132 ms
  !
 class class-default
  queue-limit 200 ms
  bandwidth remaining percent 20
  random-detect exp 0 44 ms 132 ms
  !
 !
interface Loopback0
 ipv4 address 172.16.255.129 255.255.255.255
 !
interface tunnel-te1
 description Yosemite[P]->Pieman[P]
 ipv4 unnumbered Loopback0
 priority 2 2
 signalled-bandwidth 2500000
 autoroute announce
 destination 172.16.255.130
 path-selection metric igp
 path-option 10 dynamic
 !
interface tunnel-te2
 description Yosemite[P]->Opo[P]-1
 ipv4 unnumbered Loopback0
```

Example 5-10   *Node with DiffServ and DS-TE Configuration in Cisco IOS XR (Continued)*

```
 priority 2 2
 signalled-bandwidth 1000000
 destination 172.16.255.131
 path-selection metric igp
 path-option 10 dynamic
!
interface tunnel-te3
 description Yosemite[P]->Opo[P]-2
 ipv4 unnumbered Loopback0
 priority 1 1
 signalled-bandwidth 400000 class type 1
 destination 172.16.255.131
 affinity 1 mask 1
 path-option 10 dynamic
!
interface POS0/3/0/0
 description CONNECTS TO Caroni[PE]
 service-policy output OUT-POLICY
 ipv4 address 172.16.0.1 255.255.255.254
 encapsulation ppp
!
interface POS0/3/0/1
 description CONNECTS TO Pieman[P]
 service-policy output OUT-POLICY
 ipv4 address 172.16.192.0 255.255.255.254
 encapsulation ppp
!
interface POS0/3/0/2
 description CONNECTS TO Opo[P]
 service-policy output OUT-POLICY
 ipv4 address 172.16.192.2 255.255.255.254
 encapsulation ppp
!
interface POS0/3/0/3
 description CONNECTS TO Mongebeck[PE]
 service-policy output OUT-POLICY
 ipv4 address 172.16.0.5 255.255.255.254
 encapsulation ppp
!
interface POS0/3/0/4
 description CONNECTS TO Jostedal[PE]
 service-policy output OUT-POLICY
 ipv4 address 172.16.8.1 255.255.255.254
 encapsulation ppp
!
route ipv4 172.16.255.2/32 tunnel-te2
route ipv4 172.16.255.102/32 tunnel-te3
router isis DEFAULT
 is-type level-2-only
 net 49.0001.1720.1625.5129.00
 address-family ipv4 unicast
  metric-style wide
```

continues

Example 5-10 *Node with DiffServ and DS-TE Configuration in Cisco IOS XR (Continued)*

```
 mpls traffic-eng level 2
 !
 interface Loopback0
  passive
  address-family ipv4 unicast
  !
 !
 interface POS0/3/0/0
  address-family ipv4 unicast
   metric 1024
  !
 !
 interface POS0/3/0/1
  address-family ipv4 unicast
   metric 64
  !
 !
 interface POS0/3/0/2
  address-family ipv4 unicast
   metric 64
  !
 !
 interface POS0/3/0/3
  address-family ipv4 unicast
   metric 1024
  !
 !
 interface POS0/3/0/4
  address-family ipv4 unicast
   metric 1024
  !
 !
!
rsvp
 interface POS0/3/0/1
  bandwidth rdm bc0 10000000 bc1 2500000
 !
 interface POS0/3/0/2
  bandwidth rdm bc0 10000000 bc1 2500000
 !
!
mpls traffic-eng
 interface POS0/3/0/1
  admin-weight 200
 !
 interface POS0/3/0/2
  admin-weight 50
  attribute-flags 0x3
 !
 ds-te mode ietf
 ds-te te-classes
  te-class 0 class-type 0 priority 0
```

Example 5-10 *Node with DiffServ and DS-TE Configuration in Cisco IOS XR (Continued)*

```
    te-class 1 class-type 0 priority 1
    te-class 2 class-type 0 priority 2
    te-class 3 class-type 0 priority 3
    te-class 4 class-type 1 priority 0
    te-class 5 class-type 1 priority 1
    te-class 6 class-type 1 priority 2
    te-class 7 class-type 1 priority 3
   !
  !
 mpls ldp
  interface POS0/3/0/0
  !
  interface POS0/3/0/1
  !
  interface POS0/3/0/2
  !
  interface POS0/3/0/3
  !
  interface POS0/3/0/4
  !
  interface tunnel-te1
  !
  interface tunnel-te2
  !
  interface tunnel-te3
  !
 !
```

Adding MPLS TE FRR

You can use MPLS TE FRR with any of the designs that this chapter described. FRR will increase the availability of the network during network failures (connectivity protection). Furthermore, you can use FRR to protect against certain network failures and still meet the performance guarantees for your traffic (bandwidth protection). FRR also gives you granular control over what traffic you protect. Given that each individual TE LSP signals whether it requires protection, you can signal different TE LSPs with different protection requirements. In this manner, you can control what traffic FRR protects by appropriately selecting what traffic travels through specific TE LSPs.

You can still use FRR for those designs that use a best-effort or DiffServ backbone exclusively. Figure 5-17 illustrates the two alternatives: full mesh of TE LSPs and one-hop TE LSPs.

Figure 5-17 *Full-Mesh and One-Hop Alternatives for FRR Without Performing TE*

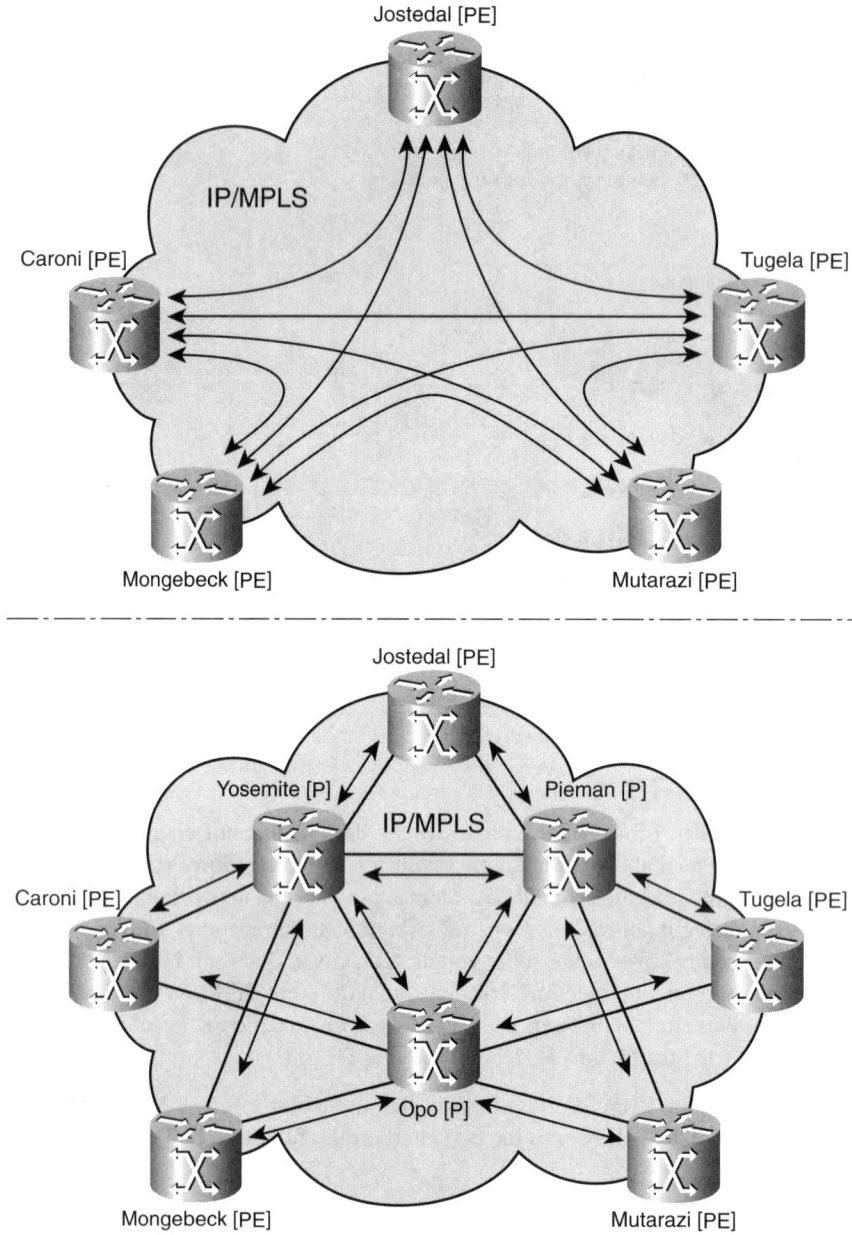

When using a full mesh, you need to configure all your tunnels to request protection, but without any constrains (bandwidth or affinity), and let your IGP use the tunnels using the autoroute feature. With the second alternative, one-hop tunnels, each node needs a one-hop tunnel to its adjacent neighbors. The tunnels have the same characteristics as the full-mesh design. These tunnels should request protection, do not make use of any constraints, and use autoroute to forward traffic.

In both cases, you are using only MPLS TE to set up TE LSPs that FRR can protect. The network forwards traffic using the IGP shortest path as if you had not enabled MPLS TE. When comparing the two approaches, notice that a full mesh of tunnels requires a greater number of primary TE LSPs than the approach using the one-hop tunnel. However, a full mesh of tunnels can benefit from link and node protection, whereas the one-hop tunnels can only benefit from link protection. In both cases, you must make sure the network has the proper backup tunnels. There is certainly an increased level of complexity with bringing FRR to a network that does not require MPLS TE for resource optimization. However, many users find the benefits worth the complexity.

TIP   Cisco IOS can create a full mesh or one-hop tunnels using the Auto-tunnel feature. In addition, it can generate backup tunnels as the network requires them. A detailed description of this feature is beyond the scope of this book. See the software documentation for information about this feature.

MPLS TE FRR represents a relatively small incremental effort for those designs that already make use of MPLS TE. The first requirement is to identify the tunnels that will require protection. You can select all or just a subset of the tunnels. The tunnel configuration requires only minor configuration to make sure the TE LSP request protection along its path. The second requirement is to establish the backup TE LSPs. You can configure the backup tunnels manually to protect against selective failures. Alternatively, you can have nodes automatically signal backup TE LSPs as a response to the protection requirements of primary tunnels. Finally, you can use offline modeling. This approach enables you to design a complete protection solution that can provide both connectivity and bandwidth protection.

Example 5-11 illustrates an implementation that combines DiffServ and DS-TE with a sophisticated FRR scheme using Cisco IOS. This implementation uses the default TE-Class definitions (see section "Class-Types and TE-Classes" in Chapter 4) that supports two Class-Types with priority zero and seven for each of them. It uses the default RDM bandwidth constraint model with BC0 and BC1 on each link representing 100 percent and 20 percent of the interface bandwidth. The DiffServ configuration uses four classes. CLASS1 represents priority traffic that will receive low latency. DS-TE CT1 will provide admission control for CLASS1. CT0 will provide bandwidth optimization for CLASS2, CLASS3, and class-default.

Example 5-11 *Node with DiffServ, DS-TE, and FRR Configuration in Cisco IOS*

```
hostname Caroni[PE]
!
mpls traffic-eng tunnels
mpls traffic-eng ds-te mode ietf
mpls traffic-eng auto-tunnel mesh
mpls label protocol ldp
!
class-map match-all CLASS1
  match mpls experimental topmost 5
class-map match-any CLASS2
  match mpls experimental topmost 4  6
  match  dscp cs6
class-map match-all CLASS3
  match mpls experimental topmost 1  2
!
policy-map OUT-POLICY
  class CLASS1
    priority
    police rate percent 40 burst 20 ms
  class CLASS2
    bandwidth remaining percent 30
    queue-limit 50 ms
  class CLASS3
    bandwidth remaining percent 60
    random-detect
    random-detect precedence 1 15 ms 44 ms 1
    random-detect precedence 2 44 ms 132 ms 1
    queue-limit 200 ms
  class class-default
    bandwidth remaining percent 10
    random-detect
    random-detect precedence 0 44 ms 132 ms 1
    queue-limit 200 ms
!
interface Tunnel1
 description Caroni[PE]->Tugela[PE]
 ip unnumbered Loopback0
 tunnel destination 172.16.255.2
 tunnel mode mpls traffic-eng
 tunnel mpls traffic-eng autoroute announce
 tunnel mpls traffic-eng priority 7 7
 tunnel mpls traffic-eng bandwidth 20000 class type 1
 tunnel mpls traffic-eng path-option 10 explicit identifier 1000
 tunnel mpls traffic-eng path-option 20 dynamic
 tunnel mpls traffic-eng fast-reroute
 tunnel mpls traffic-eng exp 5
!
interface Tunnel2
 description Caroni[PE]->Mutarazi[PE]
```

Example 5-11   *Node with DiffServ, DS-TE, and FRR Configuration in Cisco IOS (Continued)*

```
 ip unnumbered Loopback0
 tunnel destination 172.16.255.5
 tunnel mode mpls traffic-eng
 tunnel mpls traffic-eng autoroute announce
 tunnel mpls traffic-eng priority 7 7
 tunnel mpls traffic-eng bandwidth 20000 class type 1
 tunnel mpls traffic-eng path-option 10 explicit identifier 1001
 tunnel mpls traffic-eng path-option 20 dynamic
 tunnel mpls traffic-eng fast-reroute bw-protect
 tunnel mpls traffic-eng exp 5
!
interface Auto-Template1
 description CT0-MESH-GROUP-1
 ip unnumbered Loopback0
 tunnel destination mesh-group 1
 tunnel mode mpls traffic-eng
 tunnel mpls traffic-eng autoroute announce
 tunnel mpls traffic-eng path-option 10 dynamic
 tunnel mpls traffic-eng auto-bw
 tunnel mpls traffic-eng fast-reroute
 tunnel mpls traffic-eng exp default
!
interface Loopback0
 ip address 172.16.255.1 255.255.255.255
!
interface POS0/1/0
 description CONNECTS TO Yosemite[P]
 ip address 172.16.0.0 255.255.255.254
 encapsulation ppp
 mpls traffic-eng tunnels
 mpls ip
 service-policy output OUT-POLICY
 ip rsvp bandwidth rdm bc0 622000 bc1 124400
!
interface POS1/0/0
 description CONNECTS TO Opo[P]
 ip address 172.16.0.2 255.255.255.254
 encapsulation ppp
 mpls traffic-eng tunnels
 mpls ip
 service-policy output OUT-POLICY
 ip rsvp bandwidth rdm bc0 622000 bc1 124400
!
router ospf 100
 log-adjacency-changes
 passive-interface Loopback0
 network 172.16.0.0 0.0.255.255 area 0
 mpls traffic-eng router-id Loopback0
 mpls traffic-eng area 0
 mpls traffic-eng mesh-group 1 Loopback0 area 0
!
ip explicit-path identifier 1000 enable
```

continues

Example 5-11   *Node with DiffServ, DS-TE, and FRR Configuration in Cisco IOS (Continued)*

```
   next-address 172.16.0.1
   next-address 172.16.192.1
   next-address 172.16.4.0
  !
 ip explicit-path identifier 1001 enable
   next-address 172.16.0.1
   next-address 172.16.192.1
   next-address 172.16.4.4
  !
```

This node is part of an automatic mesh of protected CT0 TE LSPs. The **interface Auto-Template1** command defines a tunnel template that the node will use to build TE LSPs to any other node that is a member of mesh group one. Nodes flood their mesh group membership using their IGP. In this case, the OSPF configuration indicates that this node is a member of group one. The TE LSPs will signal their desire for FRR protection. Notice that the template does not indicate the amount of bandwidth to reserve, because it is unlikely that similar amounts of traffic will flow between all mesh group members. Each CT0 TE LSP will adjust automatically its bandwidth reservation according to periodic measurements of how much traffic is flowing through the TE LSP.

This node signals protected CT1 TE LSPs to those destinations that require them. In this case, Tunnel1 signals a CT1 TE LSP toward Tugela[PE], and Tunnel2 signals one toward Mutarazi[PE]. Both tunnels use two path options. When signaling the TE LSP initially and during reoptimization, they first try an explicit path that specifies every hop along the path. As a second alternative, they rely on CSPF to compute a dynamic path. In addition, both tunnels signal the desire for protection. However, Tunnel2 explicitly signals the need for bandwidth protection. If a node along the path can provide bandwidth protection, it will give precedence to the protection of Tunnel2 over other tunnels, such as Tunnel1, that do not signal explicitly this requirement.

Example 5-12 shows the configuration of a PLR node using Cisco IOS XR that complements the design in the previous example. This node has two backup tunnels, tunnel-te1 and tunnel-te2, which have a next-hop node as the destination and protect against the failure of interface POS0/3/0/1. However, tunnel-te1 provides bandwidth protection for CT1 TE LSPs for a maximum of 2 Gbps. On the other hand, tunnel-te2 provides connectivity protection only for primary TE LSPs requesting it. If you follow the selection rules for backup tunnels in Chapter 4, you will notice that tunnel-te1 will protect Tunnel1 and Tunnel2 in Example 5-11. Similarly, tunnel-te2 will protect any CT0 TE LSPs that the mesh group in Example 5-11 generates.

Example 5-12   *Node with DiffServ, DS-TE, and FRR Configuration in Cisco IOS XR*

```
 hostname Yosemite[P]
 explicit-path identifier 100
   index 1 next-address ipv4 unicast 172.16.192.3
   index 2 next-address ipv4 unicast 172.16.192.4
```

Example 5-12 *Node with DiffServ, DS-TE, and FRR Configuration in Cisco IOS XR (Continued)*

```
!
explicit-path identifier 101
 index 1 exclude-address ipv4 unicast 172.16.192.1
!
router-id Loopback0
class-map match-any CLASS1
 match mpls experimental topmost 5
!
class-map match-any CLASS2
 match mpls experimental topmost 4 6
 match dscp ipv4 cs6
!
class-map match-any CLASS3
 match mpls experimental topmost 1 2
!
policy-map OUT-POLICY
 class CLASS1
  police rate percent 40 burst 20 ms
  priority
 !
 class CLASS2
  queue-limit 50 ms
  bandwidth remaining percent 30
 !
 class CLASS3
  queue-limit 200 ms
  bandwidth remaining percent 60
  random-detect exp 1 15 ms 44 ms
  random-detect exp 2 44 ms 132 ms
 !
 class class-default
  queue-limit 200 ms
  bandwidth remaining percent 10
  random-detect exp 0 44 ms 132 ms
 !
!
interface Loopback0
 ipv4 address 172.16.255.129 255.255.255.255
!
interface tunnel-te1
 description Yosemite[P]->Pieman[P]-BACKUP-CT1
 ipv4 unnumbered Loopback0
 backup-bw 2000000 class-type 1
 destination 172.16.255.130
 path-option 10 explicit identifier 100
!
interface tunnel-te2
 description Yosemite[P]->Pieman[P]-BACKUP-CT0
 ipv4 unnumbered Loopback0
 destination 172.16.255.130
 path-option 10 explicit identifier 101
!
```

continues

Example 5-12 *Node with DiffServ, DS-TE, and FRR Configuration in Cisco IOS XR (Continued)*

```
interface POS0/3/0/0
 description CONNECTS TO Caroni[PE]
 service-policy output OUT-POLICY
 ipv4 address 172.16.0.1 255.255.255.254
 encapsulation ppp
!
interface POS0/3/0/1
 description CONNECTS TO Pieman[P]
 service-policy output OUT-POLICY
 ipv4 address 172.16.192.0 255.255.255.254
 encapsulation ppp
!
interface POS0/3/0/2
 description CONNECTS TO Opo[P]
 service-policy output OUT-POLICY
 ipv4 address 172.16.192.2 255.255.255.254
 encapsulation ppp
!
interface POS0/3/0/3
 description CONNECTS TO Mongebeck[PE]
 service-policy output OUT-POLICY
 ipv4 address 172.16.0.5 255.255.255.254
 encapsulation ppp
!
interface POS0/3/0/4
 description CONNECTS TO Jostedal[PE]
 service-policy output OUT-POLICY
 ipv4 address 172.16.8.1 255.255.255.254
 encapsulation ppp
!
router ospf DEFAULT
 area 0
  interface Loopback0
  passive
  !
  interface POS0/3/0/0
  !
  interface POS0/3/0/1
  !
  interface POS0/3/0/2
  !
  interface POS0/3/0/3
  !
  interface POS0/3/0/4
  !
 !
 mpls traffic-eng area 0
!
rsvp
 interface POS0/3/0/0
  bandwidth rdm bc0 622000 bc1 124400
 !
 interface POS0/3/0/1
```

Example 5-12   *Node with DiffServ, DS-TE, and FRR Configuration in Cisco IOS XR (Continued)*

```
   bandwidth rdm bc0 10000000 bc1 2000000
  !
 interface POS0/3/0/2
   bandwidth rdm bc0 10000000 bc1 2000000
  !
 interface POS0/3/0/3
   bandwidth rdm bc0 622000 bc1 124400
  !
 interface POS0/3/0/4
   bandwidth rdm bc0 622000 bc1 124400
  !
 !
mpls traffic-eng
 interface POS0/3/0/0
  !
 interface POS0/3/0/1
  backup-path tunnel-te 1
  backup-path tunnel-te 2
  !
 interface POS0/3/0/2
  !
 interface POS0/3/0/3
  !
 interface POS0/3/0/4
  !
 ds-te mode ietf
 !
mpls ldp
 interface POS0/3/0/0
  !
 interface POS0/3/0/1
  !
 interface POS0/3/0/2
  !
 interface POS0/3/0/3
  !
 interface POS0/3/0/4
  !
 !
```

This example illustrates bandwidth protection through the overprovisioning of CLASS1 and the careful placing of tunnel-te1. In Examples 5-11 and 5-12, CLASS1 bandwidth is consistently twice the BC1 value. This overprovisioning allows the network to guarantee low latency to CT1 traffic that tunnel-te1 carries during a failure. However, tunnel-te1 does not reserve any bandwidth. Zero-bandwidth backup tunnels improve the sharing of the excess capacity in CLASS1 and do not limit unnecessarily the creation of other primary CT0 TE LSPs. This approach relies on the careful design of backup tunnels using an offline tool to guarantee that a failure does not cause a CLASS1 oversubscription. A simpler, but suboptimal, approach is possible if tunnel-te1 reserves the backup bandwidth explicitly.

NOTE	Cisco IP Solution Center provides optimization of primary and backup tunnels, including bandwidth protection. See the product documentation for further details.

What Design Should I Use?

Any design that this chapter presented has the potential of meeting a diverse range of performance requirements. On one end, a best-effort backbone can meet the most stringent requirements given an appropriate amount of bandwidth overprovisioning. On the other end, DiffServ with DS-TE can satisfy those same requirements while providing greater control and demanding less bandwidth. Other approaches sit somewhere between those two ends. Figure 5-18 illustrates the impact that each design option in this chapter has on resource optimization and the capability of the network to provide service differentiation. You should identify to what extent traffic differentiation in the backbone and resource optimization are desirable in your network.

Figure 5-18 *Impact of Different QoS Designs on Service Differentiation and Resource Optimization*

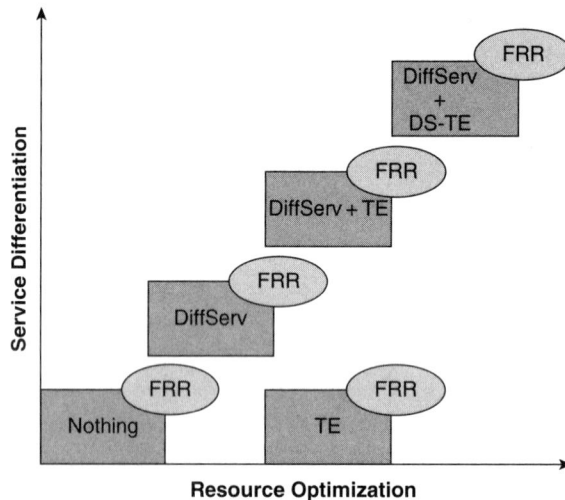

Bandwidth and operational costs are critical factors in the selection of the most appropriate design for a particular network. The implementation of DiffServ, MPLS TE, DS-TE, or FRR improves network efficiency and optimizes different network resources. However, they introduce their own level of complexity into the network. Unfortunately, control has a cost. The selection process needs to consider link transmission costs, operational cost, equipment costs, technical expertise, technology familiarity, and market conditions (among other factors). These conditions vary widely from network to network and from country to country.

Most next-generation carrier networks will demand more than just best-effort designs. Current new architectures embrace the concept of network convergence around an IP/MPLS network. Constraint-based routing, admission control, and fast restoration play an important role in the migration of real-time voice and video, among other services, to new network infrastructures. Historically, many carrier networks used similar capabilities in their ATM networks. New carrier networks are likely to require a combination of DiffServ and some type of implementation of MPLS TE to satisfy the requirements of converging their connectionless and connection-oriented network into a single IP/MPLS network.

Summary

The implementation of QoS in a backbone offers multiple design options varying in predictability and complexity. All these design options have the potential to support a given set of backbone performance requirements. DiffServ and MPLS TE serve as key tools to manipulate bandwidth utilization throughout the network. You can control this utilization by managing the offered load on a link or performing appropriate capacity planning. DiffServ and DS-TE enable you to control this supply-and-demand equation at a class level within a link. An IP/MPLS network offers greater traffic load control than a pure IP network, which has to rely mainly on capacity planning (at a link or class level). FRR is an additional mechanism that you can integrate into any of the design options to improve the performance characteristics of the network.

References

Cisco IP Solution Center Traffic Engineering Management

Clarence Filsfils, Deploying Tight-SLA Services on an Internet Backbone - ISIS Fast Convergence and Differentiated Services Design

draft-chan-tsvwg-diffserv-class-aggr-02.txt, *Aggregation of DiffServ Classes*

draft-ietf-tsvwg-diffserv-service-classes-01.txt, *Configuration Guidelines for DiffServ Service Classes*

Guido Appenzeller, Sizing Router Buffers

http://www.icir.org/floyd/red.html

http://www.nanog.org/mtg-0206/filsfils.html

http://www.nanog.org/mtg-0302/optimal.html

http://www.nanog.org/mtg-0501/horneffer.html

http://www.nanog.org/mtg-0505/telkamp.html

http://www.cisco.com/en/US/partner/products/ps6163/index.html

http://pdos.csail.mit.edu/~rtm/papers/icnp97-web.pdf

http://www.cisco.com/en/US/products/sw/iosswrel/ps1829/
products_feature_guide09186a008022564f.html

http://yuba.stanford.edu/~appenz/pubs.html

ITU-T G.1010, *End-user multimedia QoS categories*

ITU-T Y.1541, *Network performance objectives for IP-based services*

ITU-T Y.1541 Amendment 2 – Appendix XI, *Concatenating QoS values*

Leland, W.E., M. S. Taqqu, W. Willinger, and D. V. Wilson, "On the self-similar nature of
Ethernet traffic (extended version)," IEEE/ACM Transactions on Networking, Vol. 2, pp.
1–15, Feb 1994

Martin Horneffer, IGP Tuning in an MPLS Network

QoS: Classification of Locally Sourced Packets

RFC 2309, *Recommendations on Queue Management and Congestion Avoidance in the
Internet*

RFC 4128, *Bandwidth Constraints Models for Differentiated Services (Diffserv)-aware
MPLS Traffic Engineering: Performance Evaluation*

Robert Morris, TCP Behavior with Many Flows

Sally Floyd WRED Page

Sridharan, A., R. Guerin, and C. Diot. Achieving Near-Optimal Traffic Engineering
Solutions for Current OSPF/IS-IS Networks

Thomas Telkamp, Best Practices for Determining the Traffic Matrix in IP Networks

V. Paxson, and S. Floyd, "Wide Area Traffic: The Failure of Poisson Modeling," IEEE/
ACM Transactions on Networking, Vol. 3, pp. 226–244, 1995 (http://www.icir.org/vern/pa-
pers.html)

Command Reference for Cisco MPLS Traffic Engineering and RSVP

This appendix provides a command reference for *Multiprotocol Label Switching Traffic Engineering* (MPLS TE) and the *Resource Reservation Protocol* (RSVP). Chapter 4, "Cisco MPLS Traffic Engineering," illustrates some of these commands but does not provide an exhaustive command enumeration to facilitate presentation of Cisco MPLS TE. This appendix groups MPLS TE and RSVP commands separately. The command sequence follows the logical steps that you are likely to follow for the configuration and operation of Cisco MPLS TE. The tables do not illustrate the complete syntax for the **show** and **debug** commands. You can get further command details in the Cisco IOS documentation.

The upcoming command lists intentionally exclude *Generalized MPLS* (GMPLS) and per-flow RSVP-specific commands. Those topics are beyond the scope of this book.

MPLS TE Commands

Node-Configuration Commands

Table A-1   *MPLS TE Node Configuration in Cisco IOS281*

Syntax	Description
mpls traffic-eng auto-bw timers [**frequency** *value*]	Specify auto-bandwidth parameters
mpls traffic-eng auto-tunnel backup [[**config unnumbered-interface** *value*]**nhop-only** | **srlg exclude** [**preferred** | **force**] | **timers removal unused** *value* | **tunnel-num min** *value* [**max** *value*]]	Configure Auto-tunnel backup tunnel
mpls traffic-eng auto-tunnel mesh [**tunnel-num min** *value* [**max** *value*]]	Automatically create mesh tunnels
mpls traffic-eng auto-tunnel primary {**config** {**mpls ip** | **unnumbered-interface** *value*} | **onehop** | **timers removal rerouted** *value* | **tunnel-num min** *value* [**max** *value*]}	Automatically create one-hop primary tunnels
mpls traffic-eng ds-te te-classes	Enter the DS-TE[*] te-class map configuration mode

continues

Table A-1 *MPLS TE Node Configuration in Cisco IOS281 (Continued)*

Syntax	Description
mpls traffic-eng ds-te mode {migration ǀ ietf}	Configure standard DS-TE parameters
mpls traffic-eng fast-reroute {acl *value* ǀ **backup-prot-preempt optimize-bw** ǀ **timers promotion** *value***}**	Specify FRR* parameters
mpls traffic-eng link-management timers {bandwidth-hold *value* ǀ **periodic-flooding** *value***}**	Link-management configuration
mpls traffic-eng logging lsp {path-errors [*value*] ǀ **preemption** [*value*] ǀ **reservation-errors** [*value*] ǀ **setups** [*value*] ǀ **teardowns** [*value*]**}**	LSP* trap logging configuration
mpls traffic-eng logging tunnel {lsp-selection [*value*] ǀ **path change** [*value*]**}**	Tunnel trap logging configuration
mpls traffic-eng lsp attributes *value*	Configure LSP parameters
mpls traffic-eng path-selection loose-expansion {affinity {global-pool ǀ **sub-pool}** *value* [**mask** *value*] ǀ **metric {global-pool** ǀ **sub-pool}{igp** ǀ **te}}**	Loose ERO* expansion configuration for path selection
mpls traffic-eng path-selection metric {igp ǀ **te}**	Metric type configuration for path selection
mpls traffic-eng path-selection overload allow {head[middle[tail]] ǀ **middle[tail]** ǀ **tail}**	Overload node configuration for path selection
mpls traffic-eng reoptimize {events link-up ǀ **timers {delay {cleanup** *value* ǀ **installation** *value***}** ǀ **frequency** *value***}}**	Reoptimization parameters
mpls traffic-eng signalling {advertise implicit-null [*value*] ǀ **forwarding sync** ǀ **restart neighbors** [*value*]**}**	TE signaling parameters
mpls traffic-eng topology {holddown sigerr *value* ǀ **mesh-group accept-domain}**	Topology database configuration
mpls traffic-eng tunnels	Enable TE tunnels

* DS-TE = Differentiated Services (DiffServ)-aware traffic engineering

FRR = Fast reroute

LSP = Link switched path

ERO = Explicit route object

Table A-2 *MPLS TE Configuration Modes in Cisco IOS XR*

Syntax	Description
mpls traffic-eng	Enter MPLS TE configuration mode
rsvp	Enter RSVP configuration mode

Table A-3   *MPLS TE Node Configuration in Cisco IOS XR*

Syntax	Description
bfd {minimum-interval *value* I **multiplier** *value*}	Configure BFD[*] parameters
ds-te te-classes	Enter the DS-TE te-class map configuration mode
ds-te {bc-model {mam I **rdm}** I **mode ietf}**	Configure DS-TE bandwidth constraint model and operation mode
fast-reroute timers promotion *value*	Specify FRR configuration parameters
interface *value*	Enable MPLS-TE on an interface
link-management timers {bandwidth-hold *value* I **periodic-flooding** *value*}	Configure MPLS link-manager subcommands
maximum tunnels *value*	Maximum number of configurable tunnels
path-selection metric {igp I **te}**	Path-selection configuration
reoptimize { *value* I **timers delay {cleanup** *value* I **installation** *value*}}	Reoptimize timer frequency
signalling advertise explicit-null	Signaling options
topology holddown sigerr *value*	Topology database configuration

[*] BFD = Bidirectional Forwarding Detection

Table A-4   *MPLS TE Explicit Path Definition in Cisco IOS*

Syntax	Description
ip explicit-path {identifier *value* I **name** *value*} [**disable** I **enable**]	Enter explicit-path configuration

Table A-5   *MPLS TE Explicit Path Definition in Cisco IOS XR*

Syntax	Description
explicit-path {identifier *value* I **name** *value*}	Enter explicit-path configuration

Table A-6   *Cisco IOS TE-Class Definition*

Syntax	Description
te-class *value* {**unused** I **class-type** *value* **priority** *value*}	Configure a TE-Class

Table A-7   *Cisco IOS XR TE-Class Definition*

Syntax	Description
te-class *value* **class-type** *value* **priority** *value*	Configure a TE-Class

Interface-Configuration Commands

Table A-8   *MPLS TE Interface Configuration in Cisco IOS*

Syntax	Description
mpls traffic-eng administrative-weight *value*	Set the administrative weight for the interface
mpls traffic-eng attribute-flags *value*	Set user-defined interface attribute flags
mpls traffic-eng backup-path tunnel *value*	Configure an MPLS TE backup for this interface
mpls traffic-eng flooding thresholds {**up** *list* | **down** *list*}	Set flooding parameters
mpls traffic-eng passive-interface nbr-te-id *value* [**nbr-igp-id** {**isis** | **ospf**} *value*]	Force a flood of non-IGP[*] link
mpls traffic-eng srlg *value*	Set SRLG[*] parameters
mpls traffic-eng tunnels	Enable MPLS TE tunnels

[*] IGP = Interior gateway protocol

SRLG = Shared-risk link group

Table A-9   *MPLS TE Interface Configuration in Cisco IOS XR*

Syntax	Description
admin-weight *value*	Set administrative weight for the interface
attribute-flags *value*	Set user-defined interface attribute flags
backup-path *value*	Configure an MPLS TE backup for this interface
bfd fast-detect	Configure BFD parameters
flooding thresholds {**down** *list* | **up** *list*}	Set flooding parameters

IGP TE Configuration Commands

Table A-10   *MPLS TE Extensions for IS-IS[*] in Cisco IOS*

Syntax	Description
**mpls traffic-eng {level-1	level-2}**	Enable TE extension on link state packets of a specific level
metric-style wide	Send and receive wide link metrics (extended IS Reachability TLV[*])
mpls traffic-eng router-id *value*	Router identifier for MPLS TE

[*] IS-IS = Intermediate System-to-Intermediate System

TLV = Type, Length, Value

Table A-11   *MPLS TE Extensions for IS-IS in Cisco IOS XR*

Syntax	Description
mpls traffic-eng level *value*	Enable TE extension on link state packets of a specific level
metric-style wide	Send and receive wide link metrics (extended IS Reachability TLV)
mpls traffic-eng router-id *value*	Router identifier for MPLS TE

Table A-12   *MPLS TE Extensions for OSPF[*] in Cisco IOS*

Syntax	Description
mpls traffic-eng area *value*	**Configure an OSPF area to run MPLS TE**
mpls traffic-eng interface *value* **area** *value*	Configure MPLS TE interface for this OSPF process
mpls traffic-eng mesh-group *value value* **area** *value*	TE mesh-group advertisement
mpls traffic-eng multicast-intact	MPLS TE and PIM[*] interaction
mpls traffic-eng router-id *value*	TE-stable IP address for system

[*] OSPF = Open Shortest Path First

PIM = Protocol-Independent Multicast

Table A-13   *MPLS TE Extensions for OSPF in Cisco IOS XR*

Syntax	Description
mpls traffic-eng area *value*	OSPF area to run MPLS TE
mpls traffic-eng router-id *value*	TE-stable IP address for system

Path-Configuration Commands

Table A-14 *MPLS TE Explicit-Path Configuration in Cisco IOS*

Syntax	Description
[{**index** I **append-after**} *value*] **exclude-address** *value*	Exclude an address from subsequent partial-path segments
[{**index** I **append-after**} *value*] **next-address** *value* [**loose** I **strict**]	Specify the next address in the path

Table A-15 *MPLS TE Explicit-Path Configuration in Cisco IOS XR*

Syntax	Description
disable	Disable the explicit path
index *value* {**exclude-address ipv4 unicast** *value* I **next-address ipv4 unicast** *value*}	Specify the next entry index to add or edit

Tunnel-Configuration Commands

Table A-16 *Generic Tunnel Configuration Used for MPLS TE in Cisco IOS*

Syntax	Description
interface Tunnel *value*	Enter tunnel-configuration mode
tunnel destination *value*	Destination of tunnel (tailend)
tunnel mode mpls traffic-eng	Set tunnel as MPLS TE tunnel

Table A-17 *MPLS TE Tunnel Configuration in Cisco IOS*

Syntax	Description
tunnel mpls traffic-eng affinity *value* [**mask** *value*]	Desired link attributes for links comprising tunnel
tunnel mpls traffic-eng auto-bw [**collect-bw** I **frequency** *value* I **max-bw** *value* I **min-bw** *value*]	Specify automatic adjustment of bandwidth
tunnel mpls traffic-eng autoroute {**announce** I **metric** {*value* I **absolute** *value* I **relative** *value*}}	Define parameters for IGP routing over tunnel
tunnel mpls traffic-eng backup-bw {*value* I **unlimited**} [**class-type** *value*]	Specify bandwidth for FRR backup
tunnel mpls traffic-eng bandwidth *value* [**class-type** *value*]	Specify tunnel bandwidth requirement
tunnel mpls traffic-eng exp {*list* I **default**}	Set the MPLS EXP values allowed for this interface
tunnel mpls traffic-eng exp-bundle {*master* I **member tunnel** *value*}	Configure the tunnel as a bundle

Table A-17   *MPLS TE Tunnel Configuration in Cisco IOS (Continued)*

Syntax	Description
tunnel mpls traffic-eng fast-reroute [**bw-protect**][**node-protect**]	Specify MPLS tunnel can be fast rerouted
tunnel mpls traffic-eng forwarding-adjacency [**holdtime** *value*]	Treat this tunnel as a forwarding adjacency
tunnel mpls traffic-eng interface down delay 0	Bring tunnel interface down immediately when LSP goes down
tunnel mpls traffic-eng load-share *value*	Specify tunnel load-sharing metric
tunnel mpls traffic-eng path-option [**protect**] *value* **dynamic** [**attributes value** | **bandwidth** *value* [**class-type** *value*]]	Define a primary or fallback *dynamic*-path setup option
tunnel mpls traffic-eng path-option [**protect**] *value* **explicit** {**identifier** *value* | **name** *value*} [[**attributes** *value* | **bandwidth** {*value* | **sub-pool** *value*}] **verbatim**]	Define a primary or fallback *explicit*-path setup option
tunnel mpls traffic-eng path-selection metric {**igp** | **te**}	Configure path selection
tunnel mpls traffic-eng priority *value* [*value*]	Specify tunnel priority
tunnel mpls traffic-eng record-route	Record the route used by the tunnel

Table A-18   *MPLS TE Tunnel Configuration in Cisco IOS XR*

Syntax	Description
interface tunnel-te *value*	Enter tunnel-configuration mode
affinity *value* **mask** *value*	Desired link attributes for links comprising tunnel
autoroute {**announce** | **metric** {**absolute** *value* | **relative** *value*}}	Parameters for IGP routing over tunnel
backup-bw {*value* | **global-pool** {*value* | **unlimited**} | **sub-pool** {*value* | **unlimited**}}	FRR backup bandwidth requirement
destination *value*	Specify tunnel destination
fast-reroute	Specify MPLS tunnel can be fast rerouted
path-option *value* {**dynamic** | **explicit** {**identifier** *value* | **name** *value*}} [**lockdown**]	Primary or fallback path setup option
path-selection metric {**igp** | **te**}	Configure path selection
priority *value value*	Tunnel priority
record-route	Record the route used by the tunnel
signalled-bandwidth *value* [**class-type** *value*]	Tunnel bandwidth requirement to be signaled
signalled-name *value*	The signaling name to assign to tunnel

EXEC Commands

Table A-19   *MPLS TE EXEC Commands in Cisco IOS*

Syntax	Description
mpls traffic-eng automesh-test *value value* [*value* [*value value*]]	**Automesh test** command
mpls traffic-eng fast-reroute promote	Promote to a better backup tunnel
mpls traffic-eng reoptimize [*value*]	Reoptimize MPLS TE tunnels

Table A-20   *MPLS TE EXEC Commands in Cisco IOS XR*

Syntax	Description
mpls traffic-eng fast-reroute promote	Promote to a better backup tunnel instantly
mpls traffic-eng link-management flood	Force an immediate flooding of local MPLS TE links
mpls traffic-eng path-protection switchover *value*	Path-protection switchover
mpls traffic-eng reoptimize [*value*]	Force an immediate reoptimization

show Commands

Table A-21   *Command Prefixes for MPLS TE Verification in Cisco IOS*

Syntax	Description
show mpls traffic-eng auto-tunnel	Automatically created tunnel interfaces
show mpls traffic-eng autoroute	Autorouted tunnel destination information
show mpls traffic-eng ds-te	Show TE-class information
show mpls traffic-eng exp	Display tunnel exp information
show mpls traffic-eng fast-reroute	FRR information
show mpls traffic-eng forwarding-adjacency	Forwarding-adjacency tunnel destination information
show mpls traffic-eng link-management	Link-management information
show mpls traffic-eng lsp	Show LSP information
show mpls traffic-eng topology	Show topology commands
show mpls traffic-eng tunnels	MPLS TE tunnel status

Table A-22   *Commands for MPLS TE Verification in Cisco IOS XR*

Syntax	Description
show mpls traffic-eng autoroute	Autorouted tunnel destination information
show mpls traffic-eng chunks	Show the usage of memory chunks

Table A-22   *Commands for MPLS TE Verification in Cisco IOS XR (Continued)*

Syntax	Description
show mpls traffic-eng counters	Counters
show mpls traffic-eng ds-te	DiffServ information
show mpls traffic-eng fast-reroute	FRR information
show mpls traffic-eng forwarding	Forwarding
show mpls traffic-eng link-management	Link-management information
show mpls traffic-eng maximum	Maximum number of configurable tunnels
show mpls traffic-eng topology	Show topology commands
show mpls traffic-eng tunnels	MPLS TE tunnel status

clear Commands

Table A-23   *Commands to Clear MPLS TE Information in Cisco IOS*

Syntax	Description
clear mpls traffic-eng auto-bw timers	Clear auto-bandwidth collection
clear mpls traffic-eng auto-tunnel {backup I mesh I primary}	Clear auto-tunnel created tunnels
clear mpls traffic-eng link-management counters	Clear link-management statistical information
clear mpls traffic-eng tunnel counters	Clear tunnel statistics

Table A-24   *Commands to Clear MPLS TE Information in Cisco IOS XR*

Syntax	Description
clear mpls traffic-eng counters tunnels {all [heads I tails] I name *value* I summary}	Clear MPLS TE tunnel counters
clear mpls traffic-eng fast-reroute log	Clear FRR event log
clear mpls traffic-eng link-management statistics	Clear link-management statistics

debug Commands

CAUTION   Some **debug** commands generate a large amount of output that might negatively impact device performance. Use caution when enabling any **debug** commands.

Table A-25   *Commands for Debugging MPLS TE in Cisco IOS*

Syntax	Description
debug mpls traffic-eng adj-sb	Traffic Engineering adj subblock API
debug mpls traffic-eng areas	Area configuration change events
debug mpls traffic-eng auto-tunnel	Debug automatic TE tunnels
debug mpls traffic-eng autoroute	Automatic routing over tunnels
debug mpls traffic-eng exp	Exp based routing over tunnels
debug mpls traffic-eng forwarding-adjacency	Forwarding-adjacency routing over tunnels
debug mpls traffic-eng ha	TE high availability
debug mpls traffic-eng link-management	Link management
debug mpls traffic-eng load-balancing	Unequal-cost load balancing over tunnels
debug mpls traffic-eng lsd-client	Traffic Engineering LSD client API
debug mpls traffic-eng mibs	MPLS TE MIBs
debug mpls traffic-eng path	Path-calculation events
debug mpls traffic-eng topology	Show topology events
debug mpls traffic-eng tunnels	MPLS TE tunnels

Table A-26   *Command Commands for Debugging MPLS TE in Cisco IOS XR*

Syntax	Description
debug mpls traffic-eng areas	Area configuration change events
debug mpls traffic-eng autoroute	Automatic routing over tunnels
debug mpls traffic-eng connections	Connections to servers events
debug mpls traffic-eng debug-events	General debugging information
debug mpls traffic-eng ds-te	DS-TE events
debug mpls traffic-eng errors	MPLS TE error debug information
debug mpls traffic-eng frr	FRR events
debug mpls traffic-eng link-management	Link management
debug mpls traffic-eng load-balancing	Unequal-cost load balancing over tunnels
debug mpls traffic-eng path	Path-calculation events
debug mpls traffic-eng temib	MPLS TE MIB[*] debug information
debug mpls traffic-eng topology	Show topology events
debug mpls traffic-eng tunnels	MPLS TE tunnels

[*] MIB = Management Information Base

RSVP Commands

Node-Configuration Commands

Table A-27   *RSVP TE Node Configuration in Cisco IOS*

Syntax	Description
ip rsvp authentication [[**neighbor** {**access-list** *value* | **address** *value*}] **challenge** | **key-chain** *value* | **lifetime** *value* | **type** {**md5** | **sha-1**} | **window-size** *value*]	Enable RSVP neighbor authentication (RFC 2747)
ip rsvp msg-pacing [[**burst** *value*][**limit** *value*][**maxsize** *value*][**period** *value*]]	Enable RSVP Output msg-pacing
ip rsvp policy {**default-reject** | **local** {**acl** *list* | **default** | **origin-as** *list*} | **preempt**}	Policy control commands
ip rsvp signalling hello	Enable neighbor-down detection for FRR
ip rsvp signalling hello graceful-restart {**dscp** value | **mode help-neighbor** | **refresh** {**interval** *value* | **misses** *value*}}	Configure RSVP graceful restart
ip rsvp signalling hello statistics	Enable hello extension statistics
ip rsvp signalling initial-retransmit-delay *value*	Time to wait before first retransmit (in milliseconds)
ip rsvp signalling patherr state-removal [**neighbor** *value*]	PathError state removal for LSP sessions
ip rsvp signalling rate-limit [**burst** *value*][**limit** *value*][**maxsize** *value*][**period** *value*]]	Limit rate at which RSVP messages are sent to neighbors
ip rsvp signalling refresh {**interval** *value* | **misses** *value* | **reduction** [**ack-delay** *value*]}}	Configure RSVP refresh behavior

Table A-28   *RSVP TE Node Configuration in Cisco IOS XR*

Syntax	Description
interface *value*	Enable RSVP on an interface
signalling graceful-restart [**restart-time** *value*]	Configure RSVP graceful restart
signalling hello graceful-restart refresh {**interval** *value* | **misses** *value*}	Configure graceful restart hello refresh parameters
signalling prefix-filtering {**access-list** *value* | **default-deny-action drop**}	Enable prefix filtering for an access list

Interface-Configuration Commands

Table A-29   *RSVP TE Interface Configuration in Cisco IOS*

Syntax	Description
ip rsvp authentication [**challenge** I **key** *value* I **key-chain** *value* I **lifetime** *value* I **type** {**md5** I **sha-1**} I **window-size** *value*]	Enable RSVP neighbor authentication (RFC 2747)
ip rsvp bandwidth [*value* [{**rdm** I **mam max-reseruable-bw** *value*} **bc0** *value* [**bc1** *value*]]]	RSVP reservable bandwidth (kbps)
ip rsvp neighbor [*value*]	Select permissible RSVP neighbors
ip rsvp signalling dscp value	DSCP* for RSVP signaling messages
ip rsvp signalling hello	Enable neighbor-down detection
ip rsvp signalling hello fast-reroute {**dscp** *value* I **refresh** {**interval** value I **misses** *value*}}	Configure RSVP hello refresh behavior for FRR
ip rsvp signalling hello reroute {**dscp** *value* I **refresh** {**interval** *value* I **misses** *value*}}	Configure RSVP hello refresh behavior for FRR

* DSCP = DiffServ Code Point

Table A-30   *RSVP TE Interface Configuration in Cisco IOS XR*

Syntax	Description
bandwidth [*value* {**rdm** I **mam max-reservable-bw** *value*} **bc0** *value* [**bc1** *value*]]]	Configure RSVP bandwidth parameters
signalling dscp *value*	Set DSCP for RSVP signaling messages
signalling hello graceful-restart interface-based	Configure Interface-based Hello
signalling rate-limit [**rate** *value* [**interval** *value*]]	Configure message rate-limit (pacing) options
signalling refresh {**interval** *value* I **missed** *value* }	Set interval between successive state refreshes and the maximum number of consecutive missed messages for state expiration
signalling refresh reduction {**bundle-max-size** *value* I **disable** I **reliable** {**ack-hold-time** *value* I **ack-max-size** *value* I **retransmit-time** *value* I **summary-refresh**} I **summary max-size** *value*}	Configure refresh reduction options

show Commands

Table A-31   *Cisco IOS Commands for Verifying RSVP*

Syntax	Description
show ip rsvp authentication	RSVP security associations for authentication
show ip rsvp counters	RSVP counters
show ip rsvp fast-reroute	RSVP FRR database
show ip rsvp hello	RSVP hello extension
show ip rsvp host	RSVP endpoint senders and receivers
show ip rsvp installed	RSVP installed reservations
show ip rsvp interface	RSVP interface information
show ip rsvp listeners	RSVP listeners
show ip rsvp neighbor	RSVP neighbor information
show ip rsvp policy	RSVP policy information
show ip rsvp request	RSVP reservations upstream
show ip rsvp reservation	RSVP reservation requests from downstream
show ip rsvp sender	RSVP path state information
show ip rsvp signalling	RSVP signaling information

Table A-32   *Cisco IOS XR Commands for Verifying RSVP*

Syntax	Description
show rsvp counters	Counters
show rsvp fast-reroute	FRR state information
show rsvp graceful-restart	Local graceful restart information
show rsvp hello	RSVP hello subsystem information
show rsvp interface	Interface information
show rsvp neighbors	RSVP neighbor information
show rsvp request	Request information
show rsvp reservation	Reservation information
show rsvp sender	Path information
show rsvp session	Session information

clear Commands

Table A-33   *Cisco IOS Commands for Clearing RSVP Information*

Syntax	Description
clear ip rsvp authentication [**from** *value*][**to** *value*]	Clear RSVP security associations
clear ip rsvp counters	Clear RSVP counters
clear ip rsvp hello {**instance** {**counters** | **statistics**} | **statistics**}	Clear RSVP hello counters
clear ip rsvp high-availability	Clear RSVP HA state
clear ip rsvp reservation	Clear RSVP Resv state information
clear ip rsvp sender	Clear RSVP path state information
clear ip rsvp signalling {**rate-limit** | **refresh reduction**}	Clear RSVP signaling counters

Table A-34   *Cisco IOS XR Commands for Clearing RSVP Information*

Syntax	Description
clear rsvp counters all	All message and event counters
clear rsvp counters chkpt	RSVP check-pointing counters
clear rsvp counters events	Event counters
clear rsvp counters messages	Message counters
clear rsvp counters oor	Out-of-resources counts
clear rsvp counters bprefix-filtering	Prefix-filtering counts

debug Commands

CAUTION   Some **debug** commands generate a large amount of output that might negatively impact device performance. Use caution when enabling any **debug** commands.

Table A-35   *Cisco IOS Commands for Debugging RSVP*

Syntax	Description
debug ip rsvp all	RSVP messages for all categories
debug ip rsvp api	RSVP API[*] events
debug ip rsvp authentication	RSVP authentication events and messages
debug ip rsvp cli	RSVP CLI[*] events
debug ip rsvp database	RSVP database debugging
debug ip rsvp dump-messages	Dump RSVP message contents
debug ip rsvp errors	RSVP errors
debug ip rsvp fast-reroute	RSVP FRR support for LSPs

Table A-35 *Cisco IOS Commands for Debugging RSVP (Continued)*

Syntax	Description
debug ip rsvp filter	RSVP filter information
debug ip rsvp handles	RSVP database handles events
debug ip rsvp	hello RSVP hello events
debug ip rsvp high-availability	RSVP HA information
debug ip rsvp messages	RSVP messages (sent/received via IP) debugging
debug ip rsvp msg-mgr	RSVP Message Manager events
debug ip rsvp path	RSVP PATH messages
debug ip rsvp policy	RSVP policy information
debug ip rsvp proxy	RSVP proxy API trace
debug ip rsvp rate-limit	RSVP rate-limiting messages
debug ip rsvp reliable-msg	RSVP reliable messages events
debug ip rsvp resv	RSVP RESV messages
debug ip rsvp routing	RSVP routing messages
debug ip rsvp signalling	RSVP signaling (PATH and RESV) messages
debug ip rsvp snmp	RSVP SNMP[*] events
debug ip rsvp sso	RSVP sso events
debug ip rsvp summary-refresh	RSVP Srefresh[*] and Bundle messages events
debug ip rsvp traffic-control	RSVP traffic control events

[*] API = Application programming interface

CLI = Command-line interface

SNMP = Simple Network Management Protocol

Srefresh = Summary refresh

Table A-36 *Cisco IOS XR Commands for Debugging RSVP*

Syntax	Description
debug rsvp dump-messages	Dump contents of messages
debug rsvp errors	Generate only error messages
debug rsvp filter	Filter RSVP debug messages
debug rsvp frr	FRR events
debug rsvp gr	Graceful restart events
debug rsvp hello	Hello events
debug rsvp interface	Interface events
debug rsvp packet	Packet input/output events

Table A-36 *Cisco IOS XR Commands for Debugging RSVP (Continued)*

Syntax	Description
debug rsvp path	Path events
debug rsvp prefix-filtering	Prefix-filtering events
debug rsvp process	Process and system database events
debug rsvp resv	Reservation events
debug rsvp routing	Routing events
debug rsvp signalling	Signaling (PATH + RESV)

INDEX

D

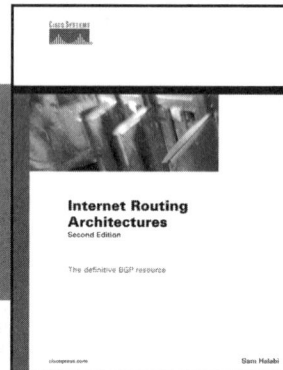

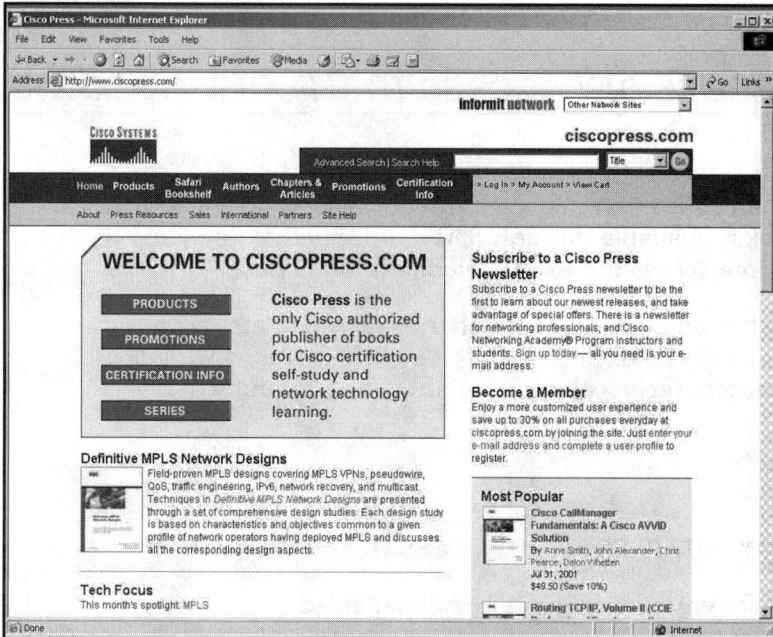

Safari
BOOKS ONLINE
ENABLED

THIS BOOK IS SAFARI ENABLED

INCLUDES FREE 45-DAY ACCESS TO THE ONLINE EDITION

The Safari® Enabled icon on the cover of your favorite technology book means the book is available through Safari Bookshelf. When you buy this book, you get free access to the online edition for 45 days.

Safari Bookshelf is an electronic reference library that lets you easily search thousands of technical books, find code samples, download chapters, and access technical information whenever and wherever you need it.

TO GAIN 45-DAY SAFARI ENABLED ACCESS TO THIS BOOK:

- Go to **http://www.ciscopress.com/safarienabled**

- Complete the brief registration form

- Enter the coupon code found in the front of this book before the "Contents at a Glance" page

If you have difficulty registering on Safari Bookshelf or accessing the online edition, please e-mail customer-service@safaribooksonline.com.